Gay American Autobiography

Living Out
Gay and Lesbian Autobiographies

Joan Larkin and David Bergman
SERIES EDITORS

Raphael Kadushin
SERIES ACQUISITIONS EDITOR

Gay American

AUTOBIOGRAPHY

Writings from Whitman to Sedaris

EDITED BY

David Bergman

THE UNIVERSITY OF WISCONSIN PRESS

The University of Wisconsin Press
1930 Monroe Street, 3rd Floor
Madison, Wisconsin 53711-2059

www.wisc.edu/wisconsinpress/

3 Henrietta Street
London WC2E 8LU, England

5   4   3   2   1

Printed in the United States of America

Library of Congress Cataloging-in-Publication Data
Gay American autobiography : writings from Whitman to Sedaris /
edited by David Bergman.
    p. cm.—(Living out)
  ISBN 978-0-299-23044-9 (pbk. : alk. paper)
  1. Gays—United States—Biography. 2. Gay authors—United States—
Biography. I. Bergman, David, 1950– II. Series.
PS508.G39G39   2009
920.0086'64—dc22
[B]
2008039537

For Raphael Kadushin

Contents

Acknowledgments

IT TAKES NO LESS THAN A VILLAGE to publish a book, and since the editor is often the town fool, please excuse me if I fail to mention an important name. I first need to mention Raphael Kadushin and Joan Larkin, my coeditors in the Living Out series. For a decade we have worked together on a project that Raphy first envisioned. He has come through for me when I felt that I absolutely could go on no further. Joan has been a dear friend and a wonderful reader and source of inspiration.

One of the challenges of this book was gaining permission to reprint works long out of print from publishers long out of business. My good fortune was to contact Michael Rumaker, who has been extraordinarily generous in identifying people who might help me. One of those contacts is Michael Williams, who represents the estate of Samuel M. Steward and the Grey Fox Press. I want to thank Steve Watson at Flower-Beneath-the-Foot Press, who exchanged many emails with me so I could get everything right. I want to thank Ira Silverberg for leading me to Wayne Kawadler, executor of David Feinberg's estate, and Jim Hubbard for getting me in touch with Tom Rauffenbart, the executor of the David Wojnarowicz estate. Taylor Stoehr put me in touch with Sally Goodman. I want to thank Greg Wharton at Suspect Thoughts Press and Bob Sharrad at City Lights. Many authors have generously allowed me to publish their works, but I want to thank especially my good friend Edward Field, who permitted me to print his unpublished manuscript about being in the army. Richard Howard produced a short list of the pieces I absolutely needed to include, and I have tried to follow it.

Richard Canning and Frederick Luis Aldama were extremely useful readers of the manuscript.

John Lessner, my partner of over twenty years, was, as always, patient and sensible when I was anxious and irrational. He is the indispensable part in making these lives come together.

Permissions

Introduction

GAY AMERICAN AUTOBIOGRAPHY. A simple enough title, utterly straightforward and unassuming, and yet the three words are each very problematic. Consider, for example, *American.* Is a work American because it was written in the United States? Is it American because the author was living in the United States when he or she wrote it? Is it American because it deals with events in the United States? Where do we place Alexander Berkman's *Prison Memoirs of an Anarchist?* Berkman was born in Russia but immigrated to the United States when he was seventeen. His prison memoirs were written in English while he lived in this country, and they are about his experiences in an American jail. Nevertheless, Berkman did not stay in the United States. He was deported after residing only twenty-one years in this country and died in France in 1936, seventeen years later. Is Berkman's work *American?* Or is it Russian or French? It was written here, it was published here, and it is about his experiences here. Yet Berkman lived less than half of his life in America and never became an American citizen. And what do we do with Henry James, who lived most of his life in Europe, wrote nearly all of his work in Europe, and became a British citizen in the last year of his life, yet is almost universally considered an American writer, one of the greatest.

Some people have argued that we should get rid of national labels such as *American* because they are indefinable. But if we did so, we would be unable to explain or understand how the experiences and culture of same-sex desire in Yukio Mishima, the great Japanese writer, are different from the ones encountered by Justin Chin, the Asian American writer. Hard-and-fast rules about what constitutes American literature may be impossible to make, but the term is helpful if in no other way than divvying up what would be an unmanageable number of works.

Gay is an even more problematic term. When the word *gay* began to be used as a rough synonym for *homosexual* has not been settled, but the earliest unambiguous uses appear in the first third of the twentieth century. Consequently, using it to refer to men in the nineteenth century is anachronistic. Even the term *homosexual* has problems, for although it was coined in Hungary in 1869, it did not come into general use in English until around the turn of the twentieth century. So it, too, is anachronistic when applied to Whitman or Thoreau. Neither man would have thought of his desires in those terms. Whitman used the term *adhesiveness* and *comradeship* to describe his feelings for men; the former term is now completely forgotten and the latter is colored by ideology. The most neutral term used today is *same-sex desire*, and while it has many advantages, it is neither flexible grammatically (it can't be used as an adjective) nor very euphonious. Generally, in the notes I will use *same-sex desire* for works before 1900 and *gay* for works after 1900, but since all the terms have problems of one sort or another, I do not adhere strictly to any one term.

If this issue of terminology had been about only the choice of synonyms, scholars would not have spilled so much ink on the subject. But each word has not only an historical significance but an ideological significance as well. Gilbert Herdt and Andrew Boxer identify four cohort systems: one for those who came of age after World War I, another for those who came of age during and after World War II, yet another for those who came of age after the Stonewall Riots and the advent of gay liberation, and finally one for those who came of age in the era of AIDS.[1] For Herdt and Boxer the term *homosexual* would better categorize the men who came of age before the era of gay liberation, men who lived in a period when people regarded same-sex relations as sinful and unhealthy as well as illegal. Men who came of age after or on the advent of gay liberation think of themselves (for the most part) as gay and reject the moral, medical, and legal stigmas of a homophobic culture and regard themselves as a loosely connected minority group. Finally, as Herdt and Boxer discuss, many men who have come of age after AIDS label themselves as *queer*. The term *queer* is more expansive than gay; it is open to women and men, bisexuals, transgender people, and others who see themselves as outsiders. Identifying oneself as queer is a political act transforming a word used in derogation into one of approbation. As a result, the term has not been universally embraced by those in the cohort.

In his examination of gay autobiography Bertram J. Cohler, a psychoanalyst, sees even more differences among gay men, that their outlook changed in every decade of the last sixty years of the twentieth century.[2] Readers of this anthology may well identify how men of a certain period face similar problems, but the diversity of gay men defies, I feel, anything more than the roughest groupings. All the biographies that Cohler examines at length are by white middle-class men. If *Brokeback Mountain* is to be believed (and I think it is), there were men in same-sex relations during the age of gay liberation who never felt its impact and were untouched by the effects of AIDS. To speak personally, I am of the same generation-cohort as the men represented in *Brokeback Mountain*, and their experiences and attitudes bear little resemblance to mine. Social and psychological changes come at different speeds, depending on region, class, race, education level, psychological makeup, and chance encounters in an individual's life. What the best life writing captures is the specificity and particularity of lives even as they participate in larger social and historic contexts.

Such thoughts lead to the final two questions: What do I mean by *autobiography*? In what sense is an autobiography *gay*?

The book includes excerpts from rather traditional autobiographies, works in which an author writes about a broad span of his life. But the book also includes samples from memoirs, journals, letters, and oral history—genres lumped together under the broad term *life writing*. Each of these genres has a different audience, style, concerns, and resonance. The earliest authors included here obviously did not write autobiographies that explicitly discuss their sexual orientation. What we have instead are their journals and letters. Yet even in the privacy of his journal Henry David Thoreau is circumspect, and Walt Whitman, who was much more explicit about his erotic passions, remained tight-lipped about his domestic arrangements. His letters to Peter Doyle reveal a man uneasy and ultimately unwilling to commit himself to living with Doyle. The letters of Henry James to Hendrick Andersen begin ardently and flirtatiously but end with exasperation and coolness as James comes to understand that Andersen will be neither the companion nor the artist James desires. These letters may appear to give us an intimate candid look into the lives of their authors, but letters are, in fact, themselves performances, and the letters that Russell Cheney, the painter, wrote to his life partner, the scholar and critic F. O. Matthiessen, are both elaborately staged and spontaneous, deeply considered and spur of the moment. Cheney and Matthiessen would never have thought of revealing these letters to a wider public at the time, but their editor, Louis Hyde, a longtime friend of the two, speculates that, because Matthiessen mentions the letters in his will, he "probably had some intention, perhaps only partly formed about their future" publication after his death. Hyde feels that the letters contain "no indication whatever that an outside eye should never see them."[3] No matter how personal the letters appear, they were, for Hyde, always intended for others to read. Thus, personal letters, which we may think of as private, may be written with a public audience in mind.

Even journals are not necessarily private, intimate works, meant for a select number of readers. The pseudonymous author "Jeb Alexander," a government clerk like Whitman, had no intentions of publishing his journal, and neither did Glenway Wescott, whose *Continual Lessons*, published posthumously, was really, as his editor, Robert Phelps, describes, "scrapbooks" consisting of "literally hundreds of ring binders, into whose pages its author had pasted every sort of memo, newspaper clipping, letter carbon, etc."[4] But other journal writers have publication clearly in mind. Perhaps Ned Rorem began his journals as a private record, but he soon got in the habit of seeing them into print. There are now five volumes in addition to several collections of letters. Similarly, only six years after the last entry, Paul Goodman started preparing his journal for publication, having sufficiently disengaged himself from the period in which he was writing. Even this short delay was caused not by concerns over privacy but by being without a publisher. We like to think that in letters and journals we get to see the "real" author freed from the more public displays of the memoir or autobiography, and in some cases, no doubt, it is true that writers are more willing to lay their hearts bare in the privacy of their diaries or in the intimacies of their letters. But we can, I think, exaggerate this difference.

What may be more significant in determining how these texts were read is the manner in which they were presented to the public. Claude Hartland's *The Story of a Life*, perhaps the earliest gay autobiography in America, was published in St. Louis in 1901 for "the consideration of the medical fraternity." His intended readers were doctors, and clearly the work is directed to win over the hearts (if not the minds) of doctors treating men for same-sex attraction. For the sake of science, Hartland was quite candid if never sexually explicit. Whether any doctors were influenced in their treatment by Hartland's writing is subject to doubt. Hartland's autobiography was reprinted in 1985 by Don Allen and his Grey Fox Press, an important gay publishing house. This little green paperbound edition of *The Story of a Life* was meant, like all of the books published by Grey Fox Press, particularly for gay readers, and it is not surprising that two other excerpts in this book—Michael Rumaker's *A Day and a Night at the Baths* and Samuel Steward's *Chapters from an Autobiography*—were also published by Grey Fox Press. All of these books have the intimate scale that indicates they were not meant for big publishers or mass readership. Grey Fox books were prominently displayed in the gay bookstores that were emerging at the time. Several other readings in this anthology also first appeared in small press publications. Ned Rorem's *Paris Diary* was first published by George Braziller, a small New York publisher, in 1966; Gil Cuadros's *City of God* was published by City Lights Publishing in San Francisco. Even when big New York houses publish gay autobiographies, they often do so as paperback originals, which are not generally given the same attention by reviewers as clothbound books. Gay life writing has found its home most frequently in small presses or private (or semiprivate) publications.

Minette's *Recollections of a Part-Time Lady* is an especially good case in point. Minette was a transvestite entertainer, not a writer. The text that appears here is a highly edited transcription of tapes she made with Steve Watson, a noted cultural historian. Minette kept scrapbooks, and the original text was printed with lots of pictures that were reworked by Ray Dobbins. The edition created by Flower-Beneath-the-Foot Press was not printed but photocopied and bound between snap-on plastic covers. Copies were either given away or sold for a pittance. In short, this "underground" publication defied all the conventions of commercial publishing. The book was available only to a small, select readership, and the publishers—Watson and Dobbins—produced the book out of love rather than for money. In this respect, Minette's *Recollections of a Part-Time Lady* is hardly unique; it is an example of how gay autobiography grew out of the community it served.

Gay autobiographies have had a difficult time finding acceptance with heterosexual readers. Edmund White, whose essay "Writing Gay" is included here, is one of America's most distinguished authors. But although his autobiography *My Lives* was published by a large New York firm and received a respectable round of reviews, it met with a response from heterosexual reviewers that is worth examining. Laura Miller, writing in the *New York Times Book Review*, tries to be unshocked by White's account of his "sadomasochistic affair with a much younger man" while at the same time wishing that he had concentrated more on his marriage-like relationship with his partner, Michael Carroll.[5] Why, she wonders, did White spend so long on such sexually disturbing behavior (especially disturbing since he is a man in his sixties) and give so little space, "by contrast, [to] the man with whom White has lived for 10 years in (nonmonogamous) 'marital harmony'"? For Miller, "marital harmony" is the proper subject of an autobiography, not the psychologically shattering relationship White had with the young man, even though, as she admits, it "might be telling us obliquely about his grief for his dead lover and his anxieties about getting old." Miller is willing to credit only relationships that look like heterosexual marriage as worthy of lengthy examination; White's feelings at the conclusion of his sadomasochistic affair are, Miller insists, "out of proportion with the actual loss." She condescendingly concludes, "There is indeed something very Continental about the belief that just because an emotion is extreme and stylized it is also interesting and revealing," as if no red-blooded American girl would ever be taken in by the psychological pain of anything other than marriage. Europeans might be fooled by "extreme and stylized" emotions, but not she. Miller is blind to the fact that the bourgeois marriage is just as "stylized" in its own way as a gay relationship and often filled with its own sadomasochistic practices. The review shows her failure—which I think is a fairly common failure—to engage with a gay life other than through a heterosexual lens, one whose focus is on marriage and children. As a result, it is unsurprising that gay autobiographies and memoirs rarely attract large numbers of readers and have mostly been issued by small publishers.

Is there such a thing as a gay autobiography? Of course, there are books by gay men in which they tell their life stories, but how would the sexual orientation of an author (or even of the publisher) influence the very nature of an autobiography? What, if anything, makes gay autobiography different from straight autobiography? No one can tell for certain, but there does seem to be one feature of gay men's lives missing in the lives of straight men: coming out. People in general have to face issues about their sexuality, but gay men and women need to reflect on their sexual choice as an issue. They need to be concerned about how others will react to it. Whereas heterosexual men may need to be aware of how others might respond to their interest in a *particular* woman, they do not have to confront hostility for being interested *in* women. In contrast, gay men, no matter how meritorious their partner, must face the stigmatization of being sexually attracted to *men*. The coming-out process—no matter how *coming out* is defined—is at least one important experience that separates gay men's autobiographies from straight men's autobiographies.

Paul Robinson, in his study *Gay Lives*, claims that "there are no American gay autobiographies . . . written before the 1970s," but he has a fairly limited definition of the term. For Robinson gay autobiographies are works by men "whose chief concern is to describe and explain their love of men."[6] But even by that standard Robinson ignores Claude Hartland's *The Story of a Life*, originally published in 1901, and Earl Lind's *Autobiography of an Androgyne*, published in 1918 (excerpts from both works are included here). If we include diaries and letters and works in which homoerotic experiences are related (without being the chief concern), we can find works that go back to the middle of the nineteenth century.

The selection of works for this book has been made difficult not by the paucity of examples but by their abundance. To be sure, Robinson is correct that after 1970 the number of published works in which gay men wrote about their lives increased geometrically. I have limited the selection to works that are explicitly nonfiction. This decision means that some wonderful examples of autobiographical fiction have been excluded, and gay writers often have blurred the generic distinctions, especially as they tried to break out of the fictional stereotypes that beset them. Only by going directly to their own experience could they find reliable figures to replace the commonly received representation of gay men. Nevertheless, the works here have been labeled as nonfiction by their authors.

Although I have tried to limit the selection to explicitly nonfictional works, I am uncertain whether the distinction between fiction and nonfiction is very helpful. The stories we fabricate about our own lives are as much an imaginative creation as the novels we might produce. The difference is that we act upon the stories we tell about ourselves. Martin Duberman told himself for years that if he only worked harder he could free himself of his homosexual desires. That narrative caused him immeasurable pain. But life writing is also fictional in that even the most candid writers are very careful of just what sort of face they project to the reader. The biggest fiction is that an autobiography is perfectly faithful to the truth. Samuel Delany, for example, confronts the problem between historical truth and remembered fact. Delany wrote to a scholar researching his life that "my father died of lung cancer in 1958 when I was seventeen." The scholar pointed out that since Delany was born in 1942 he could not have been seventeen in 1958. Only later did Delany discover that he'd gotten the date of his father's death wrong. He had died in 1960, when Delany was eighteen. Why this confusion? Psychologists have all sorts of explanations, but what is clear is that remembered time and historical chronology are very different things. Events in our lives take on a life of their own. We reconstruct them or blot them out to suit our needs. Nevertheless, our conscious attempts to tell our lives as honestly as we can are different from the works created to be satisfying fictions. I have, therefore, made the decision to reprint only works that purport to be nonfiction.

The tension between nonfictional accounts of same-sex attraction and fictional ones appears early on. Herman Melville published *Typee*, for example, as a memoir. We now know it is mostly fictional, and since it is now read as a novel, it is not included here. Melville chose to present *Typee* as nonfiction to increase its sales because accounts of adventures in the South Pacific were very popular at the time. Yet there is no doubt that Melville traded on a good deal of firsthand experience when writing the book. *Typee* illustrates not only the porous boundaries of fiction and nonfiction but the role of ethnography in the history of gay writing. Just as the *National Geographic* was allowed to print photographs of naked "primitive" people in the name of science, so too writers could safely describe same-sex relations within the context of ethnography and medicine. Charles Warren Stoddard's "Chumming with a Savage: Kána-aná" is a good example. The title suggests the problematic balance that Stoddard needed to maintain to get his work published. On the one hand, he uses the benign word *chumming*, but, on the other hand, he matches it with *savage*. Roger Austen refers to "Stoddard's half-shrewd, half-bumbling technique of constructing sentences and paragraphs so as to cover his tracks with confusion."[7] The primitive gave Stoddard the cover he needed. The tradition of the ethnographic also finds its way into Tobias Schneebaum's writing.

What strikes me about gay autobiography—particularly the less literary autobiographies—is the urgency of the writing. Behind the most matter-of-fact tone is a fervent desire for understanding, and this desire for understanding has not necessarily been reduced over the years even as homosexuality has become more accepted. David Feinberg, David Wojnarowicz, and Essex Hemphill are as much in need of understanding and compassion as Claude Hartland. In fact, because of AIDS, their need for understanding is all the more urgent. All autobiography derives from a desire to make one's self understood, but gay autobiography is inevitably colored by a greater need for understanding because it is written against a culture indifferent at best and rabidly hostile at worst.

For the most part I have included works by professional writers, but several of the entries—those by Claude Hartland and Minette, for example—are by people who were not especially literary. Jeb Alexander wanted to be a writer, but his diary was never intended for publication. I have included these accounts because they are well written and provide pictures of gay life that are less often seen. Although I could not produce an exhaustive collection of gay autobiography, I have attempted to suggest the breadth of gay autobiography. I have tried to represent writers of every generation since the nineteenth century. I have tried to represent journals, letters, essays, and extracts from book-length autobiographies and memoirs. I have included African American writers, Latino writers, and one Asian American writer. There are Protestant, Jewish, and Catholic writers, musicians, painters, tattoo artists, drag queens, and hustlers. There are accounts of life in prison, on the beaches of Hawaii, and in the swamps of New Guinea.

There have been several important collections of autobiographical writing. Among the finest are Patrick Merla's *Boys Like Us* (1996), Clifford Chase's *Queer 13* (1998), and John Preston's series of books—*Hometowns* (1991), *Sister and Brother* (1994), edited with Joan Nestle, and *Friends and Lovers* (1995), edited with Michael Lowenthal. I have not reprinted material from any of these anthologies because they are still widely available. Rather, I have been especially interested in including works that are harder to find. Minette's autobiography was published by a small press that used photocopy. Paul Goodman's *Five Years* (1966), Michael Rumaker's *A Day and a Night at the Baths* (1979), and Samuel Steward's *Chapters from an Autobiography* (1981) are all out of print and difficult to find. Young writers struck down by AIDS—David Wojnarowicz, David Feinberg, Essex Hemphill, and Gil Cuadros—did not have time to produce a large body of work, and their works are in jeopardy of being lost. This collection thus serves to bring to light writers who never got the attention they deserved and whose work is hard to get even from large libraries.

Autobiography is about the tenuousness of memory, the rapidity of forgetting. It is an attempt to staunch the disappearance of our lives, to preserve a sense of our past and, in that way, build a sense of continuity with the future. Gay people have had a particular need to pass on those memories and large obstacles in their way. Censorship is, of course, the major obstacle. It was difficult for publishers to find a way to bring this writing to readers. But unlike most ethnic groups, gay men could not pass down their stories from one generation to another by reciting them to children on their knees. AIDS especially caused a break in the process by which older men communicated to younger ones a sense of history. This collection tries in its small way to give a glimpse of the various lives gay men have lived, how they understood their experience, and what they felt for each other. The stories are horrifying and mundane, hilarious and grim, wistful and insistent. They are anybody's life because they are like no lives anyone else has ever had.

NOTES

1. Gilbert Herdt and Andrew Boxer, *Children of Horizons: How Gay and Lesbian Teens Are Leading a New Way Out of the Closet* (Boston: Beacon Press, 1996), 9.

2. Bertram J. Cohler, *Writing Desire: Sixty Years of Gay Autobiography* (Madison: University of Wisconsin Press, 2007), xiv.

3. Louis Hyde, "'Continual Journal': An Introduction," in *Rat and the Devil: The Journal Letters of F. O. Matthiessen and Russell Cheney*, ed. Louis Hyde (Boston: Alyson, 1988), 13.

4. Robert Phelps, ed., with Jerry Rosco, *Continual Lessons: The Journals of Glenway Wescott, 1937–1955* (New York: Farrar, Straus and Giroux, 1990), vii.

5. Laura Miller, "The Bearable Lightness of Being," *New York Times Book Review*, 9 April 2006.

6. Paul Robinson, *Gay Lives: Homosexual Autobiography from John Addington Symonds to Paul Monette* (Chicago: University of Chicago Press, 1999), xi, ix.

7. Roger Austen, introduction to *Cruising the South Seas* by Charles Warren Stoddard (San Francisco: Gay Sunshine Press, 1987), 14.

Gay American Autobiography

Henry David Thoreau

Henry David Thoreau (1817–1862) is best known for his book *Walden* (1854), the account of living for a year by himself at Walden Pond in Concord, Massachusetts, the town where he was born. In addition, he wrote *A Week on the Concord and Merrimack Rivers* (1849) and left behind manuscripts that were published after his death, including his massive set of journals.

Like Henry James, Thoreau seems to have been a lifelong celibate, but, unlike James, he proposed marriage to a woman, Ellen Sewall, whose brother Edmund was a "gentle boy" and for whom Thoreau developed strong feelings. He wrote that Edmund and he were "one while we did sympathize," but unfortunately this very sympathy "withheld" Thoreau from acting further on his desires. Edmund Sewall was only one of a number of men for whom Thoreau developed strong feelings.

"My friend," Thoreau wrote in his journal, "must be my tent companion," and after the movie *Brokeback Mountain* it is hard to read such a statement as entirely innocent of sexual feelings. Walter Harding, in his article "Thoreau's Sexuality" (*Journal of Homosexuality* 21.3 [1991]: 23–45), concludes that Thoreau was fundamentally attracted to men. However, in the extract from his journal that follows Thoreau's "peculiar love" stays unfulfilled, and he remained throughout his life "a busy body without pleasure."

From Thoreau's Journals

Sep 25th 1840

Social yearnings unsatisfied are the temporalness of time.

Birds were very naturally made the subject of augury—for they are but borderers upon the earth—creatures of a subtler and more etherial element than our existence can be supported in—which seem to flit between us and the unexplored.

As I sat on the cliff to-day the crows, as with one consent, began to assemble from all parts of the horizon—from river and pond and field, and wood, in such numbers as to darken the sky—as if a netting of black beads were stretched across it. After some tacking and wheeling the centre of the immense cohort was poised just over my head. Their cawing was deafening, and when that ceased the winnowing of their wings was like the rising of a tempest in the forest. But their Silence was more ominous than their din.—At length they departed sullenly as they came.

Prosperity is no field for heroism unless it endeavor to establish an independent and supernatural prosperity for itself.

In the midst of din and tumult and disorder we hear the trumpet sound.

Defeat is heaven's success. He cannot be said to succeed to whom the world shows any favor. In fact it is the hero's point d'appui, which by offering resistance to his action ennables him to act at all. At each step he spurns the world. He vaults the higher in proportion as he employs the greater resistance of the earth.

It is fatal when an elevation has been gained by too wide a concession—retaining no point of resistance, for then the hero like the aeronaut, must float at the mercy of the winds—or cannot sail for calm weather, nor steer himself for want of waves to his rudder.

When we rise to the step above, we tread hardest on the step below.

My friend must be my tent companion.

Saturday Sep 26th 1840

The day, for the most part, is heroic only when it breaks.

Every author writes in the faith that his book is to be the final resting place of the sojourning soul, and sets up his fixtures therein as for a more than oriental permanence—but it is only a caravansery which we soon leave without ceremony—We read on his sign only—refreshment for man and beast—and a drawn hand directs us to Isphahan or Bagdad.

"Plato gives science sublime counsels, directs her toward the regions of the ideal; Aristotle gives her positive and severe laws, and directs her toward a practical end." Degerando.

Sep 27th 1840

Ideas which confound all things must necessarily embrace all.

Virtue will be known ere long by her elastic tread.—When man is in harmony with nature.

Monday Sep 28th 1840

The world thinks it knows only what it comes in contact with, and whose repelling points give it a configuration to the senses—a hard crust aids its distinct knowledge. But what we truly know has no points of repulsion, and consequently no objective form—being surveyed from within. We are acquainted with the soul and its phenomena, as a bird with the air in which it floats. Distinctness is superficial and formal merely.

We touch objects—as the earth we stand on—but the soul—as the air we breathe. We know the world superficially—the soul centrally.—In the one case our surfaces meet, in the other our centres coincide.

Tuesday Sep 29th 1840

Wisdom is a sort of mongrel between Instinct and Prudence, which however inclining to the side of the father, will finally assert its pure blood again—as the white race at length prevails over the black. It is minister plenipotentiary from earth to heaven—but occasionally Instinct, like a native born celestial, comes to earth and adjusts the controversy.

All fair action in man is the product of enthusiasm—There is enthusiasm in the sunset. The shell on the shore takes new layers and new tints from year to year with such rapture as the bard writes his poem. There is a thrill in the spring, when it buds and blossoms—there is a happiness in the summer—a contentedness in the autumn—a patient repose in the winter.

Nature does nothing in the prose mood, though sometimes grimly with poetic fury, as in earthquakes &c and at other times humorously.

Saturday Oct 3d 1840

No man has imagined what private discourse his members have with surrounding nature, or how much the tenor of that intercourse affects his own health and sickness.

Wednesday Oct 7th 1840

When one hears a strain of music he feels his blood flow in his veins.

Saturday Oct 10th 1840

All life must be seen upon a proper back ground—else, however refined, it will be cheap enough—Only the life of some anchorite or nun or moody dweller among his fellows will bear to be considered—Our actions lack grandeur in the prospect—they are not so impressive as objects in the desert, a broken shaft or crumbling mound against a limitless horizon.

The fuel on the hearth sings a requiem—its fine strain tells of untrodden fields of virtue.

Oct 11th 1840

It is always easy to infringe the law—but the Bedouin of the desert find it impossible to resist public opinion.

The traveller Stevens had the following conversation with a Bedouin of Mount Sinai. "I asked him who governed them; he stretched himself up and answered in one word, 'God.' I asked him if they paid tribute to the pasha; and his answer was,

'No, we take tribute from him.' I asked him how. 'We plunder his caravans.' Desirous to understand my exact position with the sheik of Akaba, under his promise of protection, I asked him if they were governed by their sheik; to which he answered, 'No, we govern him.'"

The true man of science will have a rare Indian wisdom—and will know nature better by his finer organization. He will smell, taste, see, hear, feel, better than other men. His will be a deeper and finer experience[.] We do not learn by inference and deduction, and the application of mathematics to philosophy but by direct intercourse. It is with science as with ethics—we cannot know truth by method and contrivance—the Baconian is as false as any other method. The most scientific should be the healthiest man.

Deep are the foundations of all sincerity—even stone walls have their foundation below the frost.

Aristotle says in his "Meteorics" "As time never fails, and the universe is eternal, neither the Tanais, nor the Nile, can have flowed forever."

Strabo, upon the same subject, says, "It is proper to derive our explanations from things which are obvious, and in some measure of daily occurrence, such as deluges, earthquakes, and volcanic eruptions, and sudden swellings of the land beneath the sea."—Geology.

Marvellous are the beginnings of philosophy—We can imagine a period when "Water runs down hill" may have been taught in the schools. That man has something demoniacal about him who can discern a law, or couple two facts.

Every idea was long ago done into nature as the translators say—There is walking in the feet—mechanics in the hand climbing in the loose flesh of the palms—boxing in the knuckles &c, &c.

In a lifetime you can hardly expect to convince a man of an error—You must content yourself with the reflection that the progress of science is slow. If he is not convinced his grand children may be. It took 100 years to prove that fossils are organic, and 150 more, to prove that they are not to be referred to the Noachian deluge.

Oct 12th 1840

The springs of life flow in ceaseless tide down below, and hence this greenness everywhere on the surface. But they are as yet untapped—only here and there men have sunk a well.

One of the wisest men I know, but who has no poetic genius — has lead me round step by step in his discourse this afternoon, up to the height of land in these parts; but now that I am left alone, I see the blue peaks in the horizon, and am homesick.

Tuesday Oct 13th 1840

The only prayer for a brave man is to be a doing — this is the prayer that is heard.

Why ask God for a respite when he has not given it. Has he not done his work and made man equal to his occasions, but he must needs have recourse to him again? God cannot give us any other than self help.

The workers in stone polish only their chimney ornaments, but their pyramids are roughly done — There is a soberness in a rough aspect, as unhewn granite — which addresses a depth in us, but the polished surface only hits the ball of the eye.

In all old books the stucco has long since crumbled away, and we read what was sculptured in the granite.

To study style in the utterance of our thoughts, is as if we were to introduce Homer or Zoroaster to a literary club thus, — Gentlemen of the societies — let me make you acquainted with Sir Homer. — Think you if Socrates were to come on earth, he would bring letters to the prominent characters? But a better than Socrates speaks through us every hour and it would be a poor story if we did not defer as much to him by waving impertinent ceremony.

True politeness does not result from a hasty and artificial polishing, but grows naturally by a long fronting of circumstances and rubbing on good and bad fortune.

The elements are yet polishing the pyramids.

The draft of my stove sounds like the dashing of waves on the shore, and the lid sings like the wind in the shrouds.

The steady roar of the surf on the beach is as incessant in my ear as in the shell on the mantelpiece — I see vessels stranded — and gulls flying — and fishermen running to and fro on the beach.

Wednesday Oct 14th 1840

> I arose before light
> To work with all my might,
> With my arms braced for toil
> Which no obstacle could foil,

For it robbed me of my rest
Like an anvil on my breast.

But as a brittle cup
I've held the hammer up,
And no sound from my forge
Has been heard in the gorge.

I look forward into night,
And seem to get some light;
E're long the forge will ring
With its ding-dong-ding,
For the iron will be hot
And my wages will be got.

Oct 15th 1840

There is not a chestnut in the wood but some worm has found it out. He will seem to be at home there, and not far from the highway. Every maggot lives down town.

Men see God in the ripple but not in miles of still water. Of all the two-thousand miles that the St. Lawrence flows—pilgrims go only to Niagara[.]

Saturday Oct 17th 1840

In the presence of my friend I am ashamed of my fingers and toes. I have no feature so fair as my love for him. There is a more than maiden modesty between us. I find myself more simple and sincere than in my most private moment to myself. I am literally true *with a witness*. We should sooner blot out the sun than disturb friendship.

Sunday Oct 18th 1840

The era of greatest change is to the subject of it the condition of greatest invariableness. The longer the lever the less perceptible its motion. It is the slowest pulsation which is the most *vital*. I am independent of the change I detect.

My most essential progress must be to me a state of absolute rest. So in geology we are nearest to discovering the true causes of the revolutions of the globe, when we allow them to consist with a quiescent state of the elements. We discover the causes of all past change in the present invariable order of the universe.

The pulsations are so long that in the interval there is almost a stagnation of life. The first cause of the universe makes the least noise. Its pulse has beat but once—is now beating. The greatest appreciable revolutions are the work of the light-footed air—the stealthy-paced water—and the subterranean fire. The wind makes the desert without a rustle.

To every being consequently its own first cause is an insensible and inconceivable agent.

Some questions which are put to me, are as if I should ask a bird what she will do when her nest is built, and her brood reared.

I cannot make a disclosure—you should see my secret.—Let me open my doors never so wide, still within and behind there, where it is unopened, does the sun rise and set—and day and night alternate.—No fruit will ripen on the common.

Monday Oct 19th 1840

My friend dwells in the distant horizon as rich as an eastern city there. There he sails all lonely under the edge of the sky, but thoughts go out silently from me and belay him, till at length he rides in my roadsted. But never does he fairly come to anchor in my harbor—Perhaps I afford no good anchorage. He seems to move in a burnished atmosphere, while I peer in upon him from surrounding spaces of Cimmerian darkness. His house is incandescent to my eye, while I have no house, but only a neighborhood to his.

Tuesday Oct 20th 1840

My friend is the apology for my life. In him are the spaces which my orbit traverses.

There is no quarrel between the good and the bad—but only between the bad and the bad. In the former case there is inconsistency merely, in the latter a vitious consistency.

Men chord sometimes, as the flute and the pumpkin vine—a perfect chord—a harmony—but no melody. They are not of equal fineness of tone.

For the most part I find that in another man and myself the key note is not the same—so that there are no perfect chords in our gamuts. But if we do not chord by whole tones, nevertheless his sharps are sometimes my flats, and so we play some very difficult pieces together, though the sameness at last fatigues the ear. We never rest on a full natural note—but I sacrifice my naturalness and he his. We play no tune though—only chromatic strains—or trill upon the same note till our ears ache[.]

Sunday Oct 25th 1840

To yield bravely is infinitely harder than to resist bravely. In the one course our sin assists us to be brave, in the other our virtue is alone. True bravery has no ally yet all things are with it.

We do not see in a man all he promises, but certainly all he is. Just as the aspirations do not completely appear in the features, but they are always in a transition state—The past is in the rind, but the future is in the core. The promise of a man must have become experience and character before it can be expressed in his face.

So this outward expression is after all a fair index of his present state, for virtue is not all van, but needs to be viewed both before and behind. In his aspirations virtue is but a superficies and I know not if it be thick or thin—but the features are made up of successive layers of performance—and show the thickness of the character[.] The past and future met together make the present.—Virtue is not virtue's face.

Nov 1st 1840

The day is won by the blushes of the dawn[.]

I thought that the sun of our love should have risen as noiselessly as the sun out of the sea, and we sailors have found ourselves steering between the tropics as if the broad day had lasted forever. You know how the sun comes up from the sea when you stand on the cliff, and does'nt startle you, but every thing, and you too are helping it.

Monday Nov 2nd 1840

It is well said that the "attitude of inspection is prone." The soul does not inspect but behold. Like the lily or the crystal in the rock, it looks in the face of the sky.

Francis Howell says that in garrulous persons "The supply of thought seems never to rise much above the level of its exit." Consequently their thoughts issue in no jets, but incessantly dribble. In those who speak rarely, but to the purpose, the reservoir of thought is many feet higher than its issue. It takes the pressure of a hundred atmospheres to make one jet of eloquence. For the most part the thoughts subside like a sediment, while the words break like a surf on the shore. They are being silently

deposited in level strata, or held in suspension for ages, in that deep ocean within—
Therein is the ocean's floor whither all things sink, and it is strewed with wrecks.

Tuesday Nov 3d 1840

The truth is only contained, never withheld—As a feudal castle may be the head quarters of hospitality, though the portal is but a span in the circuit of the wall. So of the three circles on the cocoa nut one is always so soft that it may be pierced with a thorn, and the traveller is grateful for the thick shell which held the liquor so faithfully.

Wednesday Nov 4th 1840

By your few words show how insufficient would be many words. If after conversation I would reinstate my thought in its primary dignity and authority, I have recourse again to my first simple and concise statement.

In breadth we may be patterns of conciseness, but in depth we may well be prolix[.]

We may have secrets though we do not keep them.

Dr. Ware Jr. said today in his speech at the meeting house—"There are these three—Sympathy—Faith—Patience"—then proceeding in ministerial style, "and the greatest of these is," but for a moment he was at a loss, and became a listener along with his audience, and concluded with "Which is it? I do'nt know. Pray take them all brethren, and God help you."

Nov 5th 1840

Truth is as vivacious and will spread it self as fast as the fungi, which you can by no means annihilate with your heel, for their sporules are so infinitely numerous and subtle as to resemble "thin smoke; so light that they may be raised into the atmosphere, and dispersed in so many ways by the attraction of the sun, by insects, wind, elasticity, adhesion, &c., that it is difficult to conceive a place from which they may be excluded."

Saturday Nov 7th 1840

I'm guided in the darkest night
By flashes of auroral light,

Which over-dart thy eastern home
And teach me not in vain to roam.
Thy steady light on t'other side
Pales the sunset, makes day abide,
And after sunrise stays the dawn,
Forerunner of a brighter morn.

There is no being here to me
But staying here to be.
When others laugh I am not glad,
When others cry I am not sad,
But be they grieved or be they merry
I'm supernumerary.
I am a miser without blame,
Am conscience striken without shame
An idler am I without leisure,
A busy body without pleasure.
I did not think so bright a day
Would issue in so dark a night,
I did not think such sober play
Would leave me in so sad a plight,
And I should be most sorely shent
When first I was most innocent.
I thought by loving all beside
To prove to you my love was wide,
And by the rites I soared above
To show you my peculiar love.

Monday Nov 9th 1840

Events have no abstract and absolute importance, but only concern me as they are related to some man. The biography of a man who has spent his days in a library, may
be as interesting as the Peninsular campaigns. Gibbon's memoirs prove this to me. To
my mind he travels as far when he takes a book from the shelf, as if he went to the bar-
rows of Asia. If the cripple but tell me how like a man he turned in his seat, how he
now looked out at a south window then a north, and finally looked into the fire, it will
be as good as a tour on the continent or the prairies. For I measure distance inward
and not outward. Within the compass of a man's ribs there is space and scene enough
for any biography.

My life passes warmly and cheerily here within while my ears drink in the pattering rain on the sill. It is as adventurous as Crusoe's—as full of novelty as Marco Polo's, as dignified as the Sultan's, as momentous as that of the reigning prince.

Thursday Nov 12th 1840

Mathematical truths stand aloof from the warm life of man—the mere cold and unfleshed skeletons of truth.

Perhaps the whole body of what is now called moral or ethical truth may have once existed as abstract science, and have been only gradually won over to humanity.— Have gradually subsided from the intellect into the heart.

The eye that can appreciate the naked and absolute beauty of a scientific truth, is far rarer than that which discerns moral beauty. Men demand that the truth be clothed in the warm colors of life—and wear a flesh and blood dress. They do not love the absolute truth, but the partial, because it fits and measures them and their commodities best—but let them remember that notwithstanding these delinquencies in practice—Science still exists as the sealer of weights and measures.

Sunday Nov 15th 1840

Over and above a man's business there must be a level of undisturbed serenity, only the more serene as he is the more industrious—as within the reef encircling a coral isle, there is always an expanse of still water, where the depositions are going on which will finally raise it above the surface.

He must preside over all he does—If his employment rob him of a serene outlook over his life, it is but idle though it be measuring the fixed stars. He must know no distracting cares.

The bad sense is the secondary one.

Walt Whitman

One of the greatest American poets, Walt Whitman (1819–1892) placed "manly love" squarely in the middle of his masterwork *Leaves of Grass*, which went through many editions. Born in West Hills, Long Island, he moved to Brooklyn as a young man. He learned to be a printer and later became a newspaper man, one of the many jobs he had. In the 1840s he worked for the *New York Aurora* and then became editor of the *Brooklyn Daily Eagle*. His interest at the time seemed to be in prose, and he published a novel entitled *Franklin Evans* (1842) and several short stories.

In 1855 he published the first edition of *Leaves of Grass*. He was to add, revise, and rearrange the book many times during his life. In 1863 he came to Washington to nurse his brother George, who had been wounded in the Civil War. He stayed on in Washington, working as a clerk and dedicating himself to the care of the sick and dying in the crowded military hospitals.

In 1865, immediately after the war, Whitman met Peter Doyle, who was then nineteen; Whitman was in his late forties. Doyle was an Irish immigrant who had fought for the Confederacy and was then working as a trolley conductor. One stormy night a man who seemed like "an old sea-captain" kept riding the trolley; he and Doyle were alone. Doyle went into the back of the trolley with Whitman and became "familiar at once—I put my hand on his knee—we understood." According to Doyle, Whitman went "all the way back with me." Whitman taught Doyle, who was illiterate, how to read, write, and do arithmetic. Their correspondence is a sign of Whitman's success.

Although Whitman and Doyle never lived in the same house, they saw each other nearly every day until 1872, when Whitman, too sick to take care of himself, moved to Camden, New Jersey, to be with his family. However, they kept in contact until Whitman's death. The letters below are from 1868 to 1870.

From Whitman's Letters
to Peter Doyle

N. Y.
September 25, 1868

Dear Boy,

I rec'd your second letter yesterday—it is a real comfort to me to get such letters from you, dear friend. Every word does me good. The *Star* came all right, & was quite interesting. I suppose you got my second letter last Wednesday. There is nothing new or special to write about to-day—still I thought I would send you a few lines, for Sunday. I put down off hand, & write all about myself & my doings, &c. because I suppose that will be really what my dear comrade wants most to hear, while we are separated.

I am doing a little literary work, according as I feel in the mood—composing on my books. I am having a small edition of the Leaves of Grass for 1867, fixed up & printed. This & some other things give me a little occupation. Upon the whole though I don't do much, but go around a great deal—eat my rations every time, sleep at night like a top, & am having good times so far, in a quiet way, enjoying New York, the society of my mother, & lots of friends. Among other things I spend a portion of the day, with the pilots of the ferry boats, sailing on the river. The river & bay of New York & Brooklyn are always a great attraction to me. It is a lively scene. At either tide, flood or ebb, the water is always rushing along as if in haste, & the river is often crowded with steamers, ships & small craft, moving in different directions, some coming in from sea, others going out. Among the pilots are some of my particular friends—when I see them up in the pilot house on my way to Brooklyn, I go up & sail to & fro several trips. I enjoy an hour or two's sail of this kind very much indeed. My mother & folks are well, & are engaged just these times in the delightful business of moving. I should assist, but have hired a substitute in the shape of a stout young laboring man.

I send you, by mail, a copy of *the Broadway*, with the piece in the same as I had in the car one day. It will not interest you much, only as something coming from me.

I think of you very often, dearest comrade, & with more calmness than when I was there—I find it first rate to think of you, Pete, & to know that you are there, all right,

& that I shall return, & we will be together again. I don't know what I should do if I
hadn't you to think of & look forward to.

Tell Tom Hasset, on No. 7, that I wish to be remembered to him particular. Pete, I
hope this will find you entirely well of your cold. I am glad to hear that your mother
is all right of her cold. This is the time of year when they are apt to be pretty trouble-
some. I should like to have seen that match played between the Nat. & Olympics.

October 9, 1868

Dear Pete,

It is splendid here this forenoon—bright and cool. I was out early taking a short
walk by the river—only two squares from where I live. I received your letter of last
Monday—also the *Star* same date—& glad enough to hear from you—the oftener
the better. Every word is good—I sent you a letter, on the 6th, which I suppose you
rec'd next day. Tell Henry Hurt I received his letter of Oct. 5 all right, & that it was
welcome. Political meetings here every night. The coming Pennsylvania & Ohio elections cause much talk & excitement. The fall is upon us. Overcoats are in demand. I already begin to think about my return to Washington. A month has nearly passed away.
I have received an invitation from a gentleman & his wife, friends of mine, at Providence, R. I. & shall probably go there & spend a few days, latter part of October.

I am grateful to these young men on the RR. for their love & remembrance to
me—Dave, & Jim & Charley Sorrell, Tom Hassett, Harry on No. 11.

Every day I find I have plenty to do—every hour is occupied with something.
Shall I tell you about it, or part of it, just to fill up? I generally spend the forenoon in
my room, writing &c., then take a bath, fix up & go out about 12, & loafe somewhere,
or call on some one down town, or on business, or perhaps if it is very pleasant & I
feel like it, ride a trip with some driver-friend on Broadway from 23d street to Bowl-
ing Green, three miles each way. You know it is a never-ending amusement & study
& recreation for me to ride a couple of hours, of a pleasant afternoon, on a Broadway
stage in this way. You see everything as you pass, a sort of living, endless panorama—
shops, & splendid buildings, & great windows, & on the broad sidewalks crowds of
women, richly-dressed, continually passing, altogether different, superior in style &
looks from any to be seen any where else—in fact a perfect stream of people, men too
dressed in high style, & plenty of foreigners—& then in the streets the thick crowd of
carriages, stages, carts, hotel & private coaches, & in fact all sorts of vehicles & many
first-class teams, mile after mile, & the splendor of such a great street & so many tall,
ornamental, noble buildings, many of them of white marble, & the gayety & motion
on every side—You will not wonder how much attraction all this is, on a fine day, to
a great loafer like me, who enjoys so much seeing the busy world move by him, & ex-
hibiting itself for his amusement, while he takes it easy & just looks on & observes.

Then about the Broadway drivers, nearly all of them are my personal friends. Some have been much attached to me, for years, & I to them. But I believe I have already mentioned them in a former letter. Yesterday I rode the trip I describe with a friend, on a 5th Avenue stage, No. 26—a sort [of] namesake of yours, Pete Calhoun. I have known him 9 or 10 years. The day was fine, & I enjoyed the trip muchly. So I try to put in something in my letters to give you an idea of how I pass part of my time, & what I see here in N. Y. Of course I have quite a variety—some four or five hours every day I most always spend in study, writing, &c. The other serves for a good change. I am writing two or three pieces.

I am having finished about 225 copies of Leaves of Grass bound up, to supply orders. Those copies form all that is left of the old editions. Then there will be no more in the market till I have my new & improved edition set up & stereotyped, which it is my present plan to do the ensuing winter at my leisure in Washington.

Mother is well, I take either dinner or supper with her every day. Remember me to David Stevens & John Towers. Tell Harry on No 11 I will go [to] the Hall again & see if I can find that man in the Sheriff's office. I send you my love, & *so long* for the present. Yours for life, dear Pete, (& death the same).

October 14, 1868

Dear boy Pete,

There is great excitement here over the returns of yesterday's elections, as I suppose there is the same in Washington also—the Democrats look blue enough, & the Republicans are on their high horses. I suppose Grant's success is now certain. As I write, the bands are out here, parading the streets, & the drums beating. It is now forenoon. Tonight we will hear the big guns, & see the blazing bonfires. It is dark & cloudy weather here to-day. I was glad to get your letter of Friday, 9th which is the last—also a Star at same time. Also this morning, Star and Express to 12th. I suppose you rec'd mine of the 9th & the papers. I am about as well as usual. Mother is well, & my brothers the same. I am going to-morrow to Providence, R. I., to spend a few days. Should you write any time within four or five days after receiving this, direct to me *care of Hon. Thomas Davis, Providence, R. I.*

My friend O'Connor is quite unwell, and is absent from Washington away down on the New England coast. I received a letter from him yesterday. I believe I told you I was finishing up about 230 copies of my book, expecting to sell them. I have had them finished up & bound &c. but there is a hitch about the sale, & I shall not be able to sell them at present. There is a pretty strong enmity here toward me, & L. of G., among certain classes—not only that it is a great mess of crazy talk & hard words, all tangled up, without sense or meaning, (which by the by is, I believe, your judgment about it)—but others sincerely think that it is a bad book, improper, & ought to be denounced & put down, & its author along with it. There are some venemous but laughable squibs occasionally in the papers. One said I had received 25 guineas for a piece in an English magazine, but that it was worth all that for any one to read it. Another, the *World*, said "Walt Whitman was in town yesterday, carrying the blue cotton umbrella of the future." (It had been a drizzly forenoon)—So they go it. When they get off a good squib, however, I laugh at it, just as much as any one.

Dear Pete, I hope this will find you well & in good spirits. Dear boy, I send you my love. I will write you a line from Providence. So long, Pete.

Walt

I have been debating whether to get my leave extended, & stay till election day to vote—or whether to pair off with a Democrat, & return (which will amount to the same thing.) Most likely I shall decide on the latter, but don't know for certain.

Providence R. I.
October 17, 1868

Dear Pete,

According to announcement in my last, I have made a movement & change of base, from tumultuous, close-packed, world-like N. Y., to this half-rural, brisk, handsome, New England, third-class town. I came on here last Thursday. I came as guest of Thomas Davis, formerly M. C. from this city—arrived between 8 and 9 o'clock at night—found his carriage at the depot waiting for me—at the house (a sort of castle built of stone, on fine grounds, a mile & a half from the town) a hearty welcome from his hospitable wife, & a family of young ladies & children—a hot supper, a tip-top room &c. &c.—so you see, Pete, your old man is in clover. I have since been round the city & suburbs considerably. I am going down to Newport before I return. Invitations &c. are numerous. I am, in fact, already dividing myself between two hospitalities, part of the time with Mr. & Mrs. Davis, and part with Dr. & Mrs. Channing, old acquaintances of mine in another part of the city. I stopt last night at the house of the latter. It is on a high & pleasant hill at the side of the city, which it entirely overlooks. From the window of my room, I can look down across the city, the river, and off miles upon miles in the distance. The woods are a real spectacle, colored with all the rich colors of autumn. Yesterday it was beautiful & balmy beyond description, like the finest Indian summer. I wandered around, partly walking, partly in a carriage, a good part of the day. To-day there is an entire change of scene—As I sit writing this—what do you think, Pete?—great flakes of *snow* are falling, quite a thick flurry—sometimes the wind blows gusts—in fact a real snow storm has been going on all the forenoon, though without the look or feeling of actual winter as the grass & foliage are autumnal, & the cold is not severe yet. Still it [is] disagreeable & wet & damp & prevents me from going out. So I will make it up by writing a couple of letters—one to mother, & one to you, telling you about things. Providence is a handsome city of about 70,000 inhabitants—has numerous manufactories in full operation—every thing looks lively. From the house up here, I can hear almost any time, night or day, the sound of factory bells & the steam whistles of locomotives half a mile distant. Then the lights at night seen from here make a curious exhibition. At both places I stop, we have plenty of ripe fresh fruit and lots of flowers. Pete, I could now send you a bouquet every morning, far better than I used to, of much choicer flowers.

And how are you getting along, dearest comrade? I hope you are well, & that every thing is going on right with you. I have not heard from you for a good while, it seems. I suppose you got my last letter, 14th, from N. Y. I expect to return to N. Y. about the 22d. Should you feel to write after receiving this, you might direct to 331 East 55th st. as before. I am well as usual. I am luxuriating on excellent grapes. I wish I could send you a basket. At both places I stop they have vineyards, & the grapes are very good & plenty this year. Last night, when I went up at 11 o'clock to my room, I took up three great bunches, each as big as my fist, & sat down and ate them before I turned in. I like to eat them this way, & it agrees with me. It is quite a change here from my associations & surroundings either in Washington or New York. Evenings & meal times I find myself thrown amidst a mild, pleasant society, really intellectual, composed largely of educated women, some young, some not so young, every thing refined & polite, *not* disposed to small talk, conversing in earnest on profound subjects, but with a moderate rather slow tone, & in a kind & conciliatory manner—delighting in this sort of conversation, & spending their evenings till late in it. I take a hand in, for a change. I find it entertaining, as I say, for novelty's sake, for a week or two—but I know very well that would be enough for me. It is all first-rate, good & smart, but too constrained & bookish for a free old hawk like me. I send you my love, dear Pete. *So long.* Will write from N. Y. soon as I return there.

W W

P.S. Just after 12 o'clock—noon—as I am just finishing, the storm lightens up—I am sure I see a bit of blue sky in the clouds—yes, the sun is certainly breaking out.

Providence, R. I.
October 18, 1868

Dear boy & comrade,

I sent off a letter to you yesterday noon, but towards evening Mr. Davis brought me up from the p. o. yours of the 15th, which I was so glad to get that you shall have an answer right off. After the flurry of snow I told you of yesterday morning, we had a pleasant clear afternoon. I took a long walk, partly through the woods, and enjoyed it much. The weather was pretty cold & sharp, & remains so yet. As I left my over-coat in Washington, I have been compelled to get something here—so I have bought me a great iron-grey shawl, which I find very acceptable. I always had doubts about a shawl, but have already got used to mine, & like it first rate. In the evening, I went by invitation to a party of ladies & gentlemen—mostly ladies. We had a warm, animated talk, among other things about Spiritualism. I talked too, indeed went in like a house afire. It was good exercise—for the fun of the thing. I also made love to the women, & flatter myself that I created at least one impression—wretch & gay deceiver that I am. Then away late—lost my way—wandered over the city, & got home after one o'clock.

The truth is, Peter, that I am here at present times mainly in the midst of female women, some of them young & jolly—& meet them most every evening in com-pany—& the way in which this aged party comes up to the scratch & cuts out the youthful parties & fills their hearts with envy is absolutely a caution. You would be as-tonished, my son, to see the brass & coolness, & the capacity of flirtation & carrying on with the girls—I would never have believed it of myself. Brought here by destiny, surrounded in this way—& as I in self defence would modestly state—sought for, seized upon & ravingly devoured by these creatures—& *so* nice & smart some of them are, & handsome too—there is nothing left for me—is there—but to go in. Of course, young man, you understand, it is all on the square. My going in amounts to just talking & joking & having a devil of a jolly time, carrying on—that's all. They are all as good girls as ever lived. I have already had three or four such parties here—which, you will certainly admit, considering my age & heft, to say nothing of my repu-tation, is doing pretty well.

I go about quite a good deal—this is as handsome a city, as I ever saw. Some of the streets run up steep hills. Except in a few of the business streets, where the buildings are compact—in nine-tenths of the city, every house stands separate, & has a little or quite a deal of ground about it, for flowers, & for shade or fruit trees, or a garden. I never saw such a prosperous looking city—but of course no grand public buildings like Washington.

This forenoon I have been out away down along the banks of the river & cove, & making explorations generally. All is new to me, & I returned quite tired. I have eat a hearty dinner. Then I thought I would come up & sit a while in my room. But as I did not feel like reading, I concluded to write this precious screed. Fortunate young man, to keep getting such instructive letters—aint you? It is now four o'clock & bright & cool, & I have staid in long enough. I will sally forth, on a walk, & drop this in the P. O. before supper. So long, dear Pete—& my love to you as always, always.

                                                                                    W

Brooklyn, N. Y.
August 21, 1869

Dear Pete—

I have been very sick the last three days—I dont know what to call it—it makes me prostrated & deathly weak, & little use of my limbs. I have thought of you, my darling boy, very much of the time. I have not been out of the house since the first day after my arrival. I had a pleasant journey through on the cars Wednesday afternoon & night—felt quite well then. My Mother & folks are all well. We are in our new house—we occupy part & rent out part. I have a nice room, where I now sit writing this. It is the latter part of the afternoon. I feel better the last hour or so. It has been extremely hot here the last two days—I see it has been so in Washington too. I hope I shall get out soon. I hanker to get out doors, & down the bay.

And now, dear Pete, for yourself. How is it with you, dearest boy—and is there any thing different with the face? Dear Pete, you must forgive me for being so cold the last day & evening. I was unspeakably shocked and repelled from you by that talk & proposition of yours—you know what—there by the fountain. It seemed indeed to me, (for I will talk out plain to you, dearest comrade,) that the one I loved, and who had always been so manly & sensible, was gone, & a fool & intentional murderer stood in his place. I spoke so sternly & cutting. (Though I see now that my words might have appeared to have a certain other meaning, which I didn't dream of, insulting to you, never for one moment in my thoughts.) But I will say no more of this—for I know such thoughts must have come when you was not yourself, but in a moment of derangement—& have passed away like a bad dream.

Dearest boy, I have not a doubt but you will get well, and entirely well—& we will one day look back on these drawbacks & sufferings as things long past. The extreme cases of that malady, (as I told you before) are persons that have very deeply diseased blood, probably with syphilis in it, inherited from parentage, & confirmed by themselves—so they have no foundation to build on. *You* are of healthy stock, with a sound constitution, & good blood—& I *know* it is impossible for it to continue long. My darling, if you are not well when I come back I will get a good room or two in some quiet place, (or out of Washington, perhaps in Baltimore,) and we will live together, & devote ourselves altogether to the job of curing you, & rooting the cursed thing out entirely, & making you stronger & healthier than ever. I have had this in my mind before, but never broached it to you. I could go on with my work in the Attorney General's office just the same—& we would see that your mother should have a small sum every week to keep the pot a-boiling at home.

Dear comrade, I think of you very often. My love for you is indestructible, & since that night & morning has returned more than before.

Dear Pete, dear son, my darling boy, my young & loving brother, don't let the devil put such thoughts in your mind again—wickedness unspeakable—murder, death & disgrace here, & hell's agonies hereafter—Then what would it be afterward to the mother? What to *me?*—

Pete, I send you some money, by Adam's Express—you use it, dearest son, & when it is gone, you shall have some more, for I have plenty. I will write again before long—give my love to Johnny Lee, my dear darling boy, I love him truly—(let him read these three last lines)—Dear Pete, *remember*—

Walt

Brooklyn
September 3, 1869

Dear Pete,

I thought I would write you a letter to-day, as you would be anxious to hear. I rec'd your letter of Aug. 24, & it was a great comfort to me. I have read it several times since—Dear Pete, I hope every thing is going on favorably with you. I think about you every day & every night. I do hope you are in good spirits & health. I want to hear about the face. I suppose you are working on the road.

There is nothing new or special in my affairs or doings. The weather is pleasant here—it is pretty cool & dry. My folks all continue well—mother first rate, & brothers ditto. I do not have such good luck. I have felt unwell most every day—some days not so bad. Besides I have those spells again, worse, last longer, sick enough, come sudden, dizzy, & sudden sweat—It is hard to tell exactly what is the matter, or what to do. The doctor says it is all from that hospital malaria, hospital poison absorbed in the system years ago—he thinks it better for me in Washington than here.

About one third of the time I feel pretty well. I have taken three or four of my favorite rides on Broadway. I believe I described them to you in my letters a year ago. I find many of my old friends, & new ones too, & am received with the same warm friendship & love as ever. Broadway is more crowded & gay than ever, & the women look finer, & the shops richer—then there are many new & splendid buildings, of marble or iron—they seem to almost reach the clouds, they are so tall—some of them cost millions of dollars.

Staging in N. Y. has been very poor this summer—9 or $10, even on the big Broadway lines—Railroading has also been slim. New York is all cut up with railroads—Brooklyn also—I have seen Jimmy Foy—he was over to Brooklyn, looking for work on a road. He was well & hearty, & wished to be remembered to you. They pay $2½ on many of the roads here, & 2¼ on the rest. The work is pretty hard, but the hours not so long as in Washington.

There is all kinds of fun & sport here, by day & night—& lots of theatres & amusements in full blast. I have not been to any of them—have not been to see any of my particular women friends—though sent for, (the papers here have noticed my arrival)—have not been down to the sea-shore as I intended—In fact my jaunt this time has been a failure—Better luck next time—

Now Pete, dear, loving boy, I don't want you to worry about me—I shall come along all right. As it is, I have a good square appetite most of the time yet, good nights' sleep—& look about the same as usual, (which is, of course, lovely & fascinating beyond description.) Tell Johnny Lee I send him my love, & hope he is well & hearty. I think of him daily. I sent him a letter some time ago, which I suppose he rec'd about Aug. 26, & showed you—but I have not had a word from him. Lend him this letter to read, as he will wish to hear about me.

God bless you, dear Pete, dear loving comrade, & Farewell till next time, my darling boy.

Walt.

101 Portland av. opposite the Arsenal, Brooklyn, New York

Brooklyn
September 10, 1869

Dear Pete—dear son,

I have received your letter of the 8th to-day—all your letters have come safe—four altogether. This is the third I have sent you (besides that one by Adams' Express, Aug. 23d.)

Pete, you say my sickness must be worse than I described in my letters—& ask me to write precisely how I am. No, dearest boy, I wrote just as it really was. But, Pete, you will now be truly happy to learn that I am feeling all right, & have been mainly so for the last four days—& have had no bad spells all that time. Yesterday I thought I felt as strong & well as ever in my life—in fact real young & jolly. I loafed around New York most all day—had a first-rate good time. All along Broadway hundreds of rich flags & streamers at half-mast for Gen. Rawlins' funeral—From the tall buildings, they waved out in a stiff west wind all across Broadway—late in the afternoon I rode up from the Battery to look at them, as the sun struck through them—I thought I had never seen any thing so curious & beautiful—On all the shipping, ferry boats, public buildings &c. flags at half mast too. This is the style here. No black drapery, for mourning—only thousands of flags at half mast, on the water as well as land—for any big bug's funeral.

To-day I am all right too. It is now towards 3—Mother & I have just had our dinner, (my mammy's own cooking mostly.) I have been out all the forenoon knocking around—the water is my favorite recreation—I could spend two or three hours every day of my life here, & never get tired—Some of the pilots are dear personal friends of mine—some, when we meet, we kiss each other (I am an exception to all their customs with others)—some of their boys have grown up since I have known them, & they too know me & are very friendly.

Pete, the fourth week of my vacation is most ended. I shall return the middle of next week.

Give my love to Johnny Lee—let him read this letter, & then return it to you. Dear Jack, I rec'd your affectionate letter of Sept. 5th.

Pete, I have seen Tom Haslett—he is well—he is working extra on Broadway & 42d st. RR. He does not think of going home till Christmas. Jimmy Foy has not got work yet.

I suppose you got "Kenilworth" I sent.

Well, boy, I shall now take a bath, dress myself & go out, cross the river, put this letter in the p. o. & then ramble & ride around the City, awhile, as I think we are going to have a fine evening & moonlight &c.

Good bye, dear son—We will soon be together again.

Walt.

Brooklyn
July 30, 1870

Dear Pete,

Well here I am home again with my mother, writing to you from Brooklyn once more. We parted there, you know, at the corner of 7th st. Tuesday night. Pete, there was something in that hour from 10 to 11 oclock (parting though it was) that has left me pleasure & comfort for good—I never dreamed that you made so much of having me with you, nor that you could feel so downcast at losing me. I foolishly thought it was all on the other side. But all I will say further on the subject is, I now see clearly, that was all wrong.

I started from the depot in the 7:25 train the next morning—it was pretty warm, yet I had a very pleasant journey, & we got in New York by 5 o'clock, afternoon. About half an hour before we arrived, I noticed a very agreeable change in the weather—the heat had moderated—& in fact it has been pleasant enough every day since. I found mother & all as well as usual. It is now Saturday between 4 & 5 in the afternoon—I will write more on the other side—but, Pete, I must now hang up for the present, as there is a young lady down stairs whom I have promised to go with to the ferry, & across to the cars.

Sunday—6 P.M.

Pete, dear boy, I will write you a line to-day before I go. I am going over to New York to visit the lady I went down to the ferry with—so you see I am quite a lady's man again in my old days—There is nothing special to write about—I am feeling in first-rate spirits, & eat my rations every time.

Monday, Aug 1

The carrier brought quite a bunch this forenoon for the Whitman family, but no letter from you. I keep real busy with one thing & another, the whole day is occupied—I am feeling well quite all the time, & go out a great deal, knocking around one place & another. The evenings here are delightful and I am always out in them, sometimes on the river, sometimes in New York—There is a cool breeze & the moon shining. I think every time of you, & wish if we could only be together these evenings at any rate.

Tuesday—Aug 2

Well, Pete, you will have quite a diary at this rate. Your letter came this morning—& I was glad enough to get word from you. I have been over to New York to-day on business—it is a pleasure even to cross the ferry—the river is splendid to-day—a stiff breeze blowing & the smell of the salt sea blowing up, (sweeter than any perfume to *my* nose)—It is now 2 o'clock—I have had my dinner & am sitting here alone writing this—Love to you, dear Pete—& I wont be so long again writing to my darling boy.

Walt.

Henry James

Henry James (1843–1916) was one of the greatest American novelists. His works include *The American* (1877), *Portrait of a Lady* (1888), *What Maisie Knew* (1897), *The Ambassadors* (1903), *The Wings of the Dove* (1902), and *The Golden Bowl* (1904). James brought to the American novel a subtlety of language, psychology, and realism it had never had before and may never have again.

As far as is known, Henry James remained a celibate throughout his life, yet he developed deep emotional ties with a number of men and women, none as passionate in its way as the relationship he developed late in life with the young sculptor Hendrik Andersen (1872–1943), who, although born in Norway, was raised in Newport, Rhode Island.

Before meeting James, Andersen had had a relationship with Lord Gower, a wealthy English homosexual artist, critic, and patron. Thus, Andersen's friendship with James follows a pattern of involvement with older, more powerful men who might advance his career. James certainly hoped to help Andersen, and his early letters are filled with careful praise and explicit advice. But, as the letters show, James became increasingly alarmed by what he called Andersen's megalomania, an obsession with enormous, unrealizable projects. While his disillusionment with Andersen did not end James's affection for the man, it did put a damper on his enthusiasm. Yet James's most tender feelings of sympathy had nothing to do with art; his letter of February 1902, occasioned by the death of Andersen's brother Andreas, is the work of a man very much conscious of the loss of a loved one.

From James's Letters to Hendrick Andersen

Lamb House, Rye.
March 9, 1900.

My dear (by which I mean my dear young,) old Hans!

I've had your last good letter too long unacknowledged. Yet I've waited also on purpose, in order not to produce with you the feeling of pressure & overfrequent appeal—in respect to our interchange. All the same it's charming to hear from you, & I welcome & respond to every touch of your hand. "Charming" I say, in spite of my sense of your uphill winter, your alien & exiled state (as it were—after Rome the artists' *own,*) & your generally stiff conditions. I figure to myself these things & I figure you *in* them, & I sigh, & I think, & I hope; & I count the gleams of light that seem to spot a little your gloom. The biggest gleam, for both of us, will be having you here, a few months hence—if so be it that, when the time arrives, you *can* come; for which I shall earnestly pray.... May your pall be lifted and your light diffuse itself. I don't see how this can fail. I've told you that before—& it may irritate you to hear me *bêtement* repeat it, while your fate does hang fire: & yet I do repeat it, while I pat you ever so tenderly on the back—as obstinately as if you had swallowed something & were choking. I'm afraid I've no news for you that will amuse you.... It's when nothing happens that one is most at ease. I'm very quiet, very busy, & very uncompanied. But I go up to London for a fortnight day after tomorrow. There I shall see some old friends & taste a little of the cup of the world. Then I shall come back here for a long go—another—of tranquillity & production. That's the only thing that makes life tolerable—to forget everything in some sort of creation. That's what *you* can do;—none better. It's probably what you *are,* a little, doing, *Dio vuole!* Only when you speak of "lessons" I groan. I'm glad you've got them if you need them—yet I gnash my teeth to think they've got *you.*——As the time comes round that makes the anniversary of my Italian journey of last year, a deep nostalgia seizes me, a melancholy yearning to be there again, to feel the Roman May & June. I think of the day you lunched & dined with me. But it's out of the question *this* spring, & when I go again you must be there. Good night, my dear Hans—lift up your heart. We shall again be shoulder to shoulder—or, better still, face to face, and I am yours always

Henry James

P.S. Forgive this stupid blank side—which I accidentally skipped. I would undertake still to cover it were it not one o'clk in the A.M. & my hand weary & weak. Felicissima notte———[On flap of envelope] Have stupidly lost your New York address and have to reach you thus *indirectly*.

105 Pall Mall. S.W.
January 12, 1901.

My dear Boy Hans.

It has been a great joy to me to hear from you in such good sort, & I think of you, in your temple of art on the banks of the Tiber, with uncommon satisfaction & sympathy. I'm delighted to gather that you established yourself without great worry or wait, & I send you my blessing on all you do & are. If good old Lincoln does hang about you, so much the better, & if you've really got him I pray you may hold him tight. And on all the bright company in which you take him to dwell with you, may peace & abundance descend. How jolly it must be to be restored to Rome & the old life & the old light, at least, & the old loves—I mean, more particularly, as regards the last-named, the pure & independent passions of the mind & of the imagination. I rejoice that you saw my admirable sister-in-law, who mentioned to me your visit with very marked appreciation. She views you with extraordinary favour. But I hope you won't fail altogether of a sight of my brother himself—he has a wondrous sense of things plastic, things modelled, things wrought. And he is a very delightful man— better even than I! We have both, you see, you & I, such endowed brothers that we can boast of them.——I am not, as you see, at Lamb House; the winter there had ceased to be tolerable, & I've come up to town for 3 months. It's a very dusky, dingy, fog-smothered town just now; but it is also many other things else, & is the place in the world in which the state of the atmosphere, on the whole, least matters. But I shall revert, about April 1st, with a long breath & a great glee. I hope with all my heart that the summer will bring you to England. If it does I shall lay my hand on you firmly & expect you to have a good bit of a fairy tale to tell me. May the fairies meanwhile then—by which I mean the felicities that an artist knows when he doesn't know the black devils of despair—smother you with their favours. Think of me as thinking of you very tenderly & confidently, & believe me yours, my dear Hans, always & ever

Henry James

P.S. Don't think of this as a thing to be "answered"—*damn* answers!

105 Pall Mall, S.W.
February 9, 1902.

My dear, dear, dearest Hendrik.

Your news [of the death of Andersen's brother Andreas] fills me with horror &
pity, & how can I express the tenderness with wh: it makes me think of you & the aching wish to be near you & put my arms round you? My heart fairly bleeds & breaks at
the vision of you *alone*, in your wicked & indifferent old far-off Rome, with this haunting, blighting, unbearable sorrow. The sense that I can't *help* you, see you, talk to you,
touch you, hold you close & long, or do anything to make you rest on me, & feel my
deep participation—this torments me, dearest boy, makes me ache for you, & for
myself; makes me gnash my teeth & groan at the bitterness of things. I can only take
refuge in hoping you are *not* utterly alone, that some human tenderness of *some* sort,
some kindly voice & hand *are* near you that may make a little the difference. What a
dismal winter you must have had, with this staggering blow as the climax! I don't of
course know *what* fragment of friendship there may be to draw near to you, & in my
uncertainty my image of you is of the darkest, and my pity, as I say, feels so helpless. I
wish I could go to Rome & put my hands on you (oh, how lovingly I should lay them!)
but that, alas, is odiously impossible. (Not, moreover, that, apart from *you*, I should
so much as like to be there now.) I find myself thrown back on anxiously, & doubtless
vainly, wondering if there may not, after a while, [be] some possibility of your coming to England, of the current of your trouble inevitably carrying you here—so that I
might take consoling, soothing, infinitely close & tender & affectionately-healing *possession* of you. This is the one thought that relieves me about you a little—& I wish
you might fix your eyes on it for the idea, just, of the possibility. I am in town for a few
weeks, but I return to Rye April 1st, & sooner or later to *have* you there & do for you,
to put my arm round you & *make* you lean on me as on a brother & a lover, & keep
you on & on, slowly comforted or at least relieved of the first bitterness of pain—this
I try to imagine as thinkable, attainable, not wholly out of the question. There I am,
at any rate, & there is my house & my garden & my table, & my studio—such as it
is!—& your room, & your welcome, & your place everywhere—& I press them upon
you, oh so earnestly, dearest boy, if isolation & grief & the worries you are overdone
with become intolerable to you. There they are, I say—to fall upon, to rest upon, to
find whatever possible shade of oblivion in. I will *nurse* you through your dark passage. I wish I could do something *more*—something straighter & nearer & more immediate; but such as it is please let it sink into you. Let all my tenderness, dearest
boy, do *that*. This is all now. I wired you 3 words an hour ago. I can't *think* of your
sister-in-law—I brush her vision away and your history with your father, as I've feared
it, has haunted me all winter. I embrace you with almost a passion of pity.

Henry James

Lamb House, Rye, Sussex.
February 28, 1902.

Dearest, dearest Boy, more tenderly embraced than I can say!—How woefully you must have wondered at my apparently horrid & heartless silence since your last so beautiful, noble, exquisite letter! *But*, dearest Boy, I've been dismally *ill*—as I was even when I wrote to you from town; & it's only within a day or two that free utterance has—to *this* poor extent—become possible to me. *Don't waste any pity, any words, on me now*, for it's, at last, blissfully over, I'm convalescent, on firm ground, safe, gaining daily—only weak & "down" & spent, & above all like a helpless pigmy before my accumulation of the mountain of a month's letters, &c. To make a long story of the shortest, I was taken in London, on Jan. 29th—2 days after getting there, with a malignant sudden attack, through a chill, of inflammation of the bowels; which threw me into bed, for a week, howling. Then I had a few days of false & apparent recuperation—*one* of which was the Sunday I wrote you from the Athenaeum on receipt of *your* direful letter. But I felt myself collapsing, *re*lapsing again, & hurried down here on Feb. 11th just in time to save, as it were, my life from another wretched siege out of my own house. I tumbled into bed here & had a dozen wretched days of complicated, aggravated relapse: but at least nursed, tended, cared for, with all zeal & needfulness. So I've pulled through—& am out—& surprisingly soon—of a very deep dark hole. *In* my deep hole, how I thought yearningly, helplessly, dearest Boy of *you* as your last letter gives you to me, & as I take you, to my heart. I determined, deliberately, *not* to *wire* you, for I felt it would but cruelly worry & alarm you; & each day I reached out to the hope of some scrawl—I mean toward some possibility of a word to you. But that has come only now. Now, at least, my weak arms still can fold you close. Infinitely, deeply, as deeply as you will have felt, for yourself, was I touched by your 2d letter. I respond to every throb of it, I participate in every pang. I've gone through Death, & Deaths, enough in my long life, to know how all that we *are*, all that we *have*, all that is best of us within, our genius, our imagination, our passion, our whole personal being, become then but aids & channels & open gates to suffering, to being flooded. But, it is better so. Let yourself go & *live*, even as a lacerated, mutilated lover, with your grief, your loss, your sore, unforgettable consciousness. *Possess* them & let them possess you, & life, so, will still hold you in her arms, & press you to her breast, & keep you, like the great merciless but still *most* enfolding and never disowning mighty Mother, on & on for things to come. Beautiful & unspeakable your acct. of relation to Andreas. Sacred & beyond tears. How I wish I had known him, admirable, loveable boy—but • you make me: I *do*. Well, he is *all* yours now: he lives in you & out of all pain. Wait, & you will see; hold fast, sit tight, *stick hard*, & more things than I can tell you now will come back to you. But you know, in your courage, your genius & your patience, more of these things than I need try thus to stammer to you. And now I am tired & spent. I only, for goodnight, for five minutes, take you to my heart. And I'm better, better, better, dearest Boy; don't think of my having been ill. Think only of my love & that I am yours always & ever

Henry James.

Lamb House, Rye, Sussex.
August 10, 1904.

My dear dear Hendrik.

No letter from you was ever more charming & touching to me than your last from Montefiascone—wonderful romantic spot of which I envy you (even till I *ache* with it,) the so intimate & friendly knowledge. Every word of you is as soothing as a caress of your hand, & the sense of the whole as sweet to me as being able to lay my own upon *you*. It's so much money in my pocket—that of my otherwise so baffled spirit—to know you are at your ease in a good high place, with rest & peace & idleness & cool airs & brown cheeks & glorious wine all keeping you company; to say nothing of your still more human companions,—whose being with you I more & more rejoice in & to whom I am particularly glad (both for him & for you,) to know that your brother Arthur is added. Make him a sign of my ever so kindly remembrance. Stay as long & lie as loose as you by a stretched possibility can—you will be of ever so much more value to yourself & to the world in the end—to say nothing of your being of more, my dear, dear Hendrik, to your poor fond old H.J. I only groan over its being so beastly long, of necessity, before I can hope to get from your lips the charming echo & side-wind of your Italian summer—even as I had from you so beautifully, last year, the story of your primitive Norcia. I "sail", heaven help me, on Aug. 24th—not to return, very probably, till late in the spring—all of which means, doesn't it?—dreary and deadly postponements. But may the time be full, for you, of triumphant completions & consummations—without a solitary blink of giddiness. It was after I last wrote you that your photos. arrived, & I haven't as yet so much as thanked you for them directly. But I find them, dear Hendrik, difficult to speak of to you—they terrify me so with their evidence as of *madness* (almost) in the scale on which you are working! It is magnificent—it is sublime, it is heroic; & the idea & composition of your group-circled fountain, evidently a very big thing. Only I feel as if it were let loose into space like a blazing comet—with you, personally, dangling after like the tail, & I ask myself where my poor dear confident reckless Hendrik is being whirled, through the dark future, & where he is going to be dropped. I want to be there, wherever it is, to catch you in my arms—for my nerves, at all events, give way, with the too-long tension of your effort, even if yours don't. And I yearn, too, for the *smaller* masterpiece; the condensed, consummate, caressed, intensely filled-out thing. But forgive this obscure, this wild & wandering talk. The photographs are admirably interesting & give the impression of an immense effect; but to know where I am, & where *you* are, I ought to *be* there, in front of each group, with my questions to ask & your brave answers to take, while my arm is over your shoulder; & for all that *ci vuol' tempo*, alas. Meanwhile, at any rate, my dear boy, I pat you on the back lovingly, tenderly, tenderly—& I am, with every kindest message to your blessed companions, yours, my Hendrik, always and ever

Henry James

Lamb House, Rye, Sussex.
August 6, 1905.

My dear, dear Hendrik!

Your letter from Gibraltar is a sad enough story—which I bear a little less badly, however, for having felt myself, as the days have gone on, prepared for it. That I *should* have you here at this lovely moment (for it is of the loveliest here) was somehow too good to be true, & as your silence lengthened out I felt, more & more, that I was losing you. It is very horrible—but I understand well how difficult, how not to be managed, with your so much more direct & economic road to Italy it must have been for you to come this way. It was only that, in those last hours at Newport, you seemed to believe the thing possible. So *I* believed for a while—& I looked forward, & the pang of the loss is sharp; but, clearly, you have done the right thing. Short & scant—pitifully—with this annihilation, do those few American moments seem to me—& lighted with the strange light of our common uneasiness & outsideness there. But I remember ever so tenderly our first hour together in Boston, & our drive to the Railroad with my trap & then our other & better & longer drive at Newport (which was quite lovely,)—coloured with the beauty of our seeming then destined soon to meet again. When the Devil *shall* we meet, at this rate?—& when, ah when, shall I be able to go back again, at the right moment & in the right way, to the loved Italy? The grim years pass, & don't bring me that boon! Still, we *must* meet, & I must somehow arrange. What consoles me a little is to hear that your weeks in America did tend, did eventuate, in some way, to your profit & your gain—though I wish to heaven I were near enough for you to tell me more without the impossible trouble of your writing it. *That*, about nothing, must you have. Yet it's all pretty wretched, this non-communication—for there are long & weighty things—about your work, your plan, your perversity, your fountain, your building on & on, & up & up, *in the air*, as it were, *& out of relation to possibilities & actualities*, that I wanted to say to you. We could have *talked* them beautifully & intimately here, these things—but now it's as if they had to wait & wait. Yet they mustn't wait too long. *Make the pot boil at any price, as the only real basis* of freedom & sanity. Stop building in the air for a while & build on the ground. *Earn* the money that will give you the right to conceptions (and still more to executions,) like your fountain—though I am still wondering *what* American community is going to want to pay for 30 & 40 stark naked men & women, of whatever beauty, lifted into the raw light of one of their public places. Keep in relation to the *possible* possibilities, dearest boy, & hold on tight, at any rate, till I can get to you somehow & somewhere & have you *bust* me. But good night, dearest boy; it's ever so late, & it's hideous that you're not here & that you won't be. How long & close, in imagination & affection, I hold you! Feel, Hendrik, the force & the benediction of it & all the applied tenderness of your constant old friend

Henry James

P.S. It's a delight to me that you can speak of yourself as so cleared off, physically, & so confident, & oh, how I yearn after you to Montefiascone!

Lamb House, Rye, Sussex.
January 31, 1906.

Bravo, bravo, dearest Hendrik, for the vivid little note & the still vivider little photos. of the vividest big group: a more than adequate & altogether beautiful response to my poor New Year's letter, which was only meant to bless & cheer you & never to hurry & worry you at all. Noble & admirable your two Lovers united in their long embrace, & quite, to my sense, the finest of all your fine contributions to this wonderful (& interminable!) series! It won't, by its nature, help the great nude Army to encamp in the heart of the American city, but when I have said *that*, I shall have exhausted the sum of my strictures upon it—with the exception perhaps of saying that I don't think I find the *hands*, on the backs, *living* enough & participant enough in the kiss. They would be, in life, very participant—to their finger-tips & would show it in many ways. But this you know, & the thing is very strong & (otherwise) complete. There is more flesh & *pulp* in it, more life of *surface* & of blood-flow *under* the surface, than you have hitherto, in your powerful simplifications, gone in for. So keep at *that*—at the flesh & the devil & the rest of it; make the creatures palpitate, & their flesh tingle & flush, & their internal economy proceed, & their bellies ache & their bladders fill—all in the mystery of your art! How I wish (to God!) I could stand there with you in your crowded workshop & talk of these things. But patience, patience; that *still* will happen! You say no word of your head & your health—so I try to take the Kissers for favourable evidence, & I scan the so handsome fatigued face of the rabbit-picture for signs reassuring & veracious. I don't know to what extent I make them out: you're so beautiful in it that I only hope you're really exempt from physical woe. I take hold of you ever so tenderly & am yours ever so faithfully

Henry James

[On back of envelope] *His* hand is the better & his knees ever so interesting & *magnificent.*

Lamb House, Rye, Sussex.
July 20, 1906.

My dearest old Boy.

. . . Your fertility & power seem to me marvellous, & the 2 Kodak-figures of your note to testify to that as wondrously as ever. They are very beautiful to me, as to everything but their faces—I am quite impertinently unhappy (as I told you, offensively, the last time,) about your system of face. Also I sometimes find your sexes (putting *the* indispensable sign apart!) not quite intensely enough differentiated—I mean through the ladies resembling a shade too much the gentlemen (perhaps, as in the case of this last *ballerina*, through your not allowing her a quite sufficient luxury—to my taste— of hip, or, to speak plainly, Bottom. She hasn't *much* more of that than her husband, & I should like her to have a good deal more.) But no matter—they are both full of life & beauty & power—though I fear they will presently, in the mazes of the dance, tear their baby limb from limb. How many babies they do have—how they do keep at it, making you, to a tremendous tune, a grandfather! Admirable this back view of them in especial. But who, all this while, is *seeing* them, Enrico mio? & to what degree is the world the wiser? . . .

H.J.

Lamb House, Rye, Sussex.
November 25, 1906.

My dear, dear Hendrik.

I have *had* to wait to acknowledge your touching, quite harrowing letter: a friend had just arrived (from Paris) to spend a week with me; complications of work piled themselves on top of that, & in short every minute was taken. Now the friend has departed, the air is a little clearer, & I seize the pen to tell you that I yearn all tenderly over you & your new visitation—I mean the indigestion & dyspepsia you tell me about. I wish to goodness I could get *near* to you for a while & intervene somehow between you & these sorry fates which your manner of life & of work seem so disturbingly (& by no *intentional* perversity of your own, I fully recognise,) to draw down upon you. I am *trying*, all the while—I am laying out plans for our coming together somehow—somehow that will permit of my laying the firmest & kindest & closest of all arms about you & talking to you, "for your good," for three uninterrupted days & nights. For the root of these afflictions & disasters strikes me as lying in the *lonely insanity* (permit me the expression, dearest boy,) of your manner of work: the long, unbroken tension of your Scheme itself, the scheme of piling up into the air this fantastic number of figures on which you are *realizing nothing* (neither money, nor judgement—the practical judgement, practical attitude towards them, of the purchasing, paying, supporting, rewarding world;) on which you are not even realizing that benefit of *friction with the market* which is so true a one for solitary artists too much steeped in their mere personal dreams, & which wakes them up to a measure of where they are and what they are doing & not doing—for practical value or no-value. You are attempting what no young artist *ever* did—to live on air indefinitely, by what I can make out, putting all your eggs into one extremely precarious & perforated basket, & declining the aid of the thing done meanwhile *to live*, to bring in its assistance from month to month: the potboiler call it if you like, the potboiler which represents, in the lives of all artists, some of the most beautiful things ever done by them. Stop your multiplication of unsaleable nakednesses for a while & hurl yourself, by every cunning art you can command, into the production of the interesting, the charming, the vendible, the *placeable* small thing. With your talent you easily *can*—& if I were but near you now I should take you by the throat & squeeze it till you howled & make you do *my Bust!* You ought absolutely to get at Busts, at any cost of ingenuity—for it is fatal for you to go on indefinitely neglecting the *Face*, never doing one, only adding Belly to Belly—however beautiful—& Bottom to Bottom, however sublime. It is only by the Face that the artist—the sculptor—can hope *predominantly* & steadily to live—& it is so supremely & exquisitely interesting to do! The impossible effort to *ignore* all this wisdom that I thus pour out on you is what is working havoc in your nerves & digestion by the abnormal sort of tension & fever (the *monstrous* nature of the effort,) it requires. Dear, dear Hendrik, have patience with my words & shut yourself up with them a while & judge of the affection that prompts them. . . .

                                                              Henry James

Lamb House, Rye, Sussex.
January 24, 1908.

My dear dear Hendrik!
     . . . I am extremely interested in the casting of the Bust—though rather scared & abashed that you should think me worthy (even though I think *you* so,) of imperial & eternal bronze. I shall be infinitely anxious to hear how I come out, and am rather hoping, if you will pass me the indiscretion, that I shan't be in very yellow or shiny metal. However, I shall be in whatever you think good & fit, & grateful for any form or hue my poor old struggling sleepyhead (with which you had such generous patience, though you must have so hated it,) will take. Beautiful, dearest Hendrik, your saying

the thing is to be a gift to me. That will never do in the world; I shall not be in the *least* able to appropriate coolly & unrequitingly that amount of your ardent living labour, & if you will have a little *more* of the same long patience with me you will duly receive the well-earned wage of your toil. This you should already have done had it not happened that, truth to tell, my poor old perforated pocket has been this autumn & winter exceptionally empty of ready money. I came back from my 4 or 5 months' foreign tour last summer decidedly depleted — & haven't as yet quite got on my feet again in the sense of having "realized". But I shall now, before long, *be* realizing, & then you shall distinctly hear from me in a form that will give *me*, dearest Hendrik, great pleasure, whatever it may do to you.——As for showing the Bust in London, I am already — from old observation & knowledge — sufficiently master of the subject to be able to inform you definitely. There is no use *whatever* in trying to get the thing into — in sending it, as a stranger & foreigner unknown here, *to* the Royal Academy. That is practically for British artists alone; the accommodation for sculpture is small, the flood of things sent huge, & I've *never known* any "outside" thing to get in (having had frequent occasion to watch & hope, on behalf of friends.) Your one chance is to try for the New Gallery. To that end the bust must be seen in London, privately, by Comyns Carr or Charles Hallé, & then they if thereto moved, will *invite* you to send it. I myself would really (for my own interest in it) rather you *didn't* send it; & I don't quite know where to ask, or to tell you to address it, in London, so that it may be on view by those — or one of those — gentlemen. But if it *were* where they could see it, I should be able to manage that they come — though of course quite unable to answer for their often unaccountable & quite irresponsible *decision*. The thing is first, I think, to get it cast — & then if possible photographed (without too high lights;) & then to send me the photograph. I *might* be able to do something with that; & would willingly *try* (if the photograph seems favourable or fortunate.), . . . your tenderly affectionate old friend

Henry James

[On envelope flap] P.S. I send you by bookpost registered, with my blessing, a copy of *The American Scene.*

105, Pall Mall, S.W.
April 14, 1912.

Dearest Hendrik.

Not another day do I delay to answer (with such difficulty!) your long & interesting letter. I have waited these ten days or so just *because* of the difficulty: so little, (as you may imagine or realise on thinking a little) is it a soft & simple matter to stagger out from under such an avalanche of information & announcement as you let drop on me with this terrific story of your working so in the colossal & in the void & in the air! Brace yourself for my telling you that (*having*, these days, scrambled a little from under the avalanche,) I now, staggering to my feet again, just simply flee before the horrific mass, lest I start the remainder (what is hanging in the air) afresh to overwhelm me. I say "brace yourself", though I don't quite see why I need, having showed you in the past, so again & again, that your mania for the colossal, the swelling & the huge, the monotonously & repeatedly huge, breaks the heart of me for you, so convinced have I been all along that it means your simply burying yourself & all your products & belongings, & everything & Every One that is yours, in the most bottomless & thankless & fatal of sandbanks. There is no use or application or power of absorption or assimilation for these enormities, beloved Hendrik, anywhere on the whole surface of the practicable, or, as I should rather say, impracticable globe; & when you write me that you are now lavishing time & money on a colossal ready-made City, I simply cover my head with my mantle & turn my face to the wall, & there, dearest Hendrik, just bitterly *weep* for you—just desperately & dismally & helplessly water that dim refuge with a salt flood. I have practically said these things to you before—though perhaps never in so dreadfully straight & sore a form as today: when this culmination of your madness, to the tune of five hundred millions of tons of weight, simply squeezes it out of me. For that, dearest boy, is the dread Delusion to warn you against—what is called in Medical Science *Megalomania* (look it up in the Dictionary;) in French *la folie des grandeurs*, the infatuated & disproportionate love & pursuit of, & attempt at, the Big, the Bigger, the Biggest, the Immensest Immensity, with all sense of proportion, application, relation & possibility madly *submerged*. What am I to say to you, gentle & dearest Hendrik, *but* these things, cruel as they may seem to you, when you write me (with so little *spelling* even—though that was always your wild grace!) that you are extemporizing a World-City from top to toe, & employing 40 architects to see you through with it &c? How can I throw myself on your side to the extent of employing to back you a single letter of the Alphabet when you break to me anything so fantastic or out of relation to any reality of any kind in all the weary world??? The idea, my dear old Friend, fills me with mere pitying Dismay, the unutterable Waste of it all makes me retire into my room & lock the door to howl! . . . Cities are *living* organisms, that grow from within & by experience & piece by piece; they are not bought, all hanging together, in *any* inspired studio anywhere whatsoever, and to attempt to plank one down on its area prepared, or even just merely projected, for use is to—well, it's to go forth into the deadly Desert & talk to the winds. Dearest Hendrik, don't ask me to *help* you so to talk—don't, don't, don't; I should be so playing to you the part of the falsest, *fatallest* friend. But do *this*—realise how dismally unspeakably much these cold, hard, desperate words, withholding sympathy, cost your ever-affectionate, your terribly tender old friend

Henry James

Lamb House, Rye, Sussex.
September 4, 1913.

Dearest Hendrik.

If I have been silent so long it is because distress & embarrassment have kept me so; & now your letter today received makes me write, makes me unable *not* to write even with this regret at having to—having to about the matter you insist on my speaking of, I mean, & in the only sense in which, with my hand so forced, I *can*. I seem to remember that I some time ago wrote you more or less in that sense, & under your pressure—after you had sent me your plan of a "World Centre" & then again your 1st instalment of your pamphlet on a "World Conscience"; wrote you in a manner expressive of my pain in having to pronounce on these things which I understand & enter into so little. But you appear to have forgotten the impression I tried then to give you—or I seem quite to have failed of giving it; for you urge me again as if I had said nothing—had uttered no warning. Do you think, dearest Hendrik, I *like* telling you that I don't, & can't possibly, go *with* you, that I don't, & can't possibly, understand, congratulate you on, or enter into, projects & plans so vast & vague & meaning to me simply nothing whatever? . . . Evidently, my dear boy, I can only give you pain that it gives *me* pain to be forced to give you, by telling you that I don't so much as *understand* your very terms of "World" this & "World" the other & can neither think myself, nor *want* to think, in any such vain & false & presumptuous, any such idle & deplorable & delirious connections—*as they seem to me*, & as nothing will suit you, rash youth, but that I should definitely let you *know* they seem to me. They would so seem even if I were not old & ill & detached, & reduced to ending my life in a very restricted way—the ground on which I begged you to let me off, some time back, from a participation impossible to me, & in spite of my plea of which you again ask for what you call my *help*. You see, dear Hendrik, to be utterly & unsparingly frank, & not to drag out a statement I wd. so much rather not have had to make, I simply *loathe* such pretensious forms of words as "World" anything—they are to me mere monstrous sound without sense. The World is a prodigious & portentous & immeasurable affair, & I can't for a moment pretend to sit in my little corner here & "sympathise with" proposals for dealing with it. It is so far vaster in all its appalling complexity than you or me, or than anything we can pretend without the imputation of absurdity & insanity to do to it, that I content myself, & inevitably *must* (so far as I can do anything at all now,) with living in the realities of things, with "cultivating my garden" (morally & intellectually speaking,) & with referring my questions to a Conscience (my own poor little personal,) less inconceivable than that of the globe. . . . Reality, Reality, the seeing of things as they *are*, & not in the light of the loosest simplifications—come back to *that* with me, & then, even now, we can talk! . . .

Henry James

Charles Warren Stoddard

Charles Warren Stoddard (1843–1909) was born in Rochester, New York, but when he was a teenager his family moved to California. As a journalist, writer, and friend of Ambrose Bierce, Bret Harte, and Mark Twain, he is closely associated with the lively bohemian and artistic community that developed in San Francisco.

Stoddard was awakened to his homosexuality by reading Whitman's *Leaves of Grass*, but it was not until he arrived in Hawaii that he acted on his feelings. This outpouring of delight is found in his two collections, *South-Sea Idylls* (1874, 1892) and *The Island of Tranquil Delights* (1904). Like Herman Melville and Robert Louis Stevenson, among others, Stoddard found in the islands of the Pacific a culture that was free of the restrictions of Western culture. Stoddard also wrote a novel about life in San Francisco (*For the Pleasure of His Company*, 1903), travel books, and essay collections as well as poetry.

Stoddard tried college teaching, first at Notre Dame and then at Catholic University, but his health was very poor, and finally in 1905 he returned to California, where he died four years later in Monterey.

Chumming with a Savage: Kána-aná

THERE WAS A LITTLE BROWN rain-cloud, that blew over in about three minutes; and Bolabola's thatched hut was dry as a haystack in less than half that time. Those tropical sprays are not much, anyhow; so I lounged down into the banana-patch, for I thought I saw something white there, something white and fluttering, moving about. I knew pretty well what it was, and didn't go after it on an uncertainty.

The Doctor looked savage. Whenever he slung those saddlebags over his left shoulder, and swung his right arm clean out from his body, like the regulator of a steam-engine, you might know that his steam was pretty well up. I turned to look back, as he was strapping up his beast of burden till the poor animal's body was positively waspish; then he climbed into his saddle, and sullenly plunged down the trail toward the precipice, and never said "Good-by," or "God bless you," or any of those harmless tags that come in so well when you don't know how to cut off your last words.

I solemnly declare, and this without malice, the Doctor was perfectly savage.

Now, do you know what demoralized that Doctor? how we came to a misunderstanding? or why we parted company? It was simply because here was a glorious valley, inhabited by a mild, half civilized people, who seemed to love me at first sight. I don't believe I disliked them, either. Well! they asked me to stop with them, and I felt just like it. I wanted to stop and be natural; but the Doctor thought otherwise of my intentions; and that was the origin of the row.

The next thing I knew, the Doctor had got up the great precipice, and I was quite alone with two hundred dusky fellows, only two of whom could speak a syllable of English, and I the sole representative of the superior white within twenty miles. Alone with cannibals—perhaps they were cannibals. They had magnificent teeth, at any rate, and could bite through an inch and a half sugar-cane, and not break a jaw.

For the first time that summer I began to moralize a little. Was it best to have kicked against the Doctor's judgment? Perhaps not! But it is best to be careful how you begin to moralize too early; you deprive yourself of a great deal of fun in that way. If you want to do anything particularly, I should advise you to do it, and then be sufficiently sorry to make it all square.

I'm not so sure that I was wrong, after all. Fate, or the Doctor, or something else, brought me first to this loveliest of valleys, so shut out from everything but itself that there were no temptations which might not be satisfied. Well! here, as I was looking about at the singular loveliness of the place—you know this was my first glimpse of its abrupt walls, hung with tapestries of fern and clambering convolvulus; at one end two exquisite waterfalls, rivalling one another in whiteness and airiness, at the other the sea, the real South Sea, breaking and foaming over a genuine reef, and even rippling the placid current of the river that slipped quietly down to its embracing tide from the deep basins at these waterfalls—right in the midst of all this, before I had been ten minutes in the valley, I saw a straw hat, bound with wreaths of fern and *maile*; under it a snow-white garment, rather short all around, low in the neck, and with no sleeves whatever.

There was no sex to that garment; it was the spontaneous offspring of a scant material and a large necessity. I'd seen plenty of that sort of thing, but never upon a model like this, so entirely tropical—almost Oriental. As this singular phenomenon made directly for me, and having come within reach, there stopped and stayed, I asked its name, using one of my seven stock phrases for the purpose; I found it was called Kána-aná. Down it went into my note-book; for I knew I was to have an experience with this young scion of a race of chiefs. Sure enough, I have had it. He continued to regard me steadily, without embarrassment. He seated himself before me; I felt myself at the mercy of one whose calm analysis was questioning every motive of my soul. This sage inquirer was, perhaps, sixteen years of age. His eye was so earnest and so honest, I could return his look. I saw a round, full, rather girlish face; lips ripe and expressive, not quite so sensual as those of most of his race; not a bad nose, by any means; eyes perfectly glorious—regular almonds—with the mythical lashes "that sweep," etc., etc. The smile which presently transfigured his face was of the nature that flatters you into submission against your will.

Having weighed me in his balance—and you may be sure his instincts didn't cheat him; they don't do that sort of thing—he placed his two hands on my two knees, and declared, "I was his best friend, as he was mine; I must come at once to his house, and there live always with him." What could I do but go? He pointed me to his lodge across the river, saying, "There was his home and mine." By this time, my *native* without a master was quite exhausted. I wonder what would have happened if some one hadn't come to my rescue, just at that moment of trial, with a fresh vocabulary? As it was, we settled the matter at once. This was our little plan—an entirely private arrangement between Kána-aná and myself: I was to leave with the Doctor in an hour; but, at the expiration of a week we should both return hither; then I would stop with him, and the Doctor could go his way.

There was an immense amount of secrecy, and many vows, and I was almost crying, when the Doctor hurried me up that terrible precipice, and we lost sight of the beautiful valley. Kána-aná swore he would watch continually for my return, and I vowed I'd hurry back; and so we parted. Looking down from the heights, I thought I could distinguish his white garment; at any rate, I knew the little fellow was somewhere about, feeling as miserably as I felt—and nobody has any business to feel worse. How many times I thought of him through the week! I was always wondering if he still thought of me. I had found those natives to be impulsive, demonstrative, and, I feared, inconstant. Yet why should he forget me, having so little to remember in his idle life, while I could still think of him, and put aside a hundred pleasant memories for his sake? The whole island was a delight to me. I often wondered if I should ever again behold such a series of valleys, hills, and highlands in so small a compass. That land is a world in miniature, the dearest spot of which, to me, was that secluded valley; for there was a young soul watching for my return.

That was rather a slow week for me, but it ended finally; and just at sunset, on the day appointed, the Doctor and I found ourselves back on the edge of the valley. I looked all up and down its green expanse, regarding every living creature, in the hope of discovering Kána-aná in the attitude of the watcher. I let the Doctor ride ahead of me on the trail to Bolabola's hut, and it was quite in the twilight when I heard the approach of a swift horseman. I turned, and at that moment there was a collision of two constitutions that were just fitted for one another; and all the doubts and apprehensions of the week just over were indignantly dismissed, for Kána-aná and I were one and inseparable, which was perfectly satisfactory to both parties!

The plot, which had been thickening all the week, culminated then, much to the disgust of the Doctor, who had kept his watchful eye upon me all these days—to my advantage, as he supposed. There was no disguising our project any longer, so I out with it as mildly as possible. "There was a dear fellow here," I said, "who loved me, and wanted me to live with him; all his people wanted me to stop, also; his mother and his grandmother had specially desired it. They didn't care for money; they had much love for me, and therefore implored me to stay a little. Then the valley was most beautiful; I was tired; after our hard riding, I needed rest; his mother and his grandmother assured me that I needed rest. Now, why not let me rest here awhile?"

The Doctor looked very grave. I knew that he misunderstood—placed a wrong interpretation upon my motives; the worse for him, I say. He tried to talk me over to the paths of virtue and propriety; but I wouldn't be talked over. Then the final blast was blown; war was declared at once. The Doctor never spoke again, but to abuse me; and off he rode in high dudgeon, and the sun kept going down on his wrath. Thereupon I renounced all the follies of this world, actually hating civilization, and feeling entirely above the formalities of society. I resolved on the spot to be a barbarian, and, perhaps, dwell forever and ever in this secluded spot. And here I am back to the beginning of this story, just after the shower at Bolabola's hut, as the Doctor rode off alone and in anger.

That resolution was considerable for me to make. I found, by the time the Doctor was out of sight and I was quite alone, with the natives regarding me so curiously, that I was very tired indeed. So Kána-aná brought up his horse, got me on to it some way or other, and mounted behind me to pilot the animal and sustain me in my first bare-back act. Over the sand we went, and through the river to his hut, where I was taken in, fed, and petted in every possible way, and finally put to bed, where Kána-aná mo-nopolized me, growling in true savage fashion if any one came near me. I didn't sleep much, after all. I think I must have been excited. I thought how strangely I was situ-ated: alone in a wilderness, among barbarians; my bosom friend, who was hugging me like a young bear, not able to speak one syllable of English, and I very shaky on a few bad phrases in his tongue. We two lay upon an enormous old-fashioned bed with high posts—very high they seemed to me in the dim rushlight. The natives always burn a small light after dark; some superstition or other prompts it. The bed, well stocked with pillows or cushions of various sizes, covered with bright-colored chintz, was hung about with numerous shawls, so that I might be dreadfully modest behind them. It was quite a grand affair, gotten up expressly for my benefit. The rest of the house—all in one room, as usual—was covered with mats, on which various recum-bent forms and several individual snores betrayed the proximity of Kána-aná's rela-tives. How queer the whole atmosphere of the place was! The heavy beams of the house were of some rare wood, which, being polished, looked like colossal sticks of peanut candy. Slender canes were bound across this framework, and the soft, dried grass of the meadows was braided over it—all completing our tenement, and making it as fresh and sweet as new-mown hay.

The natives have a passion for perfumes. Little bunches of sweet-smelling herbs hung in the peak of the roof, and wreaths of fragrant berries were strung in various parts of the house. I found our bedposts festooned with them in the morning. O, that bed! It might have come from England in the Elizabethan era and been wrecked off the coast; hence the mystery of its presence. It was big enough for a Mormon. There was a little opening in the room opposite our bed; you might call it a window, I suppose. The sun, shining through it made our tent of shawls perfectly gorgeous in crimson light, barred and starred with gold. I lifted our bed-curtain, and watched the rocks through this window—the shining rocks, with the sea leaping above them in the sun. There were cocoa-palms so slender they seemed to cast no shadow, while their fringed leaves glistened like frost-work as the sun glanced over them. A bit of cliff, also, remote and misty, running far into the sea, was just visible from my pyramid of pillows. I wondered what more I could ask for to delight the eye. Kána-aná was still asleep, but he never let loose his hold on me, as though he feared his pale-faced friend would fade away from him. He lay close by me. His sleek figure, supple and graceful in repose, was the embodiment of free, untrammelled youth. You who are brought up under cover know nothing of its luxuriousness. How I longed to take him over the sea with me, and show him something of life as we find it. Thinking upon it, I dropped off into one of those

delicious morning naps. I awoke again presently; my companion-in-arms was the occasion this time. He had awakened, stolen softly away, resumed his single garment—
said garment and all others he considered superfluous after dark—and had prepared
for me, with his own hands, a breakfast which he now declared to me, in violent and
suggestive pantomime, was all ready to be eaten. It was not a bad bill of fare—fresh
fish, taro, poe, and goat's milk. I ate as well as I could, under the circumstances. I found
that Robinson Crusoe must have had some tedious rehearsals before he acquired that
perfect resignation to Providence which delights us in book form. There was a veri-
table and most unexpected tablecloth for me alone. I do not presume to question the
nature of its miraculous appearance. Dishes there were—dishes, if you're not particular as to shape or completeness; forks with a prong or two—a bent and abbreviated prong or two; knives that had survived their handles; and one solitary spoon. All
these were tributes of the too generous people, who, for the first time in their lives,
were at the inconvenience of entertaining a distinguished stranger. Hence this reckless
display of tableware. I ate as well as I could, but surely not enough to satisfy my crony;
for, when I had finished eating, he sat about two hours in deep and depressing silence,
at the expiration of which time he suddenly darted off on his bareback steed and was
gone till dark, when he returned with a fat mutton slung over his animal. Now, mutton doesn't grow wild thereabout, neither were his relatives shepherds; consequently,
in eating, I asked no questions for conscience' sake.

The series of entertainments offered me were such as the little valley had not
known for years: canoe-rides up and down the winding stream; bathings in the sea
and in the river, and in every possible bit of water, at all possible hours; expeditions
into the recesses of the mountains, to the waterfalls that plunged into cool basins of
fern and cresses, and to the orange-grove through acres and acres of guava orchards;
some climbings up the precipices; goat hunting, once or twice, as far as a solitary cavern, said to be haunted—these tramps always by daylight; then a new course of bathings and sailings, interspersed with monotonous singing and occasional smokes under
the eaves of the hut at evening.

If it is a question how long a man may withstand the seductions of nature, and the
consolations and conveniences of the state of nature, I have solved it in one case; for I
was as natural as possible in about three days.

I wonder if I was growing to feel more at home, or more hungry, that I found an
appetite at last equal to any table that was offered me! Chicken was added to my already bountiful rations, nicely cooked by being swathed in a broad, succulent leaf, and
roasted or steeped in hot ashes. I ate it with my fingers, using the leaf for a platter.

Almost every day something new was offered at the door for my edification. Now,
a net full of large guavas or mangoes, or a sack of leaves crammed with most delicious
oranges from the mountains, that seemed to have absorbed the very dew of heaven,
they were so fresh and sweet. Immense lemons perfumed the house, waiting to make

me a capital drink. Those superb citrons, with their rough, golden crusts, refreshed me. Cocoanuts were heaped at the door; and yams, grown miles away, were sent for, so that I might be satisfied. All these additions to my table were the result of long and vigorous arguments between the respective heads of the house. I detected trouble and anxiety in their expressive faces. I picked out a word, here and there, which betrayed their secret sorrow. No assertions, no remonstrances on my part, had the slightest effect upon the poor souls, who believed I was starving. Eat I must, at all hours and in all places; and eat, moreover, before they would touch a mouthful. So Nature teaches her children a hospitality which all the arts of the capital cannot affect.

I wonder what it was that finally made me restless and eager to see new faces! Perhaps my unhappy disposition, that urged me thither, and then lured me back to the pride of life and the glory of the world. Certain I am that Kána-aná never wearied me with his attentions, though they were incessant. Day and night he was by me. When he was silent, I knew he was conceiving some surprise in the shape of a new fruit, or a new view to beguile me. I was, indeed, beguiled; I was growing to like the little heathen altogether too well. What should I do when I was at last compelled to return out of my seclusion, and find no soul so faithful and loving in all the earth beside? Day by day this thought grew upon me, and with it I realized the necessity of a speedy departure.

There were those in the world I could still remember with that exquisitely painful pleasure that is the secret of true love. Those still voices seemed incessantly calling me, and something in my heart answered them of its own accord. How strangely idle the days had grown! We used to lie by the hour—Kána-aná and I—watching a strip of sand on which a wild poppy was nodding in the wind. This poppy seemed to me typical of their life in the quiet valley. Living only to occupy so much space in the universe, it buds, blossoms, goes to seed, dies, and is forgotten.

These natives do not even distinguish the memory of their great dead, if they ever had any. It was the legend of some mythical god that Kána-aná told me, and of which I could not understand a twentieth part; a god whose triumphs were achieved in an age beyond the comprehension of the very people who are delivering its story, by word of mouth, from generation to generation. Watching the sea was a great source of amusement with us. I discovered in our long watches that there is a very complicated and magnificent rhythm in its solemn song. This wave that breaks upon the shore is the heaviest of a series that preceded it; and these are greater and less, alternately, every fifteen or twenty minutes. Over this dual impulse the tides prevail, while through the year there is a variation in their rise and fall. What an intricate and wonderful mechanism regulates and repairs all this!

There was an entertainment in watching a particular cliff, in a peculiar light, at a certain hour, and finding soon enough that change visited even that hidden quarter of the globe. The exquisite perfection of this moment, for instance, is not again repeated on to-morrow, or the day after, but in its stead appears some new tint or picture, which, perhaps, does not satisfy like this. That was the most distressing disappointment that came upon us there. I used to spend half an hour in idly observing the splendid curtains of our bed swing in the light air from the sea; and I have speculated for days upon the probable destiny awaiting one of those superb spiders, with a tremendous stomach and a striped waistcoat, looking a century old, as he clung tenaciously to the fringes of our canopy.

We had fitful spells of conversation upon some trivial theme, after long intervals of intense silence. We began to develop symptoms of imbecility. There was laughter at the least occurrence, though quite barren of humor; also, eating and drinking to pass the time; bathing to make one's self cool, after the heat and drowsiness of the day. So life flowed out in an unruffled current, and so the prodigal lived riotously and wasted his substance. There came a day when we promised ourselves an actual occurrence in our Crusoe life. Some one had seen a floating object far out at sea. It might be a boat adrift; and, in truth, it looked very like a boat. Two or three canoes darted off through the surf to the rescue, while we gathered on the rocks, watching and ruminating. It was long before the rescuers returned, and then they came empty-handed. It was only a log after all, drifted, probably, from America. We talked it all over, there by the shore, and went home to renew the subject; it lasted us a week or more, and we kept harping upon it till that log—drifting slowly, O how slowly! from the far mainland to our island—seemed almost to overpower me with a sense of the unutterable loneliness of its voyage. I used to lie and think about it, and get very solemn, indeed; then Kána-aná would think of some fresh appetizer or other, and try to make me merry with good feeling. Again and again he would come with a delicious banana to the bed where I was lying, and insist upon my gorging myself, when I had but barely recovered from a late orgie of fruit, flesh, or fowl. He would mesmerize me into a most refreshing sleep with a prolonged and pleasing manipulation. It was a reminiscence of the baths of Stamboul not to be withstood. From this sleep I would presently be awakened by Kána-aná's performance upon a rude sort of harp, that gave out a weird and eccentric music. The mouth being applied to the instrument, words were pronounced in a guttural voice, while the fingers twanged the strings in measure. It was a flow of monotones, shaped into legends and lyrics. I liked it amazingly; all the better, perhaps, that it was as good as Greek to me, for I understood it as little as I understood the strange and persuasive silence of that beloved place, which seemed slowly but surely weaving a spell of enchantment about me. I resolved to desert peremptorily, and managed to hire a canoe and a couple of natives to cross the channel with me. There were other reasons for this prompt action.

Hour by hour I was beginning to realize one of the inevitable results of time. My boots were giving out; their best sides were the uppers, and their soles had about left them. As I walked, I could no longer disguise this pitiful fact. It was getting hard on

me, especially in the gravel. Yet, regularly each morning, my pieces of boot were carefully oiled, then rubbed, or petted, or coaxed into some sort of a polish, which was a
labor of love. O Kána-aná! how could you wring my soul with those touching offices
of friendship!—those kindnesses unfailing, unsurpassed!

Having resolved to sail early in the morning, before the drowsy citizens of the
valley had fairly shaken the dew out of their forelocks, all that day—my last with
Kána-aná—I breathed about me silent benedictions and farewells. I could not begin to do enough for Kána-aná, who was more than ever devoted to me. He almost
seemed to suspect our sudden separation, for he clung to me with a sort of subdued
desperation. That was the day he took from his head his hat—a very neat one, plaited
by his mother—insisting that I should wear it (mine was quite in tatters), while he
went bareheaded in the sun. That hat hangs in my room now, the only tangible relic
of my prodigal days. My plan was to steal off at dawn, while he slept; to awaken my
native crew, and escape to sea before my absence was detected. I dared not trust a
parting with him before the eyes of the valley. Well, I managed to wake and rouse my
sailor boys. To tell the truth, I didn't sleep a wink that night. We launched the canoe,
entered, put off, and had safely mounted the second big roller just as it broke under us
with terrific power, when I heard a shrill cry above the roar of the waters. I knew the
voice and its import. There was Kána-aná rushing madly toward us; he had discovered all, and couldn't even wait for that white garment, but ran after us like one gone
daft, and plunged into the cold sea, calling my name over and over as he fought the
breakers. I urged the natives forward. I knew if he overtook us I should never be able
to escape again. We fairly flew over the water. I saw him rise and fall with the swell,
looking like a seal; for it was his second nature, this surf-swimming. I believe in my
heart I wished the paddles would break or the canoe split on the reef, though all the
time I was urging the rascals forward; and they, like stupids, took me at my word.
They couldn't break a paddle, or get on the reef, or have any sort of an accident. Presently we rounded the headland—the same hazy point I used to watch from the grass
house, through the little window, of a sunshiny morning. There we lost sight of the
valley and the grass house, and everything that was associated with the past—but
that was nothing. We lost sight of the little sea-god, Kána-aná, shaking the spray from
his forehead like a porpoise; and this was all in all. I didn't care for anything else after
that, or anybody else, either. I went straight home, and got civilized again, or partly
so, at least. I've never seen the Doctor since, and never want to. He had no business to
take me there or leave me there. I couldn't make up my mind to stay; yet I'm always
dying to go back again.

So I grew tired over my husks. I arose and went unto my father. I wanted to finish
up the Prodigal business. I ran and fell upon his neck and kissed him, and said unto
him, "Father, *if* I have sinned against Heaven and in thy sight, I'm afraid I don't care

much. Don't kill anything. I don't want any calf. Take back the ring, I don't deserve it; for I'd give more this minute to see that dear little velvet-skinned, coffee-colored Kána-aná than anything else in the wide world—because he hates business, and so do I. He's a regular brick, father, molded of the purest clay, and baked in God's sunshine. He's about half sunshine himself; and, above all others, and more than any one else ever can, he loved your Prodigal."

Alexander Berkman

Alexander Berkman (1870–1936) was born in Vilna, Russia, to a wealthy Jewish family, but, following his parents' deaths, he came at age eighteen to America. There he met Emma Goldman, the extraordinary radical feminist writer, orator, and activist, with whom he lived. In 1892 Berkman attempted to assassinate Henry Clay Frick, one of America's greatest robber barons, who used armed Pinkerton agents to break a strike at the Carnegie Steel Works plant in Homestead, Pennsylvania. The Homestead strike, one of the most violent in American labor history, ended with several dead and many wounded. In revenge Berkman entered Frick's office, shot him twice, and stabbed him several times. Frick soon recovered, but Berkman served fourteen years in Pennsylvania's Western Penitentiary.

In 1906 he was released and rejoined Emma Goldman, who lectured in support of homosexual rights. Together they went on to edit and write. In 1919 he and Goldman were deported during the Palmer Raids, a purge of the country's politically dissident immigrants, for their radical and anarchist views. They went first to Russia and then to France, where, poor, weak, and suffering enormous physical pain, Berkman committed suicide.

In 1912 Berkman published *Prison Memoirs of an Anarchist*, in which he not only writes sympathetically and explicitly about homosexuality in prison but suggests his own homosexual feelings. The title of this chapter, "Love's Dungeon Flower," alludes to the imagery of the turn-of-the-century aesthetic movement, in which homosexuals were pictured as delicate flowers. Boss Quay referred to in the passage below is Matthew Quay (1833–1904), the most powerful politician in Pennsylvania; he was forbidden for a time to take his seat in the U.S. Senate because of his misuse of public money.

Love's Dungeon Flower

THE DUNGEON SMELLS foul and musty; the darkness is almost visible, the silence oppressive; but the terror of my former experience has abated. I shall probably be kept in the underground cell for a longer time than on the previous occasion,—my offence is considered very grave. Three charges have been entered against me: destroying State property, having possession of a knife, and uttering a threat against the Warden. When I saw the officers gathering at my back, while I was facing the Captain, I realized its significance. They were preparing to assault me. Quickly advancing to the Warden, I shook my fist in his face, crying:

"If they touch me, I'll hold you personally responsible."

He turned pale. Trying to steady his voice, he demanded:

"What do you mean? How dare you?"

"I mean just what I say. I won't be clubbed. My friends will avenge me, too."

He glanced at the guards standing rigid, in ominous silence. One by one they retired, only two remaining, and I was taken quietly to the dungeon.

The stillness is broken by a low, muffled sound. I listen intently. It is some one pacing the cell at the further end of the passage.

"Halloo! Who's there?" I shout.

No reply. The pacing continues. It must be "Silent Nick"; he never talks.

I prepare to pass the night on the floor. It is bare; there is no bed or blanket, and I have been deprived of my coat and shoes. It is freezing in the cell; my feet grow numb, hands cold, as I huddle in the corner, my head leaning against the reeking wall, my body on the stone floor. I try to think, but my thoughts are wandering, my brain frigid.

The rattling of keys wakes me from my stupor. Guards are descending into the dungeon. I wonder whether it is morning, but they pass my cell: it is not yet breakfast time. Now they pause and whisper. I recognize the mumbling speech of Deputy Greaves, as he calls out to the silent prisoner:

"Want a drink?"

The double doors open noisily.

"Here!"

"Give me the cup," the hoarse bass resembles that of "Crazy Smithy." His stentorian voice sounds cracked since he was shot in the neck by Officer Dean.

"You can't have th' cup," the Deputy fumes.

"I won't drink out of your hand, God damn you. Think I'm a cur, do you?" Smithy swears and curses savagely.

The doors are slammed and locked. The steps grow faint, and all is silent, save the quickened footfall of Smith, who will not talk to any prisoner.

I pass the long night in drowsy stupor, rousing at times to strain my ear for every sound from the rotunda above, wondering whether day is breaking. The minutes drag in dismal darkness. . . .

The loud clanking of the keys tingles in my ears like sweet music. It is morning! The guards hand me the day's allowance—two ounces of white bread and a quart of water. The wheat tastes sweet; it seems to me I've never eaten anything so delectable. But the liquid is insipid, and nauseates me. At almost one bite I swallow the slice, so small and thin. It whets my appetite, and I feel ravenously hungry.

At Smith's door the scene of the previous evening is repeated. The Deputy insists that the man drink out of the cup held by a guard. The prisoner refuses, with a profuse flow of profanity. Suddenly there is a splash, followed by a startled cry, and the thud of the cell bucket on the floor. Smith has emptied the contents of his privy upon the officers. In confusion they rush out of the dungeon.

Presently I hear the clatter of many feet in the cellar. There is a hubbub of suppressed voices. I recognize the rasping whisper of Hopkins, the tones of Woods, McIlvaine, and others. I catch the words, "Both sides at once." Several cells in the dungeon are provided with double entrances, front and back, to facilitate attacks upon obstreperous prisoners. Smith is always assigned to one of these cells. I shudder as I realize that the officers are preparing to club the demented man. He has been weakened by years of unbroken solitary confinement, and his throat still bleeds occasionally from the bullet wound. Almost half his time he has been kept in the dungeon, and now he has been missing from the range twelve days. It is. . . . Involuntarily I shut my eyes at the fearful thud of the riot clubs.

The hours drag on. The monotony is broken by the keepers bringing another prisoner to the dungeon. I hear his violent sobbing from the depth of the cavern.

"Who is there?" I hail him. I call repeatedly, without receiving an answer. Perhaps the new arrival is afraid of listening guards.

"Ho, man!" I sing out, "the screws have gone. Who are you? This is Aleck, Aleck Berkman."

"Is that you, Aleck? This is Johnny." There is a familiar ring about the young voice, broken by piteous moans. But I fail to identify it.

"What Johnny?"

"Johnny Davis—you know—stocking shop. I've just—killed a man."

In bewilderment I listen to the story, told with bursts of weeping. Johnny had returned to the shop; he thought he would try again: he wanted to earn his "good" time. Things went well for a while, till "Dutch" Adams became shop runner. He is the stool who got Grant and Johnny Smith in trouble with the fake key, and Davis would have nothing to do with him. But "Dutch" persisted, pestering him all the time; and then—

"Well, you know, Aleck," the boy seems diffident, "he lied about me like hell: he told the fellows he *used* me. Christ, my mother might hear about it! I couldn't stand it, Aleck, honest to God, I couldn't. I—I killed the lying cur, an' now—now I'll—I'll swing for it," he sobs as if his heart would break.

A touch of tenderness for the poor boy is in my voice, as I strive to condole with him and utter the hope that it may not be so bad, after all. Perhaps Adams will not die. He is a powerful man, big and strong; he may survive.

Johnny eagerly clutches at the straw. He grows more cheerful, and we talk of the coming investigation and local affairs. Perhaps the Board will even clear him, he suggests. But suddenly seized with fear, he weeps and moans again.

More men are cast into the dungeon. They bring news from the world above. An epidemic of fighting seems to have broken out in the wake of recent orders. The total inhibition of talking is resulting in more serious offences. "Kid Tommy" is enlarging upon his trouble. "You see, fellers," he cries in a treble, "dat skunk of a Pete he pushes me in de line, and I turns round t' give 'im hell, but de screw pipes me. Got no chance t' choo, so I turns an' biffs him on de jaw, see?" But he is sure, he says, to be let out at night, or in the morning, at most. "Them fellers that was scrappin' yesterday in de yard didn't go to de hole. Dey jest put 'em in de cell. Sandy knows de committee 's comin' all right."

Johnny interrupts the loquacious boy to inquire anxiously about "Dutch" Adams, and I share his joy at hearing that the man's wound is not serious. He was cut about the shoulders, but was able to walk unassisted to the hospital. Johnny overflows with quiet happiness; the others dance and sing. I recite a poem from Nekrassov; the boys don't understand a word, but the sorrow-laden tones appeal to them, and they request more Russian "pieces." But Tommy is more interested in politics, and is bristling with the latest news from the Magee camp. He is a great admirer of Quay,—"dere's a smart guy fer you, fellers; owns de whole Keystone shebang all right, all right. He's Boss Quay, you bet you." He dives into national issues, rails at Bryan, "16 to 1 Bill, you jest list'n to 'm, he'll give sixteen dollars to every one; he will, nit!" and the boys are soon involved in a heated discussion of the respective merits of the two political parties, Tommy staunchly siding with the Republican. "Me gran'fader and me fader was Republicans," he vociferates, "an' all me broders vote de ticket. Me fer de Gran' Ole Party, ev'ry time." Some one twits him on his political wisdom, challenging the boy to explain the difference in the money standards. Tommy boldly appeals to me to corroborate him; but before I have an opportunity to speak, he launches upon other issues, berating Spain for her atrocities in Cuba, and insisting that this free country cannot tolerate slavery at its doors. Every topic is discussed, with Tommy orating at top speed, and continually broaching new subjects. Unexpectedly he reverts to local affairs, waxes reminiscent over former days, and loudly smacks his lips at the "great feeds" he enjoyed on the rare occasions when he was free to roam the back streets of Smoky City. "Say, Aleck, my boy," he calls to me familiarly, "many a penny I made on *you*, all right. How? Why, peddlin' extras, of course! Say, dem was fine days, all right; easy money; papers went like hot cakes off the griddle. Wish you'd do it agin, Aleck."

Invisible to each other, we chat, exchange stories and anecdotes, the boys talking incessantly, as if fearful of silence. But every now and then there is a lull; we become quiet, each absorbed in his own thoughts. The pauses lengthen—lengthen into silence. Only the faint steps of "Crazy Smith" disturb the deep stillness.

Late in the evening the young prisoners are relieved. But Johnny remains, and his apprehensions reawaken. Repeatedly during the night he rouses me from my drowsy torpor to be reassured that he is not in danger of the gallows, and that he will not be tried for his assault. I allay his fears by dwelling on the Warden's aversion to giving publicity to the sex practices in the prison, and remind the boy of the Captain's official denial of their existence. These things happen almost every week, yet no one has ever been taken to court from Riverside on such charges.

Johnny grows more tranquil, and we converse about his family history, talking in a frank, confidential manner. With a glow of pleasure, I become aware of the note of tenderness in his voice. Presently he surprises me by asking:

"Friend Aleck, what do they call you in Russian?"

He prefers the fond "Sashenka," enunciating the strange word with quaint endearment, then diffidently confesses dislike for his own name, and relates the story he had recently read of a poor castaway Cuban youth; Felipe was his name, and he was just like himself.

"Shall I call you Felipe?" I offer.

"Yes, please do, Aleck, dear; no, Sashenka."

The springs of affection well up within me, as I lie huddled on the stone floor, cold and hungry. With closed eyes, I picture the boy before me, with his delicate face, and sensitive, girlish lips.

"Good night, dear Sashenka," he calls.

"Good night, little Felipe."

In the morning we are served with a slice of bread and water. I am tormented by thirst and hunger, and the small ration fails to assuage my sharp pangs. Smithy still refuses to drink out of the Deputy's hand; his doors remain unopened. With tremulous anxiety Johnny begs the Deputy Warden to tell him how much longer he will remain in the dungeon, but Greaves curtly commands silence, applying a vile epithet to the boy.

"Deputy," I call, boiling over with indignation, "he asked you a respectful question. I'd give him a decent answer."

"You mind your own business, you hear?" he retorts.

But I persist in defending my young friend, and berate the Deputy for his language. He hastens away in a towering passion, menacing me with "what Smithy got."

Johnny is distressed at being the innocent cause of the trouble. The threat of the Deputy disquiets him, and he warns me to prepare. My cell is provided with a double entrance, and I am apprehensive of a sudden attack. But the hours pass without the Deputy returning, and our fears are allayed. The boy rejoices on my account, and brims over with appreciation of my intercession.

The incident cements our intimacy; our first diffidence disappears, and we become openly tender and affectionate. The conversation lags: we feel weak and worn. But every little while we hail each other with words of encouragement. Smithy incessantly paces the cell; the gnawing of the river rats reaches our ears; the silence is frequently pierced by the wild yells of the insane man, startling us with dread foreboding. The quiet grows unbearable, and Johnny calls again:

"What are you doing, Sashenka?"

"Oh, nothing. Just thinking, Felipe."

"Am I in your thoughts, dear?"

"Yes, kiddie, you are."

"Sasha, dear, I've been thinking, too."

"What, Felipe?"

"You are the only one I care for. I haven't a friend in the whole place."

"Do you care much for me, Felipe?"

"Will you promise not to laugh at me, Sashenka?"

"I wouldn't laugh at you."

"Cross your hand over your heart. Got it, Sasha?"

"Yes."

"Well, I'll tell you. I was thinking—how shall I tell you? I was thinking, Sashenka—if you were here with me—I would like to kiss you."

An unaccountable sense of joy glows in my heart, and I muse in silence.

"What's the matter, Sashenka? Why don't you say something? Are you angry with me?"

"No, Felipe, you foolish little boy."

"You are laughing at me."

"No, dear; I feel just as you do."

"Really?"

"Yes."

"Oh, I am so glad, Sashenka."

In the evening the guards descend to relieve Johnny; he is to be transferred to the basket, they inform him. On the way past my cell, he whispers: "Hope I'll see you soon, Sashenka." A friendly officer knocks on the outer blind door of my cell. "That you thar, Berkman? You want to b'have to th' Dep'ty. He's put you down for two more days for sassin' him."

I feel more lonesome at the boy's departure. The silence grows more oppressive, the hours of darkness heavier.

Seven days I remain in the dungeon. At the expiration of the week, feeling stiff and feeble, I totter behind the guards, on the way to the bathroom. My body looks strangely emaciated, reduced almost to a skeleton. The pangs of hunger revive sharply with the shock of the cold shower, and the craving for tobacco is overpowering at the sight of the chewing officers. I look forward to being placed in a cell, quietly exulting at my victory as I am led to the North Wing. But, in the cell-house, the Deputy Warden assigns me to the lower end of Range A, insane department. Exasperated by the terrible suggestion, my nerves on edge with the dungeon experience, I storm in furious protest, demanding to be returned to "the hole." The Deputy, startled by my violence, attempts to soothe me, and finally yields. I am placed in Number 35, the "crank row" beginning several cells further.

Upon the heels of the departing officers, the rangeman is at my door, bursting with the latest news. The investigation is over, the Warden whitewashed! For an instant I am aghast, failing to grasp the astounding situation. Slowly its full significance dawns on me, as Bill excitedly relates the story. It's the talk of the prison. The Board of Charities had chosen its Secretary, J. Francis Torrance, an intimate friend of the Warden, to conduct the investigation. As a precautionary measure, I was kept several additional days in the dungeon. Mr. Torrance has privately interviewed "Dutch" Adams, Young Smithy, and Bob Runyon, promising them their full commutation time, notwithstanding their bad records, and irrespective of their future behavior. They were instructed by the Secretary to corroborate the management, placing all blame upon me! No other witnesses were heard. The "investigation" was over within an hour, the committee of one retiring for dinner to the adjoining residence of the Warden.

Several friendly prisoners linger at my cell during the afternoon, corroborating the story of the rangeman, and completing the details. The cell-house itself bears out the situation; the change in the personnel of the men is amazing. "Dutch" Adams has been promoted to messenger for the "front office," the most privileged "political" job in the prison. Bob Runyon, a third-timer and notorious "kid man," has been appointed a trusty in the shops. But the most significant cue is the advancement of Young Smithy to the position of rangeman. He has but recently been sentenced to a year's solitary for the broken key discovered in the lock of his door. His record is of the worst. He is a young convict of extremely violent temper, who has repeatedly attacked fellow-prisoners with dangerous weapons. Since his murderous assault upon the inoffensive "Praying Andy," Smithy was never permitted out of his cell without the escort of two guards. And now this irresponsible man is in charge of a range!

At supper, Young Smithy steals up to my cell, bringing a slice of cornbread. I refuse the peace offering, and charge him with treachery. At first he stoutly protests his innocence, but gradually weakens and pleads his dire straits in mitigation. Torrance had persuaded him to testify, but he avoided incriminating me. That was done by the other two witnesses; he merely exonerated the Warden from the charges preferred by James Grant. He had been clubbed four times, but he denied to the committee that the guards practice violence; and he supported the Warden in his statement that the officers are not permitted to carry clubs or blackjacks. He feels that an injustice has been done me, and now that he occupies my former position, he will be able to repay the little favors I did him when he was in solitary.

Indignantly I spurn his offer. He pleads his youth, the torture of the cell, and begs my forgiveness; but I am bitter at his treachery, and bid him go.

Officer McIlvaine pauses at my door. "Oh, what a change, what an awful change!" he exclaims, pityingly. I don't know whether he refers to my appearance, or to the loss of range liberty; but I resent his tone of commiseration; it was he who had selected me as a victim, to be reported for talking. Angrily I turn my back to him, refusing to talk.

Somebody stealthily pushes a bundle of newspapers between the bars. Whole columns detail the report of the "investigation," completely exonerating Warden Edward S. Wright. The base charges against the management of the penitentiary were the underhand work of Anarchist Berkman, Mr. Torrance assured the press. One of the papers contains a lengthy interview with Wright, accusing me of fostering discontent and insubordination among the men. The Captain expresses grave fear for the safety of the community, should the Pardon Board reduce my sentence, in view of the circumstance that my lawyers are preparing to renew the application at the next session.

In great agitation I pace the cell. The statement of the Warden is fatal to the hope of a pardon. My life in the prison will now be made still more unbearable. I shall again be locked in solitary. With despair I think of my fate in the hands of the enemy, and the sense of my utter helplessness overpowers me.

Claude Hartland

The man who wrote under the name "Claude Hartland" (1871–?) was born in a southern railroad town to a strong, pragmatic mother and a dreamy father who taught music and English at the local school and wrote verses and music. Hartland inherited his father's romantic spirit, which is one reason his anguish over being homosexual takes both a literary and spiritual tone.

Written for "the consideration of the Medical Fraternity," *The Story of a Life*, the first homosexual autobiography published in the United States, was designed to help doctors understand and cure an "affliction" that seemed in Hartland's mind to be ever growing. The sincerity and candor of his memoir are striking. He views his desire for men as a "dark secret," and yet he thanks "God for this sweet pure love" when he finds another man who shares his feeling. Although he tries at the advice of his doctor to have intercourse with a woman, he achieves orgasm only by blocking her out of his imagination. Hartland is torn between the way he wants to feel about his sexuality and the ways he has been taught he ought to feel. His pen name suggests his "clawed heart."

We have no knowledge of what happened to "Claude Hartland" after the writing of his autobiography.

The following chapter covers his adventures from age twenty-five to twenty-seven.

Fleeing from Self (25 to 27)

IN THE FALL of '96, my old teacher resigned the principalship of his school to the linguist and went away.

I was elected first assistant, and I now came as teacher where I had so long been a pupil.

As soon as I was separated from "My boy" in the preceding chapter, my lustful desires returned and with them the pressure on my brow.

When school opened I loved no one in particular, but I soon fell madly in love with one of my pupils, a boy about fifteen years of age.

This was the strangest affection I have ever felt.

I have never been able to decide whether it was love or lust, but I believe it was a mixture of the two.

I felt a deep interest in his welfare and progress in school, and at such times passion was dumb; at other times I yearned to clasp him in my arms and devour him with kisses, and these feelings were accompanied by erections.

I was always afraid of my love for him, and from the beginning felt guilty and unhappy, yet I could not give him up.

My love soon begot a kindred feeling in him for me.

At times he was calm and gentle in his affection, and again his face would flush to a deep crimson, and he seemed restless and uneasy.

Months passed by, and every day we loved each other more, yet we had never given expression to our love.

We met at church one afternoon, and I saw at a glance that his love or passion was unusually strong.

Mine was the same, and after services were over we instinctively lingered around the church door, waiting, one for the other.

When everyone was gone, we sat down upon the steps and talked for several moments.

We were both restless and uneasy, but I hardly knew why. At last he proposed going into the church and sitting down.

This we did, against my better judgment, for somehow I feared, for his sake, to be alone with him.

When we were seated side by side, a love stronger than I had ever felt for him before swept over me.

This was accompanied by that strange, drowsy, vaporous feeling that I had once before felt for "My boy," but now it was strongly colored with lust.

My face burned furiously.

I closed my eyes for a moment, and all was still.

During this moment the same feeling came over him, and throwing his arms around my neck, he kissed me with lips that burned with passion.

This was a warning, and we left the church at once.

After this I was very unhappy, for I feared, and still fear, that I had ruined his life; yet my love for him grew stronger every day, and I could scarcely resist his attempts to make me give it expression.

The weight on my head grew heavier till it was almost pain, and I feared I was losing my mind.

I went to the Insane Asylum and consulted the physicians in charge. I did not tell them my secret at first; but when they told me that unless I got immediate mental relief I would lose my mind, I told them the story of my life and my present love.

They did not understand my case at all, but told me I must give up my school and go away at once.

I asked them if nothing could be done for me, and they said they would search the records for a similar case, and if they could relieve me they would let me know.

I never heard from them, however, and when school closed I resigned and went to B———, a city near by, to seek medical treatment, for I was becoming alarmed.

One Dr. A. was recommended to me as a nerve specialist, and he treated me for some time, without the least effect.

This same physician recommended sexual intercourse with women as a relief from my trouble, and I made up my mind to try it, though it was the most repulsive remedy ever offered me.

I went to a first-class house of prostitution, and selecting what I called the least repulsive of the lot, we went to her room together.

Well, I have parted from several of my molars, and if sacrificing another would have answered the same purpose—that of satisfying my physician—I would gladly have gone to the dentist's chair instead of to her bed.

I had it understood with her that, "No success, no pay," and after I had failed to sum up sufficient courage for the ordeal before me, she took the matter into her own hands, and so energetically did she [flaunt] her charms (?) before me, that I was completely disgusted.

It seemed that my already flaccid organs would shrivel up and disappear entirely.

I was in a dilemma, and on this especial occasion I was thankful for one feminine gift—a woman's wits in the time of embarrassment.

To relieve myself, I resorted to the following plan:

Closing my eyes so that I could not see the loathsome object beside me, I shut her from my mind and turned my thoughts to a very handsome man, with whom I was madly in love in a passionate way.

Ten minutes passed, and when all was over, she pronounced me a grand success, at the same time modestly (?) insinuating that her charms never failed to "bring em 'round."

Not wishing to wound her vanity, I did not undeceive her, but hastened out into the street with something of the feeling that one ends his first visit to a dissecting room.

This was my first and last sexual experience with a woman, and for several days after, I was almost sick with disgust.

I could see that my physician was greatly amused when I made my report, yet he had too much respect for my feelings to give vent to the mirth that shone in his countenance.

He did not advise me to repeat the experiment, for which I was most thankful.

I then consulted a spiritualist, who offered me much encouragement, but no relief.

As an excuse to my friends at home for my long stay in the city, as much as for the benefit it brought me, I took music and penmanship, and worked very hard.

The city was full of handsome men, and I burned with passion all the time.

I soon found that many others were suffering from a disease similar to my own, and while this knowledge gave me great relief, I was grieved to find the victims so numerous.

One night, while standing upon the sidewalk listening to a public speech, a very handsome and stylishly dressed man about thirty-five years of age, began a conversation with me.

I suspected him of course, for I could see that he labored under some nervous strain, and I decided to let him take his course.

We talked for some time, when he proposed that we go for a walk. I agreed and we walked on down to the river.

When we were in a quiet and dark spot, he placed his arms around my neck and kissed me several times.

Leaning forward, he whispered something in my ear. I had an idea what he meant, but was not sure.

Passion and curiosity tempted me sorely, and I did not repulse him.

Ten minutes passed.

A new experience had been added to my life, and a half slumbering desire awakened in my breast.

One night, several months later, when I was more lustful than usual, I went on the streets actually in search of some one with whom to gratify my maddening passion.

I was passing down a dimly lighted street, when I saw in front of me a man whose form was simply perfect.

I had not seen his face, but I was sure that he must be very handsome.

I quickened my pace, and in the act of passing him I glanced at his face.

One look was enough—too much.

He was all that my passionate soul could desire, and I could not pass him by without a word.

I begged his pardon, then asked him the way to some place that I knew to be in the direction he was going, and he kindly offered to show me the way.

He talked freely, but my own voice was so choked with passion, that I could scarcely answer him.

He soon took on my condition, and before we had gone another block, he had my hand in his and—we were in love.

We turned into a still darker street, for the city was not well lighted, and at that time we did not even have a moon.

He placed his strong arms about me, strained me to his great manly breast and kissed me again and again.

I lay perfectly still against his breast, for I was completely dazed with the sweet blissful feeling his caresses brought to my soul.

He too was aflame with passion, and placing his lips close to my ear, he made a request that I could not grant and I told him so.

He gently put me from him, told me I did not care for him and turned to leave me.

I put out my hand to detain him, and he repeated his request.

I hesitated a moment, and he again placed his arms about me.

I felt my resolution giving way, for oh, how I loved him and how I longed to please him!

Placing his cheek against my own, he whispered: "Will you?"

At this moment reason returned, and springing from his arms, I firmly answered: "No, not if I die," and turning, I hurried away and left him.

I did not look back for some time, and when I did, he was gone, and I knew I had lost him.

I sat down upon a curb completely exhausted by the great strain under which I had been laboring.

I felt at that moment that I would grant any request if I only had him with me again.

I will not describe the rest of that wretched night in my room alone.

Suffice it to say that I met him again, and though men may curse me, I hope God will forgive me if I did *not* send him away.

He was a man sixty years of age, but he possessed a power, a fascination that I *could* not resist.

Even while writing these lines, my hand trembles and my face burns with passion when I remember those wild sweet moments we spent together.

Soon after this, I accidentally met a little man on the streets one night who was affected as I am. We spent the night together, and he seemed to love me very dearly.

My feeling for him was only passion and, after we separated, I gave him but little thought.

He wore a Van Dyke beard at that time, and I did not discover the beauty and sweetness of his face.

When I saw him several weeks later, I did not know him, for he had shaven, but recognizing me, he came at once and spoke to me.

Before I knew who he was, I was deeply in love with him, for without his beard he was beautiful as a dream and fascinating in every way.

We spent that night together, but sweet pure love had completely subdued my passion, and the same feeling soon came over him.

That was a night I shall never forget.

"Passion was dumb and purest love maintained its own dominion."

We lay in each other's arms all night and slept but little.

Our love was so sweet, so gentle, so tender and pure, that even wakefulness was a rest.

We talked of our dark lives, which were very similar, and tears were mingled freely.

We kissed each other a hundred times, and were so happy, the night stole by like a dream.

The next morning he went away, but I was not unhappy, for I knew we should see each other soon.

When he was gone, I fell down upon the bed where we had lain together and thanked God for this sweet pure love.

I began to improve at once.

My evil passion slunk away and hid itself, my conscience was at rest, and the great weight began to leave my forehead.

We corresponded all the time, and he told me in a letter that since our last night together, his passion for men was gone, and he loved no one but me.

I was sure he spoke the truth, for my feelings for him were the same.

He soon came to the city again, and we were so happy that we wept for joy.

He spent three nights with me, and we were so much in love that we almost forgot to take our meals.

I sought no more medical advice, for I did not need it now.

My physician was a man with a soul of love, my physic the love of his gentle soul, and I was well and happy again.

I at once began to take a new interest in life, and learning the merits of the B—— schools, I determined to enter the University there in the fall.

This I did, and all went well for a time.

My beloved friend came often to see me, and life for us both was all joy and sunshine.

I was getting on nicely in school, and the days stole by on golden wings, and the Christmas holidays began. With them came a visit from my friend, and it seemed that we were never so happy before.

He was a Christian, and (smile if you wish) having a sweet musical voice, he would sing sad religious songs to me, which often brought tears to my eyes.

We would sit for hours with our arms about each other and talk of the dark, bitter life from which our love had saved us, and the happy future we were to spend together, but alas! for dreams of earthly joy.

The holidays passed and my friend went away.

From that day to this I have never seen or heard from him again. I wrote to him several times, but received no reply, and my pride, which has always been strong, whispered: "Leave him alone," and I obeyed. I believe he is dead, for he was never very strong physically.

I knew none of his people at all, and as I never signed my name to my letters to him, there was no possible chance for them to communicate with me in any way.

My love was lost, and now the days crept wearily by.

For a time, grief and anxiety mastered passion, but when hope gave place to despair, I again became an easy prey to lust, and I was miserable.

I burned with desire for my classmates and teachers, and could scarcely hold myself in check. My head began to trouble me again, and I could not sleep at night.

When I retired, it seemed that a weight of a hundred pounds was placed between my eyes, and when I slept at all, my dreams were hideous and terrible.

I remained in the city till April, when school closed, and then went back to my father's home in the country, where I at once began a summer school.

I was again adrift on the wild sea of an abnormal passion, without chart or rudder.

I had a little niece in school whom I had always loved very dearly, and I now turned my whole attention to her educational advancement.

My last disappointment had so discouraged me that I determined to give up all hope of love and recovery, and to make her welfare and happiness the one grand object of my life.

She was fifteen years of age, very beautiful and very intelligent, and I spared neither time nor expense in giving her every possible advantage.

I made a good salary, and had no one else to share it with me.

She advanced very rapidly, and I soon found myself living for her alone.

While the brotherly love I felt for her by no means subdued my passion for men, it to a great extent held me in check, and I was about as happy as I ever hoped to be.

My school continued until about the last of October, when it closed with a concert at night.

The entertainment consisted of music and a drama of my own composition, in which my niece was the heroine, and I the leading man.

The play was very sad, and gave excellent opportunity for good acting.

She took the part of my wife, and in a drunken frenzy I had murdered her.

Then followed my grief beside her coffin, the burial, and lastly, my lunacy behind prison bars.

I had always been a perfect failure as an actor, but I was not acting now.

In these scenes I found an opportunity to pour out before the world all the bitter anguish that had filled my life for almost eighteen years.

I forgot the play, the audience—everything, but the words of the drama, which were written to express the real feelings of my suffering soul.

The audience, I afterwards learned, was deeply moved.

The men were serious and thoughtful, and the women were all in tears.

After the play, a feeling of relief came over me that I cannot describe.

All the sorrow and suffering of my wretched life I had cried out before the world, yet no one knew my secret.

Compliments were showered upon me. I was called an actor and begged to go on the stage, at the absurdity of which I could but smile.

I knew my acting was over. I had told the world of my suffering, but I could not do it again; so I did not take to the stage.

After school closed, it was decided that Violet (my niece) should go for a long visit to an uncle in Texas, and preparations were at once begun.

I had not forgotten how to sew, and with the assistance of an experienced dressmaker, many beautiful gowns were planned and created.

After two weeks of preparation all was ready, and I bade her an affectionate farewell, and went back to the University, where I was to be graduated in the spring.

I had a letter from her every week. She had reached her uncle's in safety and was very happy.

Her letters were always full of affection and gratitude, and my heart welled up with pride when I thought of the future in store for her.

I was living for her sake, and determined to make her happy.

I slept, I dreamed, and for a time forgot that no hope of *mine* could ever materialize.

Friday came, the day for a letter from Violet.

Instead, there came a telegram, which simply read: "Violet is very low. Can't live."

The next day she died, and Sunday she was buried in a strange land, away from home and hearts that loved her.

I did not weep—no.

My heart simply collapsed, and sinking into a seat, I bowed my head, and the blackness of night closed again around my gloomy life.

'Twas ever thus from childhood's hour,
   I've seen my fondest hope decay;
I never loved a tree or flower,
   But what 'twas first to fade away.

Earl Lind

Earl Lind (1874–?) was the pseudonym of a man who also called himself Ralph Werther and Jennie June. He claims to have been born in 1874 in a large village in the Connecticut hills, to have belonged to a Puritan church, and to have attended public school and a boys' prep school, but it is impossible at this point to confirm any of this information. As a man used to strapping on several identities, he may well have been stretching the truth or merely inventing it.

Earl Lind wrote two autobiographies, *The Female Impersonators* (1922) and *Autobiography of an Androgyne* (1918), from which the following excerpts come. *Autobiography of an Androgyne* is one of the earliest published defenses in America of effeminate male homosexuals and masculine lesbians and is a remarkable document for its time. In the passage below we follow Lind as he becomes "Jennie June," first as a college student, at which time he does not wear female clothing, and then later after his expulsion, when he can play Jennie June in complete drag.

Lind captures the danger of this life. He is a fairy set adrift among "ruffians," as he calls the working-class men who both allow his attentions and reject him for what he is, who rape him and then come back to comfort him. Lind expresses piety and perversion, desire and divinity. His "baby talk" is a campy strategy both to establish his sexual desires and to forestall any hostility directed at him. His tone is comically overdramatic, but, like many survivors, he is also quite practical.

From *Autobiography of an Androgyne*

DURING THESE TERRIBLE DAYS, I felt that a crisis in my life was at hand. I felt that I stood at the dividing of the ways, one leading to honor and self-approbation, the other to ignominy and the blasting of all my legitimate ambitions. As each month of my first year in the university went by, the struggle against sensuality had been growing harder and harder.

Finally, on an evening in early June, I arose from my studies and prepared for my first nocturnal ramble. I put on a cast-off suit which I kept for wear only in my room, placed some coin in a pocket and several bills in a shoe, stuffed a few matches in one pocket and in another a wet sponge, wrapped in paper so as not to dry out, and then carefully went through my clothing a second time to make sure that I had not by oversight left on me some clue to my identity.

On account of my shabby clothing, precaution was necessary to leave my place of residence—a high-class boarding-house—without being seen. I crept stealthily out of my room, closing the door softly so as not to attract attention. After listening to make sure that no one was about to ascend the outside steps leading to the street, I opened the outer door and glided out bare-headed, a cast-off soft cap crumpled up in my hand because I was ashamed to be seen wearing it by any one who knew me. Hurriedly crossing to the opposite side of the street, I put on the cap, pulling the tip down over my eyes. Walking a few blocks to a park, I took my house key from my pocket and hid it in the grass, so that it could not be stolen and I was thereby rendered unable to let myself in on my return.

The reader now beholds me for the first time transformed into a sort of secondary personality inhabiting the same corpus as my proper self, to which personality I soon gave the name of "Jennie June," and which personality was to become far more widely known in the immediately following dozen years than the other side of my dual nature, the unremitting student and scholar, was ever to be known. The feminine side of my dual nature, for many years, as a matter of conscience, repressed, was now to find full expression in "Jennie June." For it was not alone fellatio that I craved, but also to be looked upon and treated as a member of the gentler sex. Nothing would have pleased me more than to adopt feminine attire on this and my multitudinous subsequent female-impersonation sprees, as some other ordinarily respectable androgynes are in the habit of doing when going out on similar promenades, but my position in the social organism was much higher than theirs, and the adoption of female apparel would in my case have been attended with too great risk. The mere wearing of it on the street by an adult male would render him liable to imprisonment.

I made my way to the quarter of the city bordering the Hudson River that is given over largely to factories and freight yards and is known as "Hell's Kitchen" because of the many steam vents. In this lonely and at night little frequented neighborhood, perhaps the most advantageous in the city for highway robbery, where nothing else than burning passion could have induced me to go at night, I ran across a stalwart adolescent of about my own age seated alone on a beer keg in front of a bar room. By a great effort of the will I accosted him. My voice trembled and my whole body shook as if I had the ague.

I had anticipated little difficulty in securing a companion, but events showed it to be otherwise. For years subsequently I associated intimately with hundreds of unmarried toughs of the slums from seventeen to twenty-four years of age, and so I know their nature. Approximately one-third have a distaste for coitus with an invert. The other two-thirds would accommodate him provided their sexual needs were not fully met by normal intercourse—which is generally the case. Moreover, there is a difference between their attitude toward a perfect stranger who accosts them, and an invert with whom they have become somewhat acquainted. The impulse to rob a perfect stranger tends to drown out all the movings of carnality. In addition, the feeling that he is a stranger and an outlaw—the latter fact being almost universally known—prompts them to assault him.

Along with an outline of what happened on this my first nocturnal ramble, I describe below my general method of approaching strangers in the poor quarters of the city. Of course I cannot recall the exact dialogue in a particular case, but all the sample conversations given in this autobiography are woven from actual remarks passed at different times. I have taken part in hundreds of dialogues of the kind sampled here and there in this book, and the reader can be assured of obtaining a truthful impression of the words exchanged by me—an androgyne—with my youthful virile associates. On the present occasion, after a few commonplace remarks, the conversation was of the following character:

"What big, big strong hands you have! I bet you are a good fighter." My aim was to talk rather babyishly so as gradually to betray my nature.

"There's a few as kin lick me but not many."

"I love fighters. If you and I had a fight, who do you think would win?"

"I could lick a dozen like yer together."

"I know you could. I am only a baby."

"Hah hah! A baby!"

"Say, you have a handsome face."

"Me hansome! Stop your kiddin."

"Really you are handsome. I am going to tell you a secret. I am a woman-hater. I am really a girl in a fellow's clothes. I would like to get some fellow to marry me. You look beautiful to me. Would you be willing to?"

"How much does it cost yer to git married? Give me a V"—meaning five dollars— "and I'll be yourn, or else git out of here."

My statement that I had not that amount with me brought the threat of a pummeling. I was beginning to wish I was far away, but concealed my uneasiness as best I could. After a few minutes more of conversation, several pals happened to come along. He called out, "I've got a fairie here!" and clutching my shoulder with one hand, he clinched his other fist, shook it threateningly in my face, and demanded: "Hand out your money! Hand out your money!"

Frightened to death, I handed him all the coin I had, amounting to a little more than a dollar. I protested I had no more, and after they had searched my pockets and felt my clothing all over for concealed bills, one of them gave me a blow in the face. With that wonderful agility which supposedly grave danger to one's life can arouse, I sprinted away, one of the ruffians pursuing a few steps and giving me several blows in the back. But I was so terrified that I did not halt until I had run several blocks. Panting and exhausted, I seated myself on a door-step and felt that I was forever cured of seeking a paramour. I called to mind the biblical text, "The way of the transgressor is hard," and I felt glad that it was hard so as to help me never to transgress again.

But after I had rested, my intense desire for fellatio induced me to make an endeavor in another poor neighborhood. I passed many groups of ruffians congregated in front of bar-rooms, but must find some solitary adolescent. At last I ran across one standing in front of a factory, evidently, as I later concluded, its watchman. I walked past him several times, unable to pluck up courage to speak. But he called out angrily: "Who are you looking at?"

"Pardon me for my rudeness, but I was wishing I could get acquainted with you. I am a baby, and I want a big, strong, brave fellow like you to pet me. I'll give you a dollar if you'll pet me for a few minutes, and let me sit on your lap."

Much to my surprise and disappointment, he sent me away with a curse. Twice repulsed, I decided to try again in a part of the city where the immigrant element predominates. Both the neighborhoods tried were quasi-American. I strolled down the Bowery, staring longingly and beseechingly into the eyes of the adolescents I passed, but too timid to accost any. Those who had known me all my life, had they met me now, would have wondered what could have brought into the then theatre and red-light district of the foreign laboring classes of the city, at an hour approaching midnight, a timid youth, hitherto called an "innocent," naturally pious, and generally esteemed for his intellectual tastes. My friends would never have dreamed that I would frequent that red-light district near midnight, and would never have believed it if any one told them that I was there for no good purpose . . .

While I have thus in my more mature judgment considered myself practically irresponsible for the conduct just described, in that early stage of my career, I was not so sure, and during the day following this first nocturnal ramble, was overwhelmed with a sense of shame and guilt. When night came on, I made my way to a solitary spot in a large park, where I threw myself on the ground to weep and shriek and pray. The burden of my prayer was that God would change my nature that very moment and give me the mind and powers of a man. I soon heard footsteps approaching, arose instantly, and walked from the spot. The men said they were looking for an owl which they had heard hooting. It was probably only my peculiar insane, half-suppressed shrieks they had heard.

[1892]

If the reader had been on Mulberry Street between Grand and Broome on an evening in November of 1892, he would have seen meandering slowly along from one side of the street to the other with a mincing gait, a haggard, tired-looking, short and slender youth between eighteen and nineteen, clad in shabby clothes, and with a skull cap on his head. As he walks along, whenever he meets any robust, well-built young man of about his own age, who is alone, he is seen to stop and address to him a few words. If we had been able to follow this queer acting individual for the previous hour before he passed us on Mulberry Street, we would have seen him roaming about through all the streets of the then dark and criminal 4th Ward, occasionally halting near the groups of ruffians congregated in front of the bar-rooms, and then failing of courage to speak, pass along.

Finally on the corner of Broome and Mulberry Streets, he addresses a tall, muscular, splendid specimen of the adolescent (subsequently a member of the New York police force) who continues in conversation with him, and walks along by his side. The little adolescent takes the arm of the big one into his own, and presses as closely as possible against him. The spirits of the little one are visibly heightened, he appears more lively and animated, and walks along with a quicker but extremely nervous step. He is soon seized with a sort of ague—due to sexual excitement—which causes his whole body to shake, and hardly permits him to speak. If we watched closely whenever the pair passed under a shadow, we would have seen the little one throw his arms rapturously around the neck of his big companion, and kiss him passionately. They finally pass out of sight down one of the dark covered alleys leading to tenements in the rear.

When after an interval the pair again emerge, the smaller is clinging tighter than ever to his big companion, as if afraid he might escape. They walk a block together, and then the big fellow tries to get rid of the little one, much against the latter's wishes. He tells the little fellow to go on his way, but adds, "Come round again, do yer hear?"

"I don't know whether I shall or not. I am afraid we shall never meet again. How it pains me to part from you!"

"What do yer call yourself, and where do yer hang out?"

"I call myself Jennie, and I work in a restaurant up on Third Avenue. What's your name, and where could I find you again?"

"You kin find me round on this block any time. Just ask any one fur Red Mike."

"Well, good-by. The Lord bless you. I never expect to see you again, although I love you with all my heart, and would like to live with you and be your slave."

The two start out in opposite directions. The little fellow walks rapidly, turns the first corner, sprints, turns another corner and sprints, and repeats this maneuver several times, as if bent on giving the slip to any possible follower. He finally reaches the Bowery and takes a train uptown from the Grand Street station.

1893 — Fairie Apprenticeship Begins

Over five months after my previous visit, I again found myself on Mulberry Street, corner of Grand. I have always suspected that I was incited to this particular quest by an aphrodisiac. On or about that day, my physician administered a new drug. He probably hoped it would incite me to seek normal relations, but it acted along the line of my peculiar instincts.

Walking northward on the west side of the street, I encountered a mixed group of Italian and Irish "sports" of foreign parentage between sixteen and twenty-one years of age seated or standing around the portal of a warehouse. I timidly addressed them: "I am looking for a friend named Red Mike. Do any of you know him?"

One of them replied that he had just seen him up the street. Proceeding in that direction, I stopped occasionally to make the same inquiry of other adolescents. After walking several blocks in vain, I returned to the "gang" at the warehouse's portal, and asked: "Do you mind if I sit down to rest here? I am tired and lonesome. I have not been in the city long and don't know any one."

"Where did yez come from?"

"Philadelphia. I couldn't get any work there, so I came here."

It was not long before Red Mike happened to stroll by and recognized me even before I did him. An hour now passed, while they smoked and drank, hiding the beer-pail whenever a policeman went by. I had no desire to join in the drinking and smoking, and indeed up to my middle forties, when this autobiography goes to press, have never had any desire to learn to smoke, although having a few times put the lighted cigarette of a paramour in my mouth. I have always considered myself too feminine to smoke. Moreover, all my life I have been practically a total abstainer from alcoholic beverages.

But I reclined in the arms of one after another, covering face, neck, hands, arms, and clothing with kisses, while they caressed me and called me pet-names. I was supremely happy. For the first time in my life I learned about the fairie inmates of the lowest dives. They proposed to install me in one. I told them the story of my own life, only with such variations from the truth as were necessary for my own protection. We sang plantation songs, "Old Black Joe," "Uncle Ned," etc. These they had learned from Bixby's "Home Songs," published in that very neighborhood by the well-known shoe-blacking firm as an advertisement. I sang with them in the mock soprano or falsetto that fairies employ, trying to imitate the voice of a woman. Singing in this voice was not a novelty to me, as I had previously at times aped the warbling of a woman instinctively.

At the end of an hour, we adjourned down an alley, where the drinking and love-making continued even more intensely. After I had refused their repeated solicitations, one of them grasped my throat tightly to prevent any outcry and threw me down, while another removed part of my clothing, appropriating whatever of value he found in my pockets. With my face in the dust, and half suffocated by the one ruffian's tight grip on my throat, I moaned and struggled with all my might, because of the excruciating pain. But in their single thought to experience an animal pleasure, they did not heed my moans and broken entreaties to spare me the suffering they were inflicting. For two months afterward I suffered pain at every step because of fissures and lacerations about the anus.

When finally released, terror-stricken and with only half my clothing, I rushed out through the alley and down Mulberry Street, and did not halt until I reached what I considered a safe refuge on brightly lighted Grand Street. Breathless and exhausted, I seated myself on the curb. "I am cured of my slumming," I said to myself. "God's will be done. It is His hand which has brought this about, in order to drive me back to the path of virtue. Truly the Lord ruleth in all things."

Because of my exhausted condition, I remained seated for several minutes. In the meantime, two of my assailants had followed me up, and expressed their regret that one of their number had stolen my cap and coat, promising to get them back, and assuring me of their friendly feelings. "You are only a baby," they said, "and so we will fight for you and protect you."

I was so touched by their gallantry, so enamoured of them, and so sure that the assault was not committed through malevolence, that I accompanied them back to our first meeting place on the warehouse steps. I still had great fear of violence at their hands—rape, not a beating—but I was powerfully drawn toward them. Fellatio was welcome; paedicatio, horrible to my moral sense, and physically, accompanied by excruciating pain. The "gang" received me kindly, petted and soothed me as one would a peevish baby, which I resembled in my actions, fretting and sobbing in happiness as I rested my head against their bodies. To lie in the bosom of these sturdy young manual laborers, all of whom were good-looking and approximately my own age, was the highest earthly happiness I had yet tasted. With all my money gone, and cap and coat stolen besides, I finally had to walk home, a distance of several miles. Obtaining my keys in their hiding place, I succeeded in reaching my room without attracting attention.

The next day I wrote in my journal: "What a strange thing is life! Mephistopheles last night carried me through one of the experiences through which he carried Faust. . . . My carnal nature was aroused as never before. I groaned in despair. Never before in all my experience have I seen such a conflict between the flesh and the spirit. . . . How like an animal is man! Thus God has seen fit to make him."

A few days later I again wrote: "My present psychical state is most strange. I cannot yet repent of my conduct last Friday night, yet on the Sunday following I had one of the happiest experiences of nearness to God that I ever had. That afternoon I presented the Gospel in love for my Savior and for perishing souls. I have in my heart an intense desire to save from their lives of sin those in whose company I was Friday night, especially my Bill, so young, and yet so deep in sin. I want to rescue him, and make of him a strong educated champion for Christ. My heart yearns to carry blessings and peace to all those who are suffering in the slums of New York." . . .

[1897]

This autobiography has now reached my twenty-third year. I had received my baccalaureate degree with honors, and was in my second year of graduate study. I had not really degenerated morally or religiously. For the entire year ending at the date at which I had now arrived, the aggregate time devoted to female impersonation and coquetry was approximately one hundred hours, as compared with about twenty-one hundred devoted to my studies and two hundred and fifty to the worship of my Creator and religious culture. Surely I was not to be tabooed as a moral leper. While the average church member, through lack of understanding of the conditions surrounding my life, would have branded me as a hypocrite, I sincerely believed and lived up to the fundamental truths of the Christian religion.

I still enjoyed an unblemished reputation. I associated with all my beaux, including my soldier friend, incognito. Always on returning home after an evening passed as "Jennie June," I took precautions that I was not followed.

The wreck of my happy and highly successful student career was now brought about by a physician whom I had consulted in hope of a cure for my inversion, but not one of the two gentlemen already named. He happened to number the president of the university among his friends, and whispered to him that I ought not to be continued as a student. I was immediately expelled.

I earned my living in a minor capacity in the university, and expulsion also meant that my income was cut off. The shock of expulsion rendered me a mental wreck. But

I did not have the courage to return to my village home. Nor could I even apply to my father for money. Since soon after my arrest two years prior to the present date, he had, as already described, displayed a pronounced antipathy for me, rendering my visits home almost intolerable. In addition, because of the double life my nature forced me to lead, I decided I must remain in New York.

I removed to a part of the city where I would not be likely to encounter any of my college acquaintances, and began to look around for means of support. I spent several hours every day in answering advertisements. I would have been only too glad to accept such a position as shoveling coal into a furnace, but at the end of a month, had found nothing. In applying for positions, I was abashed in the consciousness that I was ranked as a degenerate and an outcast from society. I could not name as reference any member of the university or let it become known that I had been a student there. After my expulsion I called on the two professors with whom I was most intimate, and asked if I could refer to them. One replied: "Knowing your nature, I could not recommend you for any position, however menial. You cannot be trusted." (And yet shortly afterward I was for thirty months in the employ of a millionaire in the most confidential capacity, and was surpassed in faithfulness by no employee.) The other: "You must realize that you are an outcast from society."

All hope for the future and all courage for battling with the world were gone, and every day on my return from several hours' fruitless search, I would throw myself on the bed and give vent to my feelings in a violent fit of weeping. While walking the street, I would weep aloud and be on the borderline of hysterical screaming. I repeatedly entertained thoughts of suicide.

In a few weeks I was penniless and a shelterless wanderer on the streets in midwinter. I was driven for shelter to the Bowery, because there alone lodging could be obtained for fifteen cents, and a big meal of coarse and even disgusting food for ten cents. Thus I was compelled to live for nine weeks before a way was opened to something better.

During the nine weeks I was of the opinion that I must pass the rest of my days as an outcast from society, while of course living out the "Jennie-June" life to which I was apparently predestined. I was grateful to Providence that it was I and not one of my sisters who was predetermined to the life of a fille de joie and an outcast. In suffering such a fate, I believed that I was paying the penalty to God for the sin of some progenitor. I believed myself appointed by the God who visits the iniquities of the fathers upon the children to live out the rest of my life in mourning and paroxysms of grief, such as then visited me every day. . . .

Living as I was now compelled to live and necessarily mingling daily with men of loose morals, the charm of masculine beauty proved more powerful than ever before. Furthermore, it is not surprising that a person, deprived of even what are regarded as the necessities of a decent existence, should indulge immoderately in the single one of life's pleasures of which there was an abundant supply. In the environment in which forces outside of my control placed me, there was in me a practically irresistible impulse to adopt the manner of life I did. I would never have made the profession of the fairie the main business of life if it had not been for the peculiar concurrence of circumstances, expulsion from college, inability to find respectable employment, etc. That I now led the life I did was perhaps more the fault of Christian society than my own. While the world condemned, I have always believed that the Omniscient Judge pardoned because I was the victim of circumstances and of innate psychical forces.

The fact that I could now satisfy every day my instinctive yearnings to pass for a female and spend six evenings a week in the company of adolescent ruffians went far towards counterbalancing the many tears I had to shed when there was nothing to divert my thoughts from my condition of an outcast and an outlaw. I never coquetted on Sunday evenings, which I devoted to worship of my Creator at some mission. I no longer experienced any shame at displaying my feminine mentality everywhere outside of the missions, as no one knew who I was. In many neighborhoods I was hailed as "Jennie June."

Russell Cheney and F. O. Matthiessen

With his pioneering book *American Renaissance: Art Expression in the Age of Emerson and Whitman* (1941), F. O. Matthiessen (1902–1950) changed the general view of what mattered in American writing from the comfortable, genteel, "fireside" writers to the work of Thoreau, Melville, and Whitman. Matthiessen was not just a literary scholar. He was a social activist, a union organizer, and a supporter of the progressive Henry Wallace in his bid for the presidency in 1948. Matthiessen thus occupied a rare role in American culture: he was a highly regarded literary scholar and a well-known political figure. His sexuality, although not known to the wider public, was acknowledged among his friends and colleagues.

In 1925, while sailing to England to attend Oxford University, where he was a Rhodes scholar, Matthiessen met Russell Cheney (1881–1945), a painter who was about twice Matthiessen's age. The two fell in love and were partners until Cheney's death in 1945. The letters that follow are from their early correspondence, published posthumously as *Rat and the Devil* (1978), in which they try to work out their relationship. Another theme is Cheney's alcoholism, which remained a problem throughout his life. The title of the book derives from their pet names for one another. Cheney was Rat.

Cheney's death and the state of the postwar world left Matthiessen extremely depressed. On April Fool's Day in 1950, in the wake of investigations into homosexuals and Communists who might have worked for the government, Matthiessen threw himself off the roof of the Manger Hotel in Boston.

From *Rat and the Devil*

London
September 23, 1924

. . . Little by little the largeness of what has happened sweeps over me. I thought I realized it all that last night together; but first the intellect sees, and then when it has created its imaginative symbolism it gives the whole man something to live by. I saw very clearly that night and called it a marriage. The imagination has since been working, and I live body and soul in this new relationship.

Marriage is a mere term; only as a dynamic vivid thing does it dominate life. That is: you can visualize marriage or you can live it. Now I am living it.

Marriage! What a strange word to be applied to two men! Can't you hear the hell-hounds of society baying full pursuit behind us? But that's just the point. We are beyond society. We've said thank you very much, and stepped outside and closed the door. In the eyes of the unknowing world we are a talented artist of wealth and position and a promising young graduate student. In the eyes of the knowing world we would be pariahs, outlaws, degenerates. This is indeed the price we pay for the unforgivable sin of being born different from the great run of mankind.

And so we have a marriage that was never seen on land or sea and surely not in Tennyson's poet's dream! It is a marriage that demands nothing and gives everything. It does not limit the affections of the two parties, it gives their scope greater radiance and depth. Oh it is strange enough. It has no ring, and no vows, and no [wedding presents from your friends], and no children. And so of course it has none of the coldness of passion, but merely the serene joy of companionship. It has no three hundred and sixty-five breakfasts opposite each other at the same table; and yet it desires frequent companionship, devotion, and laughter. Its bonds indeed form the service that is perfect freedom.

I have hesitated about writing this. I am always afraid that I will be thought too bold. But what I am now experiencing is what I have deeply known only once before—and that vicariously, [when from my great friend Dick Tighe one night around the open fire in New Haven] I heard a story of unbelievable beauty. And now that story is my own.

How many, when reading this, would think so? Ah there's the mockery of it: those gates of society are of iron. And when you're outside, you've got to live in yourself alone, unless—o beatissimus—you are privileged to find another wanderer in the waste land. And perhaps even you think what I have written mawkish? It is infinitely difficult to make the medium of expression adequately clothe your emotions. But I have thought at length on this—between snatches of Goldsmith, and walking in St. James Park at sunset. If you dislike it, say so, and I will leave such expression to be conveyed by the touch of my hand. But it is an integral part of me.

Love—Dvl

Hôtel Royal Danieli
Venise
September 25, 1924

Dearest Dev—

Can't write a letter, got to sleep. It's all anyone ever said it was here. Gorgeous in an autumnal decay sort of way—Indian summer of a city. Arrived at noon, slowly to the hotel in a gondola, warm sunshine. Lazy sounds of water lapping the sides, and long drawn calls as you round the corners. . . .

Your last letter! God, I've read it 2 doz times. Would I rather you didn't say things like that? Not on your life. Your saying them is the very essence of my being able to hold that level, which I do not intend to pretend I do. My eyes and thoughts are not controlled, only a thousand times better than two weeks ago. Help me to get there. Boy. Love is stronger than death—"mawkish," hell. What do I carry it round all day and night and read it over and over for? Now I'll switch off my light and lie with the lapping of waves and sudden calls, and bursts of singing below—and you will be very close to me.

My love to you and good night, my Devil.

Rat.

London
September 24, 1924

Dear Rat:

Steady! Don't you see there's some difference between a kid of twenty stepping into [a new circle of friendship] and out of his habits of three years growth, and a fellow of forty trying to cut that Gorgonian knot that has been winding and twisting itself about him for I don't know how long? You've got a battle on your hands. But you've got someone who is going to fight it with you. It comes down to Goethe: the secret of strength lying in the renunciation of the things that destroy the single harmony. Well, you can't have both serenity and 3½ bottles of stout!

We're agreed with Whitman all right that:

"And if the body does not do fully as much as the soul?
And if the body were not the soul, what is the soul?"

But we're also agreed that there are other ways of using the body than by making it carry around a few quarts of angry liquor every day.

"Was it doubted that those who corrupt their own bodies conceal themselves?
And if those who defile the living are as they who defile the dead?"

In Venice you're going to start over again. You don't know where the interesting places are and you're not going to find them. You're there to paint. And you're not going to sit round the piazza with 3½ bottles of stout under your belt. Do you understand? Some of this exuberance of yours has indeed got to be pruned! If you want one of the Big Things in life, you've always got to make sacrifices for it. And your first sacrifice is approximately 3 of those 3½ bottles. Remember: I'm tugging at your sleeve every time you reach for the bottle, my hand is closing over yours every time you raise a glass to your lips.

As I write, you've been on your way to Venice about twenty-four hours. I got your second letter last night about eleven. I had unsuspectingly gone down to the office to fill my fountain pen so I could write my [friend George Norton.] "There's a letter for you, Mr. Matthiessen," So there is! "Thanks very much"—quietly filling my pen— "Good night." Up one flight of stairs at a dignified walk. The next at a jog. The third at a scamper. The last at a gallop, shaking in every limb as though I had the ague. I wrote my [friend George Norton] all right a vivid flashing letter (that's another thing: you've given a new keenness to my relationship with [even my closest friends]. I tell them what I mean now. I'm no longer pompous, self-righteous, and dull. Yes, I wrote [George], but I didn't get to sleep for hours.

My days here are uninterrupted. I've set my shoulder to the wheel. Up radiantly with a song of songs in my heart. To breakfast, usually in the company of some one or other of the wholesome simple-minded Middle Westerners who are "doing" London and staying here. A brisk walk around the square with airiness in my step that has never been there before. And to the brown and gold reading room of the British Museum for a good four hour morning. An hour off from one to two to walk around, buy a book, do an errand, (go back to the hotel and ask for mail), and get some lunch. Two and a half to three hours more in that pride of the Victorian era with its tablets around the dome revealing for all time the literary judgment of 1857: Chaucer, Caxton, Tindale, Spenser, Shakespeare, Bacon, Milton, Locke, Addison, Swift, Pope, Gibbon, Wordsworth, Scott, Byron, Carlyle, Macaulay, Tennyson, Browning. A strong list, but the last four wouldn't have much of a chance if the tablets were being erected to-day. And doesn't it cut to see Scott and no Fielding, Byron and no Shelley?

But enough of this. It's after five and I'm striding along through the opalescence of a late London afternoon. Where shall it be to-day? To St. Paul's, that "massive pile" as Dr. Johnson would doubtless have called it? To that quiet little court of the Temple—hardly a dozen yards from the busiest rush of Fleet Street where there is a dull gray stone with Here Lies Oliver Goldsmith on it? No, to-day, I'm on a bus for Marble Arch, Hyde Park. You know Marble Arch? It's notoriety is great. The place in London most flagrant. Yes, there they are. I can see them as I swing off the bus. Little crowds of them pretending to listen to the soap-box orators who keep springing up here all day. Hard faces. One, Red-hair. White flower in his button hole. Compelling eye. I look—the blood rushes hot to my face—and what then? I swing right past the whole damn bunch of them out into the broad sweep of the park where the grass is long, and there are some fallen leaves, and the kids are playing soccer in the twilight. For half an hour I walk—the park is wide—lightly, swiftly in absolute accord with the throbbing of nature. A faint line of red in the west. A slight rising of the wind. And I turn home for supper.

Of course I could have stopped in that gesturing crowd. I could have drunk in a lot of luscious slime through my eyes. But who would want to when he can throw back his shoulders, and walk into the sunset, and be at peace with his soul and you?

That eye business is just a little dirt on an open wound. It doesn't seem like much but pretty soon it begins to fester, and you find that your whole body is full of its poison. So, Rat, if you'll help me there's not going to be even a flick of dust upon me. But I must have the sense that you're with me every minute of the day and night.

I agree with you that things in letters often appear out of proportion, and so untrue. But it purges my soul to write *every thing* to you, and to know that I am getting everything in return. It's so easy to brood when you don't express. And as long as we both realize that a letter doesn't really represent life, it can't disturb our balance.

Don't worry, feller. I have absolute faith in you. I love you for yourself.

Dvl

London
October 10, 1924

Dearest [*sketch of a rat*]

   NB This *is* a RAT (What an incredible drawing!)

   Standing in the hotel office waiting to see if I had a letter. "Hello, son of Eli" That collegiate beginning makes me bristle. My returning "hello" is none too cordial. . . . We talked. He [Rudy Vallee] finished two years at Yale, now plays the saxophone in the Savoy orchestra here. A fairly attractive light-weight. Friendly, probably lonely. We lunched. Both seemed to fit in the scheme of being frankly ourselves. But when he began to talk of "the last time I slept with Kitty", I began to be a bit embarrassed. Splendid frankness, open and above board about it all, but a little too sudden for a sensitive feller.

   "Had I been to any of the Night Clubs?" No. "Would I like to go to Forty-Three, the toughest dive in Europe" My answer? An unthinking whim-of-the-moment Yes!

   . . . We get to the place, and his description proves to be hardly extreme. Such a blatant, unadulterated display of fleshly desire I have never seen. Girls dancing together until a fellow breaks in. Not drunk. Some of them fairly pretty. But the absolute vulgarity of their physical contortions. No restraint. No subtlety. A mere display of as much bodily movement as they can contrive to attract hot eyes. Poor kids. Dancing in hell.

   What do I do? I enter upon a little study in the psychology of sex! I dance. I told you you had changed me, given me confidence, and made me attractive. Even painted whores fall for me now!! These girls give me all this sensuous movement. I hold them as I never held a girl before. I dance in a way that would ordinarily land me in jail! The acme of the vulgar. Body glued to body. And the result of this scientific study—this concrete experiment? I'm left as cool as if I were sitting here in my room. A little exhilarated by the jazz. But by this unrestrained muscular contact not at all. Not disgusted. Interested in the types of people. The one observer in this den of license. I am so aloof from my actual surroundings that I can even hear some coarse voice remarking "that fellow's a virgin", and not have a shock.

   I buy my girl a drink. She tells me how her feller's gone back to the United States. I ask her if she doesn't hate the life. She doesn't understand, says this place isn't as good as some. Poor kid, what can I do for her? Nothing unless I blast her with the voice of the prophet, and I haven't the nerve to do that. She says "goodnight, dearie"—Wistful. I say "good-night", and feel half ashamed at leaving her there.

   Breathe the night air walking home. Wash off the smell of stale powder. Climb into bed, rather dissatisfied with myself, at three.

   Have I made this situation live? Sex didn't enter into it as far as any effect on me. I was as wholly yours throughout the evening as I am this minute. Although I would have been thoroughly ashamed if you had seen my "experimental dancing". For I played the part of blatant coarseness to perfection. But the whole was a mere study. The result was: no female physical attraction—which is an interesting sidelight to some of our conversations on the boat.

I hope this picture of vulgarity hasn't hurt you, Rat. It's a strange thing how I can make my sensitivity lie dormant on some occasions. . . .

Look here, feller, if you disapprove of my batting around the toughest dive in Europe at 3 A.M., why say so. You'll find that there will be frequent occasions when I will need to be given hell without restraint. . . .

Love

Hôtel Royal Danieli
Venise
October 13, 1924

Dearest Dev—

Well, well—take me a volume to answer all your letter on adventure in night life. Looks as though you had proved pretty conclusively what you set out to discover, and you needn't go again. Certainly it is not a pleasure to you and me, though it may be to your Eli friend. My reaction to the whole affair was discontent with the attitude of active Christians that they must do good to their fellow men. Why should they? who asked them to? can they if they do it consciously? (I don't think so.) Fact is I think that girl could do you more good than you could her.

Just what did you mean by feeling half ashamed to leave her there? If you meant half ashamed because you couldn't take her home and give her what she wanted, that is all right. I agree you should be; I am. If you mean something about urging her to give up "the life," I don't agree. Nothing can be done for her and she wants nothing done. She knows more about life than you or I will know if we live to be a hundred. How do you know you were the one detached observer in that "den of license"? What could be more detached than the "painted whores" who play on the particular weakness of each comer.

That "wistful" look was the play to your weakness—didn't think you had suggested ideas of a better life, did you? I'm being stinkin', hey? Sort of gets my goat the way people like Sherry [Day] think they must help people. That means they are better than the people they help. The eye is in the gallery—taking the tired look out of someone's eye. There are clichés for each good deed. The thing is to be good, be simple, be clean, be honest—and hell, forget it—

As for me—well, tonight, after all day painting (A.M. and P.M.), then a beer, then an Italian lesson, then dinner; I was walking home and passed and looked over the best built, most splendid looking feller I about ever saw—hell, a regular Greek statue.

He swung around and followed me—and I beat it for home, eyes in the boat. And since then I'm so damn mad with myself I can't see. Why should I? Oh, it's all right to do what I did. Came home to you and shut the door. Maybe tomorrow when I get up early to work I'll be glad. That is a legitimate reason—to keep myself to you; I don't know that it is. I rather think not, because that's an idea: I'm not yours and never will be. I care too much about you. Nonsense not to have two words for love like ours and love of the flesh—a need like the need for a [purge] in the morning.

Devil, while I'm being rotten I got a suggestion. I have worked on it for myself for years. Do everything possible to avoid the expected adjective in writing or speaking or thinking. That's why I "quoted" your painted whores—they are always painted. Trying to find the right word each time and trying to classify right each time are the things that count. Everything that is pigeonholed as this or that is a dead thing. You have the same weakness I fight, of having an eye on yourself. The pussy cat business—watching the thing and rather fancying the part we play—nothing in that. . . .

San Marco took a good step today and I might finish tomorrow. It is luminous and interesting. I don't know how good it is because I am too much in it. Devil dear, more than ever I want our seven weeks to come. We have so much for each other.

I hesitate about this letter. I was kind of sore—kind of thought your evening a waste—want you to live and stop watching yourself live.

It's eleven again, feller, just striking. I did my Italian exercise, and been writing this a whole lot longer than it seems. I lie back and let the sense of your nearness flow through me. I love you, and somehow this last letter makes me realize that it is not just a matter of pleasant company but a close thing inside [us], where it is necessary to be ourselves and say out what comes to our minds. God, it's a whole two months before Dec. 10, isn't it. I think I never cared more for you than I do right this minute, maybe because I feel I may have hurt you somehow here. I should hate to do that, dear feller—

Oxford, England
October 20, 1924
Dearest Rat,

. . . There was the letter you wrote on your birthday—and actually feller, I couldn't read it at first. My heart was too full—my hand shook, I couldn't sit still. So I crumpled it into my pocket, went to lunch, and calmed down a bit. Then I came back and sat relaxed in my arm chair for a few minutes, and then let the letter sink into me. When you give me the whole richness of your spirit that way, my dearest Rat, it makes me very quiet, very humble before the majesty of what has happened to us. To think that you have considered me worthy of such a trust, that you have bestowed on me the supreme gift of your life—I can say nothing. All I know is that my spirit is full within me—that I want you to have whatever fine there may be in my nature—love, devotion, companionship, protection. Yes, even protection, Rat. I know that sounds funny coming from a little feller like me. But I want to keep you from pain, from sordidness. I want to cherish the harmony of your soul, so you can give it expression.

Perhaps it could be called a coincidence that we both happened on practically the same day to write, picturing our meeting, and the moment when the door closes and we are alone. But to me it's very natural. In love we are one, inseparable. The only way I can tell how much you care for me is to look inside my heart, and see how much I love you. And o how much that how much is!

Dvl.

[*sketch of devil*]

Hotel Royal Danieli
Venise
October 24, 1924

Hello Dev—

Raining like hell still—48 hours of it anyway. As you say, it doesn't permeate. Can't make a dent on the happy peaceful outlook of our inner life together, but it does raise Cain with getting on with the new canvas I laid out of the Salute. I have half a mind to go ahead and paint it out of my head—and have such a definite idea about a late sunset, one I could probably paint with my eyes turned in anyhow, looking at the subject occasionally as a concession to the crowd of spectators.

Many times I've gone out to a subject and found it not like my impression and by gosh go ahead and stand there and paint the impression, which is the significant thing, using the actual subject only for suggestion on drawing, etc. I sure look forward to the day you turn up in my studio at home, and we can go back through the different phases I've blundered through, trying to arrive at myself. Well, at Cassis in April I thought I had arrived, and all I had to do was go back home and settle in for good—just live there and paint quietly the rest of my life. And we have seen what a mess I made of it, how the devil (not your kind) inside me raised the devil with the best laid plans and I did nothing, just nothing at all, for six months.—Well, [Cross] and [Foster] pry me out of that slough, and Devil (your kind with an accolade) takes me by the hand, and it begins to look as though I might be whole again. I'm not yet—don't think I am. But I want to be and then I did not want to be—and there is a difference. . . .

I get to thinking sometimes how much work I would have completed, say up in Vermont in the hills—or out in Colorado if I had gone out and joined the Graham family where they were up in the mountains, with the yellow aspens turning. Or at

Taos with the same yellow aspens and clear skies and little adobe villages. Take it all around the world looks pretty good, doesn't it. Thing is, it is nothing but a mirror of your inner spirit. If you are at peace and in harmony with life, wherever you are there is beauty. There at home, with every possible advantage and beauty all around me, I lost that harmony and life was hell. John Milton hit it way back, didn't he—"The mind is its own place, and of itself can make a hell of heaven, a heaven of hell."

I wish I knew whether I would end up living at home, or having to go off for periods of work and then back there. That is probably the way it will work out. It is not too unpleasant an idea to go into—the idea of you in New Haven and me settled only a couple of hours off, and one day starting in on a "great piece of decorative painting" which would have me down there the better part of a year. Will you perhaps have room for me to stay with you when I'm there? Will you perhaps have time to run in now and then to see how things are going? Judas Priest! as [my friend Cross] would squeal.

Devil, this is neither here nor there—mere vapour signifying nothing. Hell, I'd be lonely here this weather if every corner of my mind weren't filled with the sense of your company. I haven't been lonely one second. My dearest Devil, I love you—

diávolo piccolo mio—

Oxford, England
October 27, 1924

Dearest Rat,

I am sure I must repeat myself over and over again in these daily scrawls. But what difference does it make when you have given your whole self to a feller? For what Rat gets from these letters is not particularly what the Devil says, but rather the quality of Love that shines through every line. In the same way when we are together most of our conversation will be small talk—as it was on the boat, about our friends, about people we've known and books we've read, and pictures we've seen, gossip. . . . For we don't have to talk, but simply live quietly together in order to fully realize our love. I don't even believe that our conversation on the night when I get off a train some place in Italy would make very abstruse or learned reading! Somehow or other I think it will be far more like the incoherent joy of a child before a Christmas tree.

I have just come across a sort of journal I started to keep when I first reached Oxford a year ago. It was just after [my senior] year, and I was still very introspective, trying to figure out just what sort of a fellow I was, where my chief abilities lay. I did not keep it regularly or long. I don't seem to find continued interest in giving a daily expression of myself, unless it is for some one else to read. These letters to you form the first continued journal I have ever written. A jumble of half-thoughts, events, and ideas. Dear Rat, of course you know that these are not temporary only, but that every night of my life when you are not sleeping at my side, you shall have some sort of word from me? Always the letter for you to go to sleep with as I now go to sleep with yours. . . .

Hotel Royal Danieli
Venise
November 1, 1924

My devil—The 12th of May was Mother's birthday. In Connecticut that's just the appleblossom time, the first violets. Do you know what "bird in the bush" is? [*sketch of flower*] little magenta flower down close to the ground. Well, always when [we] were kids we would all get up half past five or so and go out in the sopping wet grass to hunt for all the wild things we could find, and bring back and arrange little wedgy bunches for the breakfast table—always a great surprise when she came down and found the table loaded. Great game to see who would find the greatest variety of flowers; never gave her any presents, not allowed. But she was very apt to give them to us. Later years, after we were grown up, every daughter had a flowery fancy new spring hat outside the regular outfit of clothes to be gotten.

Well, we kept up the same fool tradition of all getting out for flowers—grown men and women and of course all the kids who were there at that time carried on the idea. We still do. I almost always manage to get back home by that day. Any of the family who are near enough go home. No sickly teary stuff at all, no obligation to keep it up, just we like to. It's a sweet lovely thing to celebrate spring and family affection. I imagine an outsider would think us a great crowd of nuts.

Same way at Christmas. Even if there aren't any children at home we still hang up stockings and make a great fuss.

The first year we are home, you should spend Xmas in my house—that's a date.

Yesterday provided an unexpected spectacle. All Saints Day and the crowd about my Colleone statue surged and filled the whole square—a procession of candles and brocades, choir boys carried the Virgin high over their heads on a tippy platform down the aisle out the great doors and round the square. Colleone sitting very proud and scornful of them as she has those hundreds of years. As she passed the crowd, all knelt on the pavement—the blue insecure pale and trembly in the broad daylight, the high boys' voices, pale and sweet and high-pitched—and round the square and into the doors again—long long line of black figures of mourners each with a tall lighted candle and sad faces. Thing is, shall I try and put it all into my picture? I am very tempted to try it.

My dear, dear little Devil.

Oxford, England
November 4, 1924

Dearest Rat,

While we are on the subject of names you don't know how long it took me to get used to that one. If there is anything on earth that makes my blood cold, it is a rat. Ugh! how I loathe them! But as a name, I knew you liked it. It was short and convenient, and pleasant sounding when I could forget its meaning. So I gradually got used to it; and then came the sketch of the San Marco canvas with a Rat bent in all humility before it. That was slick, and since then I've forgotten my first prejudice. You damn black Rat—how I love you.

Isn't it strange how the sense of your nearness busts upon me in moments when I least suspect it. Take last evening: I had been out in North Oxford for an hour of German conversation with the old Fraulein I know (last year I took lessons from her, and as I know she is lonely and needs the money very badly, I go out now one evening a week). After I had left her and the miscellaneous talk on Goethe's predecessors, I was riding my bicycle homewards, hard against the sharp wind. All of a sudden something caught me. I noticed the stars were bright, that there was a growing yellow moon. I slackened my peddling almost to a standstill, and coasted along enveloped in the soft silence of the night. "The next time" said I "that a yellow moon is growing, Rat and I will be together in Italy." And then not only the black velvet night enfolded me, but your arms; and I looked at the stars and your eyes winked back at me. And as I rode slowly the rest of the way your bicycle was just beside mine.

Later when I had finished reading, I sat in my arm chair, prodding at the flickering coals with my poker. Then I leaned back and stretched and looked at the clock, and realized that I should be in bed. But I was lazy . . . and it was so comfortable . . . watching the fire.—Half an hour later I came to with a start. Fire almost out. Cold. I jumped up, unbuttoning my vest. Unconsciously I blurted right out loud: "My God, Rat, it's time I was in bed."

That shows all right how you are in every thought, every action. How you are me far more than even I realize.

As I read over your letters of yesterday I become more and more convinced that you are right on the question of "labels." "The splendid untrammeled freedom of love"—that's the essence of it all, right. Why give it a name that really doesn't belong to it? It isn't a marriage except in a very unusual mystical sense, and so don't adopt the conventional terms to speak of it. Our union has no name, no label; in the world it does not exist. It is simply the unpalpable, inexpressible fullness of our lives.

I haven't mentioned sex lately, Rat, but don't think that it doesn't bob its ugly head up where it isn't wanted. Occasionally faces attract me. Often I feel lust. But the thing is that in a sheltered academic surrounding I have never been bothered much that way. My mind and life are too busy with other things. It's only when I get into a big city—off on the loose—that the barbarian devil gives your own Devil a rotten time. But right now my body and soul are too full of you to allow any environment to really disturb them. I love you so—

Oxford, England
November 5, 1924

Dearest,

Yesterday I bought and read through Edward Carpenter's "The Intermediate Sex." It doesn't tell us anything we don't know already, but presents the position of the Uranian in society in an appealing fashion. The idea that what we have is one of the divine gifts; that such as you and I are the advance guard of any hope for a spirit of brotherhood. I have marked and checked some passages that struck me particularly, and am sending it on. You can skim through it quickly.

Reading it brought back to me the last occasion when I had a book on the subject. That was last spring—here at Oxford I was reading Ellis' volume on inversion. Then for the first time it was completely brought home to me that I was what I was by *nature*. Before that, when I told [a few close friends] I thought and all [except one] agreed that it was entirely a question of early environment, having been led into the wrong sexual channels by older boys at school. Well [Dick Tighe] doubted, and [Dick] was right. How clearly I can now see every act and friendship of my boyhood interpreted from my proper sexual temperament. But reading Ellis last spring was something of a shock. I remember coming face to face with the fact that I could probably never marry, serious and wide-eyed. I told [the same friends last June] how matters seemed to be tending, but they refused to take it seriously. Oh, no, Devil, you'll get married all right. Great fellers, they didn't want to face the possibility of my being unhappy. But I wasn't satisfied. I wanted to be understood. So when I visited [Mitch] at Colorado Springs, and we spent evening after evening when Harriet had gone to bed, sitting out in the car somewhere in the dark on Broadmoor, telling [about our lives], I outlined to him in rigid detail all my repression, how I sat reading Ellis, sexually aroused, seeing no hope of ever expressing it. I told Mitch that I didn't want to be alarmist-wasn't sure. But it seemed to me that I might very likely be altogether homosexual; and in that case I didn't know whether I could keep from getting morbid without some expression. Two alternatives: self-abuse and the old business with men. Which? "I know which I'd do" said Mitch very seriously, leaning over towards me as I sat beside him in the car, "self-abuse." "I don't know," said I. "But let's not get depressed." And I changed the subject.

Two alternatives? I had never dreamed of the third. If I had read this Carpenter book last spring I would have been surprised at the beautiful pictures he gives of love between men. Was it possible? I had known only lust. I prided myself that it had never touched the purity of my friendships. Was it possible for love and friendship to be blended into one? But before I had time to even ask the question it was answered. What is this wistful yearning I feel on these grey foggy mornings? It's not fog in my throat but an inchoate surge from my heart. What makes this new sensitive tingling in the tips of my fingers, and on my lips? It isn't the cold. It's love.

Rat, how I loved that picture of your mother's birthday. Except for my quick impatience I think we must have had exactly the same sort of relationship with our mothers. And then just when it gets to the point that after I return from Oxford she is to make her home with me in New Haven and I can maybe give her some of the culture and some of the love she has always been denied, the poor devoted little woman dies. Never did she have anyone to look after her. When I was five, my father sent my two brothers away to boarding school. Mother, my sister, and I went to California, presumably just for the winter for my sister's health. Of course any one with any worldliness, of which Mother had none, would have seen that my father never intended to give her a home again. When she wanted to come back, he'd put her off with an excuse which nobody but she would have listened to. She wouldn't listen to the mention of divorce, for in spite of his being absolutely worthless — God pity her — she loved him to the end. Finally when I was thirteen he practically forced her into a divorce, for he wanted to marry again — a Chicago social-climber from whom he was divorced on grounds of "cruelty" last year. How I remember the impotence of my thirteen year old rape, dear Rat.

"Jeb Alexander"

Jeb Alexander (1899–1965) is the pseudonym for an ordinary man who kept an extraordinary diary through his adult life, chronicling everyday events of Washington, D.C., and presenting an unprecedented window into the lives of gay men who were not famous. Jeb Alexander had literary ambitions and a good education, but he got stuck as a cog in the federal bureaucracy and in his later years became a heavy drinker.

The portion below recounts his days at Washington and Lee College, where he met C. C. Dasham, a man with whom he was in love for the rest of his life. Homosexuality was both acknowledged by the students and condemned by the authorities, and while Dasham acknowledges Jeb's infatuation, Jeb as well as other students recognize that Dash's boyfriend is Harry Agneau, who commits suicide when he and Dasham are together expelled from college.

The passage below also shows the homosexual subculture in Washington during and soon after World War I. Jeb Alexander seems well aware that Lafayette Square in front of the White House is a place not only to meet other homosexuals but also to watch them having public sex. The heartbreak that Jeb Alexander experiences when he discovers Randall Hare with other men still rings true today.

From *Jeb and Dash*

Monday, 28 October 1918 (Lexington, Virginia)

There is a chill smack of winter in the air. In the morning the bugle blows at the unearthly hour of six, and twelve minutes later we are expected to form outside beneath the starlit sky. When I got out there the detail was just leaving, so I had to run. I caught up as they started double time, so I was kept running all the way and was the last one in line.

After classes we drilled down on the athletic field. The sun was a blood-red ball showing through the fog. When we broke ranks, Poole wrestled in the ghostly fog with a pale-eyed freshman from Company C. The boy looked like a god, thrillingly beautiful. He got a good hold on Poole and wrestled him to the ground. Poole cried out, laughing, "All right, Dasham—all right!" The boy straddled him, and seemed about to whisper in Poole's ear, but Poole didn't like that and they stood up.

Tonight I asked Poole who the boy was. He looked displeased. "Oh, that one! I don't like his sort." I said, "But you were laughing—" He said, "At first I was." I asked again. Poole stared at me, then told me, "If you have your *reason* you want to know, his name is C. C. Dasham, he hails from Mississippi, he spends holidays with a married brother near Strasburg Junction, he doesn't do well in his studies, and I hope, Alexander, that he isn't your kind." Poole provided this information at top speed, but I am pretty sure I remember everything. . . .

Wednesday, 18 December 1918

Again to roam Washington's dear familiar streets! I wandered about downtown, then met Dad at the new Peking Tea Garden. I had fried rabbit, a good meal, but I dreaded the moment when Dad would begin one of our little one-sided conversations about myself. And soon he said, "Do you mean to use your education? What practical good will a literary or general cultural course do you?" I found it impossible to talk frankly about my literary ambitions. He said, "I expect you to 'mix' with other fellows, as part

of the benefit of college." He will be disappointed in that. I was feeling blue and thinking, "I shall have no path of roses at W&L," when the music, a mechanical piano affair,
struck up the "Old Gray Mare." It took me right back to W&L and I felt homesick for
the life there.

> We were only white birds, my beloved,
> White birds, on the foam of the sea.

> If only, only, *only* we were.

Tuesday, 24 December 1918

... I walked up to the public library. Finding it closed, I waited in the shelter of the
entrance. It was pouring down rain. I had no idea what I might do. A young man with
a mustache and a green hat, who looked different and intelligent, approached with a
book. He turned away when he saw the closed door. I imagined that he was a poet
without money and I took a notion to follow him. Once or twice I nearly lost him, and
several times I passed him looking into windows. Then he turned up a side street. As
I went by he was standing in the entrance of a house. Perhaps he was waiting to see if
I had been following.

Thursday, 2 January 1919

I left with only Mama to part from. I was almost sick with nervous anticipation. She
told me, "Try to make friends at school. Begin over. Don't get the reputation of being quiet." Well meant, but when the stars sing to the moon, then shall I be talkative
and likable.

My two suitcases, heavy and clumsy, were a hindrance. On Fourteenth Street hill,
from the streetcar window, I saw Henry's friends Leroy and Ford. They turned into a
tobacco store. Then to the station, and into the train and a pair of seats, red-plush covered. The train pulled out of the station and I told Washington good-bye. We flew on
through Virginia. I looked through the misty windowpanes at the sodden country in
winter. Night closed in. Beyond the pale glow from the train lights, a void of rain and
darkness. At Strasburg Junction, C. C. Dasham got on.

He looked about the car, then sat with me. He has the palest green eyes I ever saw.
He admired my tie and in his Mississippi drawl asked about my copy of *Dubliners*. He
said, "It looks like a fine book." In a while he asked me what my goals were; my goals
for life. After some hesitation I told him, "Authorship." He remarked, "I have no such
specific dream for myself. I'm still in the 'having-fun' stage of my youth." The rain

changed to snow and the flying flakes brushed against the window with a faint scratching sound. We reached Harrisburg and walked out into the storm. Dasham carried one of my valises for me, as he had only a satchel.

We climbed into the cavern of a hack and were driven to the Hotel Kavanaugh. The snow sailed horizontally into our faces. Dasham helped me bring my suitcases into the lobby. His cheeks were mottled red from the cold. We came upon two other fellows from school, and arranged to share two rooms, four beds, leaving instructions to call us at six in the morning. Dasham was in the other room.

Friday, 3 January 1919 (Lexington, Virginia)

Dasham sat across the aisle, reading. I looked out the window at brown fields, bare trees and frozen, sinister streams. Lexington looked strange and deserted. At the station, Harry Agneau, shivering, smiling, was waiting for Dasham. Agneau's father is a judge, and the family lives outside Lexington. He is refined, suggesting the far South, dark about the eyes with a sort of pleasant squint or narrowness of the eyes, finely freckled, dark hair pomaded in comely fashion. The two of them helped me with my suitcases till they turned toward Lee's. I struggled off across the campus toward East Dorm.

Sunday, 5 January 1919 (Lexington, Virginia)

Penetrating cold. I lay deep under the covers, miserably and ecstatically returning in imagination to the racketing train, *Dasham-Dasham-Dasham-Dasham*. I feel my life has changed forever.

Lexington on Sunday is the deadest town imaginable. I read some of Dante's *Inferno* and the book suddenly seemed cruel. The sexual intercourse (I hesitate to write the words, but there is no reason why I should feel prudish) seems to occur too often. Finally I took a walk. On Main Street I met Bennet, with a polite greeting and a pressure of his soft, plump hand.

Friday, 17 January 1919 (Lexington, Virginia)

Lansing Tower strolled in and sat on the arm of a chair beside me. He is only a freshman, but looks down on the world, or seems to. He has small eyes, close-set on either side of a patrician hooked nose, the eyes appraising, amused and secretive. "Alexander, do you want to join the Literary Society?" "No-o. What do they do?" "They have a weekly program, have debates." "I'm not much on debating." Tower said, "You can't learn any sooner," and left me.

After supper I saw that he, Poole, Garrison, Meek, were all going to the Literary Society meeting. I began to think that I might join after all, for it would allow me to get into the intellectual class of the students. But Tower didn't invite me again, and like a fool I didn't go. . . .

Back in the dorm I was on the front porch for a while with others. The fellow they call "Kentucky" was sitting on the railing, when there came the sound of a metal object falling and rattling on the sidewalk under him. He looked over the railing and exclaimed, "Oh, my golly! I've dropped a box of cundrums." There they lay, the box open with people walking right by it. Amid shouts of laughter of those on the porch, he rushed down and recovered his embarrassing property.

Monday, 20 January 1919 (Lexington, Virginia)

For assembly Dr. Smith and the faculty wore black robes and square-topped hats, and looked peculiar. I indulged in a harmless vanity . . . and enjoyed a sense of being well-dressed. I wore my new suit, my silk collar, iridescent rose and gold tie, white shirt with shiny silk markings, spar-rock cuff links, polished tan shoes. The idea of describing my clothes like a girl!

I waited outside the assembly until Dasham approached with Agneau. Stepping forward, I said to Dasham, "Happy birthday." He seemed surprised and amused. "Well, Alexander, did I tell you my birth date on the train?" I said yes. He said, "My birth date is the thirtieth of January, not the twentieth. Still, that was kind of you, Alexander." As they went into assembly Agneau began to tease, and Dasham laughed, and they shoved one another good-naturedly through the door. I walked home in darkest mortification. Later I gave myself a talking-to. I told myself that I must not allow obsessions to dominate my life; I must live life to the fullest and let no person or thing stand in the way. I am going to be a great author.

Saturday, 1 February 1919 (Lexington, Virginia)

Everybody turned out for the football game with Roanoke College. In the crowd I saw Dasham and Agneau sitting with Agneau's parents, the father dressed in black, the mother only slightly less somber. . . . When I was walking from the field Bennet approached me. He said, "That was a game 'worth a dollar,' was it not?" I replied, "It was a fine game, and gave me more school spirit than I have had yet." He smiled. "You should drop by my room for a 'bull session,' Alexander."

I am both attracted to Bennet and repelled by him. O, it is so hard to pour out my heart in this book. How I wish I could be a child again, sitting in the swing beside the cedar tree on a glorious June morning, when the pinks were in bloom and the lilacs filled the air with sweetness.

Sunday, 16 March 1919 (Lexington, Virginia)

Lansing Tower, sauntering along with his thin hair floating in the air, led us up a rocky hill. The cave we planned to explore was a dark hole between the rocks. We gathered about the opening so that Lansing could take pictures. I stood for the photograph beside Dasham, with Agneau on his other side.

Lansing led with a lantern. Agneau elected himself to be the one to lay down the string we would use to find our way back out. I found myself in line next to Dasham and Agneau. The way was pretty near perpendicular and the ground slippery with mud. Dasham was startled by a bat clinging to the clammy rocks about an inch above his head. I heard it hissing, and striking at it with a stick, knocked the bat down. Dasham said, "Are you all right?" I said, "I'm afraid I might step on it." He reached out his hand, and I clasped it for an instant, then plunged past the bat that shot up behind me.

Agneau's drawling voice echoed, "This isn't *my* idea of what a cave would be." Dasham replied, "Nor mine. My ideas about caves came from *Tom Sawyer.*" The two of them had foolishly thought—as I had—that the floor would be flat and the passages like hallways in houses. But the place was a honeycomb of fantastic rock formations and holes which, when investigated, were apparently bottomless. Voices echoed strangely. The ground was greasy and treacherous. . . .

A light appeared in the darkness, followed by two V.M.I. cadets. The pair had unwisely come in with no string laid to lead them back. If they had not met us, they would probably have got lost. Dasham said, "They say that several years ago, a man who brought in only one candle was lost in here, and nevermore seen." I said, "Perhaps he fell into one of those horrible pits." Dasham turned toward me. In the candlelight his eyes looked like reflecting silver. He said, "Well, Alexander, perhaps the man did fall into a pit. But that's supposing the outlandish story to be true. Do you realize that until this moment, you haven't spoken a word since you knocked down the bat? I had almost forgotten you were *here*, Alexander."

We finally clambered back, clinging to the surface until we glimpsed daylight. Hastening up the steep incline, Dasham slid, causing Agneau to lose his footing, and they disappeared frighteningly backward in the darkness. Lansing Tower called out. Up they climbed, laughing. Then out into the light. All of us were smeared with red mud. More pictures were taken and we raced down the hill to home and supper. Dasham and Agneau trailed the rest, laughing and larking about.

Sunday, 23 March 1919 (Lexington, Virginia)

As I returned from the cemetery with daffodils I had picked there, I passed Dasham and Agneau. "Hey, Alexander," said Dasham, "those are lovely." I gave some daffodils to him. On my desk as I write, the rest are radiant with beauty. O, I know I am shy and weak, but I believe that with Dasham I would be godlike, and he would be god-like with me. I declare, he is the most beautiful thing I ever saw—so wholesome and healthy, so full of youth. I imagine us on the high seas; I imagine us shipwrecked and cast adrift to lost islands. Every day I live a joyous life with him, if only in my imagination.

Sunday, 1 June 1919

D.C. sizzles under a blazing hot spell. I walked down to the National Art Gallery, and it was like walking over an oven. Still, I was glad I went. I like Corot better than any other artist. I should love to paint beautiful landscapes. It ought to be a happy life. . . .

Today is the anniversary of the death of my real mother. Who knows how much richer my life might have been had Mother lived. I was so young when she died. Henry was a sturdy lad of eight, but I was a frightened four-year old. The lilacs and the pinks were in full bloom. The nurse came on to the porch and stood looking about in her cat-and-mouse way. When she saw Henry and me, she approached us where we sat in the green swing under the cedar tree, and told us that Mother had "gone away to heaven." It hurt so much, to think my mother would leave me. And then, there came a day when Henry asked the little nurse, "Why are you going to live with us?" She told him, "He needs someone to take care of his boys." After that she and Dad were mar-ried, and she was Mama. What a starved, repressed childhood I had.

Tuesday, 12 August 1919

We were allowed time off to see the parade of the "Devil Dogs," the marines who fought at Château Thierry. Last night on the porch Eunice Martin heard me speaking of the parade to Henry, and arranged to meet me today in Lafayette Square. Through the teeming streets she strode, light of foot, wearing a blue linen dress, cleverly locat-ing me in the crowds. She complimented me, saying, "You found us a place so close to the reviewing stand, Jeb. This will be the best look at the President I have ever had." . . .

The marines were in battle array, with steel helmets and fixed bayonets, a formi-dable body of men. General Neville rode at the head of the column. The last company passed and the President and Mrs. Wilson crossed the Avenue. . . . The President and Mrs. Wilson shook hands with the wounded soldiers, sailors and marines. We were close enough so that we could hear their cheery greeting to each maimed or crippled man. Eunice told me that she "could not have found the parade half so much an inter-esting experience" had she not been with me. . . .

Later at home, after midnight, I recognized the voices of Henry and Eunice, the latter whispering so loudly that I was afraid she would be heard by Dad and Mama. When they got up to the third story Eunice staggered into my room, fell against the wall and full-length on the floor. She was drunk, drunk as a fool. I was alternately shaken with nervous mirth, and filled with fright and disgust. She got the drink in Baltimore with Henry. She fell down the stairs in going to the bathroom. My opinion of Eunice, formerly so idealistic, is considerably lowered. Henry finally got her into his bedroom and shut the door.

Wednesday, 13 August 1919

As I was walking out Fourteenth Street, Henry and Eunice stepped out of Sari's, both of them savoring ice cream cones. With a few flirting but unequivocal words Eunice made it appear that I was the one who should be chided for having seen her drunk and going into Henry's room last night, rather than herself. Henry said, "Live and let live." I said, "You are right, and 'Live and let live' is my own motto." "Good," said Eunice, smiling. They proceeded toward Sullivan's to pick up Dad's car. It is impossible not to like her. She is less an ideal, though. . . .

Friday, 5 September 1919

At breakfast Henry told me he planned to go to New York. The idea made me wildly eager to take a trip to the great metropolis. I asked him what he expected to spend. "Fifty or sixty dollars, but the trip could be done for forty. Are you going to New York?"

Why ask. Forty dollars is far too much for me to spend out of my summer savings. Henry remarked that it was almost time for me to go back to school, or as he phrased it, "return to winter rest camp." He asked what I planned to do after college, a mystery to me. He said, "Dad said that if you don't have good marks by Christmas, he is going to take you out of school." It is dreadful to think of leaving W&L in such a manner. But I could only sit there thinking that it seems hopeless for me to get good marks.

Tonight Henry began indulging in his old custom of mean nagging. He quarreled at me for being up so late, for keeping a diary, and for reading, calling me *silly fool, poor little sissy*, all sorts of damned stuff to make me mad.

Wednesday, 10 September 1919

I could hear Mama and Dad down on the porch—and listened, eaves-dropped if you want to call it that. Oh, they discussed me in and out. Dad said *he* didn't know what to do. "I can't get anything out of him. He won't speak, he won't answer a question."

Mama said, "Every time he has an opportunity to make something of his life, he runs off to the moving pictures." Henry got home and they kept on talking about me. It made me wretched. "What about his schooling? He doesn't apply himself, so what's the good of it?" "What does he want out of life?" I felt utterly alone—perched in the chilly air on a great peak while the brightness of the world passed by far below—miles and miles away. Oh, why can't they stop talking about me, and let me live my life as I will?

Saturday, 13 September 1919

I rambled about among the Saturday afternoon crowd. At Parker Bridget's corner, Ninth and the Avenue, I joined a number of people looking in the show window at a realistic wax model. . . .

While I was standing in the crowd, there came the beginnings of an experience which I hesitate to describe, the cause of which was a stoutish young man about thirty. I was aware that he was looking at me. Almost against my will, I glanced round. He murmured, "With your dark eyes, you look like a lost child . . ." He moved close behind me, continuing to talk, and I experienced that extraordinary phenomenon, so stupefying on the public street that it was far from a pleasure and indeed, was agonizing.

When I got home and attempted to hurry upstairs, Dad called me into the sitting room. . . . When he asked if I had decided on my life work, I was silent. "Well, *try* to decide." I told him I *was* trying, then hurried up to my room.

Monday, 22 September 1919 (Lexington, Virginia)

For the first day of classes Harry Agneau was wearing a bow tie—very "collegiate"— and had his hair parted in the middle, just as I wear mine. When he mentioned that Dasham wasn't arriving until tomorrow, his amused condescension was infuriating. To hell with Harry Agneau! I don't want people thinking I'm a fool. Hereafter when I see Dasham and Agneau I'll greet them as if they meant nothing to me whatever.

Friday, 26 September 1919 (Lexington, Virginia)

Lansing Tower told me that he is writing a novel; has been for almost a year. We had a long talk on the topic. Later at night I saw him at the post office and suggested going up to the cemetery. On the way up we discussed long hair and independence of ordinary conventions. Lansing spoke affectionately of "cranks," and I told him, "I should like to be considered a 'crank,' by being independent." He said, "You are pretty sure to be thought a 'crank' by at least a few." . . .

Friday, 17 October 1919 (Lexington, Virginia)

Wore my new suit and when I came down to breakfast everyone gave a W&L yell-yell for "Puny Alexander's suit." They didn't know today was my twentieth birthday. Later we had a rally at Wilson Field, with yells and singing. Agneau and Dasham sat in the bleachers. Dasham waved to me, his eyes pale green and beautiful, his face full of life. He, a young god on his throne—and I in dumb adoration and abasement, dreaming dreams of ourselves . . . and as much as I long for him, I am fearful of the slightest response, fearful that it will pull him from his pedestal, afraid that a touch of earth will destroy the celestial vision. Dear boy, would that I knew what he thinks of me, how much of that beautiful smile of his is contempt, or whether it is serene wonderment and nothing more.

Thursday, 18 March 1920 (Lexington, Virginia)

Instead of studying, tonight like a fool I went to the show, just as I have gone every night this week. The show was Mildred Harris in another splendidly true to life picture of Lois Weber's, *Home.* Like *Borrowed Clothes,* the photoplay follows the Griffith school of realism that I used to glory in at the Strand and Garden. Bennet sat beside me. Several rows ahead I saw Dasham and Agneau. Bennet and I walked home together, he with his arm in mine. Above us in the night sky there came a thunder storm. I was glad, because thunder is a sure sign of spring. Bennet talked of himself and of how much he likes me, and said I won't talk, but he never took any interest when I did try to say something. Repeatedly he has invited me to his room; again tonight I refused.

Monday, 20 April 1920 (Lexington, Virginia)

As I went down the steps I saw Dasham in front of the "bulletin board." It made me feel refreshed just to see his beautiful face. He was tanned, as he had been playing tennis. He turned about, and with a sweet, friendly smile, greeted me. It was the first warmth he has shown me in such a long time that I thrilled all over. We might have spoken more but just then Lansing passed by and asked if I were going to the library. I walked off with him before I could think of a reason not to, and immediately was filled with the bitterest grief. I glanced back and Dasham was still standing there—my beloved lad! I hardly listened to Lansing's chatter but was plunged into melancholy imagining what I might have done or said.

Walked later along the river bank. The bloodroots were getting into their prime. The hepaticas were just past it. I picked a bunch of each. I longed for my real mother, to be kneeling at her lap saying my prayers, a trusting child. Thought of a wife, which

I have not done in a long time. She was different from the woman I usually imagine. Instead of a passionate brunette creature of powerful intellect and artistic tendencies, she was a homebody, a tender, motherly woman who would coddle me and take care of me. Longed for comfort and love.

Friday, 23 July 1920

Henry has been indulging in his old pastime of scolding me for writing in my diary. I cannot imagine why he objects so idiotically to it. Tonight he tried to persuade me to go with him to the Krazy Kat, a "Bohemian" joint in an old stable up near Thomas Circle. He told me about the conversation in there, of artists, musicians, atheists, professors. I wanted to see something of the place, but was afraid I'd make a fool of myself by my backwardness. In a crowd Henry's ready tongue would give him mastery of me.

I left for town instead. Drops of rain began falling from a gloomy sky. Listened to the Salvation Army band, to "Brother Hammond," "the Ensign," "the Cadet," and "Mother," who was known in the Bowery Corps as "Sunshine." They had an organ and a trombone to aid in the work of washing sins away. The Ensign, a stout red-haired girl, sang unaffectedly, as though she were really speaking to us.

> A robe of white, a cross of gold,
> A harp, a home, a mansion fair,
> A victor's palm, and joy untold,
> Are mine when I get there ...

I don't know why I should take such pleasure in these exhibitions. The crude music attracts me, I guess, making more significant the surroundings I am looking on, as music does for me. I wandered on. I thought of writing and determined to get a theme this very night. If I can't make myself write now, how can I *ever* expect to do so? Roamed past dismal houses, steep steps and no yards, across from the Pension Building. A girl on a dim step with dreamy eyes stared into the darkness. From another house, the wistful tones of a piano in a gloomy parlor.

Saturday, 21 August 1920

The Salvation Army service was the farewell service of the Ensign and the Cadet. They will leave for Pennsylvania on Tuesday. I am sorry to see them go. It was their beautiful singing, and a personal interest in the Cadet, that has been the chief attraction for me. They sang tonight and each one gave a moving talk. Yes, the Cadet's talk moved me, because I felt sadness at the earnestness with which he spoke.

Later on I went into Lafayette Square and near the Von Steuben statue watched two fellows furtively engaged in mutual masturbation under cover of the dimness. They were frequently interrupted by the passersby. When I left, I walked close by to see their faces. Both were handsome, clean-looking chaps, refined and cultured.

Wandered down to the Union Station. The dreamy girl I used to watch in Child's is now in the Union Station soda fountain. Hair bobbed. Gazes melancholily over the great waiting rooms. Russian-looking. With a resolution to get a story written, I thought of an idea about the girl, and worked over it as I wandered about on *the* three streets whereon life concentrates, Pennsylvania Avenue, Ninth Street and F Street.

Wednesday, 25 August 1920

I have at last found a friend, a lovable, handsome fellow, a realization of the friend I have dreamed of during all those lonely nights while I walked alone through the streets. Above all, our friendship is mutual. It has burst into full blossom like a glowing, beautiful flower. It happened like this: I went to Lafayette Square and found a seat in the deep shade of the big beech. It is the best bench in the park. A youth sat down beside me, a youth in a green suit with a blue dotted tie. He has beautiful eyes and sensuous lips. He wants to become a diplomat, but is devoted to music. Earlier tonight he had been singing at the Episcopalian Church, and is taking vocal lessons. His name is Randall Hare.

We strolled down to the Ellipse, where we sat affectionately together on a dim bench. Later we came to rest in the moon-misted lawns near the Monument. With an excess of nervous caution I gazed about, watching for some prowling figure. "We are safe," Randall whispered. And he was right. Nothing disturbed us and we lay in each other's arms, my love and I, while the moon beamed from a spacious sky and the cool night breezes rustled our hair. The black trees stood like sentinels against the silvery grass. Afterward, we lay close together and gazed at the stars above, becoming fast friends, exchanging confidences. Ah, happiness! As Wilde said, "Youth! Youth! There is absolutely nothing in the world but youth!"

Sunday, 5 September 1920

Randall and his mother live with Randall's uncle in one of the oldest houses in Georgetown, a rambling stone mansion on Prospect Avenue. Several apartments occupy the house. We entered from a court. The walls are mostly of large bricks and the living room has an enormous fireplace and ceilings with heavy rafters. Randall told me that the rafters are said to have been taken from Thomas Jefferson's house in Georgetown. I was delighted. "This is most unusual, charming, quaint, artistic, ancient—" Randall smiled, "—and other adjectives. Now look at my room." He has fixed up his room in jade green, like a sunlit green bower. The whole apartment is filled with interesting objects—bric a brac, unusual furniture, paintings, and old musical instruments.

The uncle came in while we were there. He is a painter named Mr. Dieterlie. He wore yellow walking shoes, an old checkered suit and a green tie with a green-striped shirt. They showed me the painting that "Uncle Dieterlie" is working on right now. It shows a round moon rising, and fairies dancing in its light. On the right is a Lombardy poplar silvered by moonlight, and on the left is a shrub. Mr. Dieterlie showed me other paintings, various Japanese prints, and ornaments. Randall burned incense in a bronze brazier. We were late in leaving Randall's house and the streetcar trip to Brookland was a long one, but I sat back comfortably, savoring the pleasure of companionship with Randall. Out in Brookland we entered the Catholic monastery and went into a great cross-shaped hall. The service was profoundly beautiful. The monks chanted in Latin high up in the gallery. At little altars in the wings were clusters of colored candles, blazing like jewels, a wonderful sight.

During the ride back Randall had his hand lying on mine, and a girl across the aisle made an audible remark about it to her companions. But Randall in his melodious voice said, "We should worry," and kept his hand on mine. He said, "Be glad she noticed, so she won't be shocked the next time she sees it." He said there was no reason boys should not be demonstrative toward one another, as girls and Frenchmen were.

Sunday, 12 September 1920

On this day I realized complete disillusionment. My "friendship" with Randall Hare was a fabrication! Friendship indeed! We went to Washington Cathedral. As we left the beautiful open air service and strolled together across the lawns, we had an unpleasant exchange with some rudeness on his part. I became somewhat stammering. Randall said scornfully, "What *have* you been believing? Did you think that when I wasn't with you I was *singing*?" I replied, "I did think that, and I feel deceived." He leaned back looking disgusted. "If I wanted a clinging vine I'd find—a woman." End of my friendship with him! I shall never find real friendship, never!

Wednesday, 12 January 1921 (Lexington, Virginia)

In English class I told Lansing I had changed my mind concerning what he spoke about last night. He said, "This afternoon." Before supper I went to his room. There I found Howard, the light-colored negro youth who works in the kitchen. Howard had the pint of corn whiskey but said he hadn't been able to find "the $4.25 man" and had to go to another place. He wanted another dollar, and a quarter for himself. Lansing loaned me the additional money.

It is the first time I have ever drunk whiskey, except when I was a child and took it for medicine. I opened up my Keats and sipped the fiery liquid while I read the "Ode to a Nightingale"—that sensuous poetry that many a time has made me long for wine. But the poetry was more beautiful than the taste—at least of this wine of the Land of the Fire!

Friday, 11 February 1921 (Lexington, Virginia)

Scurrying clouds; flakes of snow. In the library I was reading "Modern Love" in George Meredith's poems when Dasham in his quick way strode in and seated himself to study. I gazed at that dear head bent over a publication. My fingers longed to stroke that lovely brown hair.

I want love and affection. Damn it! All that Stevenson said about journals is true. This diary of mine is a tissue of posturing. My real thoughts on such matters as sex are not admitted even to myself. I *will* be frank. I am madly in love with C. C. Dasham. "Sexual inversion," Havelock Ellis calls it. I always had some "hero" whom I adored and observed at every opportunity. It is not only Dasham with whom I've had visionary adventures, shipwrecks, desert isles, and the like. For years I have loved and worshipped other boys and youths. Before college there was Henry's schoolmate Bunny Alcott (think of it!). Then Hennessey, a god-like fellow, never seen or heard of since; and Morphew, a boy now gone to Tulane. The only one I even *spoke* to was Dasham. I have had a big-brotherly interest in some, an artistic sympathy for others. With Randall Hare the attraction was purely physical.

I left the library, not knowing where to go or what to do. Walked to the river bank, coat collar upturned, in the teeth of the chilling cold wind.

Friday, 8 April 1921 (Lexington, Virginia)

The only thing worth mentioning today is the baseball game with Roanoke, a tight little game, a well-played game. Light rain fell, almost unheeded by the drifting, shifting spectators. Observed the graceful elegance in the present styles . . . their careless simplicity, the long trousers falling loosely over the shoe tops.

Bennet and I were standing together next to the fence when Roanoke made a couple of hits, tying the score. I went angrily to the bleachers and took a seat. "There is no need to worry," Bennet said, following me. "Our best hitters are coming up next." He was right. We made the winning run. Bennet invited me to his room. I had a good talk with him and we came to an understanding. I told him I liked him a whole lot but he didn't appeal to me in a certain way. He walked with me to my room, so I could loan him Havelock Ellis's *Sexual Inversion*, which he had not read.

Now it is after midnight. I hear my dear friend the screech owl, complaining outside at the chilly night. I have come to listen for the owl every night in the trees outside.

Monday, 11 April 1921 (Lexington, Virginia)

My heart is pounding and my hand is almost too moist to hold the pen. Dasham and Agneau have been expelled from school. What is to become of me? It seems like a terrible dream. Only hours ago I stood on the upper porch watching the fellows throw and catch. Others were lying in the grass. Lansing was digging worms in the outhouse yard. I came in and lay on my bed to study Spanish, but, realizing I could never pass the exam, I set off for the river. Now all that seems so long ago. Returning, I passed some fellows from Lee's. "Hey, Alexander! You might want to know—" "Oh, *he'd* want to know!" I stood mute as a stone. Even under the calmest circumstances, I never can talk and think at the same time. "It's Dasham and Agneau. They weren't proper gents—or maybe you know that already. Those two are gone." And Poole, with a hideous grin, fluttered about with his arms in the air. I managed to come to my room where I barricaded my door with a chair. Finally realizing that I was pacing back and forth like a caged felon, I came to my desk. What is to become of me?

Thursday, 28 April 1921 (Lexington, Virginia)

Poor Agneau—living just beyond the outskirts of Lexington. More than once I've hiked out there, walking past the fences, in the hope that I might see him and talk with him. Perhaps they were sent from school with an insignificant story of poor scholastic performance. I know nothing, only that it appears almost impossible that I shall ever see Dasham again. Perhaps he was for me only a dream, a part of an obsession that threatens to ruin my life. But how could such a passion rule a human soul if there were no meaning to it, if this were the end? What, now?

Thursday, 6 May 1921 (Lexington, Virginia)

Anything, just to see the sun shine again. People are wearing overcoats. The sky is a gray mass hanging low over our heads. A letter from Dad announced that Henry and Eunice are to be married. Then a discussion of my grades, asking if it were not too late to improve my performance. I am horribly depressed, with the miserable loss of Dasham and Agneau, the dismal weather, my studies, the spying meddlesomeness of people—all of it, and the gray vista of years stretching ahead.

Saturday, 8 May 1921 (Lexington, Virginia)

Walked alone, going without coat or hat and with sleeves rolled up. "I want to be unhappy," as Stevenson said. Went up the millstream where the swift waters were reflected with shadows and leaf tracery. Returning, I saw Bennet and golden-haired little Walton, both on horseback, crossing the narrow, unsafe bridge over the mill trace. . . .

Saturday, 29 May 1921 (Lexington, Virginia)

The kitchen door swung open. Howard stood before us. "Been a boy drowned in the river." An even greater shock when Howard told us, "*Who?* That poor dead boy be Judge Agneau's son."

I started off for the river with the other fellows. It was inconceivable to think that Harry Agneau had drowned himself. We were picked up by a Ford on the road and carried to the hill above Whistle Creek. From there we ran down through an interminable yellow wheat field that rolled down to the trees on the water's edge. Underneath the steep cliff I saw Harry's father, hatless and mud-spattered. Dr. Smith directed the work. There was a crowd of townspeople and students, a silent, solemn crowd. Naked fellows worked over the water, diving or dragging grappling irons. It hurt to think of such an end for Harry Agneau. It was pitiful. Bad as this unjust world is, it is better than black nothingness. I started helping students build a fire to warm the swimmers. Nearly the whole student body was there, and I could see them still winding over the dark hill through the wheat field. Wet bodies glowed in the dusk on the dark lines, with silent onlookers on the banks, and the lurid glare of the flames over it all.

Later, when they still hadn't brought in Harry's body, Earl Podboy and I walked uptown on the dark roads. Earl mused, "Harry Agneau was a student in my Romantic Movement class. Perhaps it was the reading of melancholy poetry that brought this about." To my astonishment, dear, stupid Earl gravely recited from "Ode to a Nightingale": "Now more than ever seems it right to die . . . To close upon the midnight with no pain . . ." We walked on uptown. There some townspeople told us that Harry's body had been recovered.

Tuesday, 14 June 1921 (Lexington, Virginia)

Commencement Day. Wiedemeyer's Orchestra played outside the chapel. Dr. Flannery gave his usual speech on the Old South. I sat in the bleachers with my coat off. The sight of the golden wheat fields bordered in green trees was so beautiful that for the first time since Harry Agneau's death I had a sense of joy. I realized what heavy burdens I bring on myself. I worked on my overdue thesis later. Around two in the morning, with a great sigh of relief, I finished it. Then I dismantled everything in the room, taking down my pennants and ruining completely the little quarters that have sheltered me and my innermost thoughts. . . .

Glenway Wescott

Glenway Wescott (1901–1987) was born into a poor Wisconsin family, but through luck, talent, and personal charm he was taken up by a series of wealthy patrons and lived a life of relative ease. Among his early benefactors was Monroe Wheeler, whom he met in 1919. The two would become lifelong companions. Wescott was a perfectionist and published comparatively little. Gertrude Stein wrote of him, "He has a certain syrup but it does not pour." Nevertheless, he did complete two highly acclaimed novels: *The Grandmothers* (1927) and *The Pilgrim Hawk* (1940).

Talented, intelligent, and wealthy, Wescott and Wheeler made important and lasting friends with writers Katherine Anne Porter and Jean Cocteau as well as painters Paul Cadmus and Cecil Beaton.

In 1926, Wescott and Wheeler met George Platt Lynes, one of the important photographers of his day. His work with male nudes has become a benchmark for beauty, eroticism, and psychological insight. Lynes came to live with Wheeler and Wescott, although Lynes was much more the sexual partner of Wheeler. The complexity of their ménage à trois interested the sexual researcher Alfred Kinsey, and Wescott became one of his more important supporters and informants.

The passage below is from 1937, the first year Wescott began keeping the journal that would eventually be published after his death as *Continual Lessons* (1990). It covers a period in which Wescott tries to deal with his sexual frustrations and his writing block, conditions that would persist for the rest of his life. It shows the difficulty of maintaining a complex and open relationship. It also contains imagery of the falcon and the falconer, the first glimmers of what would form *The Pilgrim Hawk*.

From *Continual Lessons*

June 14

Dinner last night with George and Monroe at Katherine Anne's apartment in Perry Street. Her table handsomely set; raffia cloth and turkey-red napkins, wooden plates, and four silver goblets, and her new Russian forks of nugget silver, the handles enameled with dark flowers by some Muscovite William Morris.

After dinner, George drove us to Coney Island. We had been there just a year ago, but with Cecil Beaton, Marcel Khill, and Cocteau, when of course I listened and talked back more than I looked. Portals and towers in a fog are all I remember, and long wet wreaths of light bulbs. We arrived after closing time, therefore could only go up and down the street of games and freaks, where I find nothing surprising. No one ever told me of the elegance and infant splendor inside the enclosures, particularly the one called Luna Park.

Last night we saw this at its best, almost empty; it was about to rain. Clean cement esplanades; *gloriettas* and pagodas and *giraldas:* the electricity thickly dotted on the wood, which resembles paper. A child's idea of palaces, never having seen anything but tenements; or an artist's concept of what he will do, before art has begun to deflate and reform and perpetuate it. . . .

As we skirted the side shows Monroe took my arm and said, "It reminds me of 'The Runaways.'" My first, no, my second short story, written in Wiesbaden in 1922. Characteristic reminder, with his piety about writing and particular cult of what I had done and could still do. Where literature has been at work is holy ground to him; even Coney Island.

Characteristic also: a nostalgic recourse to our early experience together, whether or not we were happy at the time he happens to think of. I wasn't happy in Wiesbaden. A constant recoil of his mind toward his youth, when indeed, until his love of me began to impose penalties, alarms and fatigues, he had the happiest nature I have ever encountered.

His fanatic persistence in a stand once taken, in a hypothesis once stated: for example, that "The Runaways" is excellent. Rather rigid strength of character which makes it difficult to extricate him from any false position; such as, at present, his dubious economics, his flattered worldliness. Strength and weakness coupled; I suppose they always are. His loyalty and his inspiring willpower depend somewhat upon the fact that his grasp of present realities is not very precise or keen. Presbyopic and noble.

As a rule, a given man or woman's life is like a work of fiction that does not end when it should; thousands of pages of boring realism follow. Whatever mystic idea and meaningful pain and dramatic action there may be all occurs in a month or a year or so, immediately digging a rut, setting up a treadmill; thenceforth the hero must plod and reiterate and deteriorate, oh, how slowly! . . .

June 17

Over the weekend Paul Cadmus made a large pen drawing of me. A good likeness, I think, at least psychologically like—my sweet-sour expression, spoiled but virtuous, voluptuous but tough, heartbroken but happy. In only two photographs have I ever recognized this mood, to me most natural: one taken by the little Englewood professional who gave George lessons, the other by George himself, at my ease propped up on pillows on the daybed in the rue de Vaugirard, flattering to my profile, with my forefinger touching my upper lip.

My intimacy with Charles Rain is waning rapidly; soon I shall need someone to take his place. I must not rest long in my present equanimity and indifference about this. I know what will happen if I do, what has always happened. As I love George, I should think it wicked as well as imprudent to depend tranquilly upon his tenderness. Therefore, cheerfully, although with the usual anxieties, and resolutely, or irresolutely, I cannot tell—time will tell—I take stock of my acquaintance; try to feel some sufficient excitement about this one and that; urge myself to hurry up and make some amorous (pseudo-amorous) attempt. No matter which or what, before I get caught again by my fever and misbehavior and shame and hopelessness . . .

June 22

The night of the Braddock-Louis bout in Chicago. George and I dined uptown at Jimmie [Daniels's]: chile con carne, upon which he prides himself (and well he may). Edna Thomas, with whom he lives, a project supervisor of the Federal Theatre in Harlem, came home most melancholy, having had to lay off actors all day long as ordered by the administration: all destitute, the young ones enraged, the old in feeble desperation.

After dinner, as usual, friends wandered in to eat and drink a little, and to hear the broadcast from Chicago. A typical assembly: lovely, plumper and plumper Blanche Dunn (courtesan), in whose bed my brother spent the wee hours of certain of those delectable foolish Harlem nights in 1934–35? She had put $100 of her old white keeper's money on the white boxer, since these people believe that prizefights are all framed and scarcely care who seems the best boxer.

Alonzo Thayer, jolly and dejected, alcoholic and who knows what else? He may have been in love with someone (presumably Jimmie) all these years; and if so, doubtless has never said a word, and perhaps has kept from knowing it himself. Thus under cover (I suppose) grand passions are much commoner and unhealthier than you might think. Part-Jewish mulatto, fine-boned and getting fat; makeshift lover of mine in 1933, half a dozen nights: humble of me, and indeed I knew that then . . .

Old Caska Barnes had got one of those pink slips of Edna's (dismissal from the theater), and been presented with a consoling bottle of gin by someone, and drunk it all; therefore was irritatingly affectionate and pompous.

Feral Benga, the Dakar dancer . . . : the finest middle-aged physique in the world, heart-shaped chest, smoothly tapering legs like Josephine Bacaire's . . . Round-eyed: the whites of his eyes circularly showing as if in ceaseless apprehension or fury; nevertheless a beguiling worldly personage, and good company. During the winter he took Kenneth McPherson away from Jimmie. Then his established Austrian favorite came over from Paris, and Jimmie aptly but spontaneously seduced this one. Which flank attack threw Feral into a confused and unattractive temper; so Jimmie got his lord and master back, although on poorer terms, I fear. Not a trace of bad manners on either rival's part now. In this raffish society people really do bury the hatchet.

While we waited for the fight to begin, Jimmie played records which he has been studying with a view to some foreign engagement. . . .

During certain rounds of the broadcast Jimmie slept, his perfect hands carefully clasped on his gin-and-ginger-ale. George rolling his eyes in voluptuous admiration of him; then how gently winking at me! But luckily or otherwise, this vapid, languorously stoic, bittersweet Harlem atmosphere now has a sobering effect upon me.

The instant Louis knocked Braddock out, we hastened through the flat to the Seventh Avenue window to see the rejoicing. For an hour or so Harlem had seemed deserted: every building, as it were, talking in its sleep with a plurality of soft wireless voices; everyone indoors in parties around the radio, determined to have a good time whether or not the black protagonist should make good; even the main streets silent except for police cars coming and going with sinister although motherly cry . . . Now instantly all the young and the youthful sprang from every doorway, faintly shouting, running nowhere in particular. Proudly a man drew a woman into the shadow between two parked cars and so kissed her that she was swept off her feet, between his legs. Flimsy-looking children boxed as they ran. The less foolish and less energetic (like our party) made fun of the others, but in intimate manner, delegating their feelings. . . .

June 23

The younger generation. Charles is being visited by a friend from Chicago, a tall strong young man who teaches swimming at Northwestern. This one is allowing himself to be in love with another, somewhat older, who prefers intercourse with women; and C. is all alarmed and incensed about it. Without cracking a smile; rather, wringing his hands, he relates that one night (perhaps it was the first night) the swimming teacher took the other in his mouth; the other then offered or consented to do likewise, and, after certain odd fumbling caresses, did. Later C.'s friend discovered what the fumbling had been: his he-man surreptitiously had outfitted him with a French letter.

Dinner with Paul Cadmus in the Village. He showed me a hundred drawings or more; the nakedest and least disinterested are the best, particularly those of Jared French. Until lately they have shared this apartment, an oddly un-American interior; good shabby antiques; a quantity of books and music, charming evidence of self-education. Late in the evening a youth named Lloyd Goff, who was Paul's assistant on a government job of mural painting, wandered in, at his ease, sleepy, perhaps tipsy. Paul paid the least possible attention to him. Soon he threw himself on a bed or couch and fell asleep. With no plan, yet somehow amorous or something, I waited for him to be gone. Paul and I still sat and talked and talked, reminiscence and theory, in that peculiar mood of ours or of his: smiling relaxation, solemn boyish idealism, who knows what else . . . Goff then woke up and undertook to say good night; but the next thing I knew, there he lay again, sprawled face down on another couch, his head underneath two pillows, his clothes all drawn on the bias and tight upon his very fine little back and buttocks. At last I gave up whatever impulse it was that had kept me so late. Paul fondly (I may say) accompanied me to the subway. Perhaps, he said, he would make a drawing or two before he went to bed; our talk had been so stimulating, and a sleeping model suits him . . .

Since I can't think when, I have wanted to give some account of myself as a lover and a loved one, of the plot of my life replete with coincidences and influences, Monroe's influence especially but not solely, and now of that triumvirate in which I figure in third place, perhaps more governed than governing; who knows? Surely it constitutes a theme or a set of themes less hackneyed and possibly more significant than any other thing experienced or observed by me. But how, how, can it be dealt with clearly and interestingly and enjoyably except in an entire autobiography, painfully encroaching upon others' lives?

I came back to this thought the other day when Monroe inquired about my novel supposedly in progress, and I had to confess my despondency about it. Once more, as it appears, having imagined and promised a full-length novel, I am gradually ceasing to take a sufficient interest in its devised happenings and composite characters. Little by little a chilly complexity of form and style develops and fills the vacuum without advancing the work, slowing me up. Episode after episode, chapter after chapter, grows cold and insincere and unmalleable before I can complete it. Faithfully I sit at my desk for a certain number of hours daily, or almost daily, resisting my natural distractions and overcoming my amorous melancholy for the most part, but slower and slower, and with worse and worse skepticism.

In the course of this conversation, *in re* my amorousness, I quoted to Monroe a part of a letter that I wrote George last week, comparing him to a falconer, myself to a falcon. This impressed him as a revelation of my psychology and fate, and he said, "You must be modest and write what you can, without too much art and ambition. When personal passion interests you more than anything else, that must be your subject matter."

I should see Jack B. again and put down some of his anecdotes: of sailor-prostitutes who pretend to be doing for pay what they also evidently enjoy. The one who, having taken some active part in their intercourse or perhaps merely manifested some enthusiasm, begged Jack not to tell any of his colleagues, who would not respect him if they knew, etc. An odd and (I fancy) a new morality: commercialization of one's sex more respectable than the free gift of it. Europeans, as a rule most money-loving, would appreciate this as evidence of our love of money, but mistakenly. They never understand that with us profit is more a matter of religion or superstition than of desire. We are less avaricious (I think) than greedy, morally greedy: determined to feel free to indulge, somewhat, in every possible pleasure, without having to renounce our claim, upon occasion, to every conceivable virtue. Hence all sorts of disorderly motivation. The intimacies of true lovers of men with men who merely let themselves be loved are particularly distressing and interesting. The unsophisticated virile beloved goes to extremes of sophistry without a qualm; and the lover's docile disrespect for himself as he countenances this seems scarcely less wrong.

June 29

After dinner George sat in the blue armchair and kept falling asleep, until bedtime; and I sat in the yellow armchair and contemplated him fondly, and contemplated myself with due discomfort and dislike. For I had allowed myself to entertain the most imprudent hope of love. I fancy I played my poor part decently; surely I was afraid not to, lest George forbid me to assume it any longer. For no doubt the old hopelessness was worse than such disappointment. I tried not to make too pathetic or antipathetic a face. I said nothing spiteful, nothing ominous. Nevertheless, at last George said that it was high time I discovered for myself some new substitute lover. Of course I could not fail to appreciate what prompted him: his inability, embarrassment, compassion; and of course I agreed.

So the falconer plucks off the falcon's dark hood, and sharply exclaims, and urgently points across the plain where, somewhere, there may or may not be wily partridge, banal rabbit. But the falcon, blinded by its dream in the darkness, cannot see much; and infatuated with the master's hand upon which it sits, by which in the past it has been fed ideally, it cannot care much; and with the tight pain in its gut from long fasting and yearning, it cannot fly very well.

Paul Cadmus is one of the favorite young painters here now. He held a successful exhibition this spring; has been given a second government commission, for a post-office mural; and has had any amount of notice in the magazines. For one thing his subject matter is popular: YMCA locker rooms, sailors having fun, aging Venus and dumb Adonis up to date, etc. Also he has notable virtuosity of the classic order, real draftsmanship, sculptural modeling, interlocking composition—which our countrymen, when they have the courage to be out of the French fashion, naturally enjoy. A color reproduction of his painting of two bicyclists having appeared in *Esquire*, that rich amorous little man Cole Porter bought it. But Paul's candid romanticism about strong and sportive men is such as to appeal to the normal unsophisticated American taste as well.

Paul's mother was an immigrant Basque; and he has the bizarre, distinguished north Spanish look. Wonderful bright eyes: and he fixes them on one (on George and me) with the oddest ardor; and listens quietly, fondly; and smiles and smiles, though not exactly humorously. His teeth protrude and his gums show, consciousness of which has caused some habitual tension of his lips, as usual; but it is not nervous or ugly in his case. He has a pleasing, moderately strong body, not (I should think) of perfectly masculine measurements, yet not at all womanish either; pure-looking, also proud-looking, although he himself thinks it deplorable in every aspect. His coarse suave skin he determinedly sunburns on the sooty roof of his Greenwich Village flat.

For a number of years, here and in Mallorca, he has lived with and passionately loved one Jared French, also a painter, and of bisexual habit. Their relation has not, however, been one-sided; no sort of stylized contrast of virility and effeminacy has developed—although basically Paul is more feminine than most of us, I think. All his thought is somehow relative, partial, anti-selfish, in the way of the noblest, fondest women; his moods, as it were, atmospheric, like the weather, and mysterious, even to himself. Evidently Jared French has exercised extreme influence in the forming of his principal habits of mind: quiet disdain of society; study of literature and music; cult of the normal young man of the people, that is, of the lower classes—whom they both must think Jared resembles. Paul is frankly given to the phallic passion, and idealistic and indeed religious about it; his friend likewise, I understand. Which grand perversity I approve, indeed; the grander the better.

Some of Jared's painting is pleasanter than Paul's, though less original and less soundly skillful: scenes of rather soft abandoned baseball, homosexual *fêtes-galantes*, like Watteau or Renoir. I wish I knew him. I have met him: a commonly handsome man of my age, with a small eye and a tough little blond mustache; with a certain stolidity that highly sexed men often have, somehow lackluster, as if daydreaming of effect upon others. He has kept having relations with women. Paul has admired him all the more for this, according to a concept of ideal manhood which perhaps he has inculcated upon Paul in his own honor. Naturally the admirer and idealist has suffered: the waiting and waiting, the wanting worse and worse, the corrupt curiosity, the dreadful effort to be polite, the wanting to die, with jealousy perhaps at last a habitual stimulant—Jared coming unabashed and not exhausted from a female bed to his bed, and going likewise again. Nevertheless they have been wonderfully happy. This spring Jared decided to marry the mistress whom he has loved best. Paul doubted whether he would ever be happy again; but now that it is done, I see no indication of tragic disorder. The beloved husband still spends much time with him; and I suppose that the roles of spouse and adulterous darling have simply been reversed. In any case Paul would have borne the loss decently; for his chief strength is suppleness and a sort of deep-seated courtesy—courtesy even in his introspective dealings with himself. (How unlike me!) If he were unbearably hurt he would have to fall ill somehow and never say, perhaps never know, why. No indignation. There is not much in his art either.

July 4

Supper at Elizabeth's with our parents. I must correct my social procedure with my family; seek new subjects of conversation with them; restrict my detailed gossip with this one and that about the others' conduct; and make less comment on Lloyd's administration policy: sighing anxiety, sputtering dissent.... Over and again in this kind of domestic conference I appear (to myself at least) somehow feebly boastful and pseudo-angry; oddly, as it were *pour épater les bourgeois*.

Twenty-two years ago I broke off my first love relationship, by letter to E.R.K. Because it happened to be dated Independence Day I have not forgotten and can indulge in mild anniversary emotion. So old, how young!

July 6

Return to town. Image of American summer: the way the drivers of long-distance trucks hang their sleek biceps and golden forearms, relaxed, out the windows of the hot little coops in which they sit.

July 8

And again last night, George as falconer urged me as falcon to get after some ordinary prey, pigeon, rabbit. As there is nothing much in sight—except the too unattractive, the ill-omened, or the obviously unattainable—I have kept thinking of Eugene Loring as desirously as I could. So we asked him to hear José Iturbi play Mozart at the Stadium with us; and we both found his company pleasant.

When we returned and George retired, I simply told him that it was my intention to try to induce him to come to bed with me. Then we spent half an hour uninhibitedly though not very gaily arguing the point by word of mouth and the usual dumbshow. I was not able to have my own way. It was odd: he was somewhat excited, pleasingly potent, but resolutely unwilling; whereas I was cold and feeble but ardently aggressive. He kept assuring me of his appreciation of me in every respect; of course this might have been half vain gratification and half tact; it seemed sincere. Needless to add, I was indifferent to it by virtue of my own insincerity. So I let him go, with some little show of malice and some of sentiment.

Surely he did not mean me to think his refusal final. I fancy it had to do with something definite in his life at the moment, perhaps another amorous engagement last night. He expressed the usual doubts of my respect for him, that is, his self-respect, if I were able to have him upon such short notice. Like most such young people, alas, he is much less inclined to desire me than to aspire to my friendship.

Without any corroboration or approval of my intellect, my instinct, as it were, with faithful whisper does assure me that there is heaven and that I will go there, upon certain conditions: (a) if I do not commit suicide, and (b) if I do not go insane. An odd and, I believe, a blessed feature of my instinctive morality is this feeling that insanity is rather a crime than a misfortune: the evil heart's rape and mutilation of the imprudent brain.

July 12

George Gershwin is dead of a tumor of the brain, diagnosed too late. For several years the noted Zilbourg has been (so to speak) psychoanalyzing him for so-called imaginary headaches. Zilbourg is a White Russian who translated *He Who Gets Slapped*; then directed some little theater in Greenwich Village, where Katherine Anne knew him; then worked out a psychotherapy all his own, and has made a good thing of it. A social fellow, dear friends with his patients, he has groups of them weekend with him in Connecticut; and he goes traveling about in the way of an abbé or an augur, father-confessor, entrail-interpreter. This summer he was to have gone to Java, to dissuade the Javanese from killing themselves; Zilbourg is president of an international anti-suicide society. . . .

July 13

Monroe still urges me to write about myself.

It may be wise or it may not. For one thing, I am not sure that the old stimulus of wishing to please him will still have effect. But I may as well try it, during my failure to write fiction. It should at least somewhat prevent his little comments upon my failure, his mildly goading humor, and his hints of hopelessness about me, or pseudo-hopelessness. I do perfectly understand his goodwill and unspoken instinct in the matter. He touches upon my soreness of conscience in hopes of quickening it. In the old days when he hurt me I usually tried twice as hard, while my fit of resentment lasted. Now I react less well. Day after day my melancholy seizes upon some pessimistic remark of his as its excuse, and feeds upon it. There is no use appealing to him to be more kind or more cunning; for he neither plans what he will say nor listens to himself closely.

Jimmie Daniels dined with George and me, and we saw the Dietrich film *Knight Without Armour*. The work of Feyder and his scenic expert, Meerson, is excellent, especially in the last half: nightmare of flight into exile, trains never on time, false passports, hysterical policemen, familiar faces here and there. That in all probability is what revolution would amount to for us. Wonderful insane stationmaster marching up the platform to meet an invisible express train . . . A small tragic role is played by an actor named Clements who extraordinarily resembles Col. Lawrence: small overworked body; profile like a meat ax deeply nicked with strong painful features.

July 15

Genre picture. I sat on the toilet seat idly turning the pages of Yeats's anthology; and George came stumbling in half asleep, with a large hanging half-erection, to urinate; I got out of his way, still reading; and he kissed me good night, sleepily stooping and brushing my shoulder blade with his lips as he passed; and how happy I was! Although quite dissatisfied with what I had written all day . . . How luxurious and strange a life!

Trucks: one inscribed in large letters, AROMATIC ESSENTIALS; presumably full of same. The driver's seats of two others (belonging to different trucking companies) entirely enclosed in a grille of heavy wire, painted white, and solidly bolted to the windshield and the doors—through which those two drivers peered like two important lunatics, out for an airing, caged. Why? Do people throw things at them?

July 20

Last spring, in late April or early May, I weekended in a nineteenth-century farmhouse in Connecticut with two close friends, one still young, one very young. At the head of the stairs in that house, it so happened, the old door of their bedroom failed to meet the worn threshold under it by an inch or so. The house was on two levels; the floor of that bedroom was about two feet below that of the upstairs hallway; therefore that considerable crack or aperture corresponded almost exactly with their adjoining beds. My hosts had chanced to mention this, with reference to the drafts in winter, even in early spring; but it hadn't occurred to me how I might be taken by surprise by means of it, through it.

Katherine Anne was also staying with them, and after lunch on Sunday she and they retired for a siesta. I too went up to my room but found myself not sleepy, and presently, quite serene, without a thought, I started back downstairs; and just as my foot descended to the step that brought my eye in line with the crack or aperture and with the (so to speak) marriage bed beyond, I happened to glance just right and so saw the two friends. Both their naked bodies in ideal appearance, in intercourse, and well under way . . .

Doubtless I was in a frame of mind most apt to delight in fragmentary, momentary erotic beauty such as this, between the inadequate door and the outworn threshold, delimited and separated from me: what might have been a portion of Greek vase in graceful agitation. Do I exaggerate? I think not, or not much. In spite of loneliness and pent-up feeling, self-pitying in a way, my very admiration rose so that it amounted to thanksgiving, thanksgiving for this mishap, this miracle. There between floors in my absurd improper position, on tiptoe and weak in the knees, I might have been kneeling somewhere, in a fit of prayer or vision, far removed from ordinary human circumstances, actual individuals, social respectabilities. As it happened, I could not see any sexual organ or even erogenous zone, and both faces were turned away; which may explain why I let myself loiter there for perhaps two minutes, phenomenally full minutes.

Not ashamed, trying and failing to be ashamed, and yet afraid; like a malefactor, afraid of being found out. Even such a psyche as mine, stubborn and predestined, can be taught—and at that time, in my perhaps immature middle age, had been taught— by appropriate literature, moral treatise, precept, if not experience. I knew better than to interrupt my friends, by opening their door or knocking on it, or by calling their names. Furthermore, physically, I was not in a state at all uncontrollable or even difficult to control; no excessive energy or extreme fantasy, such as might conceivably lead to intrusion or other rape-like tyrannousness. I wasn't in the least afraid of myself. All was gentle and indeed weak—except in my own mind and heart.

Truly, what I wanted to happen had happened, was happening; *their* delight and my proximity. But changes were taking place in me; some safety valve would have to develop for me, inner or outer, some outlet and free play for my several relevant senses—so that I should not seem to myself so crazy, so silly, so morbid, so solitary. If I couldn't find or conceive any such change or escape, I might just continue like this, worshipful and, as it were, disembodied, in an inexhaustible contemplation of my lost love, my love unattainable, until I died; or perhaps die immediately, and be out of their way and the way of other such lovemakers, and out of harm's way. Death! I murmured to myself, as one often does in climaxes of the amorous life: the one and only efficacious and final form of self-control . . .

I trembled from head to foot, I failed to breathe properly, I could feel the pulse in my wrists and hear it softly surging in my ears, or at least in one ear; but, alas, not for a second did I fail to enjoy or to suffer. Sixty or a hundred seconds. Finally I dragged myself the rest of the way downstairs. What was I to do with myself? To my shame, be it said, I went back upstairs and came back past the aperture once more; luckier or (you may say) less lucky—I must have moved too fast, or my loving couple had shifted across the bed—tolerating my behavior less and less.

Intolerantly then, without a plan or idea, I crept out of doors, quite quietly, and hurried up the road to a small tumbledown barn—it seemed to me that I had not seen it until that instant—and I clambered up into the loft, which was not boarded up on one side; and from that safe distance I could still gaze upon my friends' pretty, dread dwelling, against its background of small hills, amid its modest trees. How white it was! I thought; white as an egg, out of which what in God's name was hatching? Pandora's box, utterly open and swarming.

There was a heap of fodder in the loft, dry and delicate, the fragrance of which might have blown unmixed all the way from the Wisconsin of my precocious boyhood. I lay down and undid my trousers and, in a second, simply pressed out of my scarcely tumescent, not very sensitive penis its ready drops. There was no necessity of my doing this; it didn't correspond in any real sense to my trouble. I did it deliberately, to weaken myself, to stupefy myself, as one might gulp down a small undangerous sedative drug. Then I climbed down from the loft, and pulled myself over a gate, and walked across a rather large meadow, up hill. I tore my sticky handkerchief into bits and hid it in a hollow stump. I wandered up and down the meadow, and in due time, just safely tired and humorous and dejected, reappeared at my friends' house.

We dined outdoors, on the sunset side of the house, with the hills in profile; and after dinner I talked at some length with Katherine Anne about our respective literary accomplishments to date and future prospects, in a somewhat high-flown way, vying with each other, like a couple of geniuses; with what concealed dismay and skepticism only I could know.

I couldn't wait to get back to Stone-blossom, and did in fact return next day, with my usual introspection and anxiety about myself as a writer, and about my Self, more than usual. That of course underlay my talk with Katherine Anne, and she aggravated it without intending to. I was anxious for Monroe and George to join me there, two or three days later. Perhaps my habit of never putting restraints on love, and of entering into any state of rapture which I found available, had gone too now. Might I now have to admit that my three-cornered relationship with them was untenable, destructive, or at least unconstructive; and with that admission, might it not worsen? Might I not find myself duty-bound to leave them? The duty was not only the matter of their right to love and happiness untroubled by me, but of my literary vocation; which meant as much to Monroe, in his way, as it did to me in my way. I couldn't just stay there and go to pieces before his eyes; innocent and pitying and sometimes incorrect eyes. From early manhood on, he has been a believer in willpower, especially my willpower. Whereas I felt sure that if I expended too much of my strength in self-discipline, or dissipated it too much in bouts of toxic sensibility, I might never write well again. That would disappoint dear friend number one, and disgust dear friend number two, and convict me in my own opinion of entire unworthiness of my destiny and present assignment in life, this peculiar predicament, at once blessedly included in love and wretchedly left out, with psychological miracles still apt to happen to me; no miracle more ridiculous than the weekend's epiphany in Connecticut: myself as Peeping Tom.

By the time my dear ones arrived, finally, I had decided to keep all of this to myself. Little ecstasy, followed by little disaffection and letdown and subsequent bitter humor and coarse thought, had done me good. I then noted to my amusement that the doors of two rooms in Stone-blossom also gaped a little at the base; and as a reminder and as a rite, purgatorial, pretexting my foreknowledge of the drafts of wintertime, though winter was far off, I sent for the carpenter and had the thresholds replaced.

Country details: When our housekeeper, Mrs. Smith, lived at Stone-blossom thirty years ago, there was such a plague of rats at the barn that they gnawed the horses' feet just above the hoof, until the blood ran. Not every horse, however: "There's something different about some that draws them."

Lately calves in the pasture ate off the tail of Dr. Case's spotted riding horse, so that he has had to crop it close, like a mule's.

Charles Rain is a type of young artist from out West. His father is a urologist who sends him a sufficient monthly allowance. He attended the Art Institute, then went to Germany for a year or so, then came here to practice painting and rise in the world.

He has talent but no individuality except that incident to amateurishness, no subject matter except that suggested by the Old Masters and Frenchmen in fashion, whose methods he aspires to imitate. He enjoys working hard, probably does work hard, but absentmindedly; his automatic phonograph going all the time, Forsythe and Fats Waller. He has exhibited his work at Julien Levy's at his own expense and sold a little to or through friends. He is a celebrity worshipper, perhaps not more so than other Western boys on the make, but so far he has passed the time here on a deplorable social level, the best he could get onto, I suppose: tittle-tattling queens, etc. The main outlines of his history are ordinary: mother preferred to father, irresistible naughtiness as a small boy, a hypocritical clergyman in Chicago, then the Kurfürstendamm, and around town here in the usual way. He has paired off with a number of our acquaintances, very briefly. According to him he yielded because he had accepted favors or expenditures, and was made to feel under an obligation.

There is a sister who has a beautiful head of hair cut like a sixteenth-century young man's, and pop-eyes wicked-looking or crazy-looking; she and Charles exchange confidences shamelessly. There is also a boyhood friend who also paints, less amateurishly but more imitatively; and they live and work in one large room, decorated in ordinary stylish decorator's style, as neat as can be: their paintings fussily framed and hung, their little sculptures well placed amid luxuriant bouquets.

In a fit of the worst nerves last December, out of a clear sky, and with erotic malice aforethought, and because Monroe had suggested it, I invited Charles to dinner; and he merely, as it were, could not resist me; and I was delighted by his enthusiasm and his physical fitness. So now I have enjoyed him some twenty-five times, that is, weekly. This absurdly exact count I happen to have kept in my appointment book; my referring to it is indicative of my pessimism and sense of humor about him at this point. On the other hand, I am not quite unwilling to resume this peaceful healthful intercourse upon his return from Vermont in the autumn; only my impression is that it will hardly be possible.

Our intellectual or, I should say, social relations have been artificial and tedious always. Monroe and George rather enjoy having him about because they find him comical; neither he nor I have resented this; but it was not conducive to my fooling myself in any fashion. About his hope and his hopelessness as a painter he is intense, tearful, which is hard to endure; he needs the most patient educating and he wants a constant gush of encouragement; but he stubbornly or stupidly fails to take advice; however, I have endured and been patient and somewhat quashed. . . .

Thus on two occasions his fine young sex has quite failed to function; and his sad embarrassment, and his long unsuccessful self-manipulation, and the prospect of more of the same, have had a chilling influence upon me too. Instead of behaving cleverly I talked wisely. Let us stop while all is still proud and easy, I said, and so on. Apparently he has no notion how he might blame me. It seems to him that he involuntarily is rejecting me, and (poor vain youth) he is glad of that, and so am I. Indeed I may not be as entirely to blame as I suppose; some other amorousness may have occurred, as night after night I have left him to himself. I know that he is apt to lie, and shame would unnerve him. Let that pass; the above is all true, whether or not it is the whole truth.

He is a good boy, on his humble level: he is tactful, generous, modest, credulous. He is discreet: for instance, he destroys everyone's letters and even tears out the pages of his date book as the days pass, explaining that he might be involved in some scandal and will not incriminate his friends. I should not, however, expect him to behave well in anger or in panic. His great fault is basic shame, childish fright, as the look in his eyes indicates: flickering away to the right and the left and almost back over his shoulder, as if some bully or detective were always at his heels. This apartment of ours is, he thinks, a social foothold and stronghold; my insolent humor, a bracing soothing remedy; my arms, armor. He has been so much snubbed, and so often taken by night, rebuffed by day, etc.: our easy essentially selfish courtesy, my selfish and therefore careful use of him, may well have seemed to him heavenly. Besides his experience of mean homosexual society, and dread of the hard heterosexual world, he suffers from other little self-indulgent terrors: for instance, he cannot read or sit still alone without scratching himself, raising red welts on his arms and breast, and often hopelessly acknowledges this, remarking at the same time that his mother died of cancer.

His very tall and slim figure is like that of one of the acrobats of Picasso's early manner, with strong hands and heavy feet and sexual organs of noble outline. In the bedroom, in my arms, with a blissful grimace, his face is beautiful—not at any other time, to my taste; nor has he ever seemed to me exciting until he is in potent condition and begins to act excitedly; and my failure to be thrilled at once, my evasions, my postponements, must retard his potency.

Of course, looking back upon the relationship as a whole, convenient intercourse, sufficient substitute for a love relationship, I do wish to get it back in working order. I am not as spoiled as one might expect. In my exorbitant mind, my not in the least widowed heart, my busy New York day, perhaps there is not room for much more than Charles has to offer. Then too I know the tedious mess of the search for a successor; the rarity of playmates as inexpensive and amiable and physically acceptable as he; the dangers of another stretch of celibacy, a sort of psychic scurvy, hysteria in the home, etc. I do come to the proper conclusion. Yet I am glad and say that it probably is too late.

When I have finished any such research as the above, I feel that it is shameful, petty, marginal; but I did not, it was not, at the start; what I have learned by it makes it seem so. For all this is not so much self-expression or reminiscence as laboratory experiment; literary art here is intended to be chiefly scientific, that is, exploratory, also therapeutic, God willing. If I can carry on, patient and industrious, if I can check my evil sense of humor and endure my occasional shame, something may come of it.

July 24

By the swimming hole.

Lovely peculiar color, colors, of George's sex in bright sunlight: half its length is very tawny, even sallow. Then on the tissue laid bare by circumcision (delayed until his late adolescence) there are little odd markings, like faded bloodstains, and others like stains of grape. The glans is a gray sort of pink, softly freckled, and its flange or corona vivid pink. Under which the scrotal skin, too delicate and lax and weighted, has a cold bloom and silveriness of wrinkles.

Thus his beauty gives me a great and real satisfaction, along with the impossible, constant, too keen stimulus. I told him so as we lay there on the harsh fine gravel, sunbathing. I must keep telling myself so; it helps me to content myself with my inadequate share of amorous reality . . . "That's good," he said. So he rested, his (perhaps) umber eyelids descending. I could not rest, gazing at him in my bewitched way instead, and trying to sort out a palette of adjectives for the above difficult bit of word-painting, difficult to the point of futility.

Aphrodisiac sun soaking through the colorful drooping organ meanwhile, strengthening it . . . Indeed, not only that but all his exceptionally pale flesh is fraught with many little tints: in every slender part a suffusion of veins, lightest blue; and his armpits faintly golden; and the least scratch or bruise anywhere bright, and his waistline stained by his belt all summer; and on his heavy upper eyelid a little plum-colored crescent, as if painted, and a lesser steely crescent above that when his eyes are shut; and his shaved cheeks and chin, shadowy iron.

Presently he opened his eyes, found me still looking at him, and said, "Look at something else now. You make me nervous."

Instantly ashamed, angry and sorry and sorry for myself, I wanted to cry like a baby. I retired to a log that lies there across a little backwater with minute mud-colored fish in it, and did cry, inactively, *in petto*. Cramp of face; eyes burning and blurring (the school of fish a-jitter); mind full of little panic and contradictory protest . . . Reduced to so little love; learning to do with so little; suddenly requested to do with somewhat less. Lovemaking with my eyes, and with my nouns and adjectives; nothing but that for weeks at a time . . .

If this was self-pity, it was so mixed with sense of humor as to give no comfort, not even ignoble comfort. It was not resentment. The little deprivations must follow the same rule as the great, which no one intended. George's allowance of my glances must occur or not occur like his other greater bounty, irresponsible, unpredictable. I did not lose my sense of proportion or think of this as tragedy. Indeed I was not thinking at all, I was experiencing; and what I was experiencing was a kind of reflexive psychic sob, a retching, an exhaustion.

George soon noticed my mournful posture on the log, looking down at the little dingy fish instead of at him, and complained of my having misunderstood.

Oh no, I understood aplenty: familiar truths about myself, and this and that surely to the point about him, respectfully. All morning, as it happened, I had been aware of his touchiness, kindly controlled, and I knew it was because he was tired, and I thought it was because he needed his beloved.

He went on to remark that he often finds my fixed blank look at him uncomfortable, and to express some uncertainty of the sense of it.

I have sometimes pointed out that it is like Cupid's—the dog, not the god; Cupid in his lap adoring. But I did not have the courage to repeat that bitter witticism. Also this time there must have been a sharper glance of laborious brain, vexed by my poor series of definitions of color (above). But I did not give that as an excuse, since I myself thought of it as a substitute for love; therefore it must have been subject to the same repugnance. I simply let him apologize and scold me and cheer me. And with no great delay I began to resume my better manner. Then Elizabeth and the children came down to the river.

Lincoln Kirstein

Lincoln Kirstein (1907–1996) was born in Rochester, New York, to a family that acquired great wealth. His father became one of the directors of Filene's, the Boston department store, and lavished on the son his considerable fortune. With his intelligence and ambition Lincoln, partly as a writer but primarily as a patron, used that wealth to advance the arts in America.

Kirstein went to Harvard, where as an undergraduate he founded the important literary magazine *Hound and Horn* and helped develop the Harvard Society for Contemporary Art. Soon after graduating he curated exhibitions for the fledgling Museum of Modern Art. After World War II he worked to recover art the Nazis had plundered. In his early twenties he published a novel; later he published poetry. But his principal achievement was founding the New York City Ballet with George Balanchine, whom he brought to the United States. With the School of the American Ballet, which he cofounded, he helped train dancers in what emerged as a distinctively American style of ballet. He popularized his notion of ballet in such books as *Dance: A Short History of Classic Theatrical Dancing* (1935) and *Ballet Alphabet: A Primer for Laymen* (1939).

Although he married Fidelma Cadmus, the sister of the gay artist Paul Cadmus, Kirstein's homosexuality was an open secret. He publicly came out in 1982. The memoir that follows is from the collection *By With To & From: A Lincoln Kirstein Reader* (1991). It is Kirstein's attempt to expiate his guilt for failing Hart Crane (1899–1932), a major American poet who was widely know to be homosexual and who committed suicide by jumping from the deck of a ship and drowning.

Carlsen, Crane

DICK BLACKMUR, AND LATER Bernard Bandler II, a student of Aristotle who eventually became a very distinguished psychiatrist, took care of *Hound & Horn's* Big Ideas. While I was in awe of their analytical mentation, I never considered myself an "intellectual." I had received an ignominious D+ in Whitehead's lectures on metaphysics; Varian Fry relieved my guilt by telling me that philosophy, all of it, was only vain epistemology, and that took care of my curiosity until I found Nietzsche.

Indeed, all through this period I was very much preoccupied with the social life of Shady Hill, Charles Eliot Norton's beautiful old estate, where Paul Sachs ruled his roost, and Gerry's Landing, where his partner, Edward Emerson Forbes, gave splendid parties. More glamorous was a house on Beacon Hill where the heirs of Henry Adams and Mrs. Jack Gardner continued their elevated taste and life of the mind. It was the ghost of Henry Adams that presided over *Hound & Horn* due to Dick Blackmur's infatuation with the triumphant failure of Adams's *Education*, and over my own attachment to a vanished Boston.

It may seem farfetched to blame this atmosphere for certain editorial strictures which governed the taste and tone of *Hound & Horn*. It may explain, and in part apologize for, its editors, in refusing to print Hart Crane's "The Tunnel," seventh and penultimate canto of *The Bridge*, his masterwork. We did accept a mass of inevitably mediocre and much more forgettable verse, among a small amount of distinguished poetry by well-known names.

How could ostensibly sensitive young men with notions "advanced" (for their time), with some acquaintance with advance-guard French, English, and American poetry, reject Crane's evocation of the power and grandeur of Manhattan's mystical bridge and mysterious subway? It was not refused out of hand, but after discussion, led by Blackmur the purist, Varian Fry the Latinist, and myself, who was entranced by the poem's epigraph:

To Find the Western path
Right thro' the Gates of Wrath.

I had had as my Freshman Advisor S. Foster Damon, who had just published the first important American explication of William Blake's symbols and story. To Harvard's everlasting shame, he was denied tenure and was let go to Brown; Providence then was considered provincial exile, and it was this proprietary attitude of Harvard's Department of English that *Hound & Horn* sought to contest. Blake's beautiful painting of *Glad Day*, a brilliant nude youth seen against the dazzling spectrum of a full rainbow, was my personification of Melville's Jack Chase and Billy Budd, and Walt Whitman's comrade. In arguments over the acceptance or rejection of Crane's poem, I felt he had not lived up to the oracular in Blake's lines. I was a victim of Blackmur's compensatory stringency and my own snobbery derived from my recently earned arcane knowledge of Blake's true cosmology, derived from Foster Damon. This was an early example of the academic deformation we thought we were trying to avoid— competitive vanity based on subjective attachment.

In 1927, the more energetic Americans were writing books which would provide capital for future Departments of English Literature—mainly in London and Paris. Harvard's imaginative aura lingered in a prior generation, with veterans of the recent war (Cummings, Virgil Thomson, Dos Passos) providing the exuberant foundations of our future hegemony. London seemed closer to Cambridge, Mass., than Paris, because T. S. Eliot's own teachers were still ours. Irving Babbitt lectured on Rousseau, Chateaubriand, the sources of French Romanticism, and his own brand of humanism. Still in residence was J. L. Lowes, whose *The Road to Xanadu* became a bible, and there was Grandgent for Dante, A. N. Whitehead for Plato and Pythagoras, A. Kingsley Porter for the Romanesque. We had French and some German, but compared to Christ Church or King's, small Latin and less Greek. For us, at our stage of development, Baudelaire tended to be primarily a Roman Catholic, Rimbaud an anarchist, Joyce a lapsed Jesuit, and Valéry Larbaud more "modern" than Corbière or Laforgue. The Germans were Rilke and Thomas Mann; Goethe and Heine were largely ignored.

I had met Dick Blackmur the year before I entered college. He advised me on what most recent books I should buy and what I should think of them. He regretted that he knew no Sanskrit (yet). His reading was enormous in fields I had no notion were even available, from symbolic logic to the *Nicomachean Ethics*, from Origen to Gerard Manley Hopkins, Crashaw, Hegel, Jeans, and Eddington. When he married I asked what he wanted as a wedding present: it was a pretty new four-volume edition of Herrick. He had contempt for many of my limited roster of masters. I would race down to his shop, comfortably housed in what was once an eighteenth-century tavern, eager not to miss the latest arrival from Faber & Gwyer or the Nonesuch Press. He asked me what I had "learned." Maybe I told him that Professor Babbitt had said something astonishing about Sainte-Beuve; Dick's thin lips would curl: "Oh, that. It's just his usual inane reply to M. Tel-et-tel's theory in the May number of *La Nouvelle Revue Française* (or *Le Mercure de France*)." This goes some way to define the attitude or atmosphere in which we felt free to refuse an important poem by Hart Crane.

Perhaps I might have felt less guilty if I had known sooner that there were other more eminent rejectors of Crane—Harriet Monroe of *Poetry: A Magazine of Verse*, Marianne Moore at *The Dial*; Edmund Wilson at *The New Republic*. And in reviewing the published *The Bridge* in *Poetry* (June 1930), Yvor Winters, with Allen Tate, Crane's most useful literary correspondent, turned on his entire achievement. I might mitigate my own responsibility, evoking the authority of our editorial board, which indeed exerted a common authority. Yet I was much involved with verse, daring to print some of my own. I had no interest in politics or social theory. *Hound & Horn* would increasingly be taken over by Southern Agrarians under the captaincy of Tate, and finally by a mixture of Anglican Marxists(!), Trotskyites, and "humanists." When poetic contributions came into the office I chose "the best" for Blackmur's severity. Unlike myself, he was not chastened by seeing his own verse in print, which was far more professional and justified than mine. He thought Crane's "The Tunnel" was "promising, confused, self-indulgent, inchoate, etc." It had some "good lines"; Crane would be better next time around, doubtless after a long letter from Dick, written on his thick six-by-four-inch blocks in his small, square, immaculate orthography. Perhaps a script exists; it was my duty to abstract refusals from his too extensive text.

In *Hound & Horn*'s summer issue of 1931, the excellent poet and discerning critic Yvor Winters reviewed a French study of the influence of *symbolisme* on American verse, analyzing Crane's presumed debt to Rimbaud, which was then discounted since Crane could only read him in translation. The first writing of Crane's I happened to have read, mainly for its subject matter, was dedicated to Stanislav Portapovich, a dancer in Diaghilev's Ballets Russes, who elected to stay in the United States after its disastrous 1917 season. In this poem Crane used as a rhyme "Chloe" (from "*Daphnis et Chloë*") as a monosyllable. This was enough to demonstrate how shockingly illlettered and pretentious was Crane. And Yvor Winters's analysis of Crane's beautiful "For the Marriage of Faustus and Helen" complained that

> the vocabulary of Mr. Crane's work suggests somehow the vocabulary of Rimbaud's prose and of a very little of verse, in its quality of intellectual violence and of almost perverse energy.

"Perversity" and "violence" indeed. If there were any two elements lodged in my head to justify the rejection of unworthy or uncomfortable material, unorthodox or unfamiliar, in spite of our ostensibly pro-"modern" bias, they would have been violence and perversity. We were "educated" (in a strict sense, as editors); we were sustaining humane values, traditional though progressive, against mindlessness, anarchy, and chaos. We were mandated by Eliot ("Tradition and the Individual Talent") and Pound ("Make It New"). Blackmur, severely traumatized by his permanent lack of a *summa cum laude*, used overkill. I had taken received ideas as scripture and wasn't to be budged against instruction I'd absorbed with awe. Later, listing errors of commission and omission, one could be partly consoled by the names of those who got, and didn't get, the Nobel Prize for Literature. Pearl Buck, John Steinbeck did. Marcel Proust, W. H. Auden didn't. As historic compensation, up to a point, Allen Tate reviewed *The Bridge* (*Hound & Horn:* summer 1930) under the heading "A Distinguished Poet." (For those curious about Crane's worried if deeply appreciative, yet far too troubled reaction, it is fully covered in John Unterecker's monumental biography, *Voyager.*)

I was also at this time a companion of John Brooks Wheelwright, who helped us with his very professional if eccentric analyses of architectural styles. A properly improper Bostonian, an authentic Puritan combining extremes of High Episcopal liturgy, proto-Trotskyite metaphysic, and post-Ruskinian taste, he was both monk and dandy. An important, now ignored writer of verse, he was kin to Henry and Brooks Adams: he wrote a beautiful threnody on Crane's death after a tense confrontation, entitled "Fish Food," which I came to wish I had been able to write myself as my particular personal apology. I was also a friend of Walker Evans, the photographer; with Wheelwright, we found a hundred fine nineteenth-century houses in the Greater Boston area and published photographs of some in *Hound & Horn*. Evans was living in quarters near Crane alongside the Brooklyn Bridge, and he had contributed photographic illustrations to the deluxe first edition of Hart Crane's poems published in Paris and reproduced, I never knew why, in the format of postage stamps. A little later I shared a house with Archibald MacLeish, then writing for *Fortune*, who had the happy and generous idea of commissioning Crane, who badly needed a job, to describe the construction of the George Washington Bridge. I also knew Estlin Cummings; he and MacLeish had not met, and I brought them together. They spoke of Crane's difficulties. "eec" said flatly that Crane was incapable of finishing anything; Archie should be warned.

I never knew Crane personally. I bumped into him a few times when I came down from Cambridge to New York. He never failed to frighten me. His reputation, of course, preceded him, a negative fame of lurid pyrotechnics, at once alluring and repulsive. He surely could have had small use for a supercilious college kid, some ten years younger, with firm poetic prejudices.

On March 28, 1931, I went to a party thrown by the editors of *The New Republic*, in a big penthouse above Fifth Avenue. Present were Edmund Wilson, Paul Rosenfeld, C. D. Jackson, Dwight Macdonald, and Walker Evans, among others. e. e. cummings's second wife, a termagant, baited me, deservedly, for being gratuitously rude to Crane at another party at the MacLeishes' a few weeks earlier. Cummings said that Crane's mind was no bigger than a pin, but that it didn't matter; he was a born poet. The one person present I knew at all well was Walker Evans, then about to embark on a South Seas voyage to make a film on a yacht chartered by Oliver Jennings. It was through Walker that I encountered Crane's friend Carl Carlsen, who was signed on as an able-bodied seaman.

The New Republic's party sticks in a befogged memory, illuminated by a brief thunderclap. The air was subdued, with the usual self-enclosed groups in a haze of cigarette smoke and alcohol. Abruptly, in a far corner of the high, big room, angry voices and motion. I had not noticed the spark of the fracas; now there were fisticuffs. Two men traded punches. The taller seemed in control; he held the other at arm's length and hit him, hard. Someone had called somebody else something. Whatever the source of the rumpus, music-under swelled into gathering general irritation. "Chuck the son of a bitch out!" A door onto the elevator outside opened as of itself, and Crane, slight, with rumpled shock of pepper-and-salt hair, helped by hands other than his own, was chucked out. Quiet resumed, drinks were drunk; nobody paid much mind to an interruption which scarcely had had time enough to come to serious trouble.

About half an hour later there were blunt bangings on the door. Kicks, knocks, yells; it was opened. Crane bounced back into an unastonished assembly pursued by a small but furious taxi driver. Crane had hailed him for a run to a Sands Street sailors' bar under the Brooklyn Bridge. Having arrived, Crane had no cash. Driver had pushed him into the gutter, but was persuaded to drive back to the party, where friends would take up a collection and pay for three trips. Crane, filthy, sodden, and desperate, was remorseful but morose. Cabbie, given a couple of drinks, was mollified. Crane proclaimed what a marvelous character he was; he would hire his taxi to take him to Mexico on his recently awarded Guggenheim. They left, quietly enough, together.

This eruption, which probably seemed abnormal mainly to me, was no great event for those foregathered. To others, on similar, more or less familiar occasions, this was not rousing behavior. For those who lived by the lyric imagination, whose craft and career was the play of words and imagery, Crane was not overly distressing or disagreeable—except possibly to himself, when he sobered up. When he came back with the cabdriver I was struck and humbled by his patient penitence, muffled apologies, a small boy's pathetic, instinctive good manners. At first I was inclined to be, or tried to be, surprised, horrified, and outraged. Actually, I longed to have had the guts to get drunk and pick up a character who much resembled Jimmy Cagney in *Taxi*, a brilliant Warner Brothers film. I idolized Cagney and studied his films assiduously as they appeared, seeing each one half a dozen times—from *Public Enemy, Smart Money, Blonde Crazy, The Crowd Roars,* and *Here Comes the Navy* to Max Reinhardt's beautiful *A Midsummer Night's Dream,* in which he starred as a marvelously inventive Warwickshire Bottom. Cagney, for me, provided a post-graduate course in heroic lyric realism in opposition to Harvard good taste. (Cagney liked an article I wrote about him and we were intermittent friends for fifty years.) I aimed to delete the conditioning of my schools and class, costumed myself from cut-rate Army-Navy stores, and was not wildly successful as a male impersonator. In Brooklyn bars Walker Evans taught me to keep my mouth shut, and so I penetrated the safer areas of some jungles where there was no real threat or risk except of an exotic landscape. I deceived no one; denizens of such urban areas can spot a stranger on sight. I smelled different, but I was kindly tolerated for my curiosity and adulation. It was not exactly cross-pollination, but there was some exchange in encounters between mutually bizarre tribes. In this ambiance I met Carlsen.

If he had any professional calling it was the sea, but his real ambition was to be a writer, with the sea as his subject. Walker Evans had met him through Crane's great friend Emil Opffer, a merchant seaman, and Evans had told Carl to send some of his stories to me, an editor of *Hound & Horn*. Three duly arrived, each neatly typed in its own spring binder. None of them made much of an impression. Walker pressed me concerning them. I found it hard to say anything definite. Although we were small fry compared to big-circulation magazines, we printed the first or early stories by Katherine Anne Porter, John Cheever, Erskine Caldwell, Kay Boyle, Stephen Spender, and others during seven years of publication. I read the greater part of the fiction contributions, and what I deemed best was passed on to Dick Blackmur and Bernard Bandler for final judgment. As for Carl Carlsen's quite unmemorable pieces, they had passed without comment, or at the most gained an impersonal rejection slip.

Then, one day when I was lunching at the greasy spoon near Time-Life with Walker Evans and Jim Agee, Evans brought me a scruffy bundle of typewritten yellow sheets, the rough draft of another story by Carlsen. I think its raw presentation and obvious travail attracted me, since it was so unlike the shipshape typescripts previously sent. It concerned the stoker in a boiler room of a merchant freighter. An important piece of a machine—perhaps a piston—overheated or lacking lubrication, had split and snapped. The stoker or other mechanic immediately substituted his forearm for the broken part. For some minutes the man's flesh and bone were a working replacement for steel and oil. The tragedy, while not convincing as written, obviously derived from vivid memory. The prose was by someone who knew more about metal and machinery than short-story composition. However, I could not be entirely disdainful of its stiff primitive energy, small as its wick might glow. Its strained rhetoric was influenced by Melville and his masters; it was overwritten, rhapsodic, and rhetorical. Yet somehow pretentious it was not, nor even synthetic. There was too much detailed observation to betray contrivance. The narration could not read as exactly naïve; there was the taint of absorption in Melville and Conrad. The notion was powerful, but the prose was without practice; we couldn't bring ourselves to accept so primitive a piece. I wrote its author the kindest rejection note I could manage and sent him a volume of Rudyard Kipling's riveting short stories, including "The Ship That Found Itself," in which the intransigent components of a newly commissioned steamer, after an agonizing launch run, grew to have its stubborn separate parts finally work together. It was this that brought Carlsen to our office at 10 East Forty-third Street (we were newly transplanted from Cambridge to Manhattan). He did not come in person; I was thanked by a letter slipped under the door. Carlsen found the Kipling tale unreal; its author obviously had been no merchant seaman. Fame did not forgive the fable, but his strictures made their point.

Who was Carlsen? I never discovered as much as I wished to know. Walker Evans could or would not elucidate: only "a chum of Emil and Ivan Opffer's, Gene O'Neill's and Hart's." In 1930, Crane wrote Caresse Crosby in Paris that Carl was "a former sailor who has got tired of office-work and expects to hit the deck again for a while." Crane drowned before I had real contact with Carl. Eventually, after some timorous urging, Walker took me around to Carlsen's home. This was an oversized doll's house, a picturesque miniature semisecret habitat awarded him by the guardian angels of Walt Whitman and Herman Melville. One passed through an all but unmarked gap in a row of mid-nineteenth-century brownstones in the middle of a block somewhere between far West Sixteenth and Twentieth Streets; I can't now say exactly where, since I've not been there in fifty years. Between the two blocks survived three tidy two-storied unpainted clapboard buildings with a joined narrow porch and pairs of gabled dormers. Built by 1840, these were freshly shingled, old, but without decay. In the middle house dwelt Carlsen. The single downstairs room was bare, spotless, shipshape-tidy. It might have been comfortable as a whaler's cabin anchored in Nantucket, New Bedford, or Sag Harbor. The only intrusion from the twentieth century was a small shiny upright piano with stacks of music on top. A narrow stair with a rope banister led above. Later, I would find a common lavatory in a back courtyard which served the three buildings, and there was a hand pump. Gas was laid on, but there was a total lack of heat and hot shaving water.

Evans introduced me as the man from *Hound & Horn* who had judged his offerings. Carl was a stocky, thick-trunked man, thirty-five to forty, clean-shaven, leathery, no extra flesh, and apparently hard-bitten. He had coarse, untrimmed bushy eyebrows fairer than his ash-blond, close-cropped hair. The piano obviously belonged to a stolid, self-contained woman, maybe ten years older than Carlsen. Her hair was in a stiff orange pompadour. She nodded to Walker and me without enthusiasm and abruptly disappeared up the stairs, as one might say, in a marked manner. This didn't seem to bother her companion. He wore well-worn, crisply laundered, old regulation U.S. Navy bell-bottoms, with a drop fly and thirteen buttons, in honor of the thirteen original colonies. Next to the small gas range was a wooden icebox, maple, with nicely turned legs, unpainted—perhaps a recent addition. In the icebox were cream and lemon; on the stove water, boiling. Tea was made; the master of the house took rum from a cupboard and set the full bottle before me. The—to me—exotic purity or clarity of the local weather bemused me. Speech was slow in coming. Soon enough, Walker made desultory politenesses. I studied the room. On the mantel above the wood-framed fireplace were three brass candlesticks, all different. Next to them was a portrait of Crane by Walker in an old cork mat. Inside a foot-long green bottle was the model of a full-rigged sailing vessel. I asked how it managed to get inside the bottle, which couldn't have been blown around it. Carlsen explained that the mast and rigging had been laid flat; the hull was thin enough to slip by, and a thread pulled the masts upright.

From upstairs came grunts of furniture being moved; something slammed. Carl rose from the tea table to investigate. I tried to signify to Walker in Carlsen's absence how abjectly fascinated I was by this quaint home; there was hardly enough time. Some manner of abrupt exchange was heard from the top of the stairs. Walker winked. Carl came down; there were no apologies; we were dismissed, leaving warm tea in mugs and rum untasted. He smiled without embarrassment; hoped he'd see me again "some time"; slapped Walker on the back, firmly shook my hand, and we were out in the courtyard. There had been not a word about his manuscripts.

I was loath to leave, troubled, as if, somehow, I'd done the wrong thing, for I had been enchanted. Here was a human situation, a concentrated mystery of class behavior which I might have read about or suspected, but never touched. I was torn as to what further contact I might seek. How could I warp a half-uttered invitation into some story *Hound & Horn* might print? Walker was no help. On the walk back I bombarded him with questions, but his thin answers told more of Crane than Carlsen, whom he claimed to have met only in passing. Evans had a collector's passion for ephemeral American artifacts: matchboxes, baseball and cigarette cards, old valentines, tobacco boxes, trademarked paperbags, and twine. Somehow, Carlsen and his ambiance were connected with such collecting.

In my idiosyncratic mythology, those whose fortunes followed the sea had solemn significance. The first dress-up clothes I'd been given to wear were those my father brought me (aged four), the midget uniform of a Royal Navy rating (from Rowe of Gosport), complete with a silver bosun's rope and whistle, in which I was duly photographed. At bedtimes, he read to my brother and me Dana's *Two Years Before the Mast*. His steady affairs in Britain supplied the *Illustrated London News*, with their splendid extra-colored souvenir editions celebrating the coronations of Edward VII and George V. Portraits of Princes of Wales disguised as midshipmen were linked in my mind with Mark Twain's *The Prince and the Pauper*. The rôle of sailor, ordinary and extraordinary, seemed to be that of a classless, or declassed prince. When I was a freshman at Harvard, Foster Damon, my tutor, gave me *White-Jacket* and *Israel Potter* to read. The reputation of *Moby-Dick* was at the crest of its recognition. The manuscript of *Billy Budd* lay in Widener Library. I paid a classmate to transcribe Melville's virtually illegible handwriting, since Damon told me that the recently published Constable "complete" edition was full of errors. I had been on my brother's small boat in Marble-head Harbor, but never on the open sea. In 1925, in London, I had fallen in love with the Russian ballet. Léonide Massine's *Les Matelots*, with Georges Auric's early jazz, had among its three sailors an American, borrowed from Jean Cocteau's memories of the U.S. Mediterranean cruises with gobs ashore in the bars of Toulon and Villefranche. The jolly sailors Massine choreographed for Diaghilev's Russian dancers-in-exile were domesticated acrobats, hardly sailors at sea but players ashore. Like Carlsen.

My image of him, presumably fictive, had little enough to do with any essential self; but for me, he incarnated legends. The fact that he was approachable, on the beach, and hence both estranged from his proper province and yet accessible, made his vague presence all the more exhilarating, for surely "he knew the name Hercules was called among the women and held the secrets of the sea." Perhaps he only existed between voyages, likely to ship out at any moment. How would I ever find him again unless I were able to conceive a stratagem which, so far, I had not the slyness to imag-ine? Here, again, Walker Evans was no help; he had gone as far as he could pushing Carl towards "literature"; he wasn't particularly generous, or amused by my fascina-tion. If I wanted to see the guy again, no big deal. Drop in on him, just as we had today. After all, as yet there had been no mention of his ambitious writing, nor my dubious thwarting of it.

So, breathless and in some dread, I did risk it. On my second visit, he was alone. Now my self asserted its typecasting as college critic; my sincerity was clear even if suggestions were limp. But perhaps I was almost the first to take him seriously as more than a mechanic, and thus I advanced slowly, solemnly into a hesitant friend-ship. Steps from cautious contact to relative intimacy were propelled by the abrupt arrival of his brother, a second officer on a coastal freighter on regular runs from San Diego, through the Panama Canal up to Portland, Maine. Every three or four months Nils Carlsen enjoyed a few days' liberty from Hoboken. Carl took me over to explore his command. When we first climbed aboard, there seemed to be no one anywhere. It was deserted. One custodian tended pilot fires in the furnace room. Here was surely the site of the split piston rod and the stoker's shattered arm. Carl drew no special at-tention to any single piece of machinery. I was about to ask the function of every obvi-ous object, but realized this was his private time and sacred place, not to be profaned by idle or overeager curiosity. If I, indeed, had the wit to feel awe, then let this jungle of polished brass bandings, glistening serpentine coils, and tigerine furnaces purr its hot breath. My cautious questions were answered by his ready brother. The latent power in the engines seemed to swell, filling Carl's fixed, riveted silence, in which his com-plete comprehension of mineral potency was haloed in a scent of oil, the slumbering, acrid fragrance of coal fire; an incandescent bluish gloom through thick-glazed fur-nace doors. A brutal but delicate mechanism was alive, grossly asleep, lovingly tended, waiting to be ignited into full flame. An unfired weapon, immaculately maintained, called for its own ration of love, and love is what burnished it through Nils Carlsen's professional concern. He apologized for the inadequacy of active operation. Here was power at one remove; his ship slept, not to be aroused until it met open sea. As we left, Carl astonished me by saying evenly that if we ever should ship out together, then he would let me learn what hot metal meant as the measure of energy in motion.

Initiation in the boiler room was revelation, but this abrupt personal inference or interpolation, tossed out so lightly, exploded that vein of incendiary excitement which is the rapacious flare of first love. While I realized only too well I could never bet on any specific date for a joint voyage, the fact that he had uttered so vague a proposal diffused small logic. After all, his brother was bound to this boat and could probably arrange everything easily. Why shouldn't we, some time in what glorious future, ship out together? I would teach Carl how to write as he taught me how to live.

For two good reasons, among tides of unanswerable others. First, Carl was in retirement from the sea, by will or chance. He was fixing to be "a writer." He took writing seriously; he wrote mornings, he said, every day: eight to eleven. What he wrote, Bertha, the piano teacher, his consort, typed afternoons. I could imagine that while she typed, he wandered around, did chores. She was the real hindrance for me. I never knew whether or not they "slept" together. It would have been impossible to have guessed otherwise, yet in public there was little contact. Carlsen never talked dirty, or made the exciting, outrageous, or forbidden raw jokes or references which might have been expected, and for which I knew men of his class were famous. This further distanced me from a full unveiling of the many secrets he seemed to hold. Bertha cooked; she kept their house in its pale immaculate rigor. As I ventured to drop in more often and stay longer, she made fairly polite efforts to speak, but sooner or later she retired upstairs. She even tried to make it appear that she knew Carl and I had serious things to say by which his career might be furthered. Perhaps she somehow knew his "writing" was more or less of a fantasy, but at least it was an alternative to his going back to sea, which certainly she did not want. She kept him on a loose chain; he had his "freedom." I hoped he was free enough to include me somewhere in it. He seldom spoke of her. I might have made the silly speech of setting myself up against her, but his perfect manners precluded such folly.

However, eventually I felt close enough to Carl to risk mentioning that I sensed that "Bertha didn't like me." I dared this presumption, risking a connection to which I had precarious right. All he admitted was: "You don't bother her." This was no resolution, but I knew enough not to press it. At the time when one is breaking out of post-adolescence, fright, insecurity, apprehension encourage an appetite for adventure dared. Everything I had previously experienced or felt about people seemed now on the other side of a glass wall, and my "education," *pace* well-beloved Henry Adams, was a half-conscious attempt to eliminate the self-protection from a "real world." Carlsen was my real world, and his isolation was at once nearer and farther than anyone or anything. Unfleshed imagination flickers, a vast amorphous void, filled with rainbow possibilities and doubt. Carl exploded in my life, bringing to the exercise of heart and mind the chance for a three-dimensional existence, released from the prison of prior habit. While he strove to make art out of a half-life, I tried to make come alive what heretofore I had only read of in books, which were now the models which stopped him dead.

As for any actual contact with Hart Crane, the poet, heir of Poe, Whitman, and Hopkins, this was tenuous in the extreme. Encounters with Crane were negligible; yet I depended on Crane's immediacy to certify my contact with Carl. I knew Crane would not have recognized my face. But I was rather close to those who did know him very well: Evans, Allen Tate, Katherine Anne Porter. I was not really drawn to his gift; I barely connected the man with his poetry. Both seemed outrageous and un-mannerly, although I was not ready to face the blame for fearing its obscurity. After all, there was Modern Art, and what a success that was becoming! And I was forced to feel, in spite of prejudice, that there was some irreducible courage, both in art and life, a defiance, however gross or unseemly, of which I could not help being envious. Carl was slow to speak of him; if they had been drunk and disorderly together often enough, he volunteered little that was revelatory or proprietary. He shied away from mention of violence or perversity. For these there were no apologies; he inferred such was the fiber of genius that Crane was licensed to play as he pleased. Crane was above praise or calumny. As for Carlsen's own preference or promiscuity, he let me hear nothing; when he dealt out rum, it was the classic brace at the capstan. I was forced to assume his deliberate moderation was the result of some possible earlier excess now monitored by a lady piano teacher. Yet I was eager to bring Carl into "my" world, to exhibit him to Muriel Draper and Carl Van Vechten. But he disdained entrance into alien areas, and was not eager to be exhibited as a picturesque trophy.

On April 28, 1932, I was invited to Muriel Draper's for cocktails. I wrote in a diary:

> I learned of Hart Crane's drowning. A sickening feeling, but I never really cared for him or his work, except for "Hurricane," which I thought magnificent.

> Rock sockets, levin-lathered!
> Nor, Lord, may worm outdeep

> Thy drum's gambade, its plunge abscond!
> Lord God, while summits crashing

> Whip sea-kelp screaming on blond
> Sky-seethe, dense heaven dashing—

Thou ridest to the door, Lord!
Thou bidest wall nor floor, Lord!

After this, I began to hesitate in asking Carl to show more of his writing, since my early response had been so unwelcoming. With the removal of much compulsion to connect the two of us through "literature," he grew less shy, and our relations went from friendliness to something approaching friendship. One of the impersonations requiring considerable craft is that of feigning enthusiasm about the disappointing labors of one liked or loved. Carl was never going to be much of a literary man; if his attempts had been high-school student work by a sixteen-year-old, it might have proved promising. Apt phrasing, careful observation, genuine emotion, and brief bursts of oddly personal intonation there may have been, but since he had read so little, and what he had found on his own to read—Marlowe and Melville in particular—were such monstrous models, and since his own vital experience was both so very deep and narrow, one could not hope for much quality beyond the primitive. There was yet a further, more profound impediment. From inherent shyness, good manners, or instinctive discretion he excluded from his narrative much approaching vivid personal comment. He wrote about the sea and its mariners in terms of popular magazine illustration confused by "literary" rhetoric, avoiding psychological insight, as if such realism might dull a "beauty" in expression. Carl, like Crane, his idol, was a rhapsodist not a precise analyst. The exalted rhetoric of Marlowe and Melville derived in great part from traditions of the spoken word—drama or pulpit, the heightened accents of vocal utterance. Carl's prose, like Crane's verse, was written to be read aloud, but I have yet to hear any speaker give voice to Crane as satisfactorily as one mouths it in the mind with closed lips. Carl's opacity and stumbling richness were hard enough to read and would never be printed.

He came to the world of books late in his development, receiving the key to his furnished library from a poet who canonized four overwhelming masters: Marlowe, Melville, Whitman, Rimbaud. Before almost anyone in the United States, through Yvor Winters, Crane came upon Gerard Manley Hopkins, and strove earnestly without much effect to make him better known. Crane's power was more verbal than metrical; Hopkins's shackled ferocity combined word, measure, and music with far more discipline, despite the short-circuits and elided metaphors of which both were masters. Just as Hopkins adored and was terrified of Whitman's bare-faced carnality, so Crane concealed the immediacy of his sentiment in an almost hysterical chromatics of language and compressed imagery. The alchemy of the word was a hazardous science; Carlsen, with his slight talent and less familiarity with his betters, was doomed as a writer. His awe of the potential in the English language betrayed him. Carl's longing to make literature was a means of touching magic he couldn't make. Crane came into his life as some Prospero, transforming Manhattan and Brooklyn into enchanted islands.

Did Carl have much notion of what Crane was trying to say? We had once been reading, together, from *The Bridge*:

> Whose head is swinging from the swollen strap?
> Whose body smokes along the bitten rails,
> Bursts from a smouldering bundle far behind
> In back forks of the chasms of the brain—
> Puffs from a riven stump far out behind
> In interborough fissures of the mind ...?

Carl stuck on "swollen strap." Why swollen? Now "interborough"; he could see the subway connection, but he asked: "Why in hell can't he say what he means?" In the summer of 1926, Crane had written to Waldo Frank, one of his first professional enthusiasts:

> ... work continues. The Tunnel now. I shall have it done very shortly. It's rather ghastly, almost surgery—and oddly, almost all from the notes and stitches I have written while swinging on the strap at late midnight hours going home.

In 1932, writing after the suicide, introducing the first American edition of *The Bridge*, Waldo Frank explained:

> "The Tunnel" gives us man in his industrial hell which the machine—his hand and heart—has made; now let the machine be his godlike Hand to uplift him! The plunging subway shall merge with the vaulting bridge. Whitman gives the vision; Poe, however vaguely, the method.

Now, fifty years later, Carl's innocent objection irritates like a stubborn hangnail. Here as elsewhere Crane said something less than what he hoped to mean. Rather, he relied on Rimbaud's *alchimie du verbe* to make magic more than morality or meaning. "The Tunnel," with its random mosaic of subway-mob vernacular quotations, could too easily be read as a gloss on Eliot's "A Game of Chess." To the editors of *Hound & Horn*, hypnotized by that poem and its author, any similarity would have seemed more weakening then than it does now. Perhaps it was this very likeness, or homage, which prompted Eliot to print it in his *Criterion*, for August 1927.

But, partly as a devil's advocate, partly in my rôle as professor of Modern Poetry, I tried to particularize for Carl what I conceived Crane's method proposed. I had been struck hard by an arresting image in "For the Marriage of Faustus and Helen" (Part III), which mentions "Anchises' navel, dripping of the sea—" wherein I saw some ancestral demigod striding towards a surfbound Tyrrhenian shore, Giovanni da Bologna rather than Praxiteles, an ancient marine divinity, model for a Baroque fountain, one of Bernini's gigantic epitomes. Carl asked: "Who the hell's Anchises?" Making it easy, I might have said Anchises was another name for Neptune, the sea god Poseidon, brother to Zeus, enemy of Ulysses, author of his misfortunes—or possibly merely a trisyllable Crane happened to have come across, which like so many fortuitous findings fired his prosody. There seem to be two mentions only of Anchises in the *Iliad*; he was father to Aeneas, lover to Aphrodite born of sea foam, second cousin to Priam, King of Troy. In Book III of the *Aeneid*,

> When old Anchises summoned all to sea:
> The crew, my father and the Fates obey.
>   —Dryden

Years later, a young Harvard scholar told me that in the Homeric "Hymn to Aphrodite" Anchises mates with the goddess, who bears his child in secret. Later, he is punished for presuming to couple with divinity. Mortals suffer who dare touch the immeasurable. Crane could have had something concrete in mind by naming Anchises—an autodidact; he read widely. But with Carlsen it was useless for me to pursue all this; it reduced a marvel to the academic. I did my best by trying to suggest the taut muscular belly of an ancient athlete brimming with saline, not very wine-dark liquor, chill and glistening, as from some celestial shower bath.

Meditating on Hart Crane's life, death, and residue is sobering exercise. Now enshrined, he has his niche in the mortuary of dazzling self-slayers. He's been well served by friends and students whose sympathy and industry have restored what failed ambition must certainly have granted. Before crisis framed him, his was the treasure of a small, closed audience of passionate if troubled admirers. Now widely available in paperback, griefs forgiven or forgotten, he is redeemed in posthumous sovereignty. This came without any compulsion as the inevitable slow but logical recognition of genius. To regret or complain that there are not more relics to worship, or that his legacy might be other or superior, begs the question. Crane handled, mishandled, and manipulated words, warping heard speech into an electric recalcitrance as no American has done before or since, and which few Englishmen have equaled since Father Hopkins. Nevertheless, Allen Tate, one of his closest friends, wrote in the obituary for *Hound & Horn* (July–September 1932) a judgment of "The Tunnel," which he saw as Crane's attempt to write his *Inferno*, and which is still hard to refute:

> At one moment Crane faces his predicament of blindness to any rational order of value, and knows that he is damned; but he cannot face it, and he tries to rest secure upon the mere intensity of sensation.... It [*The Bridge*] is probably the final word of romanticism

in this century. When Crane saw that his leading symbol would not cover all the material of his poem, he could not sustain it ironically in the classic manner. Alternately he asserts it and abandons it because fundamentally he does not understand it. The idea of bridgeship is an elaborate metaphor, a sentimental conceit leaving the structure of the poem confused.

Pondering the brief span of Crane's performance, one risks deciphering roots of dysfunction, tension, torment, terror, and hysteria. There are masterful studies of his times and temperament, notably Unterecker's huge *Voyager*. Crane's catastrophe can be reduced, perhaps simplistically, to two afflictions: Cleveland and Christian Science. This middle-American town early in the century stands for the basic provincial Philistine criterion, the Protestant work ethic of crippling but mandatory somnambulistic success as the guarantee and habit of salvation. C. R. Crane's candy business cannot be assigned the worst level of hell, but purgatory of the paralyzed imagination, particularly when genius is at stake, is as sad. Attempts benevolently to straitjacket his only son and heir into the patterns of industrial health were wounding and drained Hart's energy at the very moment it asserted itself towards invention. C.R. was no villain, neither ungenerous nor entirely insensitive. He loved his boy, wished him well, even when wife and mother did her damned best to kill any mutual contact.

She was and is, alas, by no means an unfamiliar American darling. "Science," for her, was true magic. And as too many others had proved, material suffering, physical and mental, was wholly imaginary; *it did not exist*. Mary Baker Eddy stated: "Nothing is real and eternal; nothing is spirit, but God and His ideal; evil has no reality." Since God is pure Good, He cannot have created, or have been responsible for aught that is not Good. Man is God's personal notion, and belongs by essence to an order in which there may be no disease, ugliness, hate, sin, sorrow, or death. Such are mere errors of Man's mortal mentation, without "reality" save as man's mortal mind admits them. Disdain them! *They do not exist!* There is only True or False, with neither degree nor choice. To the neurotic, this banishes neurosis; what we do not wish to credit, asks no credence. But this denial precipitates a terrible burden on the vulnerable lyric mechanism through the solipsism of unmeasured fantasy. The constricted, stoic self tries to force free association into passive courage, but creatures of Crane's temperament, torn between the duel of his parents' feuding, rushed roaring through the barriers of genuine suffering to drown in the only harbor he could imagine: oblivion. As Crane's wise counselor, Yvor Winters, wrote of Hart as Orpheus:

> Till the shade his music won
> Shuddered, by a pause undone—
> Silence would not let her stay.

He could go one only way;
By the river, strong with grief,
Gave his flesh beyond belief.

Yet the fingers on his lyre
Spread like an avenging fire.
Crying loud, the immortal tongue,
From the empty body wrung,
Broken in a bloody dream,
Sang unmeaning down the stream.

As a gesture of filial devotion to Grace Crane, now divorced and in lonely anguish, Crane himself tried to "practice" Christian Science, but with little confidence. He recommended his mother be more assiduous in her own practice—the amateur psychologist suggesting placebos. But she was infected, corrupting both herself and him. If human disease does not exist, there is no need to seek the means to face it, endure, handle, or use it. However, since suffering does indeed exist in omnivorous constancy, deliberate ignorance of its presence is an error majestic in consequence. Crane suffered more than most, in the depth, delicacy, and intensity of his sensibility. The pain that sprang from it, the energy taken to resist it and at the same time to bury it, somehow justified it, and absolved him from it. His short life was drained on two incompatible levels: Chagrin Falls, a well-to-do Cleveland suburb, and Sands Street, Brooklyn, a nirvana of sailor bars. Alcohol was a benison; it was as if Mrs. Eddy had handed him her witches' brew. Alcohol obliterated and at once inspired—a distillation of alchemical ink. Unraveling accommodation with his furious progenitors, patched up by his want of and need for love, plus sheer poverty, took more of a toll than bathtub gin or harbor adventures. Random encounters were seldom successful as enduring affection and became hateful payment to his "curse of sundered parentage." One-night stands are for a single night; love of one's mother, however torn, is lifelong, endless, stoked by an overkill of anguish. Physical absence may split son from father, but the tie binds. Maleness is the criterion, and Crane took sides against his own. Only the wavering is constant and consistent; wild nights are blessedly discontinuous; to make small matters better or worse, there's always tomorrow with its luckier midnight. To solve the dreadful problem—freedom, talent, genius—one can embrace a stupendous falsity: Cleveland, Chagrin Falls, according to Christian Science, don't exist.

But psychic energy nurtured by self-deceit only accelerates the false and irrelevant. The old heresy which proclaims Resurrection without Crucifixion as a material fact consoles generations of fairly affluent middle-class vulnerability in its competitive mass. While there may be unemployed Scientists, there are few born and bred as working-class folk. Carl Carlsen could never have been a practicing Christian Scientist, but I was to discover that Bertha, his piano teacher friend, was, on the side, yet importantly for her, a Christian Science healer.

My short connection with Carlsen was through Crane alone, and this was a weak link. Carl spoke little about the person, whom he knew well, but always with awe about the poet, whose lines he could barely grasp. To him, they were disparate identities, never twins. They seemed to have seen less of each other than formerly. Friends that lasted—Tate, Malcolm Cowley, Waldo Frank—were those to whom, finally, Crane could speak of ideas, the matter of his primary labor. But in some deep way for Carl, Crane was faultless; his behavior, his aberrations, were simply routes to a level of fame or feeling which was destiny.

Nevertheless, in meetings with Carl, Crane was an invisible third, spectral but manifest. I could understand well enough what he meant to Carl, but what did I mean—to him, or anyone? I was a rich college kid, twenty-three years old, whose surfeit of "education" had misprized Crane's Pindaric ode to the tunnel beneath the bridge:

> O caught like pennies beneath soot and steam,
> Kiss of our agony thou gatherest;
> Condensed, thou takest all—shrill ganglia
> Impassioned with some song we fail to keep.
> And yet, like Lazarus, to feel the slope,
> The sod and billow breaking—lifting ground,
> —A sound of waters bending astride the sky
> Unceasing with some Word that will not die ... !

Perhaps this fixation on one of Crane's buddies was an attempt to compensate for my stupidity, my wickedness. But the truth was, Carl didn't connect me with either Harvard, *Hound & Horn*, or Crane. By then the magazine had been taken over by Dick Blackmur, Allen Tate and his Agrarians, and other intellectuals with political or metaphysical preoccupations. My postgraduate studies were centered in Manhattan. Carl was amused that I was in love with him.

It wasn't easy to find him. He had his work, which I had to assume was dogged, daily typewriting—moonlighting sometimes as handyman, janitor; certainly he didn't type all day and all night. Money never seemed a problem. Maybe piano lessons paid for his drinks, because he was scrupulous about paying for them. But he was not someone I might feel free to drop in on any old time, particularly if Bertha was likely to be at home. Possibly I made more of her as a problem than she actually was. Most days, having learned to estimate his working habits, I would go over with the excuse of asking if he'd want to go for a walk. If he didn't feel like it, and if she were in, she promptly vanished upstairs. Her presence was pervasive. Some nights Carl might even walk me home to my own room on Minetta Lane, where I made him tea and a drink. I was then sharing the place with Tom Wood, an ex-cowboy who, having been trained as a blacksmith, turned into a craftsman of forged iron. He made handsome firescreens with carefully cut-out silhouettes of animals, stubby andirons, and pleasant shop signs. Carl and he shared the experience of handling metal; there were also the unspoken bonds of class and manual labor. Their immediate cool rapport made me objectively happy and subjectively sad.

One night, a clear September evening in 1932, I went around hoping to catch Carl in, and on the way bet myself he'd be out—insurance against disappointment. The city street sounds were diminished and clarified, the darkening air all the more transparent from the thin punctuation of fragmentary voices. The courtyard in front of his house was swept clean; three garbage pails were in a neat triangle, coverless and empty. Carl was alone. I expected Bertha to return shortly and spoil my fun. He was wearing a crisp pair of regulation white Navy ducks. Rum was on his table-desk; typewriter on the piano. It was almost as if he had been expecting me. Bertha had gone to Chicago to care for a sick sister (through prayer?). How long would she be gone? Don't know; you want tea or grog?

The abrupt luxury of freedom felt then I can still feel. It's a shrunken residue, and although the intensity of the explosion was a once-in-a-lifetime thrust of luck which can only erupt in youth, it was a real joy by which others would later be judged and found wanting. For the first time, I had Carl to myself, in his place, his tavern, forecastle, island. Now I could discover everything—how he felt, what he thought, who he was. It didn't turn out like that. We drank quietly for some time, in a rather oppressive silence, speaking of nothing in particular. What I wished to say rushed far and fast ahead of what I could actually say. Inside, my curiosity boiled, but he seemed perhaps even more self-centered than usual. My first wild manic propulsion subsided into apotropaic depression. I asked what he'd been up to. Writing. Evening was leaking away with each sip of rum-and-water. It would have been ordinary for him to have been drinking alone. I was an intrusion, whatever his placid courtesy; yet I couldn't bring myself to quit. Talk unraveled. Finally, I had to say: "Carl, you're bushed. I'd better go," and pushed my chair back to stand up. So did he. He put a hand on my shoulder: "Stay here, kid, if you like."

We had nightcaps. I stayed. Thus commenced a brief domestic interlude in which I played substitute housekeeper, enjoying the closeness and coolness of a creature whose mythical image was then for me no less mysterious than a unicorn or a manticore. Carl's quest for quiet, his spareness in motion, his quizzical softness, which was also a tender firmness, his nicety in consideration, his dispassionate attention or friendliness, could easily be translated into terms of love. In him, and not far below the surface, were layers of reserve that denied me any very profound exchange. He was not concealing himself; his nature, either from its poverty, discipline, or good manners, secreted some unchallenged dignity, possibly fear, but of what? Such withholding or denial was of course for me an accumulative provocation. He was not teasing; he was just Carlsen. When I too earnestly discussed all this with Walker Evans, he said only, "Oh, that Carl. He's just another one of Crane's characters; a sphinx without a secret."

Despite cold water and intermittent doubt, he remained an enthralling riddle, never more so than when he got up early, made his kettle of shaving water, washed from a wooden bucket, and set out breakfast. I stayed in bed, partly to seem to let him have his house to himself for a little; partly to observe and enjoy his singularity. I don't know whether he wandered about bare-assed when Bertha was there. With me, he never dressed until he was ready to go into the street. This wasn't "narcissism." He never drew attention to himself, nor was he particularly graced in the flesh. He might have been any age, twenty-five to forty-five, a sleek, hard, almost hairless male; easy, self-confident, and deliberate. Nakedness was this creature's kind of clothing.

Questions intruded. I couldn't accept my situation for whatever it was on his part. I must worry it, "make sense" of it. Where, and who, after all, was I? Soon, Bertha must be back; she might walk in at any moment—tomorrow morning, tonight; now . . . Each time I noticed her stubby upright piano with its sparkling black-and-white keys, its pile of music stacked neatly on top, I felt a looming adversary. Yet why should her pervasive if fragile absence cloud my present, since it in no way seemed to disturb Carlsen? How greedy can you get? We both knew she was inevitably expected; ours was no marriage, nor was it a one-night stand. If I strained trying to make myself useful, to justify proximity by offering some "contribution," Carl didn't notice. This was my business. He wouldn't have asked me to stay if he hadn't felt some need. Guilt was nowhere near, as far as I was concerned; only delight. I had hoped to have helped him with his "work," his writing, but he never seemed to have finished a story to the degree he thought it ready or worthy of being criticized. He kept his papers-in-progress in manila binders. Sometimes when I was in his house alone, I was moved to glance at a page or so, but this was a disloyalty for which I might be mortally punished. Then about a week after I'd moved in, something prompted me to start reading one of the folders straight through. There were some ten or a dozen pages, a few typed, others handwritten. Then, halfway down a page, words stopped in the middle of a sentence. This was true of all of his stuff. Nothing was finished; the fact that every one stopped seemed an odd coincidence. I suddenly realized that Carl longed to be "a writer," but couldn't write. Perhaps this was due, in some way, to the refusal from the editors of *Hound & Horn*. I guessed that he knew I knew his secret, but mutual convenience prevented it from being betrayed. He had a rare reserve of emotional energy, without any sentimental taint, and I recognized him as a classic stoic. Perhaps this is why Crane chose him. In an untidy universe, here was order, magic, however miniature, a clipper ship in a bottle.

Quiet consciousness of self, a centered, unexpressed self, trying to comprehend what is done while doing it. For myself, at the age of nineteen, I had by chance begun to engage in similar self-instruction, through the means of one system of analytical method. Hart Crane himself only touched on his astonished impression of a dramatic, then much-publicized demonstration of the corporal manifestation of this same discipline. On February 2, 1924, he had written his mother back in Ohio that he had witnessed a performance of dancing organized by George Gurdjieff, which although executed by amateurs "would stump the Russian ballet." In 1917, when Crane had first come to New York, aged eighteen, he had seen Diaghilev's company at the old Metropolitan Opera House, and later became friends with Stanislav Portapovich, to whom he dedicated an early poem:

> Vault on the opal carpet of the sun,
> Barbaric Prince Igor:—or, blind Pierrot,
> Despair until the moon by tears be won;—
> Or, Daphnis, move among the bees with Chloe.
>
> Release,—dismiss the passion from your arms.
> More than real life, the gestures you have spun
> Haunt the blank stage with lingering alarms,
> Though silent as your sandals, danced undone.

Crane came to know a number of people who had been close to A. R. Orage, whom T. S. Eliot called the best editor of his generation. Orage was designated by Gurdjieff as his first American representative. Some twenty-five students performed movements derived from Near Eastern and Central Asian sources in Manhattan, Chicago, and Boston. These drew considerable attention and had some issue. On May 29, 1927, Crane wrote from Patterson, New York, to Yvor Winters in California about his total disagreement with Gurdjieff's proposals, which claimed to impose instruction towards a "harmonious development of man" in its trinity of physical, mental, and moral capacities. He told Winters the aim was

> … a good idealistic antidote for the hysteria for specialization that inhabits the modern world. And I strongly second your wish for some definite ethical order. [Gorham] Munson, however, and a number of my other friends, not so long ago, being stricken with the same urge, and feeling that something must be done about it—rushed into

the portals of the famous Gurdjieff institute and have since put themselves through all sorts of Hindu antics, songs, dances, incantations, psychic sessions, etc. so that now, presumably, the left lobes of their brains respectively function (M's favorite word) in perfect unison. I spent hours at the typewriter trying to explain to certain of these urgent people why I could not enthuse about their methods; it was all to no avail, as I was told that the "complete man" had a different logic than mine, and further that there was no way of gaining or understanding this logic without first submitting yourself to the necessary training.... Some of them, having found a good substitute for their former interest in writing by means of more complete formulas of expression, have ceased writing now altogether, which is probably just as well.

On December 21, 1923, Crane wrote from Woodstock, New York, to his mother in Cleveland a letter replete with patient sympathy for her maddening complaints, her self-martyrizing, her distaste for his way of life.

I, too, have had to fight a great deal just to *be myself* and *know myself* at all, and I think I have been doing and am doing a great deal in following out certain natural and innate directions in myself.... Suffering is a real purification, and the worst thing I have always had to say against Christian Science is that it willfully avoided suffering without a certain measure of which any true happiness cannot be fully realized.

Crane might have been paraphrasing Gurdjieff himself. Ultimately, the essence of his teaching proposed means to utilize that suffering which is the common lot, not by avoidance, but by its positive and negative energy. Certain temperaments or "personalities" have found themselves predisposed to the magnetism of the recension of esoteric and exoteric exercises in the residue of post-Pythagorean notions. Like Crane, not a few have been moved by the apparent magic in the organization of corporal action in the Gurdjieff exercises, but have been put off by the ensuing demands of his metaphysical lucubrations. My good fortune, for I consider it the greatest luck that ever hit me, was that I encountered this cosmology when emotionally I was an adolescent, without any essential experience, and hence lacking prejudice but not appetite. I was hardly more than a child, with few "ideas" good or bad. Crane, early on, had ceased being a child. His physique, gifts, affective life were forced into prematurity. Due to over-aroused psychic activity, the furious problems of domestic tension stoked raw habits of antagonism and escape long before the boy had any capacity to diffuse them. The anguish in his prepotency withered him. He quickly became an old youth in an unresisting body and settled for a hysterical persona, laminated to his true center—brilliant, irascible, coruscating, and electric—a rocket launched towards a magnetic relief in extinction.

When, in the summer of 1927, I was in Fontainebleau for a short stay at Mr. Gurd-jieff's priory, I met a Scandinavian-American ex-farmer who might be placed (or rather, I chose to place him later) in a category similar to Carlsen's. I revered him for his undemanding straightforwardness, his unblinking devotion to the feckless jobs which Gurdjieff assigned as muscular extremities of conscious coordination or self-discipline. I had barely reached that limit where I could distinguish between positive and negative energy, but I was able, instinctively, to realize that in the superficially boring, chaotic, but exhausting games that we played there was, somewhere, some-how, a key for conduct to a life I hoped to lead. Hauling big rocks from one pile in the garden to another hole a hundred yards away for no purpose I could decipher was not the most enchanting way to inherit wisdom from the ancients, but due to my prox-imity in this "work" (rockpiles) to Swede, the sweat (his and mine) was more than tolerable. He took orders unsmiling but uncomplaining. His lack of visible protest or question somehow bespoke genuine need. If he wanted something so clearly un-defined, I could borrow whatever it must be. Mr. Gurdjieff, marking our companion-ship, grinned and said, "So. You and Swede." I was delighted at such attention. He said evenly, "Swede. Honest workman."

Honest workman. This phrase had a stubborn resonance. When I was posing for Gaston Lachaise, the sculptor, some five years later, he instructed me in his personal criteria for "modern art," in which, at that time, I was obsessively interested. I men-tioned Aristide Maillol, who in the twenties had that mandatory ubiquity now en-joyed by Henry Moore. Lachaise said, "Maillol; not great *artiste*; honest workman." Hart Crane had been friends with Lachaise and his wife since 1923 and owned a fine alabaster dove. On March 5, 1924, Crane wrote to his old friends, the Rychtariks, whom he had left behind in Cleveland: "This afternoon I went around to an exhibi-tion of sculpture by Maillol (who is an honest workman, but not very creative)."

Perhaps Gurdjieff's nomination had been transmitted through Orage, Gorham Munson, Caesar Zwaska, Wim Nylan, or others in G.'s first New York "Group." As I received it, the appellation "honest workman" did not imply peasant, day laborer, or mechanic. It was a judgment not only of a particular artisan but also of the condition and quality of art and craft in general. Here a basic integrity is not always foremost, whatever the currently accepted reputation for excellence may be. I feel certain that Crane borrowed this from Lachaise; the identity with Gurdjieff's epithet was fortu-itous. There were other odd linkages to Crane in my remote contact with him. Years later I came across two "irrelevant" facts which further diminished my superstitions concerning chance. The first artwork I collected (given me by a favorite cousin) was a Maxfield Parrish color print of Cleopatra. It portrayed a flapperish serpent of old Nile in her barge, lounging on what appeared to be an American "colonial" four-poster bed, bowered in dogwood and attended by three high-school athletes. It had been commissioned as the first of a series by C. R. Crane to adorn his five-dollar *de luxe* gift chocolate boxes. This was in 1917; I was ten years old. In 1923, Crane moved into 6 Minetta Lane with his friend Slater Brown. In 1933, I moved in there with Tom Wood, with no notion of what was a meaningless coincidence.

Crane's appreciation of art, for which his parents had prepared him, though primarily in the interests of commerce, was real. His admiration for William Sommer's undistinguished painting was inspired by his first encounter with a working artist. He adopted and adapted opinion, as also in his verse. But as to "honest workman," the simpler it sounded, the more recalcitrant the inference. Merely, honest. Only, a workman. As for the Swede, his absolute health, sanity, sense, and sweat that I imagined smelled of raw wheat—his massive softness and ready acceptance of whatever had to be practically done—were these the normal attributes merely of honest workmen? And why should such try to be any more than that—why also "creative," like Ezra Pound or T. S. Eliot, who then governed the lending library I fancied as my "mind"? Why should unadulterated animal magnetism or sweetness of spirit be allied necessarily with the capacity to paint tremendous pictures or write extraordinary poetry? What is the pay potential on a humane level? Honest work was to be judged on what range of imagination, lyric fantasy, or the responsibility which kindles the heroes and martyrs, makers or failures?

Carl Carlsen had strayed into an adventurous and dangerous area of electrical transformation which has come to be called "creativity." He had stumbled unequipped and unendowed into the field of imaginative play. His will to write, to become "a writer," licensed desire and gave it an illusion of spirit and ability which was little more than echoed promise. This honest workman had been lent a vision of unlimited possibility. He might have pursued a more profitable existence by schooling himself in physics, chemistry, or navigation, and ensured an alternate future, but the words, the fearsome sorcery of words fixed him in a situation which held only the recognition of ultimate weakness. Crane launched himself on an inevitable trajectory, only to be arrested at its peak. Carlsen never got within sight of a start.

I lost sight of Carlsen; perhaps he went back to sea as a purser, or shipped out with his brother. Maybe he married Bertha. Walker Evans didn't know. When I went around to call after I came back from abroad in 1933, there was a FOR RENT sign tacked to his front door. My conscience was assuaged somewhat by printing in the twenty-eighth and final number of *Hound & Horn* two letters of Hart Crane to his patron, Otto H. Kahn, telling him of the progress of *The Bridge*, with a letter of Kahn's to Grace Crane thanking her for a photograph of David Alfaro Siqueiros's portrait of her son, the original of which he had razored to ruin some days before he sailed from Veracruz. In the same issue we printed three large, evocative photographs by Walker Evans of downtown Havana, Crane's last port of call.

I don't think that the academic or literary renown that was beginning to collect around Crane meant much to Carlsen. To him, Hart was buddy and model, beyond any question of worldly status. Yet the ferocity of suicide must temper earlier memories, a sequence studded by signs, big or little, of ambiguous destiny. After the fact of threats, rehearsals, and the big event itself, was there, could there have been much doubt that he would have ultimately put an end to his agony? Were there no other alternatives here than with Ralph Barton, Harry Crosby, Randall Jarrell, Hemingway, John Berryman, Sylvia Plath—or even Dylan Thomas, Robert Lowell, or Ted Roethke? (And while Thomas and Lowell do not strictly fit into the coroner's casebook as self-slain, they were as much destined, self-centered victims as Delmore Schwartz or Scott Fitzgerald.) Is it only rationalizing to believe that Crane, like others, enriched language, enhanced its rhetoric, while the magnitude of negation was an exact equivalent to the intensity of talent? As to why there was not more positive energy, why suffering could not have been bridled or used, or why there was not enough spirit to exist while being consumed, perhaps the answers lie in the nature of romantic solipsism. One might wish that the dynamics of affection and revulsion that tore his parents apart, and him in the bargain, might have blessed Crane with Walt Whitman's patience, benevolence, or detachment. Whitman, whose family situation was even more disastrous (with the exception of an ignorant but loving and loyal mother), survived extreme illness, madness, and poverty into his seventies. Crane's residue was achieved in a term of some fifteen years; yet it had its own febrile harvest. His synapsis, "the conjugation of homologous chromosomes, of maternal and paternal origins respectively," exploded into electrical short-circuits which kindled magnificent verbal sparks, flares, and ever-burning torches in their positive bursts and, on the negative coil, brawls, despair, self-pity, and self-loathing. There was never to be

My hand
　in yours,
　　Walt Whitman—
　　　so—

It does not take much special pleading to propose Whitman as an "honest workman." He cast himself in a role of which the mature image was a grandiose version amplified from an impersonation of a youthful original. Cocteau said that another bard, Victor Hugo, was a madman who imagined he was Victor Hugo. Whitman invented the "Good Gray Poet," complete with a photograph of a paper butterfly wired to his fingers. He had begun as plain Walter Whitman, journeyman typesetter, printer, schoolteacher, Free Soil editor. One has no feeling that Crane ever cared or plotted to be or impersonate anyone other than his haphazardly given self. As far as his work went, he felt himself one of a band of brothers which included Poe, Rimbaud, Whitman, and even Gerard Hopkins, hoping his voice was a vatic conduit rather than a conscious and governable identity. His legitimate claims to join the company of Marlowe and Melville are his sensational elisions and impacted fireworks, so tightly compressed that the shock of their implosion lasts longer than the time it takes to scan his pages. His is a high style, an extension of the grandest rhetoric, and could only have been achieved by the most abject expenditure of sense, sentiment, and skill. Whitman's easygoing, lounging prosody betrays few hints of rewriting or emendation; he constantly altered his texts from edition to edition, but this was almost careless correction. It is hard to think of Whitman drunk or Crane sober. Crane failed as apprentice candy salesman, journalist, and professional literary man. Whitman lived as a civil servant, reporter, and lecturer: a career by pittance, but he survived.

While I was living in Carl's house, he took good care that I had my own towel, tumbler, and tar soap; he didn't like to share his old-fashioned straight bare-blade razor, and anyway, I would have cut myself. Everything was shipshape, and the days passed without memorable event. Sooner or later I would leave. Either there would be a letter or telegram from Chicago announcing Bertha's return or she might surprise us. Carl didn't think so; she had her own sort of consideration, which is why they got on so well. The delicacy that linked them need not be broken by resentment on her part, although she of course had no notion I was temporarily taking her place.

So, her special-delivery letter arrived: Bertha's mission in Chicago was a complete success. The sister was entirely recovered, although she made no boast of her "Scientific" ministrations. She planned to take such and such a train, and could be expected at such a day and hour. There was no big deal about goodbyes; in the few days of grace left we pursued our amiable routine without apprehension.

The best place to call it a day was in bed. I loved sleeping with Carl; this was no euphemism. We learned to sleep like spoons; if either had to get up in the night it was no problem to reverse positions and sleep more soundly. Vulnerability transcended? Something like that. Alone, together; cozy and quiet. What I felt most was the gravity or power of his light treatment of my fascination with him. He knew I loved him. As for him—he liked me; I was a pet or mascot.

To make a neat end to this story I could say, "You smell so good." Tar soap? Any less oppressive farewell would have been unseemly. "Yeah: that's vinegar water—but not from vinegar. Crane liked that stuff." I told him how much I had enjoyed this vacation. Abruptly, and for the first time, there was an edge to his ease. "Why didn't you like Hart?" I'd hardly known him; he scared me; I wasn't up to him. His disorder; my envy. Guilt. "Funny. You didn't like him, but you like me." I heard myself say, "Carl, why the hell do you always have to bring Crane into it?"

"Why, you silly son of a bitch. If it wasn't for Crane I wouldn't have given you the sweat off my ass."

Samuel M. Steward

Samuel M. Steward (1909–1993) is a remarkable figure in gay literary history. A novelist and member of the Stein/Toklas circle (his collection *Dear Sammy: Letters from Gertrude Stein and Alice B. Toklas* [1977] is an important contribution to our understanding of the expatriate couple), he taught English for many years at Washington State University, Loyola University of Chicago, and DePaul University. But finding teaching incompatible with writing, he abandoned academia for a career as a tattoo artist. He is best remembered as Phil Andros, the pseudonym under which he wrote, starting with *$tud* in 1968, a celebrated series of pornographic novels in the voice of a well-read, indefatigable hustler. The selection here is from *Chapters from an Autobiography* (1981), in which Steward recounts his meet with Lord Alfred Douglas, through whom Steward places himself in direct contact with Oscar Wilde. Allen Ginsberg, speaking of his friendship with Gavin Arthur (grandson of President Chester A. Arthur), who had slept with Edward Carpenter, who had slept with Walt Whitman, calls this process a "line of transmission," and it was an important way in which gay men felt themselves part of an underground heritage. See too Lincoln Kirstein's essay, which traces his desire to stand in a "line of transmission" through Carl Carlsen to Hart Crane.

The Magic Summer

SOMETIMES LOOKING BACK OVER the succession of years in a life, it is possible to pick out a watershed, a continental divide—and the summer of 1937 was that for me.

The loosely bound group at Ohio State University which embraced Marie Anderson, Robert von Riegel, Virginia Cooley, myself and others considered itself in the forefront—very sophisticated and au courant. Possibly we were by those days' standards—maybe even intellectual and avant-garde. Measured by today's we were only groping towards the kinds of esoteric knowledge that are old hat, even corny, to the young of the moment.

Robert von Riegel's channel was dramatic; Marie's was artistic; mine was literary. I had started the correspondence with Gertrude Stein to inform her of Claire Andrews' death, and her continuing letters put me just a notch above my rivals. Such success had led me to write letters of appreciation and flattery to many of the authors I admired. My list of replies, expanding, came to include Thomas Mann, Van Vechten, Cabell, Undset, Housman, Morley, O'Neill, Freud, Yeats, Maugham, Gide, Rolland, and others. The trick to getting a response, I found, was to say something intelligent about an author's work, and *never to ask any questions nor ask for anything in my letters*, not even a reply. It worked.

Tea with Lord Alfred

Naturally, whenever a literary figure came to the campus to lecture, we were all there en masse—to hear John Cowper Powys declaim like thunder, and James Stephens read Keats in a murmurous whisper—and in 1934 to listen to Hamlin Garland, who wrote *A Son of the Middle Border*, give us the October reminiscences of his long career. He was a pleasant silver-haired giant, by then somewhat diminished in reputation and obscured by men like Hemingway and Dreiser and Sinclair Lewis. But during the course of his lecture he mentioned that he had known Whitman, and that electrified me.

Afterwards I went up on the stage to speak to him. "Did you really know Whitman?" I asked in awe.

"Yes," said the patriarch. "I was very young, but he shook my hand and laid his hand on top of my head."

"Well, Mr. Garland," I said with the rash bravado of youth, "I've shaken your hand, but may I put my hand where Whitman laid his?"

He was somewhat taken aback, but he smiled.

"I want to be linked in with Whitman," I stammered, feeling my face grow red.

"Of course," he said, and bowed his head slightly. I put my left hand on his silver mane. Someone giggled, and I escaped sweating into the auditorium.

That was the genesis of the idea. The next day I wrote to Lord Alfred Douglas, finding his address in *Who's Who*. And in due time a letter from him arrived, chatty and somewhat avuncular, asking who I was and telling me about his latest book, *The True History of Shakespeare's Sonnets*. I answered, saying that I was a student working on my doctorate, and that I would try to find a copy of his book somewhere in the States. He replied that he would be glad to send me a copy but he would have to charge me for it since all his author's copies had been given out. I sent him a draft for two pounds sterling, and waited.

The book arrived. It contained the "dedication" of a full page in his handwriting, with the statement that he had corrected two misprints.

It soon became obvious from his inquiries in letters that followed, inquiries that were at first veiled and then direct, that what Lord Alfred was really looking for was someone who could help him find an American publisher for *The True History*; and I had to confess to him that I had no ties or any influence in the publishing world. And at that point our correspondence dwindled and died . . .

. . . until three years later, 1937, when I made my first trip to Europe as a literary pilgrim, to visit Gertrude Stein at her invitation, and Thomas Mann and André Gide, all of whom seemed a little curious about me. And after a little side trip to Trinity College at Cambridge University to visit Whewell's Court and Great Court B2 where A. E. Housman had lived for twenty-five years (to stand silently weeping, with chills along my spine), I wrote again to Lord Alfred and received a short note from him, asking me to come down to Hove to call on him should I find the time during my London stay.

I must honestly admit that I had no interest whatsoever in Lord Alfred Douglas as a person or as a writer, but only in the fact that he and Oscar Wilde had been lovers, and that back in those shrouded days the name of Wilde had a magic all its own for us who had to live without the benefits of liberation or exposure of our wicked lives. Besides, I was in my twenties and Lord Alfred was by then sixty-seven, and in anyone's book that's *old*. To go to bed with him was hardly the most attractive prospect in the world—it was terrifying, even repulsive. But if I wanted to link myself to Oscar Wilde more directly than I was linked to Whitman, there was no other way.

Even so, the possibility seemed remote. After Wilde's death Lord Alfred had been extremely outspoken in print in his defense of Wilde—and then suddenly changed.

He had married in 1902 and become a Roman Catholic in 1911, and thus put behind him all such childish things as fellatio, mutual masturbation, sodomy, and so on.

After returning to London from Cambridge I established myself in a small hotel in Suffolk Place called Garland's (which seemed a curious omen to me after the Hamlin Garland experience), and from there telephoned Lord Alfred in Hove.

His voice was high-pitched and tinny over the phone. He seemed cordial enough, and invited me down to tea on an afternoon two days hence. I found my way to the great blackened ugly skeleton of Victoria Station and took the train to Brighton in Sussex, which was next door to Hove where he lived, connected in those days (and perhaps still) by a kind of boardwalk along the seafront.

My nervousness increased on the way down. He was a lord of the realm, descended from the Marquess of Queensberry. I must remember not to mention the names of Robert Ross, Frank Harris, André Gide—and a host of others who had been involved in controversy with him—nor even that of Winston Churchill who had sued Lord Alfred for libel and won, with Lord Alfred spending six months in the prison of Wormwood Scrubs as a penalty, all this while he had been editor of *Plain Speech*. And I must not talk about the Jews or mention Gertrude Stein, for he was often very obviously anti-Semitic, even in print. He was the originator of the quatrain:

How odd
Of God
To choose
The Jews

What, in heaven's name, could we talk about at all?

I found out when we met. The only safe topic was Lord Alfred Douglas himself.

His address gave me no trouble—St. Ann's Court, Nizell's Avenue. The stationmaster said that it was not far, a fifteen minute walk from Brighton past the flimsy pavilions dingy from the sea air. I turned a corner and found myself facing a block of flats, perhaps in Regency architecture, little plots and gates and short sidewalk entrances. It was hardly Coleridge's countryside "enfolding sunny spots of greenery," nor Wordsworth's "pastoral farms green to the very door," but it was pleasant and British and the sort of dwelling I was used to seeing in British movies.

He opened the door himself—a man of medium height with hairline receding on the right side where it was parted, and the somewhat lackluster straight mousy hair falling down towards his left eyebrow. His nose was very large and bulbous. The red rose-leaf lips beloved by Wilde had long since vanished; the mouth was compressed and thin, pursed somewhat, and the corners turned slightly downwards. I looked in vain for a hint, even the barest suggestion, of the fair and dreamy youth of the early photographs with Wilde. None was visible. The skin of his face had not suffered the dreadful slackening of the flesh that goes with age; it seemed rather to be of the type that grows old by stretching more tautly over the bones, until—at the end—a skull-like face results. Yet the skin was not stretched tightly enough to pull out the fine network of tiny wrinkles that entirely covered his face and neck.

"Do come in," he said, but then instead of standing aside to let me precede him, he turned and walked ahead of me into the flat, leaving me to shut the door. He looked at me closely and then waved to a chair. "Do sit down," he said.

It was a pleasant room with three or four chairs, rather grimy white curtains at the windows, and a general air of crowding everywhere.

I had been in England just long enough to perceive that most British conversation was all form and no content, a kind of boneless thing, a sort of ping-pong game played without balls. There were no awkward gaps; it ran on and on, pegged to the flimsiest topics—the scenery, the weather of today and yesterday and tomorrow.

Perhaps to put me at ease but more likely to sound me out, Lord Alfred launched into that kind of talk, with a literary flavor. Hemingway was a prurient cad, and Dos Passos a proletarian, probably a Communist (like all left-wingers). Americans do not get enough exercise, and skyscrapers are too too utterly dreadful. Marriage is a mockery in America. If there is another war, the only decent thing for America to do will be to come to Britain's aid immediately; we waited too long in the war of 1914–18— and of course, as Rudyard Kipling pointed out (had I read his poem about that, "The Vineyard," the one that began "At the eleventh hour they came"?), America then took all the credit for winning.

On and on . . . I received a detailed account of the ten or eleven lawsuits he had been involved in, the trouble he had had over the money of his inheritance, his youthful passions for horse-racing and gambling, his poetry (how much of it had I read, rilly?)—thank you for saying it, yes, he *was* probably England's greatest living poet. Masefield was a poetaster, a hack who had sold his birthright, who had never written a good line after 1930 when he was made Poet Laureate; George Russell ("A.E.") wrote mystical trash . . . And of course Yeats and the other Irish ones—well, you couldn't really call them British poets, now could you?

The pale blue eyes were never still, nor were his hands, nor his feet—for he was continually crossing and recrossing his ankles or tapping his shoe against a nearby chair-leg.

"I suppose," he said suddenly, "you want to hear all about Oscar Wilde and myself!"

By then I think I had analyzed him enough to know that I must disclaim all interest. "Not necessarily," I said with a rather wan smile. "I've read everything that you have written on the subject, and the work of several others . . ."

"Including, I suppose," he said in a fierce voice, "the vile canards and lies of persons like Robbie Ross and Frank Harris and that unspeakable sod André Gide."

"Well, yes . . ." I said lamely.

"Lies, all lies," he said hoarsely, and rose to pace around the room. Had he lived later, doctors would have called him hyperkinetic. He gestured towards the untidy desk. "I am doing a final book on it," he said. "I think I will call it 'Without Apology.'"

Suddenly he sat down again, the storm having passed. "Shall we have a spot of tea?" he asked.

"That would be nice."

I took milk in my tea, largely because it was there and it helped to disguise the taste of the brew, which I hated. With the tea he served a small plateful of pink cakes, disastrously sweet, with small silver pellets sprinkled on top, possibly silver-plated buckshot to judge from the internal content.

He never stopped talking—a long monologue in which "As a poet I" and "As an artist I" recurred again and again. He seemed not ever to realize the extent to which he revealed his violent prejudices and hates, nor the immaturity of his view of himself. It became obvious before very long that he had never really grown up. He remained psychologically (and in his own eyes perhaps physically) still the radiant and brilliant adolescent beloved by the gods. He was a man of vast essential egotism yet burdened with a well-concealed inferiority, aggressively insistent on his social position, glossing over his repeated failures in business, and furious with Lord Beaverbrook ("essentially a commoner, donchaknow") for turning down the publication of his poems in the *Evening Standard*, grudge-holding for real and fancied slights, damning White's Club for closing its doors to him . . .

As for homosexual leanings and entanglements—that had all been given up when he became a Catholic—oh yes. He still got hundreds of letters from curiosity seekers and homosexuals and he could have his pick of any of them (my ears and armpits flamed), but that was all finished. Sins of the flesh were obnoxious and uninteresting. I did not know at the time of his liaison with "D.E."—a young person with whom he was infatuated after his wife left him—and all this after he had become a Catholic! These initials were those used by André Gide in telling me, later that summer in Paris, that Lord Alfred had become enamored of "une personne" (feminine gender, but referring in French to either a male or a female) and had been to bed with him/her. There were actually two recorded liaisons: the first with an American girl in 1913 who with jewels and money offered to help Lord Alfred in one of his many litigations, and with whom in his *Autobiography* he admits to "a loss of innocence." The second was a male, a young man sent down from Oxford for low grades, who always introduced himself as the reincarnation of Dorian Gray; and whose camping and good looks and "butterfly devotion" delighted Lord Alfred for over a year in 1925. It was to this young man that Lord Alfred addressed a poem: "To —— With an Ivory Hand Mirror."

The more he talked, the more I saw the possibility of linking-in with Oscar Wilde fading, along with the afternoon sun. Yet I did not give up. It was inconceivable to me that any man who had spent approximately the first forty years of his life in homosexual activity could have lost those leanings completely on joining the Catholic church. I knew from my own experience. It still seemed to me, as we said in the midwest: "Once one, always one."

And then, since this was still in my drinking days, a happy thought:

In vino veritas.

"Perhaps you will accompany me," I said, "to a nearby pub so that I may buy a round of drinks for us."

He waved his hand. "Hardly necessary, m'boy," he said. "All we need is here. Scotch? Gin and bitters? Sherry?"

"Gin and bitters, please," I had learned to drink it without ice.

And that did it. Within an hour and a half we were in bed, the Church renounced, conscience vanquished, inhibitions overcome, revulsion conquered, pledges and vows and British laws all forgotten. Head down, my lips where Oscar's had been, I knew that I had won.

After I finished my ministrations and settled back, his hand stole down to clamp itself around me. It began to move gently. Still moving it up and down, shafering me, he spoke: "You really needn't have gone to all that trouble, since this is almost all Oscar and I ever did with each other."

Genuinely astonished, I stammered: "B-b-but . . . the poems, and all . . ."

"We used to get boys for each other," he said. "I could always get the workers he liked, and he could get the intellectual ones I preferred. We kissed a lot, but not much more."

I got to Brighton for the ten o'clock train that night. Lord Alfred never wrote to me again, nor I to him. He died in 1945.

In these days it may be of no great interest to those who have graced and honored my bed since 1937 to know that they are directly linked in with Oscar Wilde. But on the other hand if they have a sense of history, they may welcome the information.

Paul Goodman

Paul Goodman (1911–1972) is impossible to categorize, and that is what he intended. He wrote plays, stories, novels, literary and social criticism, and books on city planning and psychology. With Fritz Perls and Ralph F. Hefferline he wrote *Gestalt Therapy: Excitement and Growth in the Human Personality* (1951) and founded the Gestalt Therapy Institute, where he practiced as a therapist. He was one of the central New York Intellectuals, the name given to thinkers who arose in the forties and fifties.

Goodman faced financial troubles. He was fired from a teaching position at the University of Chicago, where he earned his doctorate, because he had sex with a student; as a result, his teaching career was sporadic, and even places such as Black Mountain College, the famous experimental school that closed its doors in 1957, had difficulty allowing Goodman to join its faculty. *Five Years: Thoughts from a Useless Time*, from which the selection below is taken, is a journal of the period during the fifties when Goodman was faced with supporting his three children and his common-law wife, Sally Goodman. After the publication of *Growing up Absurd* he gained popular success. In 1967 his son Matthew died in a mountain-climbing accident. Goodman never recovered.

Martin Duberman in his study *Black Mountain* quotes someone who described Goodman as "ostentatiously homosexual and ostentatiously heterosexual at the same time." In 1959—a decade before the Stonewall Riots—he wrote "The Politics of Being Queer," an early cry for gay liberation. As a psychologist and a social theorist he was an advocate of sexual freedom.

Five Years is structured in an unusual manner. Although he presented them year by year, Goodman organized his thoughts for the year under headings. As a result, the book is both a narrative (we learn of his daughter's sudden illness from polio in the last entry) and a collection of not quite random thoughts.

Spring and Summer 1956

i. persons, places, things

[...]

: The black fellow I fuck is like a wild Fijian, with his long nigger hair starting out in all directions, his black mahogany thighs, his monumental erection. I suggest that he paint white spirals around his breasts and get a shield and a spear and appear and frighten the Coral Bar. "I'd frighten myself," says he. He seems to regard me as a kind of diabolical White Shadow.

: The chameleon is beautifully the color of the broad leaf he lies on. He is safe. But in the beating down sun, if you look from the underside of the leaf, there is the chameleon sharply drawn in silhouette.

: The big rocks terribly break off from the Palisades and tumble down at us. We line them up to make a wall along the river path to keep people from falling in the water. We make them into rustic tables and benches for picnic lunches. "Leopards break into the sanctuary," said Kafka, "—after a while it becomes part of the ritual."

: To the end of the old pier reaching into the river, where you have to pick your way in order not to fall between the broken planks, come (1) adventurous boys, (2) queers following the boys, (3) hung-over winos to sleep it off undisturbed, (4) persons in distress or elation, often weeping women, seeking calm from the sight of the water or meditating jumping in, (5) old men to sun-bathe, (6) philosophic gentlemen puffing on pipes, (7) fishers of the deep. Such is the State of Nature.

: Sweet and striking in their gaudy silk shirts, two Puerto Rican youths are petting on the corner of 23rd Street, in love, and love it is makes them brave, callous, careless.

: We say, "The mist lifted and the sun appeared." But it is the sun that lifts the veil of the mist to make his own brilliant entrance.

[. . .]

:   The small child, age 7 months, has in her eyes a look of perfected intelligence. It is only that she cannot yet manipulate the environment, for example the path from her hand to her mouth. The Gestalt-forming Attentiveness seems to be fully developed. As Plato says, the soul is like a man in a ship. Or better, as Averroes says, there is one active intellect for all mankind—and there it is.

:   In a religious rite, style of the 6th Century, the slave takes the Sacrament, his chains fall off, and he stands forth free, while his brothers sing the anthem.

ii. psychology

:   If a man becomes quickly and unreasonably angry when he is frustrated, you may suspect that his desire for the thing is shallow; he is forcing himself to seek it against his nature. He's touchy because he has to keep down his own rebellion.

:   The structure of passivity is that in the developing feeling there is an unchanging "objective" element. The structure of activity is that an objective element is destroyed.

:   Pleasantly masturbating, I have two fantasies of how things should be: (1) I am sure that my beloved loves me, she clings to me with trust. I am confronting the enemies who would prevent us, but I am confident and laughing because I have the rights, the strength, the weapons—for example, they can't stop us from just going off to Tuscaloosa. The essential premise seems to be that I am chosen; I do not have sole responsibility for the sex. (2) My enemy is gunning for me. We draw and fire. But the bullets collide in mid-air! This occurrence is so unique and interesting that it becomes the subject of lively discussion between us; and we two, who were hostile, are soon firm buddies as we engage together in this objective activity.—The meaning of homosexual love is that we both have penises and engage in sex.

:   Living to serve and so finding identity. But if they are not let to serve, they bite at you with spite, to hurt you, to get attention, not to be nothing.

[. . .]

:   The patient is sitting in a noble pose, legs crossed, small of the back straight and supporting, head up, freely breathing from the midriff—and then she begins to laugh. At first her laughter is anxious, the relief of tension. But then the laughter deepens and becomes spontaneous. It is the Homeric laughter. "What fools these mortals be!"

:   Laughter is infectious, yawning is even more infectious.

:   There are two states that balk me as a therapist: (1) Jealousy. I empathize completely. I can predict the next sentence and the course of resentment, anger, fear, and grief. I even know how to alleviate suffering by holding oneself more erect and lessening depression (the mind goes blank). But I have no perspective. I do not know how to drain energy from the insanity. It is with the patient as with myself, we are forced to rely on time and chance and flattering rationalizations and resolutions. (2) Blocked blank inability to speak or have a next thought of feeling. Here my bother is just the contrary. I often have to deal with this state and recognize it, but I have no empathy with it, I do not believe it. It leaves me out, and I don't know how to woo him forth. I myself can always think of something—except just when I am balked. I can write something even when I am balked.

iii. language

:   "Now don't be crushed if after all Bob can't take you fishing?" Matty said, "Who, me? I won't be crushed, I'll crush *him*."

[...]

:   I write pretty much as I speak, from the same impulse and with the same syntax and almost the same vocabulary. The difference is in how I feel toward the listener. When there is somebody to respond, I talk; when there is no one and yet I have something I need to say, I write, as if for the blank paper. Thus, the opposite of the usual, my writing tends to be more disconnected than my speaking. I lose the thread, I indulge myself, for there is no audience. I lose the literary audience—and they accordingly neglect me. Also, I write longer paragraphs than I speak, because when I speak I soon see that there's no point to it, no continuing response, and I swallow the ending. (Except when I give my two-bit lectures regardless.)

:   I used to write with the liveliness of my speech, and now that my speech has taken on the dullness of my propositions, I write these notes with the dullness of my speech. I used to undermine statements that had content with an irony that nullified them, and now I am left with pointing out the remarkable lack of difference between six and half a dozen.

:   Gone are the days when the editors didn't edit or cut my prose—which they didn't publish either. Now they not only edit and cut but they insist on my agreeing and revising their revisions. The problem is to reduce 304 lines to 300, and whether "shit" or "crap." Let me hasten to explain to the next happier generation that I wrote "shit" and the editor emended it to "crap." Of course the reason for most of the editing is that the editor, like anybody else, must prove to himself that he is working for his salary. The 4 lines must be pruned for "format." But often the editing of obscenities is not by the editor at all, but by the linotyper who, like anybody else, has his craft ethics.

iv. art

:   At Willy Poster's last night, we generally agreed that there was no more comedy, whether from Hollywood or *The New Yorker*. And that this was because Eisenhower is the supreme object of fun, and since they can't make *this* comedy they can't make any. We used to wait for *Punch*, now we wait for the weekly press-conference. It's Ike's rhythm—one cadence of it and you're rolling in the aisles. It never fails.

[. . .]

:   My wife has said once too often, "Soon you'll carp at this book too." My judgments are *not* bitter and overnice, they are my judgments. I cannot be sent when I am not sent, and I often find myself disappointed after a promising beginning. The author presents a new point of view, but then he is not consistent to it or he does not let it wreak itself come what may. I am tired of making allowances. I am coming to feel in me a certain iron.

:   A work of art is not in any way crippled or dismembered, but covered from head to foot with scars of battle and healed disease, ruddy of face but lined with experience.

[. . .]

:   A tragedy "ends in death specified by the circumstances of the death." So when J. finally wrecked his automobile, as indeed we had all predicted and refused to ride with him, now very clear was the proportion between this and his manner of painting, total immersion, drip, and accident. It was all of a piece, no one is surprised, but one is unprepared even so. And naturally the painting itself now becomes better—not seems better, but proves itself better. It is more fixed in its style and means its style more. When any of us dies, however he dies, his art comes into its own, for it meant all along that each of us was a dead man. Rank calls this abstraction the "imitation of immortality." The work of art is like that Emperor of China who never died because he never lived.

[. . .]

:   Here I am filling a third little notebook of thoughts, always grudgingly and disparagingly—"Are you writing anything?" "No."—as if I would rather be writing something else. Even guiltily, as if because I write this I do not write something else. Yet I know that later, when I am writing something else, these notes will seem very fine to me; even now I sometimes put something down in my notebook eagerly. I know, I know that what comes to me to write is given me in its time. I really do have this confidence and therefore am able to write — it is just this that is lacking to the lads who can't write. So rather than saying that I am only writing down little thoughts, let me say that just this year the creator spirit wills me to write down little thoughts. And there, I smile at it instead of frowning. If this is an illusion, at least it is a comforting illusion.

:   The little prayer "I do not much collaborate" was a masturbation fantasy. Now who else has such a masturbation fantasy? And who else, having this poem, remembers and calls it a masturbation fantasy? The same person, and it is I. And this is my poetic mission, "Among the Americans, to say how a thing is."

v. method

:   What is needed is a gentler curiosity.

[. . .]

:   The Hollywood movies are essentially imitations of vast, ambiguous, quasi-conscious consensual psychosexual types and life-attitudes. Parker Tyler sees this clearly, and that it is the role of the critic to name them. It is pointless to look at these films as works of art, and it seems idle to treat them sociologically rather than finding the sociology on the streets. They are psychological actions. Producers subsequently doctor the films into inconsistent and threadbare works of art; for such "secondary elaboration," as Freud called it, is necessary to make them tolerable. But what if we did not dilute them, but rather intensified and expanded the symbols in their purity? The audience would scream and panic.

:   A difference between dream and waking is that the waking world is "real," it has a feeling of possible public validation. It is not that we feel dream as fantasy, we do not. Rather, it is peculiarly conscious, phenomenally complete, not theorized or theorizable. Waking is real just in that it presents the possibility of being doubted, of its reality being questioned. Dream is not questioned, though often, dreaming, I feel that the whole thing can be turned off. But this is *not* done by pinching myself, by questioning this part or that part, but precisely by waking.

[. . .]

:   I get a vague signal to shit; I have the theory that it's good to perform animal functions without delaying; I go and shit; and *then* I get a belly-ache. It's the same with everything I do: I cruise for sex because of a vague dissatisfaction and a strong ideal ("sex is grand"); if I find anybody, I get a hard on; then, when the bout is all over and gone, I lust. Now no doubt this is neurotic, a defense against dangerous excitement, operating by safe controllable thoughts, which are also domesticated as "justified." Yet instead of just brushing my character off in this way, let me regard it as a viable psychological type, in the manner of Jung. Different characters have different styles of first contact, whether thought, conation, or feeling. What matters is that the experience is total in the end. Next, let me try to notice in which situations I begin one way and in which another. What are the structures of the various sequences?

: Freddie, the substitute bartender, is reading the story about the Parris Island marine base, and I am watching Freddie reading it, the saccadic motions of his eyes, etc., also keeping in mind his responses to the story. I am closer to the reality, the man taking in the words. I do not suffer from literary identification, a kind of fetishism. Yet still closer to the reality is the actual interpersonal situation, my lust for Freddie, Freddie's vague and avoiding behavior toward me. But *this* reality one must not observe, though one may notice it; but accept, act, risk identifying with its unknown future.

vi. society

: "What military historian," asks Marc Bloch, "would dream of ranking among the causes of a victory that gravitation which accounts for the trajectory of the shells?" Ah, the great one! the great one! the Zen master. If we took the fundamentals into account, there would also be different events to narrate.

: I am merrily fanning a wet fire at D's, smoking up the house. She pushes me aside, unmakes my fire, starts afresh, and makes a blaze. I am offended and angry, especially since my fire was getting along fine according to my standards. She imagines I have the opinion that women shouldn't make fires, the "romantic" work, but should stick to patient drudgery—as if women didn't always do the cooking and make the fires. Obviously this is *her* problem. But what I despair of making clear to her is that we sport with the fire, we piss on the fire, it is not man's work but child's ritual. Her home is blest with many things but it has the wrong kind of fire.

: "Natives" "Denizens" "Aborigines." Aborigines are savage and have wild matted hair, whereas Natives tend to be Barbaric with elaborate hair-do's that belong to the adolescent culture of decorating one's own body. But Denizens live in remote bogs and secret forests; they infest areas where something higher has established itself, either like rats who were always wild, or they are Degenerates who have retreated from a higher civilization, e.g. the Irish. One can be also, in a picture in the *Herald-Tribune*, a Denizen of the Bowery. On the positive side, Aborigines have mysterious Chthonic

Powers; and Natives have Rights to be Respected, they must no longer be extermi-
nated but kept in museums or reservations so that no aspect of Culture is Vandalized.
But nothing is done for Denizens, who are part of the flora and fauna. Denizens are
just tolerated.

: Reading C. D. Burns' *The First Europe*, I feel I have nothing to do with this European tradition, its concern for the individual soul rather than the outgoing act; in place
of immediacy, a sense of guilt, symbolic proof, vocation, etc. It's quite indifferent to
me; I guess I'm a psychopathic personality. By contrast, I feel like a classical Mediterranean, but of course I'm not that either. What frustrates me is the social problem that
the *others* do not come across, initiate, pay human attention to one another; what delights me is our sharing in achievement. Slavery and compulsion are abhorrent to me,
but no Greek would have caviled about them. Yet I take lightly the individual sense of
privacy, obligation, sexual guilt, so that the Europeans abhor me.??

: Distressing, that these handsome fellows become policemen and probably out of
circulation. But *quis custodiet custodes*? So much by way of a joke—what else is there to
do? But the case seems to be as follows: (a) The police do not much directly impede
my behavior; I have a measure of success under their noses—so they are not intolerable. (b) I shall surely be arrested one of these days, simply by probability, given the
number of occasions—I am fairly prudent, fairly careless. The prospect alarms me but
does not throw me. (c) But my spirit is spoiled by their power, and consequent right,
to molest me. This is largely an ideal consideration and therefore suspect—think of
Negroes and Puerto Ricans who catch police brutality—but there it is and I ought to
fight back. I am guilty that I did not indignantly intervene when I heard that C. was
arrested.

: In the afternoon I was with the beautiful wild boy who plays by the river, sexy,
amiable, and on the loose so that he will come to nothing. But I could happily spend
all my days with him if I dared. I would not be bored in his company—I have plenty
of resources of my own; and I'm not oppressed by not getting anywhere myself or by
my lack of prestige, except when I see how others succeed and I am envious. But in
the evening I was in the great new aeroplane flying West, and I was abashed and made
small by that machine, society with a big S. The corporation handled us psychologically to ally our discomfort, to calm our fears, to preserve each one's self-respect. In
that big operation there is no place for animal or spontaneous disturbance. Why cannot I identify with this wonderful thing? that takes me back to the campus at Tulane
which is our immortality, and whose book-store features comic books of trivial private
caprice. By the river I am myself, but I am afraid, vulnerable to the police and weak
against the hostile hoodlums who patrol there. Finally, at night I was at the conference,

leading a company of my peers who seem to accord me attention and respect, and even (as it turned out) interesting sex. I spoke well, absorbed and spontaneous; a good deal panned out; I downed my misgivings and asked for what I wanted, and somewhat got it. But that was yesterday: what is their reaction now that I am gone? I am again faced with an empty day, yet I have less impulse to throw myself back into the wild and its fears.

:   My social existence is absurd. In God's creation I'm a kind of juvenile delinquent, a little Manfred. But I move in society so devoid of ordinary reality that I am continually stopping to teach good sense, to give support, to help out, as a young gangster might help an old lady across the street on his way to the stick-up. So I cut quite a respectable figure, though on the pious and boring side. All this does nothing for me except to confuse me and use up my time. When the Devil quotes Scriptures, it's not, really, to deceive, but simply that the masses are so ignorant of theology that somebody has to teach them the elementary texts before he can seduce them. When long ago I threw in my lot with Cain and Ishmael because they were able to get to talk to God, I little realized that I was dooming myself to become a pillar of humane culture.

vii. God

:   Men don't act until the case is desperate, until there are no other alternatives and we feel desperate and those who have set their minds on inadequate alternatives are running around like chickens without their heads. Our action is compelled and this is a pity, for then it does not have the grace of free choice and divine superfluity, calm, clear, unhurried, and decorative. Nevertheless, action out of desperation has its own style, simple and close to brute nature. The gaunt and fumbling style of acting out of desperation saves man from his baroque pretensions, from missing the point altogether.

:   Some intelligent Jews nowadays, e.g. the Zionists up at *Midstream*, lay all their stress on survival, having survived. The Jews are those who have survived, and modern Zionism is not a return to sacramental glory but the engine of survival. *Is* this the way to survive? It seems to me that one in fact survives by having an idea which—surprisingly, but one was not thinking about survival—outlasts the roundabout forces of destruction; it proves to be a stronger way of organizing energy. To work at survival as such is like trying to be happy as such. Not that the "idea" is to be taken at face value, nor that survival isn't more important evidence. But to use survival pragmatically is bound to make it boring and we'll destroy ourselves just for spite. To boast of surviving tempts Nemesis, our deeper impulse.

[. . .]

: Here's a poem I hope to write, before I am robbed of it by disappointment: "Thee God we praise! I have had a stroke of luck, with all the earmarks of surprise, unlikelihood, and utility for my further activity. And not undeserved. The result has been to animate me and make me resolve to do a job, within my powers, classic in proportion and rich with baroque decoration." P.S., the premise did not pan out.

[. . .]

: Somehow I must do two things apparently incompatible. First, simply disregard evil, folly, prejudice, timidity, lethargy, and cheerfully assume that you aim at the sensible and happy-making. When I do this, I rouse your disbelief and contempt of me, then your irritation, but finally I get you to laugh at yourself. I *know* that this is right behavior. I have always done it when at my best. The defect of it, however, is that it is too thin in content. I must take more seriously your world as it is for you (and richly for me). I must *not* glibly bypass it, as I tend to. Yet I must meet it with neither frontal assault nor with acquiescence. God is in the world, including you, not in my intuitions, even the soundest.

[. . .]

: Giving up my planless and fruitless search for company, I go far off on the empty beach. And what if I were Robinson Crusoe? I would collect kinds of insects and shellfish, whatever has a will of its own. Everything—the waves, the sun—has a rudimentary will of its own. Soon the nature of things becomes a Thou for me. There is a return of the forgotten and the landscape is peopled with its gods. This company of the chosen solitude, or resigned solitude—it comes to the same thing—is what I really want, but I am so impatient.

[. . .]

: June 30, 1956: I swear, by this wild-rose bush in the bank of honeysuckle, and the visiting bee, to maintain the peace with my only world.

viii. myself

: If I breathe softly and let my underlying face reappear, it is the child crying himself to sleep. There is no complaint or demand, that's all over. Then I yawn, and at the yawn I spontaneously smile, because it's interesting how the reflex carries itself out: yawning after relaxation. So I guess I'm cut out for a philosopher. I have the two philosophic faces of final woe (Heraclitus) and merry curiosity (Democritus). I pass lightly enough from one to the other, without desire or effort. Indeed, I am *not* much in touch with the desires and disappointments that I gripe about so bitterly. And I must get *some* satisfaction from my philosophic faces, or I wouldn't have camped there so long ago. I write from these faces: my writing is sad and it is alert. It is authentic writing, though it changes nothing for me. My griping is not authentic, and it also changes nothing.

:   When I lay about me in my rages off the top of my head, then beware first those who by neglect have done me a small wrong that I can cunningly latch onto and make a symbol of the world's neglect. But treated still worse are those who like me and do me small services, for they must bear the brunt of my accusation that their efforts are worthless. I render them speechless by my implacable reasons. Yet I really don't mean to make them feel bad. I am waspish. I mean, "Don't bother me, for instance by existing." Wasps don't attack, they just sting you if you bother them—I like wasps—but it's hard to know what bothers a wasp.

:   Since I do not remember (in the fiction that I accept as my biography) a moment of confidence, of feeling that the world had great possibilities, of ambition toward an unquestioned goal, I never suffer from feeling bogged down, having lost impetus. And since I never experienced a love that was "pure, clean, gave me a good feeling," the way some people speak, I do not feel that I am no longer innocent. Paradise is lost, but *I* didn't lose it. Similarly, if I had ever wanted "to be a writer," as the kids say, I should probably suffer at how I miss the mark, at how little I do the right work that suits my genius. But since I just got half-ass involved in writing one piece after another, and so became a writer, I have often enjoyed a complacent satisfaction at how bully my writing is.

:   I see an attractive fellow far off, but as I approach along the beach I see he's with his wife, to my no small frustration. She smiles at me, and I, pursuing my New Policy of immediate impulse, of saying it out and having it out—a policy to which I was driven after I finally caught my death of boredom—I say, "Stop grinning at me. I don't lose any love on *you*. Why don't you fly a kite and lose yourself, so him and me can be men together and end up sucking off?" But he, the booby, feels that he has to protect her, and I—my immediate impulse now having changed into self-defense—hardly get off unscathed. What could I have seen in such a stupid, hen-pecked type—as it turned out?

:   I have hunted the wharves from 23rd St. to 38th St. so often that they take me as belonging there, on the job, either going about my business or having a break for lunch. This is an advantage. It makes me less strange. (But the truth is that I come from about 2 blocks further away and work at a different job!) Now curiously, even when I am elsewhere I am taken as if I came from the wharves: "Are you a seaman? Do you have a truck? work on the railroad?" Do I? am I? I have succeeded in making myself more Catholic than the Pope.

:   "You look younger than when I saw you 6 years ago." Ach, that looking younger began about 4 years ago, so now I'm growing older in that being younger, and it shows.

[...]

:   It's admirable and touching how Sally and I always carry out the mission, often a hard journey over hundreds of miles, and we drive old cars. But we suffer no mishap, we are on schedule, nothing has been left behind, we deliver safe and sound. Meantime each journey has less satisfaction and less importance for us, and we are increasingly distant from each other. Then one time it is likely that we shall *not* accomplish the mission—not arrive on schedule—something left behind—delivered *not* safe and sound. And this without any change or crisis, but just as might be expected.

:   My eyes are glazed over—something must surely crack. My daughter is very ill and it drags on. I don't know what to fear or even hope for. I go to the hospital afraid to ask. Being with her, I feel a warm affection, even simplicity, and it's not boring to spend the whole day there. But it wears me out. I know nothing about it medically and I cannot intervene, but I know that what they are doing is not good enough, is not the best that could be done. On the train there is a sexy and inviting fellow, and again my feelings are eagerly warm and simple, but I am on the way to the hospital. I remember my old guilty theory that my pleasure will bring on disaster to somebody else, yet I *know* that animal vitality creates health. Everywhere I feel disapproved—by the nurses; tonight by Dr. Northup, for my quick remarks about the ineptitude of these hospitals. My bluff manner annoys people, but I can't help it. Here, here we see the result of my good head and full heart long disused and out of touch. I no longer know anything with confidence, and I know very little; and what I do know and perceive better than anybody often contains a proposition that may be disastrously wrong. This throws me utterly. The few things I know surely and simply I cannot effectually present and execute, because of all the garbage in my head and all the garbage in other people's heads. I am anxious that the car will wreck. I am superstitiously anxious about finishing this notebook on this note, for it is the last page.

Tobias Schneebaum

Born on the Lower East Side of New York and raised in Brooklyn in an Orthodox Jewish family, Tobias Schneebaum (1922–2005) became a world traveler, visiting places Westerners had rarely or never seen and living with the indigenous people to escape the restrictions of Western culture, to which he was nevertheless indebted.

An artist by training, he won a Fulbright grant to paint in Peru. At the end of his stay he went to the extreme eastern Amazon edge of the country, where, after staying with missionaries, he ventured into the jungle alone, hoping to meet the elusive and savage Amarakaire tribe. Since no one had survived an encounter with the Amarakaire, he was presumed dead when he did not reemerge immediately. His reappearance some months later was reported in the *New York Times*. His account was the subject of his first and best-known book, *Keep the River on Your Right* (1969). In his late seventies Schneebaum returned to the Amarakaire, who now live on reservations, to make a documentary, also titled *Keep the River on Your Right* (2000). Most of his writing, however, like the essay below, is about the Asmat people, who live along the swampy southern coast of New Guinea.

Although he did not consider himself a writer, Schneebaum went on to publish *Wild Man* (1979), *Where the Spirits Dwell: An Odyssey in the Jungle of New Guinea* (1988), and *Secret Places: My Life in New York and New Guinea* (2000). The passage below is from his last book, and it concerns the continual conflict between missionaries, who wanted to change the practices of indigenous people, and Schneebaum, who wanted to become a part of every community he visited.

The Priest and the Pagans

FATHER TOON VAN DE WOUW was flushed with anger when he talked to Father Mannheim about me and my book *Wild Man*. He was getting angrier and angrier, building himself up toward the edge of madness. He seemed to be enjoying his own wrath. His body shook; perspiration poured from his forehead, some of it gathering in droplets at his upper lip. Patches of dampness blackened further his black cassock at the armpits. His trembling hands held out my book: "Here! Here! Take it! Read it! You will soon enough see what I am talking about. It is rotten, and I won't have anyone like that here.

"Had I known about him, I would not have allowed him to stay with me or anywhere in my parish. No, sir! I won't have it, and God won't have it, believe me!"

I had not been present at this scene, so this talk comes second-hand. Father Mannheim described it to me vividly, and I have heard him repeat the story more than once.

Father Mannheim took the book, flipped through its pages, and said, "I want to read it very much, now that you have told me what it is about. And I will be pleased to pass it on to all the others." There was a list of a dozen or so missionaries, Dutch and American alike, waiting to read it.

"You watch out, Father," said van de Wouw. "He is going to corrupt everyone. All the boys and all the men! I know his type, and I don't want him here. I don't want that kind of evil in my villages. There is no such thing as sex of any kind between men here, and he is not going to start it!

"Just remember," he went on, "that I stamped all that out when I was with the Marind-Anim twenty years ago. Do you know what they were doing? Have you any idea how they were defiling themselves? Do you know what abominations they were committing? They were using sperm. Yes, sperm. They were using it on everything, rubbing that filth on bows and arrows and spears, saying that it made their spears go straight into the hearts of the enemy.

"I could vomit just thinking about it. They mixed it with their own blood and with lime to make glue. They used the glue to seal the lizard skins onto the top of their drums. Ugh!

"That was nothing, of course, compared to what went on between the men and the boys. That was when they were still initiating nine-year-old boys into sodomy. Apprenticing them to their uncles, learning about sodomy and warfare and how to plant their gardens. And then, then, the friends and in-laws of the uncles also sodomized the boys, one after another, six or seven of them in the men's house. Maybe more. Who knows?

"They told me that the sperm was necessary to the health of the boys, to make them grow into great warriors. Without the sperm inside their bodies, they would not approach manhood, they would never become powerful warriors. It is the work of the Devil. And I stopped it completely. It took a while, but I assure you that it is all gone."

Father Mannheim waited while Father van de Wouw gathered himself together for further revelations. "Here in Asmat," he went on, "they used to have wife exchange— *papisj*, they call it. Of course, they had an excuse, claiming that the flow of semen was necessary to keep the cosmos in balance. I quickly put a stop to that, too. All it really was, was another excuse for an orgy. They know it is against God, just as they know that sex between men is against God."

Father van de Wouw, unlike the other Caucasian missionaries in Asmat, was not a Crosier. He was a missionary of the Sacred Heart and was rather inclined to look down on other Roman Catholic orders. He was a relatively narrow-minded man on this subject and was insistent that only missionaries of his own order had the direct line to God. He was slender and handsome, his body taut, reflexes sharp and alert. He had a long hooked nose that might have been deemed Semitic had his lips been more than a tight thin line. "No!" he insisted. "There never was any homosexuality in Asmat, and it is going to stay that way, believe me."

Father Mannheim had related the conversation to me soon after he learned that I would be traveling with Father van de Wouw to Ladakh, in India. He wanted to make sure that I knew what I was getting into, that I would be with a man who despised me and who despised all homosexuals.

I never hid my sexual proclivities during conversations with the missionaries. I did, however, restrain myself when it came to personal relationships with Asmat men. I liked to spend time in van de Wouw's villages because they were in an area rarely visited by outsiders at that time.

During my early days in Asmat, I stayed with Father van de Wouw three or four times and learned a great deal from him. His knowledge of the people, although limited in some ways, was remarkable. There was much about him, in fact, that was admirable, including his knowledge of the Asmat language. I was discreet in my behavior, not for my own sake but for that of the people themselves. Even matters of a nonsexual nature sometimes were difficult to discuss with him.

One day, an elaborate memorial celebration in honor of recently dead relatives was taking place in the village of Japtambor, close to van de Wouw's home in Basim. Both of us were invited to attend. Although the feast itself had begun several months earlier, the final formalities were to begin the following day. The feast was an exhausting and exhilarating time, an occasion into which we both entered enthusiastically—in the singing, the dancing, and the eating—with almost the same excitement as the villagers themselves.

On the morning after the celebration, church services were held in the roughly built schoolhouse that doubled as a church. No one in the village had yet been baptized, so the service was short, with no Mass being said. Almost immediately after van de Wouw began, he announced that the adults could leave, but the children were to remain for instruction in catechism. I went to the men's house to continue my questions about the carvings and the ritual works that had been made for this particular ceremony. Some minutes passed before I became aware that a group of fourteen men was standing around me. Suddenly, they were lifting me horizontally and grunting in unison, "Uh! Uh! Uh!" They carried me to one end of the structure, turned and carried me to the other end, and then carried me back to the center, where they stopped, still grunting "Uh! Uh! Uh!" I was still being held horizontally.

The men's house was full. The grunting continued while the man at my right shoulder bent down as though to kiss me, but moved instead to suck my nose. He sucked my chin, and then sucked my earlobes. He sucked my fingers one by one, sucked my nipples, opened my shorts, sucked my penis, and finally sucked each of my ten toes.

When the first man had passed my nipples, the man next to him bent and began sucking my nose, then my chin and earlobes, making the same rounds as the man before him. The third bent and then the fourth, and in this way, each of the fourteen men sucked all the extensions of my body. It thrilled me, and I was as though in a dream, floating as the men carried me, my ears and head filled with the sounds that reverberated through my body. The men took up my penis and sucked it, and I was thinking to myself, Why am I not erect? It was all without reality, without sensuality, mysterious, otherworldly. No one seemed to expect me to have an erection, nor did the men handle me in a way that might have aroused me. When they put me down, there was a great hullabaloo of shouts. I did not know the meaning of the ceremony, but it obviously had to do with adoption into the village.

Then, no sooner was I breathing normally when I heard sounds coming from outside the men's house. I heard "Uh! Uh! Uh!" I looked out. Father van de Wouw was being carried from the church to the men's house for the same ritual sucking. The number of men around him made it impossible for me to see what was going on, but from the bobbing heads, it had to be that the men were sucking his nose, his chin, and his fingers. Then it was obvious from his shouts that he would not allow them to lift his cassock. "Stop! Stop!" he yelled. "Put me down! Put me down!" Later he said to me that these practices were barbaric, and he would put an end to them.

Still later, I learned that the ceremony was performed primarily for the men to absorb my strength by ingesting the fluids of my body, part of a ritual adoption. In this way, I would be a permanent member of Japtambor, my juices already inside the bodies of other men. It excited me no end that some part of myself, if nothing more than sweat, would be spreading within the fourteen men who had absorbed my secretions. In the same way, the men ate the flesh of their enemies, taking into themselves additional power and fierceness.

The men did not neglect me during those hours of rituals when van de Wouw slept peacefully in the teacher's house. The men's house, by then, reeked of armpits, and I breathed in the air as though it were sweet and fresh. They took my hands and rubbed them on their chests, and then they rubbed them on my own chest so that I took on their sweat, the essence of their strength.

I felt completely at home in Japtambor and did not hesitate to recommend the village to a German filmmaker by the name of Friederich who came into the area. The year probably was 1979. He had had an introduction to the bishop, and the bishop introduced him to me, asking that I take him to a village in the south. Quite naturally, I chose Japtambor for the film's location, since it remained one of the few places where some aspects of traditional life continued. Father van de Wouw also agreed to take part, to make sure that all commentary and scenes were culturally correct.

During the three weeks we were together, Friederich treated me and van de Wouw like servants, even slaves. Later, neither of us would accept money for our respective roles because Friederich seemed interested only in the violent side of Asmat life. However, in lieu of financial payment, he invited us to join him on a five-week journey to Ladakh the following summer, all expenses paid.

In Asmat, Friederich showed himself to be egocentric, with everything revolving only around himself. All thoughts of possible personal problems with him, however, faded when it came to the actual moment of flying to Ladakh. Going there was too exciting a prospect. Both van de Wouw and I expected to be able to cope with his oddities, as well as with each other's. By then, there was an unspoken truce between us.

A chauffeur-driven Mercedes met us individually at the Frankfurt airport, and we spent two full days at Friederich's house. He was wonderfully generous and outfitted us with parkas, boots, and the other usual paraphernalia for trekking in high mountains. A small incident in Frankfurt should have put me on guard. Friederich brought out three small rugs that he had bought in Ladakh some years earlier. "Marvelous!" I said. I looked at them carefully, commenting on the tightness of the weave, the golden colors, and the intricate design. "Did you know," I asked in all innocence, "that all Muslim carpets have a mistake woven into them?"

"What do you mean by that? A mistake in *my* carpet? It is not possible!"

"Oh, yes," I said, wanting to show off my knowledge. "Every carpet has one."

He was upset that I had dared question his eye. I simply wanted to point out that all Muslim carpets have a small fault woven into them on purpose. Only Allah can achieve perfection.

We flew off to Moscow via Aeroflot, probably the most rattletrap airline on earth at that time. Everything on the plane seemed to be loose and shaky.

In Moscow, we changed to an equally unpleasant craft and equally unpleasant stewardesses. We disembarked in New Delhi, switched to Air India, and continued to Kashmir, a marvelous flight. Friederich had bribed all the visible Soviet officials, thus enabling us to board without payment for excess baggage for the camera equipment, the heavy luggage, the tents, the sleeping bags, and a trunk full of boots.

There were seven of us all together, five mountain climbers in their twenties and thirties, plus van de Wouw and myself, both in our mid-fifties at the time. In Srinagar, we were taken to the most luxurious houseboat on Lake Dal, had a splendid lunch, and began preparing for the sights after a brief rest.

It was already four o'clock in the afternoon when Friederich announced that we were going to a factory to look at carpets. We were herded into three horse-drawn carts and were kept at the factory for five hours. "Now," Friederich said, "we are going to the Oberoi Palace Hotel, where I lived for six weeks seven years ago, when I was making a film there. It is one of the great hotels of the world. There is nothing to see in Srinagar."

After coffee, we returned to the houseboat for supper.

"Everyone up at four o'clock tomorrow morning! No more sightseeing here," Friederich yelled at bedtime. "Set your alarms, if you want good seats in the bus!"

Van de Wouw and I, by this time, were treating each other as though we were good friends. The difficulties between us did not surface. We discussed our lack of freedom from Friedrich, but not much more. There seemed no anger on the priest's part.

It was still dark the next morning when we climbed into a bus that clattered and bumped through the eastern Hindu Kush, passing through the lushness of the Vale of Kashmir into the high arid deserts of Ladakh. The road twisted and turned above the Indus, the great river lined with trees and fields of wheat. That evening, we arrived at a small hotel in Kargil and accepted the rooms assigned to us by Friederich. Van de Wouw and I were put together. He was obviously nervous about sleeping in a room with me. He was polite but distant. He never discussed his true thoughts or feelings. The room we shared was cell-like, with two narrow beds and a small, low table. We had had separate rooms on the houseboat. I was nervous and thought I would not sleep, but slept very well.

Van de Wouw said nothing that night. He blew out the oil lamp on the table between the beds and began to undress in the dark. In the morning, I was up first and went out to wash, giving him time to dress alone. The water was fiercely cold.

"Damn!" I said when I came back. "Friederich is getting to be too much. He is out there now opening all the doors and screaming for everyone to get up. I do not know how much longer I can put up with his odd behavior. Aside from the fact that I don't give a damn about climbing mountains. I'm interested in the people and the monasteries and the religion. Climbing mountains is not my thing."

Van de Wouw agreed: "Let us figure a way out."

For two whole days, we stood in the back of a truck, shaking and bouncing, while the vehicle jolted and creaked, cracked and tilted, farted and groaned, climbed to 17,000 feet, twisted itself on twisting, rocky roads, and, finally, arrived at Padam in Zanskar on the second evening, just as it was getting dark. We had spent the previous night on a great plain in icy temperatures, in sleeping bags covered with several blankets. We slept inside a huge tent, while outside winds blew at fifty miles an hour.

We all looked ghostly getting down from the truck, covered with the fine white powder churned up from the roadway, all except Friederich, who had been sitting in the relative comfort of the truck's cab.

By then, van de Wouw and I had decided on our story: we were too old for a walking trip so high in the mountains. Not only were we sick of Friederich, but spending two weeks trekking through snow-covered mountains without seeing people or monasteries seemed wasteful. I had been reading extensively and intensely on Hindu and Buddhist religions since my early teens and felt that looking only at mountains in Tibet would devastate me. I had no interest in proving my strength through climbing rugged peaks, beautiful as they were.

The plan had been to start the trek the following morning. We asked Friederich for five minutes of his time. Van de Wouw began: "Friederich, we have a confession to make, and we are afraid you won't like it. Please be patient with us. We have now been around these mountains four days, and we both find it exhausting. The altitude is too much for us. We are afraid we will hold you up and delay your schedule. We see now that we are too old and should not have come."

"No, no," Friederich said. "No need for apologies. In New Guinea, I thought you both were strong when I saw you walking through the jungle. But now I see how difficult it will be at your time of life. After all, we Germans are a strong people, and we are used to cold climates and the difficulties of climbing mountains." There was a good deal of satisfaction in his voice. Both van de Wouw and I might have had problems on the journey, but neither of us doubted that we could make it.

"We hope you aren't too disappointed," I added. "We can take a truck back to Kargil and make our way slowly to Leh and meet you there."

"Perfect! I will give you the money. It will be an easy trip from Kargil, and if you have trouble, if you get too tired, just stop and rest wherever you are. You will have plenty of time before we get there." Friederich was suddenly solicitous, as though we were decrepit old men, which is what we wanted him to think. There was a spirit of conspiracy between van de Wouw and me.

That night, I read aloud for the first time from *The Asian Journal of Thomas Merton*.

Merton had not been in Ladakh on his last journey in 1968 when he died so tragically through a faulty electrical connection in a hotel in Bangkok. He had studied Buddhism and Tantra and had been at the court of the Dalai Lama for some time, traveling mostly in northern India, where he had written of his fascination with Eastern religions. He saw no reason for Buddhism not to act as an extension of Catholicism, believing that he could take it into his heart without allowing it to affect his Catholic tenets. In the appendix of the journal, a glossary and notes explained in detail a lot of what we were seeing and what we were about to see.

As we moved from village to village, from monastery to monastery, I read aloud more and more often, in buses, in places in which we ate, and in the small and large rooms in which we slept on stone floors. At first, van de Wouw would not listen to anything that might include sexual connotations.

"Pollution," I read, "is the spilling of the seed without union, without fertilization or discipline, without 'return' to the summit of consciousness. A mere spilling out of passion with no realization. 'The end of passion is the cause of sorrow, the precipitation of the [human consciousness]'" (Thomas Merton, *The Asian Journal of Thomas Merton* [New York: New Directions, 1975], 90).

This passage disgusted van de Wouw, even though it is difficult to understand. It seemed to be against physical and mental masturbation. But as we read on, he began listening and questioning everything. We read passages over and over again, both from Merton's pages and from the appendices. Even the word "Buddha" needed an explanation:

> Literally, an awakened or enlightened being, from the Sanskrit root "bodhati"—he awakes and understands. The name usually refers to the historic Buddha; that is, Gautama Siddhartha (563–483 B.C.), born near Kapilavastu in India, a member of the Sakya clan, and hence called also Sakyamuni, the Sakya sage.... It is important to stress that Gautama was only one of many Buddhas who have existed before him and are destined to come after him. (Merton, *Asian Journal*, 370)

Oddly, I was able to explain a great deal that was not in the book through my own knowledge. We talked, too, of Judaism and Christianity.

"But how is it that you, a Jew, should know these things?" he asked.

"What does being a Jew have to do with anything? Or being a Catholic or Muslim for that matter? I told you that I started reading of other religions right after my mother died. Buddhism had always interested me, and I could not imagine myself climbing these mountains and looking only at the landscape, when there is so much else to see and know."

We spent days in monasteries, sometimes with lamas who understood enough English to talk to us in depth. I, for one, believed their stories of reincarnation and listened to the men talking about the *Tibetan Book of the Dead*. It took us both a long time to begin to understand the differences between the Gelugpa (Yellow Hats) and the Nyingmapa (Red Hats), the two sects of Buddhism practiced in Tibet. This was partly because the lamas themselves could not verbalize it properly, and partly because Merton quotes a friend who says, "There is no difference."

It was through our talks, as well as through our reading, that it was possible to see that van de Wouw, for the moment, was opening up, beginning to expand his vision of religion and of life. He, too, seemed to believe in the reincarnation of the lamas who spoke freely to us and in such detail of their past lives. We sat listening to experiences that presumably had taken place hundreds of years ago, and we both fell under the spell of the men recounting tales of former lives. We never questioned the truth of what they were saying. The look on their faces and their manner of speech told us that they could not be lying; they believed and had an aura about them of other centuries. They often seemed enveloped in a halo of spirituality.

Van de Wouw and I shared a room everywhere we went, sometimes sleeping next to each other on carpeted stone floors. He appeared to have lost his fear of me, no longer apprehensive that I might attack him. Since we stayed in monasteries where Tantric Buddhism was practiced, we talked of Tantra, too, and of its ritual use of orgasm as a stop along the way to enlightenment. It seemed miraculous to me that we could speak of such matters openly. In my eyes, the use of sperm for magical purposes, retaining it and thereby using its power, was no different from what had been happening among the people of his parish in Asmat.

After several days of talk, van de Wouw appeared to accept the fact that sexual activity could be necessary to early stages in the training of lamas, that the act itself brought forth a dynamism that gave great strength to the spirit. He said he could understand that the orgasm might even become the ultimate form of spirituality for those deeply involved in Tantra. At least he was able to discuss it, whether or not he understood or felt its sensibility. As lamas go to the higher stages of their spiritual development and the sexual act continues, the orgasm itself is held back. Adepts are brought to the point of climax but no further, so that they might contain its power, for it is this power that leads the adept closer to Nirvana. Van de Wouw agreed that this might be possible, but he could not or would not connect it with the way of life in his own villages. He would not allow me to bring up the subject, insisting that there was no comparison between his wild and savage people and the highly civilized Tibetans.

Shortly before leaving New York for Ladakh, I had been to see a practicing Buddhist. He had lived for two years at the court of the Dalai Lama in Dharamsala, in northwestern India. There were many followers of Tantra in the Dalai Lama's retinue, and it was to that group that my new friend had attached himself. He was homosexual and, when I met him, was completely open about it, although I never would have suspected his orientation through his appearance or gestures or voice or attitudes.

Some months after his training began, he told me, he declared himself to his Superior. "There is nothing wrong with homosexuality or in practicing homosexual acts," the Superior said. "You must remember, however, that such acts should be limited to your first years here. You will learn that everything must be directed toward perfect balance, the *yin* and the *yang* equalizing each other, the male and the female balancing each other. Only through sexual acts between men and women is it possible to go on to the next stage of spirituality. You must pass beyond homosexual relations before you can begin to absorb your own semen into yourself. By retaining your semen, you will eventually transform yourself; you will move, however slowly, along the road toward becoming a bodhisattva, perhaps eventually achieving Nirvana."

To my knowledge, my friend did not reach the point of retaining his orgasms, but he was remarkably self-contained and had an inner peace that enabled him to remain calm, at least on the surface, no matter what the circumstances. I recently learned that he is now living in a remote valley in the Catskills, continuing his prayers and meditation.

Van de Wouw and I talked of the sexual act in impersonal terms, although I suspect that he had never performed any sexual act, including masturbation. However, he must have had wet dreams in his youth. We certainly could not talk of people we knew. He simply closed up when I approached the subject of the people of his parish. It is one thing to discuss sexual matters in an alien land about alien people, but quite another to discuss people we knew personally. He was horrified at the thought of the young men he knew imbibing semen to give them the strength of great warriors.

I wanted to stay on in one of the monasteries, to learn, to become involved. The square faces of the men, with their high, prominent cheekbones and their shaven heads, seemed to glow with purity and strength, and eroticism, too. They chanted, they meditated, they laughed. Their lives, from the outside, looked gracious and elegant and mysterious among the paraphernalia of their ceremonies.

With van de Wouw in such close attendance on me, it was not possible to become more friendly with the monks. I needed to be able to sleep anywhere, to enter into their religious atmosphere with complete freedom.

Van de Wouw was trying, I think, to reevaluate some of his beliefs. Perhaps, given the choice, he might have stayed on for some time longer, studying the religion a bit more in depth. Merton, although a Trappist who had obtained permission from his superiors to break his order's vow of silence, had concentrated on understanding some Eastern beliefs and had remained a deeply religious man, a true Catholic.

By the time we parted, van de Wouw appeared to like and to trust me. He acted as though he had reversed his earlier judgment. I could not be sure of his true thoughts, but after we rejoined Friederich and the others in Leh, I sometimes heard him praise me and my "vast" knowledge of the religions and the way of life in Ladakh. On the flight back to Frankfurt, he said, "You know, Tobias, I have spoken against you many times. I disapproved and still disapprove of your way of life. But I can see now that not all other ways are necessarily wrong. On this journey, I had to accept the fact that your knowledge goes deeper and wider than mine when it comes to religious life, and I admire you for that. And I must admit that I could never have made this trip without you."

Months later, I heard through Father Mannheim that van de Wouw had spoken to some of those in Holland to whom he had complained about me and had told them of his new attitude. He seemed to be another person. Soon after van de Wouw returned to Asmat, however, I heard again from Father Mannheim that he had reverted to his former self, complaining about homosexual acts and condemning the use of semen in any way but for reproduction. It saddened me that he could not keep to his new insights, but had fallen back into the pattern that had molded him as a child, as a postulate, as a young priest. Perhaps he was frightened of his own sexuality. Perhaps he realized that the men of Asmat had been lying to him for years, a fact he could not absorb.

Ned Rorem

Called "the world's best composer of art songs," Ned Rorem (b. 1923) has a distinguished career as a composer of symphonies, concertos, operas, and choral works. He is also the author of fourteen books, including five volumes of diaries and collections of lectures and criticism. Born in Richmond, Indiana, on October 23, 1923, he studied at Northwestern University, the Curtis Institute in Philadelphia, and Juilliard.

In 1949 Rorem moved to France and lived there until 1958. His years as a young composer among the leading figures of the artistic and social milieu of postwar Europe are absorbingly portrayed in *The Paris Diary* and *The New York Diary, 1951–1961*. When *The Paris Diary* first appeared it created a sensation because of its unapologetic account of Rorem's highly active sexual and artistic life among the European elite. Janet Flanner wrote that it was "worldly, intelligent, licentious, highly indiscreet."

In the spring of 1956 Rorem returned to New York for about six months. The excerpt below is his diary from that period. It opens a window not only into New York gay life of the mid-fifties but also into the music culture of the period.

From *The New York Diary*

AGES SINCE I'VE WRITTEN HERE because, as prophesied, New York with its noisy pollution is where, unlike Paris, we look at our feet instead of the sky. No "inner repose" needed for journal writing. I'm not sure this is true. *Is* it repose French diarists possess?

In any case, Americans are not especially concerned about whether they're going to hell when they die, and that's the theme of a French diary. I'm not at all interested in what I now write here after such long months, and cannot imagine adding anything not already said at more urgent minutes. It's not simple to summon sufficient interest for starting again. We all lie anyway at the really fascinating time that makes a difference. When a person has gone to pieces—really to pieces—he is no longer capable of maintaining a document about himself although this is the crucially interesting moment toward which he has been directed, because he's no longer in a position of caring. Not that I've gone interestingly to pieces, *au contraire. La preuve*, I'm writing a diary once more.

America, the new slang: goof—to miss, make a mistake. Flip—to swoon with enthusiasm. America, the new compulsion: male impersonation. In his *mépris* of women a young man refuses to caricature them; he becomes instead a male impersonator by affecting leather and dungarees (male symbols, it seems). He attends S & M meetings (i.e., sado-masochist or slave-master) where truly gory doings are rumored. Yet, when I question Bill Flanagan about the details, the Third Avenue bartender, overhearing, intrudes: "Don't kid yourself—they just hit each other with a lot of wet Kleenex!" Perhaps it's in mimicry of divine James Dean (already immortalized by our Frank O'Hara); still, it's a cause and not an effect: James Dean would not have existed without them.

America, my "success"—otherwise I'd have been a failure. I learned that a composer, whatever his reputation, must be (as opposed to a poet) on the spot. I also touched Talullah Bankhead (thanks to Bobby Lewis) and dined with Dietrich (thanks to Truman Capote). Bernard Charpentier—*de la drogue*. Myself from champagne, that easy way away from tension. Aphrodisiacs used to be put, for children, into candy which is dandy though liquor's quicker. . . . We do not need graphic sexuality in letters.

Nineteenth-century restraint's more troubling than today's one-dimensional violence. . . . Taffy-colored taffeta drag: old-fashioned.

Seven years' absence. Old friends in America are now settled into their mold. I am left out. Conservatism comes with age.

The long lazy heat of childhood summers in the first heavy odor of zinnias, hollyhocks, bumblebees, summer with his hot yellow smile at the summer maid who sniffs the dirty laundry of the boy she loves.

All we need now is one genius, just one. There aren't any more. I'm not as glamorous as my friends think. But more than they think, blind to the rich man who, in his huge and unrequited love, finances the lover of his sweetheart. The French have no word for vicarious.

Embarrassment composing at the piano when Messaoüd was in the house. Messaoüd, our Moroccan servant in Fez, 1949, in every sense a Moslem and centuries away. Embarrassment that he might find the sounds I struck too corny.

Embarrassment as a child at the semi-annual arrival of the decorators who pulled away the bed to expose the lower wall onto which for six months I had smeared deposits of mucus after picking my nose in the morning.

Sober: the awe of death is—is *sharper*. But sorrow is useless.

Drinking, like anti-Semitism, is unintelligent. But must we always be intelligent? Probably.

If through skill in false premises I annihilate a less logical yet more honest adversary, I later cringe with wonder at the pleasure in my wrongness. To be confusedly right (though ephemeral and smug) should be higher satisfaction, should it not? Does my conscience tell me *not* to kill because my wish tells me to kill?

If I've learned one thing in my travels it's that Europeans, Arabs, Negroes are not "just like everyone else" but quite different. That difference should be coveted, not thwarted, for it provides an attraction which could prevent rather than cause wars.

In war the first thing to go is the truth.

People are mostly alike; one hopes for a difference. When a crippled girl entered the restaurant tonight I mused that there at least, by definition, was a difference. But then she brought forth *The Readers' Digest*.

Discontent with work, vaguely but regularly saddened by the gorgeous weather—sentiments not wholly lacking in charm. Meanwhile the weeks slide by like a funeral procession.

Another day. . . .

The superfluous is all that counts—art, screwing, ice cream. As for sleep or taxes, they don't *count*, do they?

Painter friends accuse me of blindness. It is because I'm internally visual. Even my musical memory is visual, not auditory. For instance, if I'm on a subway or somewhere and think of a tune, I inscribe that tune on a mental staff, photograph it, store the negative elsewhere in my brain for development later.

Nor can I "just listen" anymore: whatever enters my mind must be inscribed on psychic paper. Do I *know* music too well now to enjoy it? In any event the layman's hearing is inconceivable to me; my nature always asks what makes beauty beautiful.

And silence? Becomes the sound of our world whirling through space.

A poet may look like a janitor, a janitor like a poet. Art is the only domain that resists generalities.

Why not a popular song extolling New York as the French, with accordions, have so often extolled Paris? Because one can only extol in three-four meter and Americans are too hurried for that. Why *be* in New York? Because it's where you *have* to be: for better or worse it's the center of the universe. Which is why I'll leave soon: I can only feel adjusted off-center.

If I retire forever to write, does not the very act of writing contradict retirement? How can I wish to chastise Man in words or notes unless *au fond* I want his love? Yet the most agreeable sorrow (the pleasures of pain, the pain of pleasure) is in contemplating the Jersey flats on the train to Philly and wondering where that one reed (that one in billions) will be in a year, in a minute, when the train's gone by.

Finally heard Liberace. Extraordinary, his fingerwork! He plays all the right notes wrong.

At loose ends on a Thursday evening, I phone Paul Goodman and invite myself to his group-therapy session. In preparation I wash my hair and don the famous black turtleneck jersey.

Of those eight or ten present, I know only Paul and Sally. . . . Long, very long Quakerlike silence which I finally invade by exclaiming, "Well, since I'm the new one, maybe we could break the ice with someone telling me about the procedure." Silence again, pregnant and sinister. Then Paul speaks. "Ned, the artifice of your social style, your charm, will be your downfall." This drop of blood set the group on me like sharks. At a total loss, I exposed myself to their teeth; mute myself, I was tossed from one stranger's mouth to another; following the leader, they ripped me to ribbons. At which point the session was over. (Charm or not, I *had* been the center of attention!) Then we all had tea and cookies and were filled with fraternal love. No question of a postmortem; only Paul's complaining of always being Father. But he can't have it both ways. As for me, I felt like another Faust: he sells his soul to the devil, then shows his pretty body to Marguerite, who declares, "Oh, I'm sorry, sir, but I prefer older types."

We can sing it and say so, but how can we be truly glad for what we have or are, since we cannot know until we have not or are not anymore, and then we are no longer glad? Glad for what we've gained? But at this moment we have forgotten yesterday: five minutes after weeping, our tears seem silly. Should a cruel king fall to low place, repent and do good deeds and cry loud and love God, once reascended he will again be cruel. I have never been shown that there is a connection or growth from day to day: it is as easy to forget as remember, as logical to be happy as sad. People say, "I would give my kingdom, my riches, my fame, my soul, for youth and beauty." I have beauty and youth, though how can I know their value? I want a soul, fame, riches, a kingdom.

A priceless bird hides hardly fluttering in the cage of all our chests, a bird we are not allowed to see until the moment it decides to leave us and fly away forever. How could we have known it was starving inasmuch as we ignored its existence? So as not to become tiresome to others, I oblige them to fall in love with me.

As I grow I become more and more curious about things, but about people less and less. It's rare that I am not bored by the average person within two minutes and by an intelligent one within two hours (excluding, of course, the physically attractive, who cannot be boring). My only curiosity about fellow humans concerns the waste they make of themselves. Why, I wonder, have even the ugliest been so magnificently constructed: that labyrinth of artery and nerve, more exquisite, fragile, and complex than a beehive's gentle machinery? With what is this mechanism occupied? With sleeping, eating, fornicating, nothing more. Its reason serves solely destruction. Still, it takes nine months of building, more magic and intense than for skyscrapers or ant hills, more patient than for blueprints of pyramids or atom bombs, a muscular waxing, the infinite house of the brain which finally uses about 3 percent of itself. All this emerges, works for years in spite of itself toward a total perfection which will live in the charmed construction incrusting the earth like a transparent jewel. But why, seeing that all this is good for absolutely nothing?

Unimportant that people exhaust their hearts and die at the end of a given time, if only they would ask a question one day in their lives. Yesterday evening I was exposed for hours to the laughter of five ridiculous girls. Never have I been so bored. One can say, let them giggle, it's a stage they're going through. But *I* never went through it; I read and asked questions, not of others but of myself; the others bored and frightened me. One says too: they are only girls and require gentlemen, though gentlemen serve the purpose of their mechanism to even less effect than animals or vegetation.

If in half an hour I can make an indelible impression why, when I go away, must I want to rush back for fear of being forgotten? Three seconds can inspire a lifetime of loathing. . . . If a person dies later than he thinks, only a handful more people will recall him, and already with less mystery. We are immeasurably more curious about Mozart, Lautréamont, Maurice Sachs, than about Richard Strauss, Voltaire, Gide.

How, sometimes, could I not compare myself to some god come down to earth when I look at those about me? Suppose it were true but that the knowledge for some reason were denied me: would this keep me from suffering any the less in a contest for my life? Is the trial of a god like any other when the judges are blind?

Donald Gramm and Mattiwilda Dobbs, each in Town Hall the same week, sang premières and beautifully for me. Also my little opera *A Childhood Miracle* received its television debut in Philadelphia, thanks to Plato Karyanis, Wayne Conner, Dorothy Krebill, Benita Valenti, and a bunch of instrumentalists from Curtis conducted by Donald Johanos, all of whom donated their services. But what else did I get or give in America? Since not a day passes without history, there are those who say it should be recorded or lost. But such is a chronicle, not a diary. And history recorded tonight would not be the same if recorded tomorrow. It is not what you say but what I say you say.

I drank a lot, was sober a lot, saw a thousand intimate friends, made some new ones, lost old ones, parties, parties, accumulated fans and clarified my situation with the music publishing world, was hated and well received, grew up and got younger, refound my marvelous mother and father, had a Thanksgiving, a Christmas, and Easter, and no longer believe in my own immortality.

It is the rainy month of May and next week, after six months, I'm going via London to Marie Laure's in the south of France. I'll be back in the Europe I've missed. If it please God, I'll also be able to miss home.

Is it the memory of New York friends that might make the heart ache? Or will it be rather more difficult to shake the souvenir of sitting in my late-night, early-spring apartment on 23rd, and the window-street sounds of tires on warm-winter New York rain ten stories below?

Edward Field

Edward Field (b. 1924) has lived his entire life in New York, although he has traveled widely through Asia, Europe, North Africa, and the Middle East. He fought in World War II as a navigator in the air force, the subject of the memoir below.

Returning from the war, he attended New York University, which he left to go to Paris. His daringly direct poems have won him the Prix de Rome, the Lamont Prize, and the Shelley Memorial Award. His works include *Stand Up, Friend, with Me* (1963), *Variety Photoplays* (1967), *A Full Heart* (1977), *A Frieze for a Temple of Love* (1998), and, most recently, *After the Fall* (2007).

Field also wrote the narrative to the 1964 Academy Award–winning documentary *To Be Alive* and with Neil Derrick, his partner of over forty years, several novels, including *Village* (1982) and *The Potency Clinic* (1978). In 2006 he published *The Man Who Would Marry Susan Sontag*, a memoir of the artists and writers he has known.

Gay in the Army

AT THE AGE OF EIGHTEEN, during World War II, when I went to the recruitment center to enlist in the Army Air Force, I was easily able to field the fatherly psychiatrist's question "Do you like girls?" Taking in my barely adolescent face and body, he nearly added "Sonny." And in that age of obsession with female virginity, there seemed to be no question of whether I fucked them. I just said yes, I liked them, and that was that, and moved on to the next cubicle to drop my pants for the "short-arm" inspection.

But I'd already had quite a bit of casual sexual experience of the kind any lustful schoolboy might encounter in everyday life—the psychiatrist didn't ask me about that! Hitchhiking adventures where the driver's hand on the gearshift migrated onto my conveniently close knee, and groping in the dark of the rear rows in movie theaters, and mutual masturbation with equally horny school friends. Even more thrilling, at the age of fifteen, on my paper route, I locked eyes with a young dental technician and jazz pianist, getting out of his Ford with a boner. "Ever fool around with fellas?" he asked me. Which led to a thrilling, if necessarily furtive, affair of some months. We drove out to lovers' lanes in the Long Island scrub country and somehow avoided the patrol cars, and the humiliating exposure I already so feared.

Though there was always the danger of blackmail, this was a time when the only recourse to American homosexuals, who couldn't manage to hide behind the facade of a conventional marriage, was to seek anonymity in the cities, work in the arts, or join the bohemian refuge of Greenwich Village. Or better, flee to France where there was even a gay literature—the writings of André Gide, Proust, Cocteau and others. London was also a more tolerant place, in spite of draconian laws that imprisoned many celebrities, from Oscar Wilde to Ivor Novello. But the big discovery in the military, an all-male institution at the time, was that there was a gay world built into it. And, considering the homophobia of the times, I got the first inkling that I might not have to live a criminal life after all, lurking in the shadows of the underworld to follow my perverted, illegal desires.

After finishing clerk-typist training, I was stationed at Tinker Field in Oklahoma, and assigned a job in the command headquarters on the airbase. Evenings and weekends, I was now free to go into Oklahoma City, and when I was checking out the men's room of one of the big movie houses downtown, I met two soldiers who were just hanging around in the lounge. They were show-offs, and when they saw me watching them, they both whipped powder puffs from their regulation shirt pockets and flamboyantly powdered their noses, which, considering that they were in uniform, I found hilarious. It was my introduction to camp, though I still hadn't heard the word.

I had a few casual sexual experiences off base, one with a handsome naval officer who, spotting my interest in him, simply asked me for a date and took me to a hotel. But it was obviously difficult for an enlisted man and an officer, especially from different branches of service, to go around together. I had to salute him in public! Another time, I went to a rooming house with a tough, gruff, hard-muscled Italian-American sergeant, who was nervous that I would spread the word about him, but I didn't know anyone to tell. I also went out drinking at a tavern with a bunch of Regular Army men (as opposed to draftees) from my barracks. Oklahoma allowed only the supposedly non-intoxicating 3.2 beer, but if you drank enough of it it made your head whirl. My buddies were big, friendly country boys from the South, who treated me affectionately like a little brother, teasing me and picking me up a lot in their arms—I looked about fourteen. They said things like, "if you can't get yourself a woman, take my advice, the next best thing is a boy . . . you powder his ass re-e-e-al smooth, etc. . . ." They seemed exotic to a Jew from New York, and I was delighted they accepted me.

One night, a master sergeant joined us from the next booth. A baby-faced youth with a southern accent who smoked cigars, Glenn, I learned, worked in the HQ on the floor below me in the Adjutant General's Office. This was the legal branch of the military. He was only a year or two older, but seemed very much at home in the Army, wearing tailored uniforms like a Regular Army man, and traveling with high brass around the country in Air Force planes. He was unusually bright, and could reel off military legal codes by heart. To become a master sergeant at his age was no small achievement. Glenn, as it turned out, lived in one of the private rooms at the end of my barracks reserved for noncoms, and I began joining the bull sessions in his room, during which he tied trout fishing flies, his favorite hobby. He was from Tennessee, and liked to demonstrate his down-home talent as a non-stop cusser in competition with other southern boys, whose string of obscenities he could always top. "You're such a low shit, you can't even reach up to lick a coon's asshole, etc., etc." "Oh yeah? You're so low you think your outhouse is a skyscraper, and to take a shit you've got to take a running leap up to the crapper, and half the time you fall in. . . ." The idea was to spin it out with endless folksy metaphors. When Glenn outcussed them, they would often stomp away in fury.

I knew he liked me when he gave me one of his trout flies, which I pinned to my shirt. Sometimes we would walk around the base at night, he'd light a big cigar, and in the darkness I'd be moved by the brilliant desert sky to philosophize, which he would tolerate with grown up amusement, though he was only nineteen himself.

We soldiers were transported back and forth between the airbase and Oklahoma City in the backs of personnel carrier trucks, and it was always a dash to catch the last run around 11:30 P.M. One night, on our way back to the base after a double date with a couple of civilian girls we worked with at HQ, so many GIs piled into the truck that I had to sit on Glenn's lap, and in the pitch blackness, hanging on to each other as the vehicle bounced over potholes, his lips nuzzled mine and buddyhood turned into a love affair.

Though I'd had crushes before, this was First Love for me and I boldly went around wearing his school ring, which aroused some curiosity at the headquarters, for the civilian women who worked with us noticed anything like that right off. Pulling his rank, Glenn was able to get me moved out of the open dorm of the barracks into his room at the end, though we had to be careful, since the wall planks of the partitions between the non-com rooms were loosely fitted and left gaps. The first time I was in his room after our nocturnal canoodling in the truck, we were lying together on his bed when he said, "Turn around." My heart sank. I thought he wanted to fuck me, and from some painful hitchhiking experiences I knew I didn't like it. But it quickly became clear he meant sixty-nining. That weekend we got a room in a small hotel he knew, and after experiencing a mutual orgasm, the most complete in my life, before and after, we both fell asleep. He was the only lover I ever had in whose arms I fell asleep after we came, invariably together.

My sergeant was something of a dandy who went to the barbershop of the main hotel in town every week to get "the works," including haircut, shave, manicure, head massage, and mud-pack facial, which he got me to try. Free time in Oklahoma City also included all-you-can-eat watermelon at outdoor tables, and baskets of fried chicken and shoestring potatoes, a specialty in the coffee shops, along with drinking a lot of the 3.2 beer, though sometimes we tipped a porter or bellhop in the hotel to get us a bottle of black market bourbon. There were also movies at the base theater, and I somehow found time to read. In the library I discovered Frederick Prokosch's *The Asiatics*. I had no idea that the author was a poet, but I was moved enough to write a fan letter to him. His novel of spies in wartime Lisbon *The Conspirators* was shortly to be made into a movie that starred Hedy Lamarr with one memorable scene in which, embraced by her Nazi officer lover, she slipped down his body below the screen, unmistakably to give him a blow job. After the war, when I started hearing gossip about poets, I learned that Prokosch was not only gay but a muscle man, one of the first I knew of, in an era when intellectuals didn't have respect for their bodies.

One afternoon, in one of the fly-tying, cussing-contest, bull sessions in his room Glenn grabbed me and, in front of his buddies, twisted my arm behind my back like the tough guys in school had done. I was close to bursting into tears. I couldn't understand it, but I suspect now that he probably had gotten wind of gossip about us, and this show of sadism was a device to prove to his fellow non-coms that nothing was going on between us, he felt nothing for me.

Humiliated, my feelings for him vanished instantly. It was finished between us. But I was unable to tell Glenn I'd lost interest, and went on with the affair, going through the motions—it was a terrible self-betrayal, acting what I no longer felt. My instinctive, if cowardly, way of dealing with it would have been simply to disappear, but the army doesn't allow easy escape. Anxious to get away from a relationship I could no longer tolerate, luckily, across my desk came an announcement that because of a shortage of flight personnel (they "neglected" to say the result of so many of our planes being shot down by the Germans), the air corps was opening up the aviation cadet program to qualified enlisted men. This offered me an out and I instantly applied. Glenn didn't question my sudden rush to transfer, and said he'd visit me wherever I was stationed—I brushed the repugnant thought away. But my main problem of qualifying was making the minimum weight, for I was considerably under it. After failing a few times, I loaded up on malteds and bananas and the sympathetic sergeant in charge let me pass—it was another "sonny boy" scenario. Greatly relieved to be escaping my nightmare affair, in a week I shipped out to an Air Force testing center in San Antonio, Texas.

I've never really recovered from that mysterious and devastating situation with Glenn. Glenn's betrayal, if it was that, and my duplicity in hiding my feelings from him wounded my sexuality irreparably. Nor can I blame it on the army, except that our proximity in the barracks allowed no escape or time for reflection. In my years of psychotherapy later on, no psychiatrist was interested in exploring my sexual problems, since they immediately assumed the "problem" was that I was gay, and set out to correct that. As it turned out though, being complicated is not completely a curse, but in many ways a blessing, one that forced me to examine my life. And the vast sexual experience I've had nevertheless has been tremendously rewarding, even if there's always been something missing, something that I was aware of being missing, that I lost in the collapse of that blissful love affair.

On the giant Air Force base in San Antonio, after batteries of tests, I had a supremely satisfying moment for someone who had been considered a jerk in high school. I ran into one of the star athletes who had to admit he had just washed out, while I informed him that I had passed. For the first time, I was treated with respect!

My fantasy was becoming a fighter pilot, and I could see myself in the cockpit of a P-38 with its twin tails flashing through the skies, and even more vividly, a glamorous, swaggering figure on earth. But my tests were highest in math, and since the Air Force was especially short of navigators, I was put down for navigation training. Again I would end up sitting at a desk, even if this time up in the skies. Just as well, as it turned out, since in the flying lessons we all had to take in the training program, I practically crashed the Piper Cub each time I attempted to land. I would aim it at the ground as you were supposed to do, but could never pull up the nose at the right time to stall out the engine just before the wheels touched the ground, which I found fearfully difficult to judge. Perhaps it was the same lack of coordination that prevented me from hitting a baseball with a bat, the trick that would have transformed me from jerk to one of the popular kids. So with me, the plane simply hit the ground with a fearful jolt and bounced back in the air, while my flight instructor in the cockpit behind would scream at me for risking his life. Again, it was not dissimilar to my father teaching me to drive, and pulling the brake on me when he thought the car was out of control.

Sometimes the lack of sex nearly drove me crazy, but I was still in confusion over my recent romance with Glenn, especially about the sudden turning-off of my feelings for him—the magic of sex was forever tarnished, not that that was what stopped me. It was fear. On one of the overnight train rides between training camps, my group of cadets slept the night in a Pullman car—two were assigned to each lower berth, as per regulations. My bunkmate turned out to be a husky Texan who had been bragging the whole trip about his female conquests, and whose big dick I saw when he took off his clothes. In the middle of the night he started running his hand up and down my body, while I lay rigid, too scared of exposure to respond. It didn't occur to me that he would be in as much jeopardy as me! But fear was by now built into me. Still, I started to suspect that southerners, who seemed to be in the majority in the army, were more relaxed about homosexual practices. And shortly after that, when I was stationed in Shreveport, Louisiana, a civilian hillbilly youth and I got together under a tree by a bayou, shielded from view by the thick Spanish moss hanging from its branches.

I certainly enjoyed being with men from every walk of life. And army life couldn't fail to have a sexual component with all those young men living together. But horny as I was, there wasn't even any privacy to jack off. One morning in the hot Texas summer, sleeping naked on my bunk because of the heat and on the verge of a wet dream, hearing someone say, "It's bigger than he is," I woke up with a jolt to discover a group of men standing around my bed watching as I, naked, my erection throbbing in the air for all to see, writhed in the throes as the wet dream reached its climax. I pulled up the sheet just in time before I came, and the men dispersed grinning.

After getting my commission as second lieutenant, I was stationed in Lincoln, Nebraska, waiting for assignment overseas. My buddy, Dave, another navigator on the base, was a cynical young man who laughed at me for being a devotee of the Hit Parade. He had enlisted out of Cornell University, where he had had a course in modern poetry. By then I had discovered Rupert Brooke, attracted as much by his fabled blond looks as by his verse, but Dave only sneered, and read me poetry by someone he proclaimed the greatest modern poet called T. S. Eliot, but whom I found incomprehensible. I don't think I quite understood yet that poetry was being written by living poets.

I was nuts about Dave—at twenty-one he was already bald, and I found him super-sexy, the first of several bald men in my life. And one night when we went to Omaha, in a taxi he pulled me roughly against him and roughed up my black, curly hair, but then quickly pushed me away, saying, "No, I won't do that to you." Very strange, since that's exactly what I wanted him to do, and more! A few weeks later, when we were both assigned as navigators in the same squadron ferrying a fleet of B-17 bombers overseas, we would meet at each stop on the way across the Atlantic—Bangor, Labrador, Greenland, Iceland—often only to spend the layover playing poker for a penny a point. It was in Northern Ireland, that December of 1945, on an airbase on the shores of Loch Neigh, that, walking through the fog-shrouded countryside one night, we came across a manor house that held a grand restaurant for higher officers, major and over. It was full of brass, all men. Of course, as 2nd Lieutenants we weren't eligible, but nobody objected when we sat down and ordered dinner—I think they couldn't object to two young lieutenants in the throes of a romantic friendship. Afterwards, we walked home by the lake and at one point, Dave stood in the pitch darkness under a tree and waited for me. Silly ass, afraid I was misunderstanding the situation and exposing myself, I couldn't go to him, and the moment passed.

A few days later we were sent to different airbases in England.

It was after I was assigned to Grafton-Underwood, an airbase in the Midlands, that I met my first living poet. At the bar in the officers club, a gnome of a man with a crooked grin and the beaky nose common to old aristocratic families started talking to me from a neighboring barstool. Coman had already published poetry, and had been voted by his class at Columbia University the one most likely to succeed. The irony is that Allen Ginsberg was also in the same class!

Coman, who made no bones about the fact that he was gay, had entrée into the literary world in London, and told me about going, on his passes to London, to the Gargoyle Club, where top writers such as T. S. Eliot, Rosamund Lehmann, Rose Macauley, Stephen Spender, and George Barker belonged, even a group of literary American GIs who had managed to wangle cushy posts in London—Harry Brown, Dunstan Thompson, and others. Though many of his stories seemed to involve quarrels between drunken poets and their wives, I vowed that one day I too would be part of that world.

He introduced me to the poetry of Dylan Thomas with its memorable music: "The force that through the green fuse drives the flower" and "My wine you drink, my bread you snap." Under Coman's influence, I also bought George Barker's *Noctambules* that began, unforgettably, "The gay paraders on the esplanade, the wanderers in time's shade"—there was no doubt what that was about! Coman told me that George Barker claimed to have made love with GIs from every state in the union. Stephen Spender preferred farm boys from Ohio. Among English poets, I got the impression that being married, as they both were, did not preclude any sexual possibility.

But my favorite among Coman's poet friends was the American, Dunstan Thompson, largely forgotten now, but at that time very much in vogue. A brilliant young poet from Harvard, he had already published a remarkable book, most of the poems reflecting his love affairs with soldiers, sailors and airmen, in many of which he used the word "gay" with abandon, perhaps feeling freer because the word was not yet in general circulation. I memorized "This loneliness for you is like a wound, that keeps the soldier in his bed . . . ," and "Waiting for the telephone to ring, watching for a letter in the box. . . ."

After the war, I met Dunstan Thompson in New York. We had a drink at 1-2-3, a somewhat flossy eastside bar with a cocktail pianist. Dunstan was an attenuated creature, with huge, bulging eyes, dome forehead, and no chin, whose long fingers waved expressively in the air—there is a portrait of Keats seated with his legs crossed in the National Portrait Gallery in London that looks very much like I remember Dunstan. Unfortunately, the price of being his friend would have meant going to bed with him, and I didn't want to—I've always gone for butcher types. We never met again. He left for Egypt to write a travel book, and, as I learned later, to join up with his British soldier boyfriend stationed in Cairo. After the war, they settled down together in a remote seaside town in England, where he reverted to his boyhood Catholicism, and turned his back on the worldliness of a poetry career.

After our plane crashed in the North Sea after a bombing run over Berlin, my fifth mission, what was left of my crew was sent to recover for a week in the charming seaside town of Rockport near Liverpool. There, Ray, our tail gunner, a fair, soft-spoken youth with a Boston accent, and I confessed to each other we were gay. When we'd been spotted by a British air-sea rescue boat in our rubber raft bobbing in the treacherous, wintry waters of the North Sea, Ray had been the only member of the crew who had cried openly along with me. Ray and I went into Liverpool together, which was about an hour away, and wandering around, were picked up by a refined English gent, a Leslie Howard–type, who was working for a government ministry that had been transferred out of London during the Blitz. Leslie took us to a symphony concert conducted by Sir Thomas Beecham, and then to dinner in a vast, very posh hotel dining room, where I had what was probably one of the local pigeons, sacrificed to the food shortage, but served on a silver platter and called squab. With Leslie Howard concentrating on me, Ray drifted away, and I ended up sleeping over in Leslie's huge bed in his comfortable lodgings, where I got an inkling of the style the upper class British enjoyed, especially when his landlady came in with tea on a tray for us in the morning—I could tell I was one of a series of "gentlemen guests," since the landlady didn't turn a hair. This too smelled of class privilege. For me, the experience was more sociological than sexual.

Back on duty, I resumed going on long, sometimes hair-raising bombing missions over German cities, four more times to Berlin, Hamburg, the Ruhr industrial cities, Munich, flying in a series of B-17s that kept getting shot up. We flew three days in a row, and then had a day's rest. Off-hours, I was beginning to find out more about gay life on the airbase around me, since we gay servicemen spotted each other in the PX and started talking. There was a whole network of gay GIs, I learned. The chaplain's assistant was invariably gay, I was told, and the one to go to on any new airbase to connect with the gay underground. Special Services, which included the base newspaper, the PX, and assorted recreational activities like the drama group and chorus, was full of openly gay men. I heard stories of sexual encounters with ordinary soldiers too, such as a ground officer running into one of his humpy aircraft mechanics on the train to London, and ending up in a hotel bed with him. "And he was wearing jockey shorts!" Even if it was a wish-fulfillment fantasy, sex felt very casual, and possible in all directions.

But the only sex I directly observed on the airbase itself was heterosexual, and in our barracks. Both officers and enlisted men were housed in rows of separate but identical long wooden sheds with double-decker bunk beds, and separate shower rooms between every other building. Every Friday night a dance was held on the base, and busloads of local women were brought in from town for it. Besides the men, who were scarce for English girls during the war, another attraction for the women must also have been the buffet, which was a feast by English wartime standards. After the dance, before the buses left, the couples ended up fucking in the darkened barracks, and it seems strange now that, though I always went to the dances, no one ever questioned that I didn't participate. I would lie in my bunk, as the beds creaked around me—once again, my fellow officers may have thought I was too young and innocent to participate. Or they sensed I was gay and were tolerant.

I must confess that I sometimes hung out in the shower room just to catch a glimpse of a man with the heroic proportions and thick features of one of Leni Riefenstahl's glistening Nubian wrestlers, though he was white, of course—there were no black servicemen on my airbase, or in the towns around it. The white Nubian never noticed me, or perhaps was used to all men looking at him. I managed to catch him in the showers frequently. Oddly, I never saw him in uniform.

In London on my first three-day pass, I was directed by friends to the White Room, a gay drinking club off Shaftsbury Avenue, the theater district, which was full of American and British soldiers. As a result I didn't see much of London, except going to and from the club—the whores lurking under the arcades of Piccadilly Circus and the grimy theater facades with their colorful posters. I only heard after the war from another veteran that nearby Hyde Park, pitch dark in the blackout, was a seething mass of bodies—he was straight, but confessed he didn't know whether he was being blown by a man or a woman! In the White Room, for the first time I started hearing gossip, true or not I had no way of knowing, about various English aristocrats who meant nothing to me then, among them Prince Philip, the future Prince Consort. He seems to have followed a similar pattern to many Brits, who, like the novelist Evelyn Waugh, "graduate" to straight life after a gay youth spent in Public Schools and at Oxford or Cambridge. Or they are openly gay on their ships at sea. I was told that nobody could graduate Sandhurst, the West Point of Britain, without putting out for the higher officers. And stories of British barracks where the soldiers and sailors held orgies every night. And country life where all the farm boys were available to the gentry. Of prominent homosexuals, I heard that Klaus Mann, the son of Thomas Mann, who later committed suicide, was in an American intelligence unit with the armies invading Sicily. I was told that he was the only one in his barracks to wear silk underwear instead of government issue. All this, whether exaggerated or not, was heady stuff to my innocent ears, and I suppose it's true that wartime liberates you from convention.

The only time I went home with anyone from the White Room was with a handsome, fair-haired British officer with a handlebar mustache like in the movies, who had an apartment. I don't know what I expected, but when he stripped in a matter-of-fact way, he was wearing regulation wool long johns that gaped open to reveal a huge tool like a horse cock, that unaccountably repelled me, and, to his astonishment, I grabbed my coat and escaped.

I learned about the theater as a gay activity, and started going to plays in the West End, where many in the audience seemed to be gay. A waspish civilian who played the piano at the White Room told me that he and some friends took Oscar Wilde's lover Lord Alfred Douglas, ancient by then, to see a play about Oscar Wilde's trial. "I was much more beautiful," the shrunken gnome kept croaking, whenever the actor playing him appeared on stage. "I was much more beautiful." I myself went to a musical with Ivor Novello—"We'll gather lilacs in the spring again . . ."—without knowing the famous matinee idol had just been in prison for cruising, and when he came on stage after his release the whole audience stood and applauded him.

Another Brit at the White Room quoted to me an early, never published, Stephen Spender poem written for him. I was so taken with it, I still remember some of its lines: *"You and I were playing, when suddenly I grew serious and wanted more than play with you. . . . But blinded by my will, it took me time to find, that you were playing still."*

After VE Day, my bomber wing was transferred to the south of France to fly troops to Casablanca on their first leg of the voyage home, but after the first trip, I was called in to headquarters and re-assigned to a courier run to London. This meant I could get back to the White Room from time to time. I have no evidence that the officer who chose me for this cushy job spotted me as gay, but looking back, I wonder about it. Instead of the lumbering B-17s turned into troop carriers, I was now sitting awkwardly with my maps on my knees in the cramped nose of our newest attack-bomber, a speedy two-engine plane that for our courier run had been stripped of its armor plating. Our pilot amused himself by skimming over the treetops, only pulling up sharply to avoid power lines and bridges. We were all slightly hopped up the after the combat experience.

It continually amazes me that I never walked around just looking at London or visited any of the famous museums or monuments, and I have no memory of the bomb damage in the wartime city except for soot-blackened buildings. But I think I was like most GIs in this regard, heading for bars and other entertainments.

Once, we had to fly a general to Frankfurt, and from the airfield the crew drove in a jeep through streets walled in by mountains of rubble from the bombed-out buildings. Relaxing that night in the officers' nightclub, we shared a table with a group of officers stationed in Frankfurt, who invited us back to one of the luxury apartments they were billeted in. This was actually my first gay party, and turned out to be typical, where one of the men played Broadway show tunes on the piano all evening, and afterwards everybody paired off and disappeared into the bedrooms. Though this seemed strange to me, I went along with it and, though I'd barely noticed him, ended up with a Colonel, a kindly, fatherly man—it was a friendly fuck. One straight member of our group, a family man, spent the night by himself on the sofa, appearing to accept our less-conventional sleeping arrangements as the usual thing. Even our dashing pilot went off with one of the drunker officers, a southern boy, and in the morning embarrassedly showed up at breakfast, denying anything had happened. But this made me wonder if he too had been chosen for the job by the same gay top brass that had picked me out.

My courier run allowed me other duties, and I also worked as navigator on planes flying our now-idle GIs on passes to recreational spots like Rome and Paris. Coman was on one of my flights to Rome, and did his damnedest to get me into bed in his hotel room on the Via Veneto, where we were quartered. A more cultured man than me, he went to Keats' grave and plucked a leaf from it to place in the Collected Poems. I dutifully took the GI sight-seeing tour of Rome and its churches and museums. At night, a stroll by the Tiber got me nothing but an aching boner.

I didn't actually get into bed with anyone until an overnight stop in Paris. The officers' club and dining room were on the Champs Elysées, where the truck from the airfield dropped us off, but the tree-lined boulevard meant little to me, and I was unimpressed even by the vast Arc de Triomphe. Nor did I have any interest in the literary cafés on the Left Bank, knew nothing about the Existentialists yet, had never heard of Gertrude Stein and only barely of Picasso. Any brief impressions of the glorious city of Paris are blotted out by my excitement of discovering Le Boeuf Sur Le Toit, a gay bar founded in the twenties by Jean Cocteau, that Coman had told me about.

That night, I walked into the bar crowded with American and Allied servicemen from every army—the gossip there was that even General de Gaulle had been in some weeks earlier—and in a defining moment when I stepped into the room, every head in the place turned to look at me. My cap tilted cockily on my head, I was wearing the trim, forest green Eisenhower jacket, one of the first issued, with my silver wings and battle ribbons pinned to my chest and the white silk scarf around my neck that airmen affected. It was a kind of debut. Coman liked to joke that the decision to replace the dowdy skirted dress jacket with the buttock-revealing Eisenhower jacket must have caused alarm at the Pentagon when they saw what they had allowed!

Entering that room was the first time in my life that I got a sense of being me. I had certainly never realized that I was remotely attractive before, much less desirable. It was such fun, then and in the years to come, being wanted—and I was reassured of that again and again, and I turned everybody down who came on to me—that was enough. One rough talking GI growled that he didn't stand a chance, I was officer's stuff—actually, I would have gone for him, if I wasn't being distracted by all the attention.

Nevertheless, I did go home with someone that night. A good-looking young captain named Charles told me, with complete unconcern, that he was awaiting court-martial for being caught in bed with a paratrooper, but somehow, under the gentlemen's code that applied to officers, he was free to come and go. He and I went on to the elegant El Morocco nightclub, seated on a banquette in the violin-shaped room with quilted walls, drinking champagne. Gypsy violinists, moving from table to table, serenaded each couple—they stopped before our table too, put our champagne glasses on the back of a guitar, and when the haunting melody was finished, we retrieved our glasses and drank a toast to each other. It was a recognition that we had as much right to be there as the other couples. At four in the morning the doors were closed and the proprietor served everyone roast chicken and champagne, then called for horse carriages to take us home, Charley and I to his very-French hotel room with whorey, leopard-skin drapes and bedspread, and a landlady who asked no questions.

The following week he hitchhiked on a plane to the south of France to meet me at my airbase, and with unimaginable chutzpah checked out a jeep from our motor pool. It astonishes me now to think that I just drove off the base with him without any permission or a word to anyone. And when I returned a few days later, I didn't seem to have missed any flying assignments, or have been missed. Or, perhaps, somebody in headquarters covered up for me. No one said a word about my being AWOL. Dazzled by my adventures, I was oblivious.

We checked into a charming Provençal hotel. And that night, we drove the twenty miles to Marseilles to an illegal gay dance hall in a warehouse district of the city that turned out to be full of Frenchmen. Somewhat drunk, I hazily remember us leaving with a group and going from café to café, necking together shamelessly in public, until one of the Frenchmen exclaimed in exasperation, "Everywhere, they kees! They kees!" Charley and I eventually wandered out on the docks of the night harbor and sat in the back of a fishing boat and made out under the stars in the warm Provençal night. When the fisherman, clad in beret and waistband, unexpectedly returned, he didn't seem in the least surprised to discover two male American officers embracing on his boat, but motioned to us not to disturb ourselves. We could even have one of the bunks in his cabin, he indicated, as he turned in.

Our affair ended on one of my courier flights to London, where Charley was going to meet me. Following what I imagined to be a very sophisticated scenario, I rented a suite at the Ritz Hotel, and invited him to breakfast. Sitting across from each other at the elegant table wheeled in by a tuxedoed waiter, I told him that I didn't want to go on with our affair. It was childish setting it up that way, but it does seem to me slightly more grown up than having to join the aviation cadets to break off with my master sergeant lover in Oklahoma!

On subsequent courier flights to London, I again spent many hours in my club, the White Room, and with my discharge not far off, I collected addresses of gay bars and restaurants in New York, as well as people. And when I returned to the States in the winter of 1945 and was discharged shortly after, I started exploring the complex gay scene in New York and discovering where I fit in.

I loved being in the army, physically close to all those men like in one big hormone-charged locker room. If, in Freudian terms, the army represented a father-figure, with its strict code of discipline, it was far less punitive and moralistic than my own had been. And as the Freudian mother it took care of all our needs. I also enjoyed my life in the clouds, even with bursts of flak rocking the plane—fear morphed into a "danger high" that was addictive, and toward the end of the war I found myself volunteering for extra missions.

My experience as a homosexual in the army was not at all unusual back then. Unlike today, the WWII military was relatively easy-going, even if there were pitfalls and many servicemen were caught in CID dragnets. That didn't matter much in civilian life—the threat that "your record would follow you" was simply not relevant after the war. For my part, I'd had a very good time on the whole, and regretted leaving. Besides being taken care of in every material way, the atmosphere suited my naturally promiscuous sociable and sexual proclivities. And above all, I liked the men, though when I think of it I didn't make out with many. My three years were well spent, and if I was left psychologically damaged by the combat experience, I think I'd have had to spend years on the couch anyway, from my difficult childhood.

Minette

Jacques Minette (1928–2001) was born on August 25, 1928, in Cleveland, Ohio. During his life Minette was flexible about dates and never mentioned Cleveland.

Minette's parents were artists, and his aunt performed in burlesque. To give her nephew something to do, she encouraged him to go on stage. Minette began performing in burlesque at the age of five, doing vocal impressions. During his adolescence he worked as a boy crooner. Minette began dressing as a woman at the age of sixteen and soon performed as a female impersonator in Boston's Scollay Square during the early 1950s. This was the beginning of a long career performing as "Minette." Minette worked in carnivals and vaudeville and small-town clubs. He appeared in Avery Willard's campy low-budget movies and provided key moments on the soundtrack of *The Queen* (1967), the first above-ground movie about female impersonators. Minette lived in a world of show business that has vanished, but Minette introduced that tradition to the next generation.

At the age of forty Minette embraced the spirit of the sixties, LSD, and gay liberation. Minette frequented the gay firehouse gatherings of the Gay Activist Alliance. He inspired Charles Ludlam's Ridiculous Theatrical Company and sewed costumes for them as well as other off-off-Broadway groups. The Hot Peaches drew deeply from Minette's sheet music for their shows. Minette encouraged many performers in their early careers: Jackie Curtis, Ethel Eichelberger, Taffy Titz, Agosto Machado, and Alexis Del Lago. By the 1970s Minette was regarded as a gay godmother to a generation of performers and off-off Broadway.

In his later years Minette survived by selling antiques, marijuana, and phony subway tokens. Adrian Milton's documentary *Minette: Portrait of a Part-Time Lady* (2005), presents the life of Minette. Minette died in December 2001. He was found in his kitchen in Brooklyn by a concerned friend.

The excerpt below is from *Minette: Recollections of a Part-Time Lady* (1979). The text is unlike any other, since it was transcribed from taped conversations and edited by Steven Watson. The book was not so much printed as photocopied, with photographs reworked by Ray Dobbins. It was distributed to friends as a gift.

From *Minette: Recollections of a Part-Time Lady*

Boston and Sailors

Most of these album pictures are from 1949 to 1954. It was fabulous showtime for queens. Lots of sailors during the Korean War, cheap booze, and lots of shows. Everything that was important, you know. A very campy time.

Scollay Square in Boston was the center of things, like Times Square years ago, with clubs and theaters. I remember one club that was a redo of one of the burlesque theaters when it burned. It was a whole mass of bars, and they covered the place in a snakelike network, so wherever you were there was a bartender at your disposal. So you'd drink more. See, Boston had no cover—no minimum. And there was a tradition then of big spenders. People would come into a bar and buy everybody a drink. So liquor was cheap in these huge barny places that needed decoration for the last fifteen years. Dingy looking places, but lots of acts and cheap booze. It was a good showtime, and the common people supported nightclubs. It wasn't the Coconut Grove they went to, but clubs like the Rex and the Showtime.

I opened one night at the Showtime when the Navy had just gotten paid. I wasn't used to the Showtime and I got scared to death. The Showtime was like they were all Marines, even though they were mostly sailors. I had to follow this real pig of an act, a real woman, a fat woman. "Peggy O'Day" was her name. Everything about Peggy O'Day was real pig-like. She couldn't sing and she was vulgar, but she wasn't funny. She was just dirty. As roaring drunk as the Navy was, they hated her. They threw beer bottles at her. And she cursed the Navy right back. So there it was: "bastards," and beer bottles and "sons of bitches" and worse stuff—Peggy O'Day knew them all. And I had to follow that.

The band tortured out this unrecognizable version of "International Rag" in the key of Z. But I belted it anyway and those boys were kind to me. Nevertheless, there were several free-for-alls between songs and I made that my last night at the Showtime.

In the clubs I mostly sang regular songs, but I also wrote lots of gay parody songs that I'd sing when I could get away with it. I'll sing you one called "Doodle Doo Doo." "Doodle Doo Doo" was a popular number in the twenties.

I know a belle who loves to raise hell
With doodle doo doo, doodle doo doo.
I know a dyke that says that she likes
Her doodle doo doo, doodle doo doo.
She's his big brother, he's her little sister,
Disowned by their mother, but I'll tell you mister
Wherever they cruise, they know how to choose
Doodle doo doodle doo doo.
One night they came home, but they weren't alone
'Twas doodle doo doo, doodle doo doo.
Their parents weren't wise when they rolled their eyes
At doodle doo doo, doodle doo doo.
Now mama is butch, her morals are scanty
Papa's turned too and he's an old auntie
The family's gone mad, they sure got it bad
'Bout doodle doo doodle doo doo.

Here I am with the Navy at the College Inn. I still love seafood, seafood's still my favorite. There were a lot of inexperienced ones, and they'd say, "Oh, I've never done this before." But they did it so well. And then some of them would be more honest: "Oh, we do it with each other on the ship, but when we get to port we look for real queens." Nowadays, they're ashamed to wear their uniforms and I don't blame them.

These sailors in the picture were lovely boys too. I went with one and Dixie Gordon went with the other and the one on the end passed out. I had them take me to a nice restaurant. Nothing too much—I didn't want to break these boys—they were good for about $20. They're probably old farts by now, but they were handsome young sheiks at the time.

Dixie Gordon once brought two sailors home at once, to her boudoir. She left these two sailors to prepare in her bathroom, and when she came back they were going at each other. Dixie came running down the hall to me. "Oh, Minette, what am I going to do? They're doing it to each other." "Don't complain," I told her. "You already got the money." "But I was sort of in the mood," she said, "and they were such nice boys."

Dixie Gordon comes from Cincinnati and ran away from home to work as a stripper when she was fifteen.

The manager raped her, found out it wasn't real, and didn't care. And her father finally found out and came and pulled her off the stage. She did five years in the penitentiary for armed robbery during the last Depression. Miss Gordon said the first year in the cellblock was terrible, but after that she began to get privileges. She was the mistress of one of the top guards, and the other prisoners would wait on her, like a princess in prison. When they had a show, she would borrow the wardrobe of the warden's wife—they were the same size—and she'd look capital. In drag there was no one like Dixie Gordon. When she got out she lived in drag. So, honey, if you think I've got campy tales . . .

There was always a little heat from working at the College Inn because drag was against the law and the Navy banned the sailors from coming in toward the end, afraid they might get subverted. The sailors came anyway, without their uniforms.

And, as for the law against impersonating a woman, it was fun seeing how we could push it. Boston was a semi-drag city. We could wear women's blouses and makeup, but we had to wear trousers. I wore "patio pajamas," now known as "culottes." I wore French high-heeled shoes and said, "These are men's shoes from the time of Louis XIV." And if they looked in the encyclopedia there was something to back me up. I had a woman's blouse from the last Depression and I told them it was a man's shirt from the time of George Washington. Rene Lewis used to take the paper serviettes from restaurants and she made tits out of them. She had a special way with paper tits so that if the cops walked by she could crush them just like that.

When queens started coming into the clubs it wasn't as rough. Honey, gay life wasn't like Christopher Street. The queens then were like ladies, and if they didn't act like ladies they got called "faggots." See, that's why I object to being called a faggot. To me, the faggots were the lowest common denominator, the real scuffy ones, the tearoom types.

One of the best places was the Silver Dollar. Now the Silver Dollar was a little bit of everything. They had fairies, and prostitutes, and straight people, and lots of sailors. It was called the longest bar in the world and it ran all the way from Washington Street back to Playland. On the stage they had a real woman that looked like a female impersonator, sort of a Margaret Dumont type of woman, with a campy name like Velma. She played the organ gorgeous, and it used to get real loud. We used to say, "You know, everyone thinks they're having such a good time at the Silver Dollar because the music's so loud they can never get lonely." That was the theory.

This is Murry Pickford and her Royal Canadian Doves. They were really white pigeons, but she insisted you call them doves. "Doves," she said. Murry was a deaf and dumb queen and when they closed Boston down to all the queens, Murry went to the officials and said: "Drag is the only way I can make a living, you know. I'm deaf and dumb." So they gave her a special card from the liquor board that said she could work in drag, and Murry was the only queen in all of Beantown that could work in drag. She was born deaf and dumb so she talked funny and couldn't hear anything. But she could read lips like crazy. She used to read them in the mirror when we were in the dressing room, only it would come out backwards and she thought everyone was dishing her. If you said she was terrific, it would come out you were dishing her. I worked with her when I was a little kid and then much later on. She had a lot of mileage by this time and she was hard to work with, although she kept on working until she died a couple years ago.

Her act was that she used to dance to "Beautiful Lady" or anything else that the band would play in the same tempo. She could feel the tempo in her body. But the band would play all kinds of crazy things, as long as it was in the same tempo, and Murry wouldn't know, so she'd come out to dance to "Beautiful Lady" and the band would be playing "I'll Be Glad When You're Dead, You Rascal You," in waltz time.

Closing Beantown

I was working a club in Springfield, Massachusetts, with some of my sisters and we'd drive all the way back to Boston after the show. We got back at three one morning: the hotel lobby was filled with trunks and fairies in traveling wardrobes. I said "What's happening?" and they showed me the front page of the paper. The Archbishop had written this editorial calling us the lowest crawling creatures of the earth, and he said something to do with worms. "Archie the Terrible" we called him. He later became Cardinal Cushing, and he got ill but he didn't die. We put the bitch's curse on him. He just suffered for many years, and that broken old man who sounded like a Bowery bum that officiated at Kennedy's funeral: that was what was left of him.

When they closed Beantown, they closed it. It wasn't just the impersonators, it was the strippers, too. The strippers weren't allowed to take their clothes off, so they'd have to come out with nothing on except the bra and pasties and a g-string. And they had to wear fringe. They did what was called "an exotic" but they were showing practically everything through the whole act, which is the worst. When they closed up the town you couldn't do anything you couldn't do on television. You couldn't even do a hula on a nightclub stage.

But I said to myself: I'm not leaving without any bookings. Oh, didn't I have the nerve. So I inherited everybody's johns, and I was on my way to making a fortune before the tip-off. There was a police station around the corner, but this waitress friend of mine that worked across the street overheard a conversation. The cops had my room number, but they had Dixie Gordon's name. The hotel told them Dixie Gordon had checked out, and that threw them off for a while.

I stopped sitting in the lobby like I had been, sitting in the lobby in drag after one o'clock in the evening. The night clerk was a pal of mine, an ex-hooker. When she would see someone that looked like a prospective customer, she's say, very genteel, "Minette, Minette, would you show this man to his room?" And then she'd give him room 69. I got the message. Room 69 was actually a graduated dog act.

After 1 A.M. the night clerk would lower the lighting, so it was nice soft lighting, and I'd sit down in the lobby. They'd have these real ones sitting there, too, $5 girls. I was $10 and up. And so men would try to get me down. "Oh, we can get a real women for $5." I said, "Of course you can get a real woman for $5. I'm a rare thing. I'm a queen. In Beantown. After Archie, I'm damn rare. To compare me with a real woman is like comparing a diamond to a rhinestone."

Martin Duberman

Martin Duberman (b. 1930) is one of America's most distinguished historians, having taught at Yale, Princeton, and the Graduate Center of the City University of New York, where he founded and was the first director of the Center for Lesbian and Gay Studies.

He began his career as a historian of nineteenth-century America, writing the biographies *Charles Francis Adams, 1807–1886* (1961), which won the Bancroft Prize, and *James Russell Lowell* (1966). But because these books reached a limited academic audience he began writing plays. *In White America* won the 1963–64 Vernon Rice–Drama Desk Award.

In 1972 Duberman published *Black Mountain: An Exploration in Community*, in which he came out. Two of the contributors to this volume, Paul Goodman and Michael Rumaker, were associated with Black Mountain College, Goodman as a teacher and Rumaker as a student. Duberman has devoted himself to recording gay history in works such as *About Time* (1986) and *Stonewall* (1993) and his monumental study *Lincoln Kirstein* (2007).

Duberman has published two volumes of autobiography, *Midlife Queer* (1996) and *Cures: A Gay Man's Odyssey* (1991), from which the passage below is taken. *Cures* is a harsh indictment of the past psychological treatment of homosexuals, therapies that not only hindered Duberman's development as a gay man but undermined the health of many people.

Larry

HOW TO DESCRIBE "LARRY"? Thirty-five years of sea change have intervened, repositioning the memory at every turn, smoothing over the jagged ups and downs of our years together to a hazy sweetness.

We met at the Napoleon, a few months after I broke up with Rob. Larry was twenty, three years younger than I. He lived with his devoutly Catholic, working-class Irish family in Canton, a suburb outside of Boston, commuting every day to a clerk's job with Filene's department store (from which he gradually worked himself up to be a buyer). We were different in many ways besides class status. Larry was muscular and compact in build, low-keyed, intense, essentially nonverbal. He was my somatic ideal, I was his intellectual one; he helped me learn about my body, I helped him learn about books and ideas.

Though our differences were in some ways deeply nurturing, allowing us to open up new worlds for each other, we worried from the beginning that our pervasive differences in background, education, and temperament would ultimately overwhelm our passionate feelings of attachment and our sense that we did, profoundly and illogically, belong together.

We were expected to worry. And about much more than temperamental differences. Two people of the same gender, the culture had taught us, were not meant to spend their lives together and, should they be foolish enough to try, would soon learn that Nature intended otherwise. As if that conviction was not debilitating enough, we also had to cope (as did heterosexuals) with the then-current cultural nostrum that when two partners were *really* meant for each other, neither sexual arousal nor emotional commitment ever flagged; health was defined as the absence of desire for more than one person, or at least the need to act on the desire.

Larry and I didn't vary from the acceptable pattern for about two years. From the beginning, young and hot, our eyes strayed constantly. But we were under several spells—the mainstream American injunction to be faithful, love, and the fear of losing love—and they held our hormones in check. Charles constantly told us, his voice resonant with campy amazement, how *incredibly* lucky we were to have found each other and what *utter* ingrates we would be should we *ever* do *anything* to jeopardize our good fortune.

Properly chastised and warned, Larry and I scarcely dared think about outside sexual contacts, dutifully concentrating instead on the seemly issue of whether we should or could live together. Since we were both scraping by financially (I was now self-supporting, or at least trying to get by with minimal family assists), moving in together seemed a pipe dream for the time being. This was an impasse that carried with it some relief for me, since I still felt ambivalent, even if less so under the trance of love, about settling down as a now-and-forever homosexual. We made do with weekend overnights in my single bed (by 1954 I was a resident tutor in Adams House, with far more privacy than when living in the graduate school dormitory).

But by 1955, after Larry and I had been together for two years, amorous zest and fantasies of eternal togetherness began, in tandem, to fray a bit. As they do, of course, with most couples, romantic intensity inevitably mutating (when the couple is lucky) into a more routine and comfortable domesticity. It's also commonplace for partners to view any erosion in erotic excitement with alarm, as a forecast of ultimate disaster. But the forecast seems more ominous still when the couple consists of two gay men—who have been forewarned of their incompatibility and told that sex was all they cared about and were good at anyway.

Larry and I continued to feel considerable passion for each other, but since it was no longer automatic and constant and now seemed to follow arguments rather than forestall them, we nervously wondered how much of a future we could count on. The more we wondered, the more prone we became to elevating garden-variety disagreements into the equivalent of Doomsday. And so we began to hedge our bets, slacken our commitment. (If it was only a matter of time before we broke up, maybe we ought to start looking around now for likely replacements?) Both of us, but I more than Larry, began having sexual adventures on the side. This deviation from the monogamous norm, in turn, further convinced me of my incapacity—generic, so long as I remained homosexual—for intimacy. Hadn't psychiatry long warned that homosexuals were condemned, by the very nature of their illness, to flee from relatedness to promiscuity?

Even if the culture had been supportive, Larry and I might have broken up; some of our differences, after all, did not bode well for the kind of long-term commitment that feeds best on companionable similarities of temperament and interest. But for straight couples, social values serve to counteract problems in the relationship; the high premium placed on heterosexual pair-bonding and family life provides plenty of brownie points and self-esteem for staying together. For homosexual couples, social values serve further to underscore, rather than counteract, interpersonal difficulties; being called "sick" and "degenerate" hardly gives one the needed psychic support for sustaining a relationship.

I began thinking once more about psychotherapy, thinking about "conversion" as my only hope for a happy life. Ironically, it was just at this time, the mid-fifties, that Evelyn Hooker began her research study of *non*-patient homosexuals, began to amass the counterevidence needed for challenging the notion, under which I (and most of the country) then labored, that homosexuals were sick people in need of treatment. Orthodox psychiatry had based its negative conclusions about homosexuality on studies of people who had come to therapists for help or on captive populations in prisons and mental hospitals. With a grant from the National Institute of Mental Health in 1954, Hooker matched thirty homosexual men with thirty heterosexual men, screening both groups for manifest pathology, and then subjecting the remaining candidates to a variety of projective tests. Two-thirds of both the heterosexual and homosexual men were judged (by outside evaluators, as well as by Hooker herself) as having made an average adjustment or better—and, significantly, the two groups could not be told apart psychologically.

In her later studies, Hooker would also find that far more homosexual men than earlier believed did manage to maintain long-term love relationships, despite the constant fear of public exposure and despite the culture's strenuous efforts to stigmatize those relationships. Indeed, Hooker would ultimately single out stigmatization as itself the prime cause of what pathology did exist in homosexuals.

In her first article, published in 1957, Hooker summarized her findings up to that point:

> ... personality structure and adjustment may ... vary within a wide range.... What is difficult to accept (for most clinicians) is that some homosexuals may be very ordinary individuals, indistinguishable from ordinary individuals who are heterosexual.... Some may be quite superior individuals not only devoid of pathology (unless one insists that homosexuality is a sign of pathology) but also functioning at a superior level.

These suggestions provided a striking challenge to the dominant psychiatric view that homosexuals were a homogeneous group, bound together by dysfunction and neurosis. Hooker's series of articles would grow in influence over the years, but the initial one in 1957 appeared in the specialized *Journal of Projective Techniques*. Neither my friends nor I read technical journals in psychology, and it would be another decade before I heard a word about Hooker's findings. Indeed, by 1957 I was paying regular visits to a psychotherapist whose views of my "condition" were precisely of the kind Hooker was attempting to counteract.

I began seeing "Dr. Weintraupt" in late 1955, after the spiral of recrimination and reconciliation between Larry and me had come to seem hopelessly circular. These were the years when—for the privileged, particularly those living on the Eastern Seaboard—the decision to enter therapy seemed logical and valid. In a culture that had grown apolitical and conservative, analyzing the inner life had become a primary, praiseworthy enterprise. For intellectuals and egotists especially, it was the elective choice of the moment, *the* certified path to self-knowledge.

From the first Weintraupt advised me to give up the relationship with Larry. Until I did, he warned, any real progress in therapy would prove impossible. The drama of our interpsychic struggle, Weintraupt insisted, had become a stand-in for the more basic intrapsychic conflict I was unwilling to engage—the conflict between my neurotic homosexual "acting-out" and my underlying healthy impulse toward a heterosexual union.

I resisted—not so much Weintraupt's theories, as his insistence on a total break with Larry. I accepted the need, but could not summon the will. I spent therapy hour after therapy hour arguing my inability to give up the satisfactions of the relationship—neurotic and occasional though they might be, and though my future happiness might well hang on their surrender. I resisted so hard and long that Weintraupt finally gave me an ultimatum: either give up Larry or give up therapy.

I turned to my friend Ray for advice and comfort. "I'll never find anyone as sweet or loving or loyal as Larry," I wailed over coffee cups and wine glasses. "If I give him up, I give up the best person I'll ever find."

"The best man," Ray would correct, his tone mournfully tentative, sharing all my doubts about a possible "conversion" at the advanced age of twenty-six.

"But do I have any choice but to try? After all, it hasn't been any bed of roses for Larry and me lately. And it can only get worse from here."

Dutifully leaping to the other side of the argument, Ray would halfheartedly say something about the value of "a bird in the hand." That would prompt me to defend the need to push ahead, against all odds, into the risky unknown. Which would lead Ray to a disdainful reminder that we were dealing with a real-life relationship not a soap opera. Which would cause me hastily to launch into a stringent intellectual assessment of psychoanalytic assumptions—which we would then reluctantly conclude were probably true, though unpalatable.

The dialogue and commiseration continued for weeks. Finally, torn with anguish and self-doubt, I decided I would *try* to give up the relationship with Larry, try to cast my lot, as Weintraupt had long urged, on the side of "health." But in the privacy of my diary, I went on lamenting and rethinking the decision, inadvertently revealing along the way how fully I had internalized the culture's homophobic biases:

August 29, 1956

God I miss Larry. How I wish he were here tonight waiting for me in bed, sweet, affectionate … and yet I can't really settle down with him. I have no confidence in our building any sort of a life. … Is any genuine commitment between homosexuals possible?

September 2

… went to the bars … Larry was safely on the Cape [vacationing] and couldn't directly prick my conscience ("You supposedly gave me up for analysis, and here you are a month later cruising in the bars") … Got quite drunk and came home with a youngish guy who I thought would be a good fuck. But he was lousy in bed—inexperienced physically, inane in every other way … After two hours of nonerect activity, we finally managed an orgasm. I was afterwards completely repulsed by what I'd done; this absurd compulsive intimacy with an anonymous body—and a disappointing one at that (which is perhaps why I'm so righteously repulsed).

He left early this morning. I've been moping around ever since. Came very close to rushing off to see Larry on the Cape. It's extraordinary how "right" seeing him would make everything. But I've yielded to this too many times before, and always without lasting satisfaction. It's been a full month now since we've seen each other—I've got to hold off—I cannot form any lasting relationship with him—why, I'm not sure—but this I do know, that it won't work, and I must give him a chance to free himself.

September 3

The great drought is over—with the usual awful results. Last night Larry called. I was so glad to hear from him, and under almost no pressure, agreed to meet him … eventually I was talking drunkenly—meaning it all—about giving up the analysis, about missing him terribly, etc. And finally, sex. As miraculous as ever, and followed, as ever, by panic over what I had done and remorse over what I had said.

Will it ever be resolved? When I see him I'm lost; and I can't seem to stop myself from seeing him. Yet it's never enough. Could I really give up the analysis and accept my life as it now stands? Also impossible …

September 4

Nervous about having to tell Weintraupt what happened last night. Half hoping, like a renegade schoolboy, to be "dismissed." But I was unable to goad either him or myself into it.

The confessional did me good. And now, I suppose, the usual drifting till the next crisis. What of all the promises I made to Larry last night? Today I consummate the immorality by not even calling him. What else can I do? If I call, I merely reestablish a lifeline that consists of half-promises that always remain unfulfilled, and yet always remain. If only I could know that after my physical and neurotic needs are spent, there's still something left for us to live on. I sometimes think there is—but Weintraupt had thrown so many of my feelings into doubt and confusion, I can't even be sure of "sometimes." And so I'll continue to drift; trying not to call — hoping he'll call me; continuing to go to Weintraupt — planning imminently to quit.

September 7

Just back from the bars. Larry was there and we mooned around each other — with intermittent snarls — all night. Curse Weintraupt and my bloody fine powers of resistance! I'm so sick of considering consequences, "looking ahead" — to what? To a question mark, to the bare possibility that I may someday be able to marry and have children.

1:45 A.M.: Larry called a few minutes ago. "Can I borrow your car to get home?" "Sure, I'll meet you at the gate [of Adams House] in 2 minutes." And at the gate he looked — so beautiful. Then he cried and said he loved me and swore he'd never "bother" me again. How the hell can I resist? I asked him to come upstairs. He hesitated and said he was tired of "taking the blame." We went through this 3 or 4 times. Finally, in a pique at his stubbornness, I walked away — half expecting and more than half hoping to be called back. But no, he let the gate close . . .

September 8

I'm like a stupid child who can't profit from experience. Larry returned the car during the afternoon and I invited him up, although I was playing cards. He slept while we played and then when the others left, I woke him, crawled into bed, caressed him — and that was that. I simply made no effort to resist. Why invite him up in the first place? Why not wake him hurriedly? . . . No, none of those sensible things. Attraction, tenderness, wonderfully passionate sex — and then the usual regret over the destructiveness of my lust, both to Larry and to my analysis.

September 10

I quit the analysis this morning. After months of indecision, the final action was almost unexpected. I told Weintraupt about last night with Larry — and about a dream in which my "auditing" a course evolved into a symbolic reenactment of my attitude towards the analysis — i.e., an onlooker, an auditor, rather than a participant. From there it was only a step to being told my attitude made the analysis circular and endless; and since in honesty I couldn't swear that I would be able to change it, it was mutually agreed that it would be best to stop. Yet having made the decision, I can't accept it. Accepting it means accepting my life, being satisfied with it. And I can't . . .

I told Larry immediately about my decision to quit therapy, and we met for a serious talk about our future. We began the evening by having sex ("How great not to follow it," I wrote in my diary, "with panic and guilt"). Then later, over dinner, I told him that the best I thought I could manage would be a part-time relationship, no strings attached. I was happy, I said, for us to go on seeing each other—if he was—but no longer thought an exclusive relationship would work, explaining (as I wrote in my diary) that "I remain incapable (don't all homosexuals?) of finding satisfaction permanently with one person." Larry, an accepting stoic by nature, and extraordinarily tolerant of my mercurial shifts, asked for no further details or explanations and simply agreed henceforth to a loose arrangement between us.

But in a real sense, therapy had already poisoned that well. Weintraupt's certitudes about the hopelessness of homosexual life managed to underscore all my pre-existing doubts about my—or any homosexual's—capacity for love and commitment. Like most homosexual couples in those years, Larry and I had distrusted ourselves far too much to affirm what might have been genuinely different, and creatively different, about a gay relationship, to affirm (rather than apologize for) some needed distinctions between emotional and sexual fidelity. Instead we had invested our energies, as well as our hopes for certification as *bona fide* human beings, in conforming as closely as possible to the mainstream norm of what constituted a healthy union—meaning now-and-forever monogamy. Not the least of the sabotages the conformist fifties committed was to instill the notion that "different" was the equivalent of being "disturbed" and, in the case of political nonconformists especially, "dangerous."

But being declared an unfit candidate for intimacy released me, ironically (though the irony escaped me at the time), better to enjoy the pleasures of the flesh. I was a horny young guy who had never before had license to explore the nonmonogamous urges of his body; being certified as "sick" hobbled my confidence but liberated my libido. I even had the occasional inkling that in breaking away from Larry I was *using* the insistence of orthodox psychiatry that I was incapacitated for love to justify some unorthodox and overdue sexual adventuring that the culture would sanction only for those lost souls unable to partake of the *real* satisfactions of monogamy.

I now began to roam with a vengeance, as if—being a dutiful creature of the culture—determined to live out Weintraupt's prediction that only therapy could have saved me from a life of random, disconnected promiscuity. I even called an old friend in New York City and asked him to meet me one night for a tour of the hot spots. We started decorously enough, with dinner at the East 55 restaurant, which, daringly for those years, openly catered to a homosexual clientele. I reacted to the scene with disdain. "The place was filled with babbling queens," I wrote indignantly in my diary, "who, because they can afford to spend $5 on a dinner, feel they are also entitled to talk at the top of their lungs." It was one thing to accept one's fate as a homosexual, another to be queer; I wasn't about to identify with any of that "'girl' crap." But I did have the limited grace to add in my diary, "Oh why criticize—I suppose the sick should stick together!"

From there it was down to Lennie's, a gay bar in Greenwich Village. I spent most of the evening talking to a redhead from Toronto named Rick and ended up in bed with him. Disappointed in the sex, I drew a self-lacerating moral in my diary: "Perhaps I purposely single out those to whom I'm only marginally attracted—thus ensuring disappointment. A way of punishing myself? Of preventing any further involvement?" When I attended a straight friend's wedding that same week, I enviously compared the contentment I chose to see all around me ("wives bearing, husbands beaming," I wrote in my diary) with my own empty life. But I was not yet wholly brainwashed: "Perhaps I mistake it," I added, "and am merely romanticizing."

I alternated between fits of remorse over quitting therapy ("throwing away my one chance at health") and self-recrimination over my inability either fully to commit or fully to withdraw from the relationship with Larry. He, within a few weeks, tried to bring matters to a head by putting a ban on our having sex ("We've got to try to form a new kind of relationship—friends, since lovers hasn't worked; and occasional sex with each other is merely postponing the adjustment"). Larry said he still preferred going to bed only with me, but rather than settle for occasionally, he had decided he preferred never—knowing the thought of never would frighten me more than him.

Having no choice, I agreed that we would stop having sex together, and went back to my routine of bar-hopping. But Larry himself proved unwilling to stick to the agreement, and within three weeks, at his initiation, we were back in bed. Within a week after that, we accidentally ran into each other at the Punch Bowl (the Napoleon had now become too buttoned-up for my taste). Sensing I had my eye on someone else and was reluctant to leave with him, Larry angrily vented his frustration at our on-and-off gyrations. I told him (as I wrote up the exchange in my diary that night): ". . . I hate tormenting him and yet I am incapable now of changing my insane pace of promiscuity. I said I'm useless to both of us. We agreed not to see each other any more."

The "insane pace" turns out, on rechecking my diary, to have amounted to one sexual experience in two weeks. Maybe I was exaggerating to help Larry break our stalemate. More likely, I *felt* such a pace to be insane. In forsaking the certified One-Person-Now-and-Forever model of health, I saw myself as descending into an iniquitous pit of promiscuity. Although sleeping around gave me quite a bit of incidental pleasure, it was circumscribed by guilt.

After one sexual encounter, I wrote despairingly in my diary: "I tell myself how meaningless this anonymous cycle of body and body is, but I continue to repeat it; partly, no doubt, because of the necessity to keep proving myself, but also because the means of forming a healthier, more complete relationship are slight." Another evening, having successfully maneuvered someone to bed whom I had long found attractive, and although sex with him had been enjoyable, I felt compelled to atone: "My revulsion is working overtime. All sorts of resolutions. Eager for work—never going to waste time bar-hopping again, etc. No satisfaction there anyway. All set for a return to analysis; must have a wife and family, only possible things that matter."

But I was not yet ready to give therapy another go. I was willing enough to label my sex life neurotic and compulsive, but felt myself powerless to change it: "I can neither give up my homosexual activities, nor devote myself guiltlessly to them. Paralyzed on the one side by desire and on the other by knowledge." Besides, as was soon to become clear, Larry and I were not yet finished with each other.

Despite having broken off forever, within a short time we were again having sex. This time, more than a little exhausted at all the reformulations, we avoided cementing a pact of any kind and simply let our meetings take what shape they would. By now I was nearing completion of my doctoral thesis, and both Larry and I knew that within a year I would be leaving the Boston area for a full-time teaching job. We no longer had any expectation about sharing our lives in the future—though there would be occasional pangs of longing and regret for several more years, and for several decades (for we did stay in touch) unexpected surges of deep feeling for each other.

When I took up my first teaching job at Yale in the fall of 1957, Larry and I still occasionally alternated weekends in Boston or New Haven. Saying good-bye to him after one of them, I remember tears gushing from my eyes, wondering bitterly why I let myself acknowledge the full depth of my feelings for him only when I safely knew it could be indulged infrequently. As I wrote in my diary, "If I don't love him, why did I cry so painfully when it came time for him to leave? If I do love him, why has our relationship fluctuated so wildly the last few years? A riddle I long since gave up on. Anyway, it's awful being alone again . . ."

It was so awful that within a few weeks of arriving at Yale, I decided I had to go back into therapy.

Michael Rumaker

Michael Rumaker (b. 1932) was born in South Philadelphia, one of nine children. The family was poor, and his father drank. At eighteen he was kicked out of his parents' home "for not going to church and for being gay." Yet when he heard of Black Mountain College, the now famous experimental school in North Carolina, and that it was "a hotbed of communists and homosexuals," he knew immediately it was "the place for me." In 1955 Rumaker was a member of the last graduating class. His account of that period is related in *Black Mountain Days: A Memoir* (2004).

Rumaker then moved to San Francisco, where he studied with Robert Duncan, described in his memoir *Robert Duncan in San Francisco* (1996), and published a novel entitled *The Butterfly* (1962) and a highly praised collection of short stories entitled *Gringos and Other Stories* (1966). He earned a master of fine arts degree from Columbia University in 1970 and has taught at City College of New York, the New School for Social Research, and, until his retirement, the Rockland Center for the Arts.

The excerpt published here is from *A Day and a Night at the Baths* (1979), in which he gives a self-reflective and sexually explicit account of his first visit to a gay bath house, expressing his experience of sexual freedom and inhibition, psychic isolation and community. According to George F. Butterick, Rumaker is "a kind of sensitive picaresque hero who passes through the various levels of society ... emerging enriched and with integrity intact."

From *A Day and a Night at the Baths*

AN EXCITEMENT OF SPERM-LUST, whiffs of it bleachy in the air, aerated me with an agitated impulsion to feed close. I visualized the minutest trace of blood in the sea stirring sharks to glide along the inky tentacles of its faint trail hanging in the water to ultimately zero in on the kill in a thrashing and frenzy of feeding. My face burned with a thrill of delighted shame in the comparative image, my teeth were that sharp, possessed as I was by original hungers.

Boldly, with no backstroking, I swam into the next open doorway I came to where I sighted a live, breathing body afloat on its back on a bed of rumpled sheets, its waving blood-red tendril an appetizing lure.

His name was Paolo. From Brazil, he said. A fish from far waters. And from a very good school, too: he spoke excellent English. He looked like an exotic breed from the equatorial upper-classes, he had such a sleek and privileged look and, the joint he was toking aside, an air of confidence and insouciance of manner that only old and habitual money can buy. With wavy iron-gray hair, he wasn't young but appeared expensively youthful, the body trim and tanned and well taken care of. He exuded a relaxed and antique Latin American charm. I found myself thinking about monkey gland transplants. Around his neck hung a small discreet crucifix inset with diamond chips on a fine gold chain, and I thought of the small bands of Portuguese and Spanish thugs who brought syphilis to South America in the Name of God and wondered if he was their true heir. I also wondered if one of the more light-fingered customers here, in an unguarded moment during the throes of passion, might not relieve him of his cross.

My shark teeth sharpened.

Another toke, and he told me, conversationally and with a merry, amused glint in his eye, pleased to accommodate, that he was storing up a bladderful for "a nice guy" who'd stopped in shortly before me and had extracted the promise from him.

"Said to drink a lot of water and he'd drop back later. I hope you're not into that yourself because I wouldn't want to disappoint him. I'm not much into water sports but he seemed such a sweet guy."

I assured him I wasn't either and that he could fill up as much as he wanted. Not that I wasn't willing to experiment, but I didn't add that.

"Thank goodness," he smiled, relieved. "No fun having to get waterlogged a second time. I've been wearing a trail between here and the water cooler as it is." Chin pressed on chest, tamping probing fingers over a belly flat as an ironing-board, he said, "I'm getting a bit swollen now, don't you think?"

"And down below, too," I added, rakish, baring my teeth.

"More there than here," he said, patting his belly affectionately.

With the most gracious smile, he offered me a drag from his joint. I declined but opted for a few tokes of the real thing which he allowed with a satisfied smile and a generous parting of his thighs.

He was wearing a cock ring so unusual I bent down very close to inspect it. Faint and delicate designs of looping snakes, heads biting tails, were etched in the silver band, as worn as a family heirloom. A rough leather thong of rawhide clamped the metal hoop tight behind his testicles, the thong, which he'd evidently dampened, perhaps on one of his trips to the water fountain, shrinking tighter and tighter as the rawhide strip dried against his body heat, bulging his balls out like Valencia blood-oranges, his prick increasingly ramrod stiff from the slowly squeezing pressure. It looked excitingly painful.

My nose sharpened as I nudged around purple veins swelled to bursting in a nest of ink-black pubic hair crinkled with gray the gloss and texture of watered silk. He had a scrubbed unerotic smell with a strong hint of Aramis. My tongue itched for an unadulterated taste of salt-fresh blood. Slipping a finger below the thong, I touched an anus loose and yielding for easy entry.

He brushed my cheek with well-manicured fingers. "You're a sweet guy, too," he breathed in a marijuana basso. He sighed profoundly. "Do with me whatever you like."

And I did, patiently and thoroughly, not as a shark I found out, because, even though I made use of my teeth, it wasn't blood I eventually drew. The sting of it, uncontaminated by perfumed soap or heavy cologne, was a welcome shot of carnal reality.

Straddling between his legs, I glanced up at one point and caught Paolo smiling over my head, a sparkling grin like a movie star's splitting his face. At first I thought it was ecstatic bliss and was just about to congratulate myself on my performance when, hearing distinct heavy breathing just over my shoulder, I swung around and spotted several pairs of eyes staring intently and curiously through the crack in the door. Kneeling at the foot of the bed, my butt up close to the door, my flanks exposed, so to speak, I felt very vulnerable and, reaching back with my arm (and hating my priggy rudeness), closed the door tightly.

Paolo pulled a long puss but I soon put him in a better mood, not saying a word but getting back to the work at hand until, with a kick of his legs in the air, he let out the squawk of a rooster getting its neck wrung, his arms and legs flapping, then fell back on the mattress in utter collapse. Diminished now, his cock ring slid off and dropped on the bunched up sheets between deflating testes like balloons slowly leaking air. The metal hoop lay there like a coiled and useless outsized earring.

He blew me a genteel peck from his lips. "*Obrigado*," he murmured, "*Merci*," and dropped his eyes demurely, a polite way of saying, 'I think I'll just rest now.'

Crawling off the bed I stood up and slipped my towel around my waist. I said I might stop back later and say hello if he was still there.

"Please do," he said, and pulling another joint from beneath his pillow, lit up again. After expelling the smoke in a thin, quick cloud, he said, arching his eyebrows, "*Santa Iansa*, I hope that *bicha avec les goûts particuliers* gets here soon. I don't think I can hold off much longer."

I hunched my shoulders and giving him a commiserating smile, wishing him speedy relief, reached a hand behind my head, flipped an imaginary tophat at him and, peeling out of my shark skin, strolled out the door.

After another trip to the showers I began to realize that constant showering after every escapade could really shrivel up the skin and decided next time I'd bring along a bottle of Aapri Body Satin Lotion—"Leaves Skin 'Sauna Soft' and Refreshed."

Then I climbed at last to investigate the third floor, the uppermost part of the baths. I paused near the top of the steps and looked back down, seeing all the way down the steep flights of stairs to the marble lobby floor two stories below. Towel-clad figures moved up and down on the deep-grooved rubber treads of the steps, sharp under bare soles. The long downward rush of stairs was broken only by the wide landing leading to the second floor, from which I'd just climbed and up to which a man in lumberjacket and levis, evidently just arrived, was trudging.

Wearing nothing but a sweatshirt with YALE in big block letters across the chest, a tow-haired youth with a pink, protein-fed face, open, innocent, the face of a remote pilot peering with dreamy, abstract eyes out of jet bomber plexiglas, jogged onto the third floor landing and bounced athletically past me down the steps, hands stuck straight out at his thighs, fingers tapping air, a loose, quick spring on the balls of his feet as he tripped blithely on down the stairs, pink genitalia jouncing.

On a metal folding chair on the landing just outside the doorway sat the attendant, a heavy-set, middle-aged black man in short-sleeved white cotton shirt and trousers, a benign and passive-faced guardian of the third floor entrance whose main job it was to show customers to their rooms, supply extra towels when asked for and change the linen on the beds after customers left. I soon discovered he was also involved in some moonlighting of his own. (I expect his salary wasn't much—the attendants relied on tips and my friend had suggested that a quarter would be "adequate"—and so this little business on the side that in a few minutes I would chance on, must've helped fatten his weekly income, and then some.)

I glanced at him as I passed and he nodded curtly, neither friendly nor unfriendly. He looked like he had worked here for years, at this same station, sitting on this same folding chair, perhaps even in the days when the baths were not predominantly gay — in palmier days of the neighborhood, according to my friend, when it was an exclusive turkish bath and clubhouse for wealthy, and presumably white and non-gay, men only. He had the kind of blunt, grizzled face that looked, in its guarded ruggedness, tactfully unseeing, surprised at nothing.

Once through the door, I was immediately aware, in contrast to the floor below, of the "lightiness" of the area. Looking down the first long narrow corridor just off the entry, I was relieved to see, at the far end of it, the small square dusty light of a window. I started toward it, hoping I could open it and get a breath of fresh air.

On the way, I passed many closed doors, silent within (they seemed to rent all the second floor cubicles first before letting out the third floor ones), but a few of the doors were open and I slowed my steps to glance inside them. Other men passed me, circulating in the same round of cubicle-cruising as on the floor below, but here the atmosphere seemed quieter, a little less frantic and close-quartered, the space not as broken and abbreviated by the short alleylike halls; perhaps quieter, too, because there wasn't the proximity and activity of the downstairs dorm. Here, the cubicles were lined either side along the simpler layout of three very lengthy corridors stretched parallel from front to back of the building.

One man lay on his bed wearing nothing but a jockstrap; another wore scanty, pastel briefs; another, black leather briefs with a zippered pouch. Several were nude or posed with their towels arranged in such a way as to definitely arouse curiosity. A long leanly sinuous man was totally bare-ass except for a pair of cowboy boots, the blunted points of which jutted out beyond the door so that you couldn't help but brush them as you passed, which I guess was the main idea.

In the next cubicle a man lay flat on his belly, his legs extended in a wide "V," a foot-long plastic dildo, pointing straight up, and pointedly leaning against the partition beside his bare buttocks.

The attendant suddenly pushed up behind and around me, escorting a newcomer, a bearded young man wearing a black leather jacket and form-fitting leather pants, both studded all over in curlicue designs made of brass rivets. A stiff black SS-type military cap was perched over his shaggy blond curls.

The attendant unlocked a door just ahead and turned on the light. It was a supply room with shelf upon shelf stacked with clean towels. Tacked up on the inmost walls of the closet were vivid color photos, cut out of nudie magazines, of naked women, huge-breasted and sleekly curvaceous.

Surrounded daily by the constant sight and noise of so many undressed men engaged in so much same-sex activity, the photos, exaggerated as they were, perhaps were a reminder, helping the attendant keep a grip on his own preference each time he paid a visit to the closet.

"How's your supply?" I heard the man in leather drag, sounding like an old hand, say to the attendant as I approached.

The attendant glanced at him quickly with lifted eyebrows. "You *know* I always got a *good* supply." His thumb, like glossy teak, riffled up a stack of neatly folded towels.

The blond youth grinned. "Lemme tip you now," he said and snapped out a bill, sliding it into the palm of the attendant, who then transferred it deftly into his hip pocket. He reached up between two stacks of towels, palming a small brown envelope, barely visible for the fraction of a second as he withdrew his hand, then folding the envelope neatly into a clean towel, he handed it to the young man.

"This is good *strong* stuff," he said in a low, confidential voice. "A *good* buy."

He gave a tug at the light chain, locked the door behind him and continued escorting the young man down the hall to his room. Several heads turned at the clump of the heavy boots, their militant stomp sounding until the two rounded the corner at the far end of the corridor and disappeared from sight.

A white-haired man, perhaps in his early fifties, stood naked just inside the shadowy doorway of his cubicle. He stared out at me with a flat, stolid face, the points of his eyes concentrated in unblinking and earnest solicitation. He was fingering his testicles and manipulating them in a flapping, beckoning manner. My eyes met his and I nodded but kept on walking toward the far window.

Slumped on his bed against the wall, staring with youthfully handsome but bored, indifferent eyes at the partition opposite, sat a young man with short-cropped blond hair, a narrow waist and the wide, sloping shoulders of a swimmer. The model of a "good school" type, he appeared out of place here, like a fantasy ghost of the 1950s, roaming seamier halls than the ivy-clad ones of that time.

When I glanced in he dropped his gaze, staring down at the folds of the towel in his lap, his square-jawed muscles tightening.

"You into Crisco?" he muttered.

I stopped in the doorway, not sure I'd heard him right. Sparkle of a cock ring through his parted towel, long in a thigh as sleekly muscular as a frog's.

He jerked his head to the corner of the cubicle where, in the center of the small nightstand, the only object on it, stood a one-pound can of Crisco, the smooth whorls of its snow-white surface as yet untouched.

Seeing my hesitation, he looked up at me carefully from under his brows. "There're lots of things you can do with it."

I had an image of myself, and him, smeared head to toe with the stuff and rolling around entangled in greasy sheets, then my being handcuffed and tied spread-eagle to the bed with slip-resistant rope, a prospect that for the moment was a turn off.

I also imagined him, clothing his nakedness, dressed in a striped school tie, red corduroy vest, gray flannel trousers and a navy-blue blazer with dull metallic buttons—Another dead and respectable ghost, among so many, my head was so filled with them—But all ghosts now and pretty much at rest.

I shook my head. "Not right now."

Then, slow and quiet-voiced, "Thanks for stopping by anyway," he said, and turned the humorless gaze of his eyes again to the partition.

Maybe another time I would be more adventurous, but for now my immediate tastes ran to the raw and unadorned flesh, without additives of any kind.

As I walked on, I wondered if the advertising department at Procter & Gamble was aware of a new and exciting use for their product? (Or, for that matter, if the makers of Chapstick knew that their lip balm applied to the lips beforehand lubricates the glans as an aid to deepthroating? One more reason to "Never Go Out Without It.")

Many of the rooms, as on the second floor, were in total darkness, perhaps because, dim-watted as the lights were (the frosted shades appeared to be broken in a majority of the rooms), a bare lightbulb was a bare lightbulb and, like the one in mine, irritating to the eye in such a cramped space.

The darkened room certainly served as an allurement, enlivening curiosity, suggesting mystery. Perhaps for some it was a disguise, as in one room where I could make out the stretched out figure of a very old man, propped on his bed on one thin withered arm, the door just barely cracked and the light not on. Concealed in shadow, perhaps a pathetic attempt at trickery to make him appear a little more "desirable," to fool someone, out of desperate loneliness, into entering, if only for a moment?

In a very few cubicles, there glowed soft orange and red bulbs. I wondered if these had been installed as a fluke, or because of a shortage, on the part of the management? Perhaps the occupants of these more invitingly lighted cubicles had had the foresight to bring their own bulbs, unscrewing those supplied by the baths and replacing them with their own more romantically tinged light.

Instead of the rose-colored paper perhaps I would bring a pretty lightbulb on my next trip.

From somewhere down one of the long hallways I heard a cracked, pleading voice, the grainy voice of an old man, crying, "Could somebody tell me where Room 306 is? Please help me find Room 306."

There was a bustle of footsteps and the attendant saying in an annoyed, weary voice, as if he'd done this now for the umpteenth time, "This way, pops. 306 down here," and an apologetic cackle from the old man as he said, "Damn if they don't keep moving it on me. Thank you, thank you."

Did such old men live here? Did the owners of the baths have an arrangement with the social services of the city, cut-rate prices for homeless and elderly men during slack times when the management wanted to fill up cubicles? Or perhaps it was only that they chose to be here, like everyone else, in such a spry and busy sexual atmosphere.

I stopped at an open door where, stretched on his bed, his handsome head propped up on the pillow, lay a huskily built dark-haired man with very symmetrical features, a wide neatly clipped mustache and a smartly cropped haircut, giving him the over-all appearance, *sans* work boots, levis and Sears cheap flannel shirt, of a Christopher Street clone. He was wearing only a very brief tangerine towel (undoubtedly one he had brought with him since, except for a few washed-out pink ones, most all the men were wrapped in the ordinary, threadbare terrycloth ones). Around his neck was a thin chain with two delicate gold pendants. He looked like a commercial for after-shave lotion.

I put my hand on the doorknob, thinking of the dial of a TV set, and smiled.

"How are you?"

"I'm fine, love," he said. His teeth were very white.

The broadcasting school blandness of his voice encouraged me. I clicked the knob and went in. I'd always wanted to meet one of those perfect television specimens up close.

I stood a foot or so out from his bed, not wanting to get too familiarly near, tenta-tive as to approach, glancing with uncertainty into his dark-lashed eyes. I ventured a hand on the flat muscles of his chest, lightly dusted with fine black hair. It met no re-sistance. The trace of a smile played over his lips, his black eyes watching me. I stroked his chest farther down, running my hands over his well-developed legs which were also covered with soft sooty hair. The whole of his body was in excellent shape, like he really spent a lot of time on it, exercised or swam a lot. I longed to find a scar, even some imperfection, however slight. But there was none. Perfection. And what can you do with perfection? Stick it up in a museum, I guess, or a video screen. He looked like a commercial for Jantzen swim trunks.

I lifted the pendants of his necklace but the light, as usual, was so bad I couldn't make out what they were.

"One's a good luck charm," he offered.

"And the other?"

"That's a Hebrew symbol."

I told him I liked the necklace. It seemed the most real thing about him, but I didn't tell him that.

He put a hand on my arm and said to me, in the most agreeable way, but in a tone that suggested I was wasting his time, "I'm just resting, hon."

"Sure," I said. I began thinking of the unexpected possibilities in the numerous cu-bicles throughout this floor and the floor below. I suspected the lump between his legs to be a stick of roll-on deodorant.

He was so at ease and pleasant-natured, I thought he must have smoked some dope, but I smelled none in his cubicle, not that that meant anything. I decided to change channels.

"Enjoy yourself," I said and placed my open palm lightly on his chest for a moment. There was a definite heartbeat.

The smile you could trust clicked on. "Thanks, love."

Leaving his cubicle was like walking out the front of a cathode tube.

I came to the end of the first hallway at the front of the building where the small grimy window was inset in a box-like casement. I was glad to find I could slide it open, and did, sticking my face out as far as I could through the narrow opening. Even the soot-laden and chemical air blowing over the city was a relief from the oppressive atmosphere of perspiration and genuine and artificial smegma smells, the rank underground odor of the window-sealed building. I longed for a whiff of the flowers on display behind the plateglass windows of the wholesale florists up the street.

Pedestrians were hurrying by on the sidewalks below and the block was jammed with slow-moving traffic because of the double-parked trucks at the curbs. To the north, the Empire State Building glowed with a granite light in the silvery reflection of the fast-flying clouds that were lightening up now.

As I leaned out the window I felt an unseen hand casually squeeze my ass in passing, but I didn't turn to look, just kept breathing in the cold air in deep drafts.

After a few minutes I left the window and wandered into the middle hallway, moving slowly toward the rear of the building, my head clearer now. Passing the shut door of one cubicle I could overhear husky voices inside, one saying "*That* was all *right*," and the other responding, "Yeah, put that in your roach clip and toke it." Somewhere, another voice, commanding in good humor, "Don't you *dare* cum yet." Over the wall of another cubicle a few doors down, still another voice in a resigned, factual tone, "No use knocking yourself out—I can't help you, man—It's dead."

From the attendant's station the staticky voice of the clerk down in the lobby was heard through the intercom speaker: "Room 325, tell that guy in there his time's up," and the attendant shouting back from somewhere over in the next hallway, "325—OK!"

At intervals, from someplace close by, came the sharp, repeated, almost desperate whisper of, "*Suck it!*"

A little farther on, a half dozen or so men were standing in a knot, listening intently outside the door of one room where the sounds of violent slapping and punching were heard. I squeezed my way around them and a couple of doors down discovered a youth perhaps in his early twenties, fair-skinned with dark blond hair. Slenderly muscled, he had a boyishly appealing face. He was lying flat on his back, not in a relaxed way, but holding himself in a rigidity of apprehension. His round eyes had a look of fright in them, almost of frenzy, as if he expected the very worst to happen. He was clutching his penis through his towel in a tight fist, staring out through the doorway with the expression of a frightened, frustrated boy about to cry.

Perhaps, like myself, this was his first time at the baths. Probably he'd been lying there listening to the energetic punchings going on in the room down the hall. Perhaps it was that and something else, something maybe that he carried with him all the time and had brought here to the baths, which only magnified it in these surroundings. Maybe he really was waiting for somebody with the look of a punisher.

His expression was so poignant I stood in the doorway for a long moment, not knowing what to do or say. Probably better just to go away. Humanism can be inhuman.

In spite of his display of nudity and the knuckle-whitened hand clenched at his crotch, he appeared, from the tension in his face, in no way to be awaiting some delightful erotic occurrence. If anything, he looked afraid of getting beaten up, or murdered—not uncommon fears in the backs of the minds of most gay males. But here that seemed, though not impossible, at least less likely to occur than elsewhere. Given the whole gamut of playful as well as vicious variations practiced at the baths to the widest and fullest degree, every satisfaction of taste and desire was possible and, giving assent, probable. If his pleasure was in servility and the trust of sadistic control in pain, perhaps the shaggy blond-haired youth in the SS cap I'd seen a few moments before would come strutting by.

If it was that, and if it wasn't . . .

I lifted my hand to him in a kind of wave of greeting, not knowing what else to do. I asked him if he was all right.

"I'm okay," he said, his voice strained. "Just resting."

"Are you sure?"

"Yeah—Sure." His eyes clearly told me to let him alone.

"Take care then," I said, and walked on, having seen clearly in that moment, beyond all speculation, a glimpse of an old and passing self in those wide, frightened eyes; passing on to instinctively protect the recently acquired space of this different self I felt myself becoming; no longer wanting, or needing, to be contaminated that way again, in early fear become reflex, in chronic worry, in habitual defensive alert: not able to help him either, or at least not knowing how, not yet fully healed myself, not yet the healer.

So many of us frightened here, I thought, so many faces that passed me with the look of urgent and perilous need that seemed to have nothing to do with sex, or the reason for being here.

In a dark corner a slow firm hand pushing a groper's fingers away, dissuasion enough. There were doors you stopped at where the occupant, without speaking a word, with a turning away of his eyes, or the all but barely perceptible curl of a lip to one side, told you plainer and louder than words to get lost.

And there were those I found whose cubicle you entered, deciding to risk it, who, when you touched them, slapped your hand away or turned their shoulders abruptly. Rejection learned here, as in other gay male cruising places, as readily as acceptance. But that helps oil it, and you're off, direct, busying on in search of the next and, with hope, more open and accommodating flower. Eros isn't stingy. But the unwanted are here, too, and the too wanted. The too handsome and the not handsome enough, the ugly and deformed—even one youth struggling about the halls on aluminum crutches, his twisted legs strapped in metal braces ("There is no end to desire")— And the very old and the very young, they, too, are here. The cock-teasers, too, I saw, who lured you and when you approached, aroused, pushed you away roughly, often with a sneer. Macho gays were here who needed, all ways, to be on top, to "win" at all costs, where the partner doesn't count except as a used and humiliated participant in their petty glorification. The scrawny with no chins and the chubby with too many; those with pipestem legs and those with the legs of weight lifters. The small cocked, the big cocked, the slender peckered and the stout pricked; the loose-assed and the tight-assed, the beer-bellied and the flat gutted; and all those who give better than they get—All here with all their fantasies and desires, their little lies and big ones, their bent dreams and passing straight dreams and dreams of soaring and airy gay-ety—The beautiful on the outside who are poisoned inside; and the physically ugly who keep close and quiet a loveliness within that many are blind to, often even themselves—All prowl these dreary dim halls with the same purpose and search: to find, surprised, behind the monotonous row on row of cheap plywood doors, endlessly opening and closing, the heart's desire and the awakener of the heart; the miracle of a barely imagined paradise, here in this dingy smelly place, heavy with stale body odors and decades-old perspiration of lust-sweat, and fear-sweat, and ashes of sperm-fire that encrust the walls and floors and ceilings from all the century-long years of those who have searched here in unspeakable pleasure and pain (for there is unspeakable pain here, too); searching patiently and tirelessly to discover, in sly and passionate ambush, in the litter and stink of this hidden away bathhouse in a floral market street of the city, a tiny glint of the shy and elusive flower that enfolds the secret and the meaning. And each of us brings that here, furled tight in the unconscious, in the cellar of need, prowling for it in this house where sunlight is not, nor moonlight, nor nurturing air and moisture, our vision purblind, slaking our thirst on ashes.

I leaned against the wall between the doors of two cubicles and closed my eyes for a moment, envisioning whole stretches of seacoast of briny and sunny sensuality, their beaches and environs unpolluted by attitudinal poisons; gay children, lesbian and gay peoples, giving only to sisters and brothers, giving the others nothing, depriving them of their energies, depriving them of their bodies, cleansing the flesh of patriarchal syphilis, of the poisonous gonorrheas of imbalance, the rape and violence of toxic maleness run riot; all the sons and all the daughters no longer crippled, no longer born blind, no longer living blinded, deprived and hungry; now reviving, cleansing, purifying flesh and spirit, the unpolluted energies returning strong, eros protecting those close and obedient to its ways.

Envisioned great green parks, genuine *play* grounds, too, of open pleasure, wildernesses of nudity given over to sensual disobedience, with all the obedient freedom of mutually consenting and courteous erotic play in praise of happiness and well-being, in praise of ourselves. Playgrounds without chain link fences penning in children, and never again children hanging by the neck from poisoned trees within such holding pens, legs kicking in the unimprisoned wind. And every hometown in America with a free public bath, but, unlike this one, airy and light, open to everyone, where purified mothers and other women teach the girl-children and purified fathers and other men teach the boy-children, in gentle massage, in merry bubble-winking strokes of beginning awareness, in the double cleansing of purification and fleshly acceptance, in encouraging right and clean and courteous ways, the kindliness of our bodies, to know and respect the incredible instrument of sensuous joy, received and given, the body is; and then none can ever be unkind to another, learning in ceremonies of bark and root and wild flower and herb, in open air peoples' baths, to scour ourselves and each other, perspiring in sweat lodges to sharpen vision again, sweat out the poisons, for how we will be with each other; and the gay children live again, and all the children live in us, emptying the mental hospitals and doctor's waiting rooms, depleting the populations in prisons, cutting the death-by-broken-heart rate to zero.

This vision lasted only for a moment since the clamor of perpetually jingling keys, the dull sound of restlessly moving feet sliding up and down the linoleum halls, the sharp cries and gasps and thwackings of flesh in the cubicles around me, didn't allow even the briefest moment of escape.

From over the top of the partition I was leaning against voices drifted:

"I'm fucking my dentist to get my teeth fixed."

"I did the same once with a proctologist when I had my anal warts."

"The pig."

"He said the exercise was part of the treatment."

Sputtering, snickering laugh.

"Did it help?"

"Well, you just tasted the results."

"Not bad. My thanks to Doctor Proctor."

A long sigh.

"What's a poor gay boy to do?"

Opening my eyes, I saw through the open door in the cubicle directly across the hall a redheaded youth spread-eagled on his bed. His skin was the color of ripe peaches. I crossed over and leaned on the doorjamb. After a few moments, aware of me standing there, he turned pale blue eyes to look at me.

"Want company?"

His face was expressionless, studying me. Light coppery eyelashes. He looked me up and down and finally said, "I could use some."

I entered the cubicle and stood beside him, laying a hand on his shoulder, stroking it. His skin had the furry velvet of peaches. Not changing his spreadlegged and belly-down position, he extended an arm and reached under my towel, feeling the heft and size of me, his eyes measuring, weighing. Satisfied, he jerked his head in a "come on" way and sank his face on the pillow again.

I unknotted my towel and let it fall to the floor and climbed onto the bed, kneeling between his legs. His eyes closed slowly, his mouth opening to shape a wide "O" as I ran my fingertips tickling down his spine and played them over the small of his back. The muscles of his buttocks quivered like dartings of wind over water.

He stretched his legs wider on the bed, one leg now pressed flat against the wall, the other jutting off the mattress, stiff and tensed, toes curling and uncurling. I traced a finger along the downy cleft of his buttocks, his anus exposed now to my eye, red seed in a freshly halved peach.

From my kneeling position, I leaned over and swung the door shut.

John Rechy

John Rechy (b. 1934) was born of Mexican parents in El Paso, Texas, the scene of many of his novels. After studying journalism at Texas Western College and the New School of Social Research in New York, he joined the U.S. Army and was stationed in Germany. After returning to New York City, he began a period of male prostitution (hustling), which he continued, as the passage below indicates, long after it was economically necessary.

His most important work is his first novel, the highly autobiographical *City of Night* (1963), the story of a hustler's crossing the country, a book that in pre-Stonewall America caused an enormous stir. In a stinging review in the prestigious *New York Review of Books*, Alfred Chester, who was himself gay, called the novel "the worst confection yet devised" by Grove Press, a publisher of avant-garde literature.

City of Night, although highly autobiographical, is still a novel, one of many Rechy has written, including *Numbers* (1967), *This Day's Death* (1969), *Rushes* (1979), and *Bodies and Souls* (1983). The passage below, however, is from his later book *The Sexual Outlaw: A Documentary* (1977), which is more explicitly nonfiction. It follows a weekend in the life of "Jim," a hustler in Los Angeles, where Rechy now lives. Interwoven through this documentary story are "voice-overs," essays and memoirs of Rechy's own life. The voice-over below recounts Rechy's experiences with conservative homosexuals of an earlier generation.

Voice Over: Four Factions
of the Rear Guard

1

I attend a dinner of gay gentlemen and icy ladies.

Our host is a little man who adores collecting people. He looks like a gay monk. On a black and white tiled floor multiplied by mirrors, he's explaining breathlessly in the corridor who the combatants will be tonight:

"Oh, the usual Los Angeles royalty—though of *course* they're *all* from Pasadena— and our darling Dusty, an ex–Busby Berkeley chorus boy—he'll be 5000 years old in February, and the poor thing *still* thinks he's the cutest thing in dyed feathers! You'll *adore* Natasha, she's a Russian duchess, simply *devastated* by the revolution, and now she's a lab technician but she reads cards. And the wife of Herman von Dern? She *never* says an intelligent word. Oh, there *is* a strange little man all in white and one emerald, I *think* he's famous but God only knows what *for!*—he's here with his muscleman protégé, a Mr Somebody (you two might like each other). . . . Oh, yes, and Otto, a clairvoyant from Orange County. Simply *marvelous* with earthquakes. Do you know Billy Adams?—the son of Alexa Alexandra?—the silent-movie star? Most people don't *know* it, but she was a deafmute, and you can *imagine* what the talkies did to *her*. And some others— . . ." He pauses for breath; we're at the ornate door to his apartment. He turns suddenly to me and says: "Oh, and I want to tell you I *adore* your book!"

"Which one?" I ask, somewhat irritated; I've written five, and people still refer to my "book."

"*City of Night*, of course," he says—inevitably. "Oh, it was forward of me to call you out of nowhere—but how else? how else? But let's do go in. Everyone is simply *dying* to meet you!"

Entering, I see the incredible ensemble; here and there are a few very beautiful determinedly sexless women, one in a tuxedo. I'm wearing a tight, very open shirt, and I love how I am being looked at; I am obviously the evening's fresh blood—myself, and the other muscular man, who sits rigidly throughout the evening with the man who "sponsors" him in body contests.

The chairs are all high-backed, of course. Velvet cuddles the room. The light is, oh, golden. A yellow chandelier twinkles flirtatiously.

The ladies and gentlemen are wearing emeralds, diamonds, rubies, pearls—one gentleman exhibits at least a dozen rings on a chain ("his fingers are too *fat*," our host whispers).

Dusty the Busby Berkeley chorus boy wears a tacky necklace of pukah shells. "They're quite expensive," he informs Count Etienne, a skinny man with plucked eyebrows—no relation to the duchess here.

"Hmmm," says his lordship.

"I paid fifty dollars for the necklace," the ex–chorus boy insists.

Flashing rubies and emeralds, the count says, "Oh, *nice!* But you know, dear, you have to have a certain *bubbly* personality to get away with *those* things—*you* have it, *I* don't."

Dusty waits for his turn. It comes. His lordship is narrating the shock he felt when an ordinary policeman came to his door by mistake. In Pasadena!

Dusty strikes: "And the Pasadena ladies looking out their windows said, Oh, my God, she's entertaining the military now!" He loops the pukah-shell necklace around his wrist.

Drinks about the room are like colored water in goblets: green, red, amber. Photographs of the great stars line bookshelves; the gorgeous artificial faces next to dead flowers.

When the count comments favorably on my body, I ask what he does.

"Mostly I'm a count," he answers.

And the Busby Berkeley chorus boy strikes again: "Cunt?"

His lordship smiles tolerantly. The rabble— ... "Count, dear, with an 'O.'"

"Oh," says the ex–chorus boy, and goes on to tell about the death of Hollywood and glamour.

"So many funerals," sighs Billy Adams, the son of the mute star. "So many stars dying. Gone, gone. I went to Mandy Mandeville's funeral. She looked terrible—so shriveled, so tiny. They used to be bigger. Oh, but at Forest Lawn this adorable youngman insisted I buy a plot there—before need. And I did."

"Did you buy the youngman or the plot?" asks the host.

"It overlooks Glendale," the famous son of Alexa Alexandra says.

"How chic," says his lordship.

The icy ladies sip their drinks frostily. They look like Russian spies in an American movie.

"My *God!*—I thought you were dead," Dusty the ex–chorus boy says to a new guest, a man who once played the evil scientist in dozens of movies.

Natasha the Russian duchess wants to read the cards for me—but there's only an incomplete deck, *two* incomplete decks. So she mixes them—different-sized cards. In her chubby hands, they flutter to the floor. "Fuck it," she says.

The clairvoyant tells me he doesn't need the cards to tell me I have powers I haven't even discovered yet and I'll win the contest I'm entering.

But the old gentleman "famous for God knows what"—and he *is* all in white, with just one huge emerald—says, no, no, it's *his* muscular friend—who hasn't said a word—who is entering the contest.

Oh.

Somebody tells me he loved my book.

"Which one?" I ask.

"*City of Night*, of course."

"Do you still hustle?" the ex–chorus boy asks me naughtily.

"Yes," I say defiantly.

"You know," he goes on. "I occasionally dial the telephone on the corner of Selma, and I speak to the hustlers—so exciting!"

My God, I've talked to him!

I want to affront them all, they're so uptight, reactionary. "I also go to alleys."

His lordship says he couldn't get involved with alleys because, being inbred royalty, he has to guard against disease. "It would *kill* me," he says. From his coat-of-armed blazer jacket he pulls out an ivory fan, which he spreads expertly—*swushhh!*—as if to chase away deadly germs especially those that may be coming from the ex–chorus boy.

I tell the count he could go to clean alleys.

"What kills *me*," says Dusty the Busby Berkeley chorus boy, "is that all the niggers are driving Cadillacs."

The gentleman in white asks him didn't he wear feathers in his last film?

"What happens in the alleys?" the clairvoyant asks.

"Some clairvoyant," sighs the host.

"Fucking and sucking." I don't like how I'm sounding, but I want to protest this stagnation.

"Oh, it was all more fun and sexy before the so-called sex revolution," says Billy Adams, the famous son, "before all this sexual revolution mess. *We* kept in our closets."

"My family lost their *estate* in a revolution," his lordship sneers icily.

"Mine too," echoes the duchess; "that's why I'm a lab technician."

The table is set: Silver plates shine under hypnotized candles.

The sexless beauties look like killers.

Now here's a guru in flowing robes—just out of jail for attempting to shoot his lover. "*Om, om.*"

The beauty in the tuxedo gets told not to smile—she hasn't—or she'll ruin her lovely baby face. The gentleman in white suggests that his "friend" and I armwrestle.

The guru asks me what I suggest for his sagging middle.

Someone tells the cool beauty that if she sneers she'll get wrinkles too.

Om.

Dusty laments the openness of everything sexual now. "I like it more naughty," he giggles.

The gentleman in white agrees snippily: "The closet is perfectly comfortable, thank you!"

For dinner we have meatloaf.

2

In his palatial home, the famous director courts an army of drifting youngmen. All are sure they'll become big stars. Not one has, not one will.

I hate the man, his contempt. So much wasted power! He uses it to extend a tapestry of dreams cruelly to the hungry youngmen, only to withdraw it quickly and send them to others in a sliding order back to the streets but, now, with memories of evaporated glory.

"My films extol the old truths," he says in an interview. "That is what is needed, a return to morality."

3

I meet a famous star. He gets drunk. Under the dinner table his hand gropes me. His fingers dig into my fly. I'm trying to be cool, not to embarrass anyone. Others at the table are unaware what's happening under it.

Except for the star's bodyguard-lover.

Alerted by other similar times, he stands abruptly behind the star and looks down. The star withdraws his stumbling fingers.

"I knew it," says the bodyguard-lover.

"Piss," says the star.

The bodyguard leaves.

The star gets drunker. His overtures to me increase. "Please come home with me." He's pitiful, this famous, rich, powerful man. Pitiful. Always falling in love with those who can't love him, who will only use him; surrounded by an entourage of invited sycophants who drain his need for love; always, always inviting to be used. No, I can't go with him, I say.

He leaves the party. But he calls back on the telephone. Please come to his house, just to talk. Just so he will be with someone. *Please.*

Driving to his mausoleum of a house, I see in the flash of my headlights his bodyguard-lover, spying.

Fuck it. I promised I'd come, to talk. And there he is, the lonely star, at his door.

The house is cluttered like an overbought antique store. Chandeliers like crystal spiderwebs. Devouring velvet chairs. Figurines and statues battling limply for attention. Plastic corpses of flowers.

"I want to show you my bedroom," he tells me.

I decide I have to leave.

"Please."

His bed is on a platform. It's a cross between a throne and a circus tent; drapes held at the top with a golden crown. Rows and rows of clothes hang in enormous open closets like squads of frozen guards.

He tries to kiss me, but I'm not attracted to him. "Hey, man," I say.

"Please."

He knew all along I'd reject him this way, I think suddenly. He knew it all along.

As I'm leaving, he offers to take me to Palm Springs if I stay.

4

"It's a white party," the man informs me. "Everyone has to dress completely in white." The party will be in his lovely rustic home.

What the hell. I get into it. I wear a white-bloused, see-through open Cavalier shirt, white boots, and pants with two rows of buttons in front.

A greenhouse with exotic flowers. Listen to the delicate water spray, like kisses. Oh, a brook! And alcoves. Look! A large swaying hammock. And minstrels in white, playing flutes.

Men and boys in white jockstraps wander along the multi-leveled gardens. A man turns up in tennis drag. Men sit along the tiered ledges watching the parade.

A few women idle about, ignored. There's a sultan in see-through pants. There's a man in white ballet tights, genitals exposed. A dazed-looking youngman with a very bad complexion and wearing nothing but crossed belts on his skinny body wanders aimlessly.

I think suddenly of a dull, white purgatory.

Over a hundred guests in white.

A producer arrives with harnessed "slaves." There's appreciative applause from the tiers.

"It's just lovely. Lovely. So innocent," says a man standing benignly on a balcony like a voyeuristic high priest.

Alan Helms

Edmund White has called Alan Helms (b. 1937) "the most famous piece of ass of my generation," a description that suggests both the admiration and condescension he endured. Alan Helms was not beautiful the way so many young men are; instead, he was so incredibly beautiful that he modeled for such world-famous photographers as Richard Avedon and was considered star material by the same agent who signed Robert Redford. But beyond his beauty was his intelligence. He graduated from Columbia University and was a finalist for a Rhodes scholarship, "the first big thing [he'd] ever wanted in life [and] . . . hadn't got." He was, in fact, the ideal that many have sought to become.

Nevertheless, for all its excitement and pleasure, being "the most famous piece of ass" was a misery for a man who was shy, insecure, and troubled by his own inadequacies and an alcoholic family. *Young Man from the Provinces* (1995), from which the excerpt below is a part, is Helms's attempt to show life from the point of view not of most people who seek beauty and brains but of one who has been given such gifts.

Helms went on to reject modeling, acting, and a possible movie career to become an English professor. Today he is professor emeritus of English at the University of Massachusetts, Boston, and the dance critic for *Bay Windows* and the *South End News*.

From *Young Man from the Provinces*

THE SUMMER AFTER MY JUNIOR YEAR in 1958, I remained in New York doing test shots & putting together a modelling portfolio; otherwise, I spent my time exploring the gay world. It was such a different world, & now such a vanished one, that it's not easy to explain. Intensely secretive & hidden, it went on mostly at night behind the unmarked doors of bars & in apartments where the shades were always drawn. The 415 Bar on Amsterdam Avenue was typical: you walked in, saw a few locals talking with the bartender, & figured you'd made a mistake. But through an unmarked door in the back & down a flight of stairs, you entered a cavernous basement teeming with hundreds of gay men who were dancing & laughing & cruising & kissing & drinking & passing out in the johns. No wonder that during my two years with Dick I'd not had the slightest suspicion such a world existed. It was determined to remain as hidden as possible.

The men were too. Everyone I knew was more or less closeted & spent a lot of time in the workaday world passing for straight. Save for a few artists & hairdressers & decorators & dancers, we were all terrified of being found out. Gay men regularly married for the sake of appearances or inheritances & just as regularly committed suicide. If you heard that a gay man was seeing a shrink, it meant only one thing: he was trying desperately to "go straight," which sounded more like a road sign than a way of life. Parents routinely disowned & disinherited their gay sons or had them committed to mental hospitals where they were subjected to shock treatments & lobotomies & a popular therapy of the day called "aversion therapy": "by means of hypnotic suggestion and conditioning, the author has been able . . . to create deep aversions in the male homosexual to the male body." How do you do that? "Suggestions of filth associated with the male genitalia of their partners were implanted in their subconscious and reinforced periodically during the hypnotic trance." Psychiatrists published abominations like that with pride & impunity. In their view, which was mainstream America's view made professional & scientifically unassailable, homosexuality was an abnormality to be corrected at all costs; the most barbarous treatments were justified in the name of destroying such pernicious tendencies. There were gay men walking the streets of Manhattan in those days who had been rendered incapable of sex or had their memories obliterated by electricity. For some, it would take years to put their minds back together again; for others, the effort was hopeless. Of all the enemies we had, psychiatrists were among the most dangerous. And our parents, of course. I never met anyone who was out to his parents; you had to be crazy to do such a thing.

There was no place in public where it felt safe to be gay. Even inside the gay world you weren't secure, since bars & parties were raided all the time. You'd be having a beer & a chat with someone in a bar when suddenly the police would appear at the door screaming "Stay where you are, this is a raid!" Fear would sweep over the place, followed by a stampede for the back door, people falling over each other & jamming the exit in their panic to get out. During one of my own terrified escapes, I was fleeing out the back when I saw a fat man I knew wedged in the bathroom window leading to the alley. The next day, his name appeared in the papers along with the names of the other men arrested in the raid—a couple of dozen all told, an average take. He was fired of course, & evicted from his apartment, & there was nothing he could do about it. There were no legal aid societies or political action groups for gays in those days, no gay weeklies or bimonthlies to publish his plight & raise money for his defense. What defense? Firings, evictions, arrests, entrapments, blackmail, muggings, murders— they happened all the time, they came with the territory.

At parties, you knew the instant the police had arrived. The room would fall silent & without even turning to look, you knew a couple of New York's finest were at the front door, "Fuckin' Faggots" scrawled all over their faces. Sometimes they told us to keep it down & they went away; other times they told us to break it up & then stood at the door as we filed out between them like guilty things caught in a shameful act. I never once heard anyone protest or ask why we had to break it up. We just did as we were told.

Except for the drag queens, bless their sassy, revolutionary hearts. But they always got beaten up & arrested & thrown in jail, over & over again. "Such masochists," we said. "They're really sick."

Whenever our world came into conflict with the straight world, group loyalties crumbled. Threatened with arrest or blackmail, thrown out of a party, chased down a midnight street by a gang of fagbashers, it was each gay man for himself, running for fear, lost in a panic to save his own skin. We didn't have much political awareness, partly no doubt because our enemies were so often invisible: cultural opinion, legal precedent, psychiatric theory, social convention, religious stricture—nothing you could insult or demean or punch in the face in return. The most pernicious enemy of all, & the most invisible, was our own self-hatred.

Almost all of us bought into the straight notion that there really was some-thing wrong with us, something abnormal & perverted & ultimately pathetic. It still astounds me to think how many derogatory names the straight world has invented to designate gay men: fags, faggots, pansies, perverts, inverts, aunties, flits, queers, queens, cocksuckers, nellies, sickos, homos, sodomites, pederasts, sissies, swishes, fairies, fruits, & the list goes on. The reverberations of that lexicon sounded even in our dreams, inducing a kind of concentration camp mentality. We were disposable, the scum of the earth, living crimes against nature (thank you, Thomas Aquinas), & we knew that socially, religiously, legally, psychoanalytically, & in every other way that mattered, we were beyond the pale of what was considered acceptably human. I don't remember that we talked about the sense of shame the straight world bred in us, but it was pervasive in our lives, & I don't know anyone of my gay generation who's ever been able to shake it. I certainly haven't. You can still see it in the timid gestures toward self-exposure of a John Ashbery or a Jasper Johns, & in the furtive, guilty cruising of gay men in their fifties & sixties.

With so much fear & danger hedging our lives, it's no wonder we were a wildly romantic bunch. Mainstream America was too, of course. My parents had grown up in a world fed by Hollywood fantasies of romantic love, & the lyrics of popular songs urged a desperate, eternal monogamy: "Once you have found him / Never let him go," & then the repeat in case you weren't paying attention the first time. In 1957, 96 percent of adult Americans were married, if you can imagine such a statistic. Heterosexual marriage was the only model of adult life that existed at the time, so gay America was busy coupling in imitation of its masters.

Since romance thrives on obstacles (Tristan & Isolde, Romeo & Juliet, Cupid & Psyche, Antony & Cleopatra), there was no more fertile ground for romance in those days than the gay world. I don't think I ever made love with a man without first convincing myself he was a potential long-term lover, & if the first date went well, which invariably meant the first night of sex, I was ready next morning to shop for monogrammed towels. All the frenetic cruising & partying & sexing had as its goal the paragon lover, a gay knight on a charger who would sweep us off our feet & make everything all right, compensate us for the oppression we had to put up with & for the pervasive sense there was something lacking in us that only the right man could supply. We fell in love a lot, & conducted our mostly brief affairs with operatic drama—passionate avowals of eternal devotion, fits of jealous rage, wrenching break-ups replete with nervous breakdowns & threats of suicide. The few of us liberated enough to resist the notion that gay men were incapable of sustained affection managed successful relationships, but most of us got "married" & settled down for a brief while, then broke up & broke down, then grieved & cruised until we met the next candidate for our troubled affections, & thus the same round all over again.

There was almost always an element of the frantic & the excessive about our pleasures. Parties & pimples, tricks & true loves, suicides & sales—everything was "fabulous" or "horrible," "terrific" or "terrible," with nothing in between, no "all right" or "fine" or "okay." It was all very hectic, extreme, loud, & mildly hysterical. Yet very conventional too in that gay men's relationships aped straight marriages with their clearly assigned roles of "butch" & "femme," "top" & "bottom," "husband" & "wife."

I didn't know anyone who didn't have a camp name. Two giant weight-lifter friends were dubbed "Martha" & "Hilda," & I once lived with a gorgeous Neapolitan-Sicilian we called "Gina," by which time I was "Hanya" & "Celeste." I didn't know anyone who didn't have a sunlamp or take a long time in the bathroom or wear clothes too small for comfort. I didn't know anyone who didn't belong to a gym, unless he was hopeless material, or anyone who didn't care a lot about bodies. I didn't know anyone who didn't have a type ("He'd be gorgeous if he weren't blond") or a limited repertory of sexual practices ("What do you do?" we always asked to make sure our desires could cooperate). I didn't know anyone who didn't drink a lot. A typical evening began with drinks at someone's apartment, then wine during dinner followed by a brandy or two, then more drinks at a bar afterward. I often staggered home at three & four & five A.M. with vodka & wine & brandy & beer sloshing around in my disconsolate stomach.

You can find the feel & flavor of that world in Frank O'Hara's poetry. He was on the scene a lot & he wrote about it, though usually in guarded ways that require deciphering. But he clearly conveys the sense of lots of romantic, glamorous, frenetic living & high hilarity, & beneath it all, some sadness laced with a little shame & a little self-hatred.

But this is all after the fact. I didn't analyze my experience at the time, I just lived it. "You kept from thinking and it was all marvelous," as Harry says in "The Snows of Kilimanjaro." If I bothered to think anything at the time, it was probably "Lucky me, fiddledeedee," nothing more profound than that. I was too flustered for thought, too dazzled by the sexual & social opportunities that existed for me in that world.

The sex was everywhere. The parties & bars & dances & dinners yielded a lot, but gyms were even better sources, for in a gym you could see what a man had to offer physically. A goodly portion of attractive gay Manhattan worked out at the West Side Y, & I never went to the Y without the expectation I might go home with someone afterward. At the least I usually got a telephone number or two for future reference. Sex was out in public too, walking down the street at all hours of the day & night. Noon or midnight, three in the afternoon or ten in the morning, before lunch or after the theater, on your way to the post office or in the subway—it was abundantly there for the having. I knew guys who had sex three & four times a day, & if they couldn't, they masturbated three or four times a day. Usually they got what they wanted. Some of my most exciting times happened when I connected with an attractive man in the supermarket or on the street, & fifteen minutes later we'd be curling each other's toes in one of our apartments. But you had to be careful about the sexual opportunities you encountered in public if you wanted to avoid the homophobia & violence that existed everywhere & were so easily aroused.

As for the social opportunities, I wouldn't believe them if I hadn't lived them. In the next four years, I met Noel Coward & John Gielgud, Laurence Olivier & the Lunts, Bette Davis & Gloria Swanson, the *West Side Story* crowd (Bernstein, Robbins, Laurents, & Sondheim), Katharine Hepburn, Lena Horne, Rock Hudson, James Baldwin, Judy Garland, Rex Harrison, Nat King Cole, Dali & Margaret Rockefeller (the Marquesa de Cuevas), Robert Redford & Jane Fonda, Ava Gardner & Jack Dempsey, Williams & Albee & Inge, Gore Vidal & Eleanor Roosevelt, Marlene Dietrich & Adlai Stevenson, Jackie Kennedy & the Dalai Lama. (I'm namedropping, yes, but how else can I make the point so neatly?) In the ensuing years, I met many more such prominent people. Some I met by chance or through common friends, but some became close friends & a few became lovers. If you were a presentable young gay man with manners & a good suit, there wasn't anywhere you couldn't go in the worlds of art & entertainment, & those worlds easily opened up other vistas. Because I was gay, I had much more social mobility than if I'd been straight. As for the gay world, it was much smaller & more concentrated then than now, so instead of being a small fish in a big pond, which would have been my lot as a young man coming out these days, I was vice versa. Today you can live a gay male life as a leather queen in Chicago or Houston or Des Moines without traversing the boundaries of other subworlds, but in those days, the gay world was concentrated in New York & its members inhabited several subworlds simultaneously. A Manhattan leather queen circa 1958 might well be a member of the opera queen set, which included people from the gym queen set, some of whose members were writers & painters & playwrights from the arts queen set, which spilled over into the international queen set, which boasted some tearoom queens & trade queens, & so on throughout that whole, elaborate, secret world. The result was that you knew people throughout the only concentrated gay world in America. And they knew or had heard about you—or at least about me.

Since a good body counted for so much in gay New York, that summer of '58 I joined the West Side Y. I had a perfectly good body to start with—well-proportioned thanks to Mother Nature, developed & toned from construction work & my daily mile in the Columbia pool. But always willing to find myself wanting, & now inhabiting a world where bodies counted for a lot, I had to have a better body, the best body on the beach, a body that would make people swoon.

Four times a week at the West Side Y, I lugged & hoisted & pushed & pulled & pumped & strained until I got what I wanted—a body like the Doryphorus of Polyclitus but with no Venus girdle (i.e., no love handles, only the taut line of muscle from waist to hip, a "lithe sheer of waist"). Pleased at how quickly my body responded to exercise, I turned my visits to the gym into a fetish. If I had a date or a party or any kind of evening out, I needed a thorough workout beforehand as a prop for my wobbly self-esteem. So I'd pump up the muscles, squeeze into some Levi's, & off I'd go into the night.

People did in fact say that the sight of me walking on the beach made them swoon; one man claimed he'd had to leave the beach to recover. But compliments about my body were easy for me to accept. I might doubt my looks, but never my body. From the time I became addicted to the gym, I knew that my body was superb. And luckily I was saved from the grotesque models of male bodybuilding that exist these days. Steve Reeves was the Mr. Universe of the late '50s—a handsome man of classic features with a body of classical proportions like you see on Greek statues of older gods & heroes, the mature Zeus & Poseidon for example. Nothing like Arnold Schwarzenegger has ever existed in the world of art.

Not yet a year into my gay life & already it bewildered me whenever someone didn't want me. That sexy Slavic waiter in the restaurant on Bleecker Street, with wavy blond hair & dark eyebrows & lupine eyes & an ectomorphic body all shoulders & wrists & cowboy legs showing through his tight pants, he certainly wanted me. Desire was written all over his beautiful, brooding face, so it was easy to make a date with him to come back to my place when he got off work around one in the morning.

In fact, he'd wanted me so much I wasn't worried when it got to be 1:10 & even 1:20. It was only around 1:30 that I began to pace the apartment & look out the window to see if he was coming up the street, then 1:45 when I ran downstairs to check the doorbell, first disconnecting the phone in case he called during my absence, then back upstairs fast to reconnect the phone & look out the window again & check myself in the mirror to reestablish the fact that yes, I was attractive, I was so attractive I hadn't met anyone who didn't want me, so he'd be along soon, there was some explanation, he was held after work or something until it was 2:30 & then 3:00 & 4:00 & 5:00 with the dawn coming up but still the frantic hope he would come despite the growing, horrible realization that I was being stood up for the first time in my life, was being abandoned & was thus what I feared in my worst thoughts: worthless because not really that attractive & therefore someone others would stand up, which was to say, abandon. What was happening to me simply *could not happen*, so even at 6:00 & 7:00, sitting in the window watching early risers on their way to coffee shops, I still nursed the dying hope that the phone would ring. There *had* to be a different ending from the one I was living through, for it was intolerable, a kind of hell, & so back to the window to search the street now filling with people on their way to work, & me alone, not really that attractive after all, a fraud the Slavic waiter had seen through just as everyone else would soon see through me. I was unattractive & worthless: it all showed in the mirror.

It would take me more than twenty years to work my way through that confusion. During that time, legions of men offered me their company & their affection, their bodies & their secrets, but it was usually the ones who turned me down or stood me up or didn't call or somehow rejected me who made the most lasting impressions. Given my childhood, rejection always felt like abandonment, & whenever it happened it was devastating. I'd been out maybe nine months & established an extraordinary record of social & sexual triumphs, but all of that counted for nothing the night the Slavic waiter didn't show.

"Never mind, my dear," said Sam Sloman, "for*get* that Slavic slut. You are di*vine*, do you *hear*? *Absolutely di*vine! Now pay attention to your mother!"

Sam Slomon—*aka* Sally Slomon, your Aunt Sally, your mother, & the Sobo heiress (his father invented Sobo Glue)—was the Elsa Maxwell of New York gay society in the '50s & '60s. Every few weeks Sam gave a party in his over-decorated Village apartment for sixty or seventy of New York's most beautiful gay men, along with a sprinkling of the older rich &/or famous. Most attractive gay men about town eventually found their way to one of Sam's loud, jampacked, giddy, trick-fix drunkfests. The first time I went, I was in the bathroom when Sam barged in to change for his drag number. He stripped & got in the bathtub as I started to piss. "Over here, my dear. Go ahead, your Aunt Sally's a golden shower queen. Oh come *on*, for heaven's sakes, just a little bit, don't be such a tight-assed *WASP*. Right here on my leg. Come on now, do what your mother says." I did what my mother said. "Ohhh, I may just *faint* with joy. Well, *that* was certainly refreshing. What a *kind* young man you are, every bit as *sweet* as you are *beautiful*." A short time later, Sam emerged from the john to entertain us in a hula skirt, with breasts & wig of shaving cream. When he wasn't falling down drunk, Sam's drag numbers could be hilarious.

Sound sort of pathetic? Not really. "Humani nil a me alienum puto," says Terence ("Nothing human is alien to me"), & besides, considering Sam's story it was a miracle he could function at all. When he was sixteen & living with his family in Brooklyn, he sneaked out one night to attend a drag ball in Manhattan. Returning home drunk & wobbly in high heels, he saw a man cruising him in a car, so he flounced & teased the man all the way home. When he turned up his front walk, the driver pulled in behind him. Sam's father had been cruising his son, having mistaken him for a woman, & a loose one at that—one of the more startling ways to discover that your namesake & heir is gay. A week later, according to Sam, his father tried to push him into a two-thousand-gallon churning vat of Sobo glue.

Sam had grown up in a world even more benighted about gaydomry than the world of the 1950s. In the '20s & '30s, there wasn't even a *Giovanni's Room* or *The City and the Pillar* to read as a young man. Sam's early passions were for drag & trade, & he remained faithful to both his whole life long. He told me that his first sex occurred when Harpo Marx seduced him as a boy vacationing with his parents at Grossinger's.

Sam boasted of the experience as a grown man, but if in fact it happened, it must have been unnerving for a boy of twelve. Though a real mensch & full of street smarts, he'd often been beaten up cruising the docks for trade. It had to be harder for Sam to be gay in the 1930s & '40s than it was for us in the '50s. Constantly fortified by booze & pills & a succession of unsuccessful shrinks, he was one of the people who helped pave the way for gay men of later generations. But everyone's heard about prophets in their own countries.

I met Sam when he was forty-five, & he was then an interior decorator who'd done some well-known New York restaurants. (Why do so many gay men become decorators? It's a way to design alternative worlds, or at least to improve on the existing one.) Short, stocky, balding, an inveterate camp & very butch, Sam was like most gay men I knew then, & many I know now, in that he thought he was missing a piece, a part, a something that could only be supplied by the right man, which in Sam's case meant the right straight stud — a sailor or Marine or carpenter or bricklayer or telephone line repairman or . . . well, you get the type. The illusion kept him cruising so constantly that I often thought he must have cruised in his dreams. Sam would walk up to a stud in broad daylight & exclaim "You are the *most* gorgeous & sexy man I have *ever* seen in my *entire life!* Do you *realize* how *gorgeous* you are?" A Santa Claus laugh in here, then "My dear, a man like *you* deserves the *best* blow job of his *life,* & that's the *least* I'm offering you." More often than not, he got the guy — through flattery or jokes or promises to pander or persistence or money. Sam's life was a continual demonstration that where there's a will, & sometimes money, there usually is a way.

I saw a lot of Sam that first summer of being out in gay New York. He adored me, but he didn't lust after me. He paid my way & pandered for me. He made sure I met all the attractive young men he knew, & he served as a go-between for older men too shy to approach me on their own.

"Remember Joe Hastings, the advertising queen? Tall, skinny, nervous, looks like a dachshund? Matter of fact, she *has* a dachshund. Well, you've done it again, my dear. She's *mad* for you, says she'll do *anything,* I can't get her off the phone. Would you consider dinner? the theater? a trip to Europe? adoption? I can't remember it all, but I *do* remember a firm offer of a thousand dollars if you'll spend the night with him."

A thousand dollars for a single night of sex (equivalent to roughly five thousand dollars today)? That was the offer, & the best proposition I've ever heard of. I turned Joe down for the simple reason that I didn't find him attractive, but by way of compensation I let him buy me a custom-tailored sport jacket from Dunhill & take me to a few opening nights. Also a few parties — the most closeted parties of all, attended by diplomats & politicians, heads of corporations, top military brass, the gay men most terrified of exposure. Aside from occasional remarks about attractive men, those gatherings could have passed for stag parties, the men were so resolutely masculine.

Their dates were West Point cadets, college athletes, Olympic medalists—impeccably butch young men beyond a hint of suspicion; young men like me.

Surely one reason for Joe's munificent offer was the fact that in a world of so many effeminate men, I was masculine. I enjoyed the camping of others but wasn't good at it, & I wasn't about to do anything in public I didn't excel at. I could pass for straight except when some hawk-eyed homophobe found me slavering at high noon over an Italian demigod. With little to lose, I was more out than most (away from Columbia anyway), which meant that though I felt shame at being gay, I didn't show it. And a lifetime of learning how to please plus the knack of altering myself to suit the moods & needs of others meant that I was well prepared for success in that world.

Since society is essentially a form of theater (something the French have always understood), people devoted to social success need to be adept actors or they'll end up with bit parts. I was ready for most leading roles in that world of sexual fantasy. I couldn't satisfy anyone's need for a leather or S&M type or your average slackjawed sheet-metal worker, but otherwise I had several roles in my repertory:

Ivy League student intellectual? Down pat.

College athlete lifeguard with body of death? No problem.

All-American boy next door oozing with Hoosier? The Norman Rockwell boy-man type which was then the reigning image of the attractive American male? That's exactly what I looked like.

Soulful aesthete who swooned at Balanchine, haunted museums, & could quote reams of poetry from memory? I put my heart & soul into that one.

Withdrawn, tormented, meditative young man? Right up my alley.

Spoiled, self-centered, unavailable brat star of the gay world? Watch me do my stuff.

In short, there was the face for the face queens, the body for the body queens, the mind for the mind queens, the brat for the brat queens, & a deeply confused, worthwhile young man for those who wanted to rescue someone. Also the carefree young man who didn't seem ashamed of being gay (an impression greatly aided by the eight hundred miles between me & home). I was able to serve as a multipurpose screen on which men could project their different desires, & I served eagerly, with a desperate neediness, for the more people wanted me, the more I mattered, right? "That's right," the voices said.

I didn't think of it this way at the time; I just thought, "Wow, everybody wants me, I really *am* unique." I was aware however that the life I was living was a lot of work & took a lot of time, but I figured that, as the French say, "Il faut souffrir pour être beau"—One must suffer to be beautiful. I had to show up at a lot of social events, & endure a lot of flattery, & spend a lot of time at the gym, & make sure the clothes fit right, & balance a bewildering number of demands on my time. Just going to a party could consume half the day. The preparations included going to the Y for a thorough workout, concluding with a two mile run & a mile swim, after which I had a sunlamp treatment. Then home for a nap before showering & shaving & dressing & preening. At last I was ready, except for a glass of milk & a tablespoon of olive oil to coat my stomach as a guard against hangovers. And that was just a single party.

The payoff for all this effort? I was becoming the most celebrated young man in all of gay New York.

I was taken on for a tryout period by the Hartford Model Agency (owned by the A&P heir Huntington Hartford, who soon sold it to Eileen & Jerry Ford). Odd that I would persist in modelling since I hated being photographed, worried as I was that the fuss over my looks was mistaken & convinced that the other male models were better looking than me. But the money was so good & the strokes for my ego so gratifying that I swallowed my diffidence & showed up for bookings.

Clearly, I thought, I needed to know more about my looks, the better to tend them, the better to nurture my fledgling career. I don't know how it is for other models, but for me it wasn't possible to think about my looks & body & hair & skin & teeth only from nine to five Monday through Friday. I came to think about them around the clock. I developed an extraordinarily acute sense of my physical self that I lost only when drunk or asleep or in the throes of sex. I studied myself until I knew every square millimeter of my body, from the beauty mark on my left cheek to the shape of my toenails. The really beautiful, I thought, are flawless—the ones like gods, that is. Whenever I arrived at a party or restaurant or anywhere I knew people would be ogling me, I headed straight for the john to check myself out in the mirror to make sure the gift of the look was in prime working order. Always my comb, never my glasses. I learned which was my better side & positioned myself so that side faced whomever I wanted to impress. Whenever there was no one to impress, I had a boring evening.

The modelling jobs began coming in on a regular basis. They sometimes interfered with my classes at Columbia, but no great matter. It was enviable to be a model & my career was taking off, hip hip hurrah. One more thing I'd wanted a lot & managed to get.

My advisor at Columbia was Andrew Chiappe, a brilliant polymath who was legendary on campus for his incisive mind & immense knowledge. Lionel Trilling & Meyer Schapiro used to drop into his office to have him decipher a phrase of Hegel, or translate some medieval Latin, or explain the essentials of Rajput painting. I found him so intimidating that his innocuous "How are you, Mr. Helms?" used to render me speechless.

When Professor Chiappe suggested I apply for a Rhodes Scholarship, I therefore took it as a sign from on high. I applied, & after a couple of preliminary rounds I became one of the midwestern finalists, which meant a trip to Indianapolis for the interview that would winnow a field of eighteen or so to the two who would go to Oxford in the fall. Chiappe's recommendation augured well. I had a custom-tailored three-piece suit (a gift from an admirer), & I could count on a first-rate education to support me in the interview. I headed for Indianapolis, nervous but hopeful.

The morning interview was exciting—questions about structural relations between Bach's music & mathematics & other such ingenuities posed by a genial group of a dozen former Rhodes scholars seated on the far side of a large table. Clearly I performed well, clearly they liked me.

After lunch, three of us were called back for a final interview. When my turn came, the examiners began with questions that seemed somehow odd.

"If you were to go to Oxford, Mr. Helms, would you miss the world of Broadway theater?"

"Probably not. If I did, I could take a train to London."

"Have you ever been in the homes of any of your professors?"

"I've often been in the home of Professor Webb, and I once attended a wedding reception at Professor Hofstadter's."

"When you lived in the dormitory, you sometimes had guests?"

Their drift became clear & I began to panic.

"Now & then, yes."

"Where do you go when you go to Greenwich Village?"

"No place in particular . . . that is, movies mostly, & the Amato Opera Company. It's not expensive. The operas aren't very good, I mean the performances, but I go there and . . . sometimes a restaurant . . . nowhere in particular. Mostly I just walk around."

"You live off campus?"

"Yes."

"And you have a roommate?"

"Yes."

"Would you tell us about him, please?"

How in God's name had they found out about my roommate? If they knew about him, they knew everything.

"He's . . . a dancer. I like ballet and . . . it's a temporary arrangement. I thought it would be good experience to live off campus my last year. He was looking for a place at the same time, & . . . anyway it's temporary, so . . ."

I blushed & stammered, forgot my place, repeated myself & stopped in mid-sentence, trapped & defeated, the Rhodes lost.

"Thank you, Mr. Helms, that will be all."

A few minutes later, or an eternity later, I couldn't tell which, the examiners called us together & announced the winners—the other two students who'd been called back after lunch. Then a receiving line, a gauntlet for me, to shake hands with the examiners. I wanted to scream insults, weep, run out of the room, but I went down the line & minded my manners. There was one man, however, a college dean, who detained me to say that if he could ever be of help, he hoped I would contact him. There was that at least, which at the time seemed like small pickings but now seems magnanimously humane under the circumstances.

The Rhodes was the first big thing I'd ever wanted in life that I hadn't got. (Oh sure, there was Dad's drinking, but I mean the first *possible* thing.) And to think I'd lost it because I was gay, & had been spied on & set up like a clay pigeon, & then, full of hope & trust, shot down by that company of urbane, genial humanists. But I didn't despise them for what they'd done to me, or the culture that told them it was a necessary & right & moral thing to do; I despised myself for the fact that in constructing a gay life in a straight world, I'd been heedless, had left clues to my sexuality lying about for the straight world to find & use against me.

It was clear I would pay dearly in the straight world for being gay. I'd lost Jay, my only friend at Columbia, & some of Dad's feeble love as a result of our last fight when he'd finally confronted me with my homosexuality. My relations with Bob & Patti were strained because of the duplicity I practiced with them. I'd been spied on in the dorms & now lost the Rhodes. Maybe it was better to cut out of the straight world completely, leave it as far behind as possible—which meant leaving behind a world I identified with my intelligence & academic accomplishment, although that didn't occur to me at the time. I just wanted to get away from being despised & humiliated. I would be safe from all of that in the gay world, & safe in modelling, a world where in those days half the male models & photographers were gay & no one was punished for his sexual proclivities.

Arnie Kantrowitz

Arnie Kantrowitz (b. 1940) is a writer, a professor (now retired), and an activist. Kantrowitz was an officer of the Gay Activists Alliance (1970) and the Christopher Street Liberation Day Committee (1976) and later a co-founder of the Gay and Lesbian Alliance Against Defamation (1985). He was close friends with those who fought for gay liberation in the days after the Stonewall riots.

Born in New Jersey, Kantrowitz has lived his adult life in New York City and is an associate professor of English at the College of Staten Island. The passage below is from his 1977 autobiography *Under the Rainbow*. It was one of the first autobiographies written by a gay activist, and it gives, as few accounts do, the day-to-day sense of those early activist years.

From *Under the Rainbow*

I SAW AN AD in *The Village Voice* announcing a meeting of the Gay Activists Alliance. I had never liked going to meetings, especially with strange people. But maybe there would be something there that would explain what was happening to me. Maybe I wouldn't feel strange with these people. Maybe we had something in common. I had to know if they existed, or if what I had seen in the streets that Sunday had been a mirage invented out of my own needs. I had to find out if there was such an animal as a healthy, self-respecting homosexual. Maybe I could even become one if there was, by playing birds of a feather.

On Thursday I took a taxi to the Church of the Holy Apostles at Ninth Avenue and Twenty-Eighth Street. The meeting was in a hall attached to the side of the church. There were about sixty people there, mostly men, mostly white, mostly butch. But a handful of blacks and women and feminine men could be seen. The chairs were arranged in a semicircle facing a long table where a few people sat. I slipped into a back row, timidly hoping to observe the proceedings unnoticed. They spoke of the Snakepit demonstration I had seen and of their plans for petitioning the City Council. Jim Owles chaired with an aggressive insistency on the cause of gay rights that turned me on to it immediately. Wonderful people rose to speak, with anger, with philosophical wisdom, with cleverness, with strength. And each one was clearly an individual.

There were long-haired radicals and short-haired conservatives. No one was simply the stereotype I had been deluded into accepting, even in spite of myself as evidence. I had thought that I wasn't even any good at being a homosexual. I was learning that homosexuals, like every other group, are human beings, as different from one another as one would expect an Eskimo to be different from a Parisian. And I felt that I, who had never fully belonged to any group, always holding something in reserve because I hid the fact that I was gay everywhere except the analyst's couch and the waterfront streets at midnight, had at last found my people.

There was a lot of work to be done, and volunteers were needed to do it. I assumed I would only be able to work behind the scenes, perhaps offering my English teacher's skills in writing leaflets or statements, or at least in editing and proofreading them. I wasn't sure what I could do, but I knew I wanted to do something, and I knew that I would be back the next week. And somehow, when the list was circulated for volunteers to help gather signatures petitioning our City Council representative to work for our civil rights, I already felt I would be denying my best instincts if I failed to put down my name and phone number.

Saturday morning I received a call from Keith Robertson, a young social worker, saying he had been assigned to petition with me in Sheridan Square, right near where I lived. What had I gotten into?

If audience response counts for anything, Keith Robertson was the best-looking man in GAA: a well-turned-out five foot ten, with dark-blond hair that always seemed to fall in his bedroom eyes, leaving observers to bemoan the even momentary obscuring of his handsome features. When he spoke, he revealed a Middle Western simplicity and directness that was refreshing in cynical Manhattan. And so, accompanied by a sight most gay men (even considering the variety of taste) would be proud to be seen with, I took to the streets to fight for the rights that a week before I hadn't even believed I deserved.

We stopped in the neighborhood store where I hadn't bought *Gay* because it was too close to home, and we received a warm reception and two signatures. After that I bought *Gay* there—without *The New York Times* to hide it in. We passed a friend of my cousin's on the street. I had always walked around the block when I was cruising near the antique shop she owned; but I was coming out of the closet, and my entire family would find out eventually. She gave us her signature, looking at me with surprise. It was all much easier than I had ever dreamed. My years of cowering had been unavoidable, but in vain.

The afternoon in Sheridan Square was a revelation. People were interested, amused, willing, rarely hostile. Neighbors, strangers, one of my colleagues from school: all sorts of people signed. But the moment that justified all of my internal *Sturm und Drang* occurred when a man of about seventy came up to me. As he signed the petition, he said, "This is too late for me, but I'm so glad it's happening. Maybe it will make your life better." I wanted to hug him and cry.

When the day's work was finished, Keith came over to me to say good-bye. Right there in broad daylight, under the glowing sun, in front of strangers and neighbors and heterosexuals, he kissed me good-bye—on the lips, and his lips weren't closed! I hadn't even considered that—the right to be more than verbally open, to be like other human beings, to kiss a beautiful man when you like and where you like. I walked home three feet off the ground.

That night I accepted the invitation to see *The Wizard of Oz*. I felt like a different person from the one who had been invited only a week before. It turned out to be the first gay party I had ever been to in my twenty-nine years of closetry. Half a dozen of us watched Judy Garland's vulnerable innocence as Dorothy made her way to the Emerald City and back, daring to dream in Technicolor. I made new friends, and when the film was over, we went out to the Lower East Side (which in those days bore the Day-Glo label of "East Village") to a bar called The Hippodrome, where for the first time I saw men dancing with each other. Only then did I realize how, when I'd danced with women, I would lower my eyes if seduction seemed to threaten in theirs. It took me about two minutes to join the men at The Hippodrome, right up front, eye to eye, dancing with intent to fuck.

The gay world was a consuming infatuation, and liberation a vision we were reaching for, a vision of a world in which everyone could be honest, a world without pretending, where men could love men and women love women openly. Our Emerald City glistened in my newly shining eyes. Within weeks I moved from lonely pork chops in the frying pan to hurried sandwiches gobbled before or during GAA meetings. My life revolved around meetings. There was little time for anything else. I dropped out of Supernova, leaving educational experiment in order to devote all my spare time to "The Movement."

General membership meetings were at seven-thirty on Thursday nights, and the rest of the week was structured around that fact, with committee meetings and political intrigue and demonstrations interspersed. The weekly meetings were growing wildly, and along with them blossomed more and more committees dealing with every issue from pleasure to police. At first, small committee meetings were held in someone's apartment—mine, sometimes, if the group was small enough. Despite the conspiratorial air about our gatherings, we conducted our business according to Robert's *Rules*, and when we were finished, we relaxed our political selves and became people. That was how my consciousness got "raised."

We compared sexual notes, and I found that though my experience, like everyone's, is unique, I had a lot in common with my newly discovered peers. Among them I could at last feel "normal." GAA was anxious to avoid the radical style of its forerunner, the Gay Liberation Front, so there was never any actual consciousness-raising group. We were simply friends, clustering according to our interests, our politics, and our personalities. I made a host of new, gay friends, "brothers and sisters," who called me not Arnold but Arnie.

Jim Owles and Vito Russo and I soon formed a tightly knit triad, sharing fun and crisis and "dishing the dirt" on our mutual acquaintances with equal candor. Vito seemed a firefly, darting from meetings to movies he digested whole at the rate of several a day when he wasn't at work as a waiter. His brown eyes brightened with fervor at the mention of Judy Garland, pictures of whom adorned every room in his house—including the john. His soft round features stood ready with easy sentiment for all the celebrities who had acted and sung the fantasies I had grown up on. His wiry body hurtled more than it walked, forcing him to rush even when we were pacing a slow circle on a picket line. His tongue was sharp: "We're not 'girls,' lady; we're men who fuck each other, and you'd better get used to it!" His tears were quick when he was hurt, his smile radiant when he was pleased. We beamed at each other across rooms full of people like happy kids.

Jim was a more sober sort. He was the president of GAA, a good politician, angering some with his rigidity, but refusing to surrender his firm hand to the sway of fashion. His features looked pale and measured, yet sensuous, his glance steady and clear. There was a military no-nonsense air about him: "Don't bother me with your Sunday-school morality." But there was a person beneath the surface that few people got to see. He bore the burden of public position well—in public. In private he wept over its weight. Our friendship was a love affair without sex. We could walk with synchronized strides. One of us proposed; the other disposed. We played private games: sometimes the potentate and the sage, sometimes Pinocchio and Jiminy Cricket, sometimes Harry and Midge, a typical suburban couple. Midge's voice had a twang: "Harry, put on your galoshes. It's snowing. If I've told you once, I've told you a thousand times. . . ." Either Jim or I could play Midge to the other's Harry, but they lived in private. We would let Vito see them, but not the public.

In public we all showed our anger. Almost as fast as I recognized I had any rage about the subject of gay oppression, I was out in public airing it. Displaying my emotions was awkward at first, but I had been encouraged in group therapy. I was being encouraged here too, by Jim and Vito and a whole community of new acquaintances to chat with on Christopher Street. I was encouraged into doing things I had never imagined I could do. We shook Mayor Lindsay's hand in a receiving line at the Metropolitan Museum of Art's anniversary party, and we didn't let go until we could say, "What are you going to do about civil rights for homosexuals, Mister Mayor?" I probably sounded more like a reporter than a revolutionary, but I felt like a revolutionary, defying my own timidity in order to change the world as suddenly as I had changed my mind. Our sense of community allowed us to do more and more outrageous things. We encouraged each other into more and more nonviolent "zaps": into dancing together in front of a crowd of straight people in Central Park and into disrupting the taping of the mayor's television show.

Letting out the anger was never easy for me. It was embarrassing. But letting out the pride was a pleasure. My favorite demonstration was simply holding hands in the streets. We kissed hello and good-bye wherever we went; we held hands and embraced as lovers and friends. Strangers rarely let us know they noticed, but when I walked behind a couple of men holding hands, I could see people turning to stare and trade nervously amused looks with each other. Holding hands in the street took all the strength I had. It's difficult not to be self-conscious when first you flout custom. But as part of a gay crowd I could yell "Two-four-six-eight: Gay is just as good as straight" with a feeling I'd never had when I'd yelled "Peace! Now!" I had never worn political buttons, but buttons were in style along with politics, and I wore the gay liberation lambda symbol as a matter of honor, just hoping people would ask what it meant, so I could tell them. Even when there wasn't a man's hand there to hold, I wanted to make my gay presence real wherever I went.

I maintained a dwindling interest in other causes. Ralph, the other gay man in group therapy, came along when I went to spend the weekend in Washington for the 1970 annual peace march with a group of gay friends, all of us huddled together in the back of a chugging Volkswagen bus. Along the way I got into a little foreplay with someone named Bob, and we spent the night together. The peace march the next day was as much a picnic in the park as it was marching and oratory. It was definitely not a popular uprising. Our gay contingent drew plenty of surprised stares but few comments, even as we relaxed on the lawn with a little more than fraternal closeness. My head was comfortably ensconced in Bob's lap, looking up at the sky, our friends in similar postures strewn around us. Slowly, out of the corner of one eye, I realized that not only was Bob stroking my brow with one hand, he was holding Ralph's with the other. Still accustomed only to anonymous contact, I was just beginning to have sex with the same people I mixed with socially, and I didn't know how to behave. Then they excused themselves to go for a walk. I was so angry I went home in another car.

I arrived at group therapy the next night just in time to overhear Ralph confiding to one of the other patients, "I stole a trick from Arnie in Washington yesterday." The people in the group had become used to our being open. We had taken to sitting with our arms around each other during sessions, which had established us as comrades and as different. His gloating turned immediately to red-cheeked embarrassment when he saw my angry face in the doorway.

"I was just . . ." he tried to explain.

"I know what you were 'just,'" I mimicked, "and I don't think it's very cute."

We began the group discussion with what had happened to us the day before. Everyone listened patiently for a while, and then they passed their judgment. It had been my fault for not asserting myself, for not saying to Bob that I minded what he was doing, for not reminding Ralph of my feelings. Ralph and I had a good deal to work out. He had sexual feelings for me that weren't mutual. The others lost interest and drifted away piecemeal to discuss other matters, eventually re-forming as a circle in another corner of the room. It wasn't long before Ralph and I had resolved our problems and glued together a cracked friendship.

"I wish the others could have seen how we resolved our feelings," I said. "What are they doing over there anyway?"

"They're busy with their own problems," he said. "They probably thought this was just a homosexual bitch fight. *Fuck them!* I'm not staying after the two of us are finished."

"I'm angry too," I said, "but I want to stay. Walking out won't make the message clear." I wanted to be different but not separate, and I wanted the rest of them to know it.

We kissed lightly, and he left without saying a word to the others, who were so busy they didn't even notice him go. I went to join them, standing at the edge of their seated circle.

"Where's Ralph?" one of them asked, noticing me.

"He left because he was insulted," I said.

"Did you fight?" he asked, hesitating a moment as if he feared another installment of soap opera.

"No. We worked out our problems directly. He left because *you* insulted him, all of you. And you insulted me too."

"I don't understand," the doctor said. "I thought we listened to your story."

"The story wasn't the point. The resolution of the problem between us was. And that's where all of you ignored us. It's not even something we take personally. It's something we're used to as homosexuals. For the first time in this group something real happened between two members—out there, in the real world." I felt the authority born of just grievance, and they obviously felt it too. They were all listening raptly. "It's easy to be in this room and discuss things like why somebody chose to sit in a certain place. But it isn't easy to cope with a real situation. Something important was happening between Ralph and me. What you all did by walking away was to tell us our situation wasn't real, and there's only one possible reason for that. It's because we're gay. You ignored the real feelings we were working out as people, because you decided that gay people's problems with each other weren't your concern. Well, you're wrong. Problems are problems, and people are people, and what happened between Ralph and me could have taught you all something, but you blew it, all of you. You blew it because you're prejudiced. You think our lives are just imitations of yours and that our feelings aren't real. Well, I'm telling you they are. I'm standing right here in front of you, and I'm a real human being, and I'm a real homosexual, and I'm a real angry man. Put yourself in my place. Now are Ralph and I equal members of this group, or aren't we?"

The whole group stared at me in wide-eyed silence. Nobody had ever talked to them like that before. And I had never talked like that to anybody before. My feelings were coming out at last, and they were more powerful than I had imagined. They were so intense they scared even me, but I liked them already. I felt stronger than ever before.

Finally the doctor spoke. "You're right," he said. "The only thing we can say is that we're sorry and it won't happen again." A few people seconded. No one demurred. I sat down. I was a victor.

So when Jim asked me to run for the secretary of the rapidly growing GAA, I let him talk me into it. It was a campaign that won points for its modesty. My opponent was Keith Robertson, the man who had first kissed me on the street. I was afraid his handsome face would outweigh my academic background. There were cries of "Take it off" whenever he stood to speak.

I accepted the nomination with honest fervor: "I believe that GAA has done something for me, and now I'd like to do something for it." In spite of myself, I was elected. I had become a politician. I felt like a dignitary as I dressed for the first gay pride march on a bright Sunday in June, 1970. It was the first anniversary of the Stonewall riot, and we wanted to commemorate it as our own St. Patrick's Day, Steuben Day, or Columbus Day in New York. We were going to have a parade. We would leave our Greenwich Village "ghetto," where our numbers made it safer to be gay, and march up Sixth Avenue, through parts of Manhattan less tolerant of our lifestyle, to Central Park, where we would hold a "Gay-In." The number of people who appeared would matter to me much more than the head count at the Be-In I'd attended at the same site a few years before. The future of The Movement depended on it. Gay activists claimed to represent a mass of invisible constituents, and we needed their appearance to prove it. So I was nervous as I spread an array of political buttons across the chest of my gay liberation lambda T-shirt: "Gay Is Good," "Gay Revolution," "Fellatio."

We were gathering along Waverly Place because there weren't enough of us to rope off Christopher Street for. I was going to be a marshal, which added to my nervousness, since the rudiments of nonviolent crowd control taught to us the day before by a team of Quaker pacifists didn't seem certain of containing the hostility we might meet along our way. I put on my red armband and went out to meet my date, Donald Shaugnessy.

When I got to Waverly Place, only a few people were milling around. Marty Robinson was an energetic carpenter who articulated our dream handsomely: "The 'cure' for homosexuality is rebellion." He was there ahead of me. I kissed him hello.

"What do you think?" I asked him.

"It's still early," he said with nervous rapidity.

"Do you think there'll be enough?"

"I'll be happy if we get a few hundred," he said reassuringly. "If that's who's willing, then that's who'll march."

"But we've notified the media and everything. We'll look silly with only a few people."

"It's a celebration, not a zap. Why shouldn't people come? Do you know how many gays there are in Manhattan alone? They'll come."

Nobody knew how many gays there were in Manhattan. The Movement claimed 10 percent of the population, based on Kinsey's statistics, but who listens to Movement figures? For blocks around, people were sprinkled in small knots, waiting to see who was going to march and who wasn't before they committed themselves, but slowly more and more gathered behind the police sawhorse on Waverly Place until we had several hundred.

"Maybe we announced too early a starting time." I greeted Donald, kissing him at the same time.

"They'll come," he said.

"But we've been having events all week. People are tired, and it's Sunday morning besides. What self-respecting homosexual would get up before noon on Sunday? It would look like he—or she—went home alone after last night's dance, as if that weren't exhausting enough!"

"Don't worry," he calmed.

By noon, when we were scheduled to start, we were packed along Waverly Place for two-thirds of a block. It looked like a little over five hundred to me. I was more disappointed than elated, but I was damned if I was going to show it. Whatever we were, we were going to be proud of. We started along the sidewalk, because we didn't have a street permit. But within blocks, with cries of "Out of the closets, and into the streets," we took to one lane of Sixth Avenue's easily diverted traffic. Balloons went up. Signs appeared in the crowd: "HI, MOM," and "BETTER BLATANT THAN LATENT," and "I AM A LESBIAN, AND I AM BEAUTIFUL." The Mattachine Society, which had been working to help homosexuals while I was back in high school, held clusters of small flowered signs. The Gay Liberation Front raised its white banner, adorned with large pairs of same-sex symbols, lovingly linked. Donald and I marched with the large blue-and-gold lambda banner of GAA, our arms around each other.

Curious crowds began to string along the sidewalks as we passed up the avenue, flaunting our hearts on our sleeves. There were smatters of gigglings, but they were quickly stifled. We were a few too many to offend. The spectators' faces showed amazement, confusion, shock, resignation, unconcern, affirmation. Ours showed two emotions: pride and determination. We were coming out of our closets, however many of us could, but we were coming out together.

At Fourteenth Street I passed my psychoanalyst standing quietly at the curb, smiling. I ran up and kissed his embarrassed cheek, and he introduced me to his lover of nearly thirty years.

"Join us," I invited. "Out of the closets and into the streets!"

The doctor shook his head. "Not in my profession," he said. I sympathized, but I ran back to my place in the march. Within the month both my doctors agreed that I was healthy and ready to cope, and both analysis and group therapy ended.

I could see for a few blocks ahead and a few behind that the march was moving in a narrow but steady stream. When we got to the Chelsea Flea Market, shoppers abandoned their bargains to line the curbs and stare. Students waved good wishes at us from the window of their ballet school. Construction workers did an enigmatic jig high above the street. At Forty-Second Street a stern-faced Bible thumper held aloft a sign that warned: "Sodom and Gomorrah." And we chorused, "Out of the closets and into the streets," and "Out of the theaters and into the streets," and "Out of the bars," and "Out of the stores and into the streets." At Radio City a line of men stopped to do their impression of the Rockettes' chorus line kicks. A few blocks later a self-styled

"Fairy Queen" appeared at the head of the parade—some guy dressed in a tulle gown and a golden crown and wand, looking like Billie Burke as Glinda the Good Witch of the North, with everything but the pink bubble. When we got to the entrance of Central Park, we jibed, "Out of the bushes and into the streets," which, given the park's reputation, may well have flushed a few blushing guys out, zipping up their flies.

At last we came to the Sheep Meadow, our feet hot and tired. I got to the crest of a small knoll before I turned around. There behind us, in a river that seemed endless, poured wave after wave of happy faces. The Gay Nation was coming out into the light! There was hardly a dry eye on that hill. What had begun as a few hardy hundred had swollen all along its route, until we filled half the huge meadow with what the networks and newspapers estimated as five to fifteen thousand people, all gay and proud of it!

We needed a rest. Somebody started a chant: "Everyone standing is straight!" and thousands of people sat down where they were. We began to hug and kiss, to show off our clothes and take off our clothes, to play games and sing songs and begin that night's lovemaking early.

Donald and I wandered around, visiting friends, playing, stopping to embrace. Beneath a tree at the meadow's eastern edge lay two male couples who had been there since dawn locked in one long kiss, breaking the heterosexual world's record. I wandered among the crowd. There were men who wore dresses and women who wore denim overalls. Some wore their faces painted and sparkling with glitter. Some were utterly plain. Fanciful costumes were here and there amid the prevailing blue jeans: costumes made of shredded crepe paper, or dripping with rhinestones, or patchworked a hundred motley colors.

We were leathermen and cha-cha queens, and we were glad bright-eyed women with flowing manes, black transvestites and young Orientals and a few old faces; we were gentle bicycle riders and proudly strutting superstuds, questing wanderers, fierce feminists, revelers and rioters, seers, politicians, artists, cowboys, philosophy teachers, husbands and lovers, loners, pot heads and patriots. We were transsexuals and opera queens and Judy Garland fans and hardhats and hairdressers and poets and fops, and we were totally honest poseurs. We were panhandlers and executives, mothers, anarchists, veterans, bank robbers, barflies, Catholics, and at least one twenty-nine-year-old Jewish Assistant Professor of English from Newark, who was having the time of his life. Arms linked, the legions of gays were marching to Oz. We were off to see the Wizard. We were coming out.

Edmund White

Born in Cincinnati, Ohio, Edmund White (b. 1940) grew up in Chicago. On the one hand, he was a child of wealth and privilege (his father was a highly successful businessman), but on the other hand, after his parents divorced, he lived with financial anxiety and social dislocation as his mother tried to make ends meet. These social contradictions are central to his work, in which an exquisite, sophisticated, and elevated style is often matched by grungy subject matter. It is fitting that he wrote *Jean Genet* (1993), a biography of a man who, though born in poverty, raised in reform school, and arrested multiple times for theft, became one of the greatest and most elegant of French writers.

During the 1980s White was part of the Violet Quill, a short-lived group of gay writers that included Andrew Holleran and Felice Picano. One of the important issues facing that group was the need for an autobiographical novel that would change the stereotypical image of gay men. During that time he began the trilogy of autobiographical novels for which he is best known, *A Boy's Own Story* (1982), *The Beautiful Room Is Empty* (1987), and *The Farewell Symphony* (1997). His novel *The Married Man* (2000) also is highly autobiographical. He has written a memoir, *My Lives* (2006), that reads like one of his novels.

But White has also worked in highly unrealistic forms. His first novel, *Forgetting Elena* (1973), takes place in an imaginary kingdom that bears an uncanny resemblance to Fire Island, while *Fanny* (2003), an historical novel, seems to take place in a complete fantasy America. In addition he wrote the allegorical novel *Caricole* (1985).

White has also taken his place as a public intellectual, frequently appearing on television and speaking on radio in England and France, where he is better known and more revered. He was, for example, made a commander in the French Order of Arts and Letters. In the United States he has been an important early advocate of gay liberation, and he was one of the founding members and briefly president of the Gay Men's Health Crisis (GMHC), the first organization created to fight AIDS.

A writer's life is, however, mostly about writing, which is a very dull and lonely practice when viewed from the outside. "Writing Gay" is the opening essay in his collection *Arts and Letters* (2004), and it gives a vivid account of what it means to be a gay writer.

Writing Gay

SOME FORTY YEARS AGO I won a college literary award for a play I'd written that was called *The Blueboy in Black*. The prize money I spent buying cases of a terrible sweet fizzy Italian wine named Asti Spumante, which I considered wildly elegant. Though the award money was quickly dissipated, my name and the name of my play were announced in the *New York Times*, which led to an agent contacting me. Through her a production was arranged and two years later my play, starring the black actors Cicely Tyson and Billy Dee Williams, opened off-Broadway. The play, partly because at the time I was out-of-touch with the newest trends, was a bit démodé, a recycling of the Theatre of the Absurd and Jean Genet's *The Blacks*, and I was criticized for being dated. Worse, in 1964 we were at the height of the Civil Rights Movement when the race problem was supposed to have been solved, but I was showing angry blacks on stage who were taking revenge on their white employers. The critic for the *Times*, Bosley Crowther, said, "Negroes in America have enough problems without Mr. White." The most positive review, by Alan Pryce-Jones in *Theatre Arts*, called it one of the two best plays of the year. But when I met Mr. Pryce-Jones twenty years later (and this is the Proustian part) and thanked him for his kindness, he had no recollection of my play.

The play was not only about race but also about homosexuality. When my ultra-conservative Republican father came to the opening night with a business associate he asked me privately, "What's it about—the usual?," which was his way of referring to a gay theme. I had to confess that it was a little bit about the usual. Of course for him discussion of race was almost as offensive, so it must have made for a rather uncomfortable evening.

When I was a junior at the University of Michigan I had won a somewhat smaller award for a collection of short stories, and there again "the usual" had been a recurring theme at a time when almost no gay literature existed—and when even the very term was unknown. To be sure, Baldwin had recently published a despairing homosexual-themed novel, his beautiful book *Giovanni's Room*, and Gore Vidal and Paul Bowles and Tennessee Williams were all experimenting with short gay fiction, much of it extremely deft and sophisticated, but none of them became celebrated or successful for their gay fiction. They all had to go on to quite different work in order to achieve their immense fame.

I suppose I never had much of a choice. For some reason I had a burning need to explore my own gay identity in fiction. I'd written my first gay novel when I was just fifteen and a boarding student at Cranbrook boys school in Bloomfield Hills, outside Detroit. Since I didn't play sports I had the long afternoons in which to do my home-work and then the official two-hour enforced study hall in the evenings to work on my novel, which I called *The Tower Window*. It was all about a boy much like myself who turns to an adult man, a handsome Mexican, because he's been rejected by a girl his own age. I had a highly developed fantasy that I would sell this novel and make a fortune, which would allow me to escape my dependence on my parents—but even though my mother's secretary typed it up for me I never got around to sending it off. Perhaps I didn't know where to send it.

No matter what I wrote, even at the very beginning, it was bound to have homo-sexual subject matter. I studied fiction in a creative writing class at the University of Michigan in a workshop conducted by Allan Seager. The one time I had a conference with him he thoroughly frightened me by saying, "The nouns in a paragraph should be arranged like the heads in a painting by Uccello." "Utrillo?" I asked. "Aw, get out of here," he said, fed up and waving me out.

In those years, long before gay liberation, no one could write a proud, self-respecting, self-affirming gay text, since no gay man, no matter how clever, had found a way to like himself—not even Proust, the sovereign intellect of fiction, had man-aged that one. But a homosexual writer could be impertinent, elusive, camp—and that was a tone I adopted in a novel I submitted to the Hopwood Committee in my senior year, a book called *The Amorous History of Our Youth*, which was quite an arch performance, starting with its title, an allusion to two books—Lermontov's *A Hero of Our Times* and a scandalous character attack of the seventeenth century called *The Amorous History of the Gauls* by Bussy-Rabutin, Mme de Sévigné's cousin. Louis XIV exiled him for his book. I remember that the Hopwood judge, a woman novelist, was quite rightly so irritated by the flipness of this novel—an account of a sexual love between two brothers, one rich and one poor, separated at birth—that she couldn't contain her rage and gave it a severe drubbing (I rather fear I wasn't meant to see this evaluation and pulled strings in order to read it). Of course she was right—the novel must have been appallingly grating. But I suspect that in that period, when no homo-sexual could defend his identity as anything other than an illness, a sin or a crime, our inexpressible anger came out in bizarre forms—as a hostile and inappropriate super-ciliousness, for instance.

And though I was a fairly bright student I had almost no skill as a writer. I wrote in a trance, almost unconsciously, because I was writing to stay sane, to conduct my own autoanalysis, to drain off my daily dose of anguish, remorse and hostility. That was the era of the bitchy queen, since there were no available modes of open anger, of self-legitimizing affirmation. I wrote as drag queens bitched at each other on the street corner—to claim attention, to shock, even to horrify the straight people passing by. Later, after gay liberation, we were able as people and as writers to redefine ourselves as members of a minority group who could mount campaigns for our rights and against societal stereotyping, but back then, forty years ago, such a program would have caused us to puff on our cigarettes and to say, "Get *you*, Mary."

This terrible unconsciousness and obsessiveness continued to mark my writing after graduation. I'd found a job in the very bastion of American conservatism, the halls of *Time* and *Life*. I worked in New York for Time-Life Books, writing essays about everything from the giant molecule to the Japanese garden, but every night I grimly returned to my office after a solitary supper and wrote many, many bad plays, which my agent refused even to send out—and a long novel. The novel rather confusingly bore a title, *The Beautiful Room Is Empty*, which I used years later for an entirely different book. This book was confessional, despairing, and all about a hopeless, one-sided love affair with a handsome, brilliant guy my age who became temporarily insane, so guilty was he about being a homosexual at all. This book, which I finished in 1966, three years before the advent of gay liberation, was sent out to some twenty publishing houses, all of which rejected it. Two of the editors who read it were clandestinely gay and were afraid to accept it lest they be labeled as gay themselves and fired—or so they told me years later.

After this defeat I thought I should write a good book—it sounds ludicrous, but it only then occurred to me that I could and should write a book that was obviously impressive. For if I'd never bothered to write well myself, I was a connoisseur of good writing done by others. I loved Firbank and Proust and Colette and Jean Genet and at this time specially Nabokov. I could suddenly imagine what it would be like to bring to the page the same pleasure I took in reading the fiction of these geniuses. Not that I hoped to emulate their art; I just wanted to exercise in my own writing the taste that made me respond to theirs.

The Usual was still part of my new novel, *Forgetting Elena*, except now it was as obscure as the rest of the book. The narrator is an amnesiac who doesn't want to admit he's lost his memory and who struggles to second-guess from other people's reactions what sort of person he must be. He has no idea what sex and love are, and the heterosexual love scene, which must be one of the most peculiar in literature, he construes as something like a dangerous and ultimately painful religious rite. A man named Herbert displays all the signs (at least to our eyes) of being in love with the narrator. The whole thing takes place in an island kingdom (which may or may not be real—or perhaps just a distorted vision of Fire Island), an ambiguity which in some ways recalls the real or unreal kingdom in Nabokov's *Pale Fire*. *Forgetting Elena*, my first book to be published, was not perceived as a gay-themed book at all; three years after it had come out to no acclaim whatsoever, Nabokov singled it out as one of his favorite American novels. By then, of course, most of the first edition had been pulped.

I don't want to recapitulate my writing career, such as it has been; I'd rather focus on two or three aspects of gay writing that have interested me in recent years. Most importantly, I'd like to talk about the writing of biographies of gay men and how that has affected some of my own fiction.

In 1982 I published what has possibly become my best-known book, *A Boy's Own Story*. At the time the craze for memoirs had not yet taken off. Of course generals who'd won the battle of Iwo Jima might write their memoirs, but the interest in their historical accomplishment was firmly established in advance. Back then few nobodies wrote their memoirs, and I was quite happy to call my piece of autofiction a novel. First of all calling something a novel, at least back then, protected a writer from pesky personal questions of the sort, "Why did you betray your high school teacher when he was so nice to you?"

Second, by calling my book a novel I could take all sorts of liberties with the truth without being held accountable for the discrepancies. I could change around the chronology to make it more dramatic. I could reduce the cast of characters, so messy and redundant in real life. And, in my particular case, I could nudge my own weird case towards the norm, at least the gay norm, and hope to pick up a bit more reader identification along the way. Whereas in real life I had been bizarrely brazen (or perhaps driven) sexually, and just as unpleasantly precocious intellectually, in the fictional derivation from my life I could make my stand-in shy and not outstanding in any way. In short, I could make him much more likable.

In the summer of 1983 I moved to Paris, where I stayed for the next sixteen years except for a few short intervals. When I finally moved back to the States four years ago I was surprised by many things: the institutionalization of identity politics, which had still been struggling to impose itself when I'd left; the concurrent ascendance of a rather Stalinist brand of political correctness; and finally the parallel growth of *Oprah*-style programs and the memoir industry. I suppose all three phenomena—identity politics, political correctness and the memoir (usually linked to a disability or an oppressed minority or a childhood trauma)—could all be labeled aspects of the culture of complaint, though I see them more as parts of a very American tradition of bearing witness and of commandeering that testimony into a political program: the personal as political, which may be America's most salient contribution to the armamentarium of progressive politics.

I followed up *A Boy's Own Story* with two other books in a trilogy—*The Beautiful Room Is Empty* (1987) and *The Farewell Symphony*, ten years later, in 1997. Already, with *The Beautiful Room Is Empty*, I had discovered that whereas there is something eternal about childhood, that the strong nameless moods of that first period of life are undated, there is something highly historical about early adulthood. The sheltered if miserable childhood I had in Cincinnati and Texas as a boy could just as easily have been led in the nineteenth century as in the twentieth. My childhood, at least, was all yearning and brooding, running through woods and fields, and much of it was spent in isolation or with maids who resented all of us. As a result I never indicated when or where the action was taking place in *A Boy's Own Story*. Even the narrator's all-male boarding school has a distinctly nineteenth-century feel to it. The one thing that was undeniably American about the book, as I learned later from talking with European readers, was how free and unsupervised the boy was. But that sort of freedom was something Europeans had noticed about American children already in the nineteenth century.

By the time I got to describing my protagonist's early adulthood in *The Beautiful Room Is Empty* I knew it was crucial that I show exactly when and where he came of age. Coming out in New York in the 1960s was obviously something very different from what coming out in London in 2000, say, would be. Moreover, I decided to have my narrator-protagonist enter directly into a major historical turning point—the beginning of gay liberation. That breakthrough occurred in June 1969 at the Stonewall Uprising, the first time gays resisted arrest en masse and rose up against the cops after the raid of a popular gay bar in Greenwich Village. As it happened, I had witnessed this event firsthand and it had had a direct impact on me.

In fact in planning the book I started with the violence that would come at the end, with Stonewall, and decided to construct a book leading up to it that would prompt even the most conservative heterosexual reader to become impatient with the hero's self-hatred and his years spent in therapy seeking in vain to go straight. I wanted that reader to say out loud, "Oh, for crissake, get on with your life and leave us all in peace." I was pleased when the daily *New York Times* critic wrote something almost exactly like that.

In the ten years that intervened between the publication of this second book and that of the third I had devoted seven years to researching and writing my biography of Jean Genet.

I would like to tell you a little bit about that experience and then eventually lead the discussion back to how my Genet affected the shape of *The Farewell Symphony*.

Genet died in 1986 and a year later my editor, Bill Whitehead, asked me if I knew anyone interested in writing his biography. Without much reflection I said, "Me!" I thought the project would take no more than three years of researching and writing. But at the end of three years I'd written not one word and knew almost nothing about my subject. I lied to my new editor (Bill in the meanwhile had died of AIDS) and said it was coming along swimmingly, but in fact I was in a complete panic and considered stepping in front of an oncoming bus just to get out of my contract. I didn't dare admit I didn't even know the name of the village where Genet had been born (no one did). Although I'm considered brash, I could be defeated by the slightest refusal from a stranger, and in the world Genet had left behind everyone was very strange indeed.

Genet was completely unlike most subjects of literary biography, who are middle-class prodigies, adored by their mothers; the mothers save every scrap of their juvenilia and as the little darlings grow up they are surrounded by friends who are also writers or at least highly literate. These other people all keep journals, send letters, now even print up the e-mails they receive from distinguished friends, publish accounts of their own lives and create fictional portraits of one another. The parents and mates of the middle-class writer save every scrap they write and their movements are widely reported in the press.

Writing a biography of someone such as Sartre, for instance, is primarily a question of what to exclude in an overly documented life.

Genet, by contrast, was an orphan, raised in a village—but which one?—and had already entered the French penal system by the time he was an adolescent. He had no literary friends until he was in his early thirties and was briefly taken up by the gay men around Cocteau as well as by Cocteau himself. Even that Parisian literary interlude lasted less than ten years. Throughout most of his life Genet's friends were criminals, fellow soldiers, fellow prisoners, shady boyfriends, thieves for whom he worked as a fence, Black Panthers, Palestinian soldiers—in other words, people hard to identify and locate, people who die young, people who are suspicious of a white American interviewer, people who in any event scarcely know what a biography is. Criminals in particular are people who die young, who can't be found (if they're still alive), who if they're found won't talk, who if they talk are not to be believed and who in any event want to be paid. I knew perfectly well that Genet would have disliked me, since he detested whites, members of the middle-class, Americans, writers and avowed homosexuals—on five counts I was out. Why should his friends and survivors like me anymore? Moreover, Genet detested the idea of anyone ever writing his biography, partly because a "real" life would challenge and even overthrow his own account of things in his so-called autobiographical novels such as A Thief's Journal.

In addition, Genet had eventually rejected and abandoned all his friends, so each time I met one of them I was dealing with a wounded person, someone who remembered Genet only as a painful episode in his or her life, yet sometimes as the most important one.

After three years of fruitless research I was so obsessed with Genet that I'd virtually forgotten I'd ever written novels of my own. Once in England when I was giving a talk about Genet someone asked me about my own fiction and I blinked, uncomprehending for a moment.

In my ignorance and arrogance I had initially hired a beautiful American boy and girl to help me with my research, though they had no special skills as scholars and had never read Genet's oeuvre (nor did they get around to it now). They had no idea of where to start, no more than I did. Unwittingly we had stumbled onto the most challenging and intransigent of all modern literary biographical subjects. Nevertheless, each of these two beauties provided me with one vital link in the story. The young woman I hired to pretend to take French lessons from Paule Thevenin, someone who had refused to grant me an interview. Paule was an extremely difficult older woman who had befriended Genet in the 1960s and helped him prepare the final version of his great play *The Screens*. Although my young American spoke excellent French she engaged Paule for a year as her coach (all at my expense); at last she'd become sufficiently close to her to be able to ask her to give me an interview, which was finally granted. After an initial coldness Mme Thevenin opened up and shared freely with me hundreds of specific and enlightening memories—and even showed me X-rays of Genet's kidneys! (Her husband had been Genet's doctor and had provided him with the powerful sleeping pills he'd consumed by the handful.)

The young handsome American man also had a find. A friend of his sent him a clipping from *Le Morvandiau*, a newspaper published in Paris for people who'd moved to the capital from the rather primitive district known as the Morvan. In this paper was an article by a certain M. Bruley about "my classmate, Jean Genet." The article itself was a whitewash of Genet's highly questionable character but it did give us the name of the village (Alligny) and M. Bruley eventually led us to a dozen other villagers who'd grown up with Genet and considered him to have been a highly dubious character.

As the years went by I teamed up with the world's leading Genet expert, Albert Dichy, who prepared me a complete chronology of Genet's life and who established Genet's elaborate police record in every town and village in France. He also introduced me to key people in Genet's life including his three heirs (a seven-year-old Moroccan boy, a circus horse trainer and an ex–race car driver). Through Albert I met Genet's literary lawyer and several criminal lawyers who'd worked with his legal dossier as well as Leila Shahid, the Palestinian ambassador to Paris. I interviewed a woman who pointed a pistol at the lion when her husband put his head in the animal's mouth during their circus act.

Genet was as assiduous a traveler as I myself am, so I took some pleasure in following him to Damascus and to Morocco, where I visited his grave, which looks out on the local prison, a bordello and the sea—three of the great tropes of his fiction. I interviewed Jane Fonda, the mother of one of my former students, Vanessa Vadim. She had met Genet at a benefit for the Panthers in the early 1970s in Hollywood. Genet had grabbed onto her because she was one of the few people present who could speak French at the party (for years she'd lived in France when she'd been married to the

French film director Roger Vadim). Genet took her phone number and called her the next morning at six. He'd awakened in a strange house, he didn't know where he was and he wanted his coffee. Miss Fonda said, "Okay, I'll come right away but where are you?" Genet didn't know. At last she, who'd grown up in Hollywood and knew every house, said, "Go outside and come back and describe the pool to me." He did so and she said, "Oh, you're at Donald Sutherland's. I'll be right over."

One of the valuable keys to Genet's American period that Albert Dichy tracked down was the testimony of a Swiss woman named Marianne de Pury. Albert had seen that Genet had written her several letters, which she had sold or given to the library at Kent State University. We tracked her down just as she was moving back to Switzerland from Santa Fe, New Mexico, after some twenty-five years in the States. She had been a pretty upper-class Swiss girl with blonde hair and a pearl necklace who'd moved to the States and almost immediately become involved with the Panthers and in particular their minister of information known as Big Man. It was she who had translated for Genet almost everywhere he went in the States—and fortunately she had a good memory.

I read the interviews that Genet had given to Japanese papers and Arab papers and Spanish theatrical magazines and Austrian and Italian magazines—none of them previously collected. I got my hands on some rather stiff and literary love letters Genet had written in his late twenties to Lily Pringsheim, a German leftist living in Czechoslovakia in the mid-1930s, a woman who had harbored him when he was fleeing the authorities after he'd deserted from the army. I interviewed the English journalist who'd interviewed Genet on television—a memorable occasion during which Genet, insisting that every person in the room had as much to say as he did, or more, turned the cameras on the technicians and interrogated them. I went to a garage outside Cannes where one of Genet's lovers now worked in what he called the Garage Saint Genet. His wife spoke freely and interestingly to me, but her husband gunned the motors he was repairing louder and louder to drown out our voices. I interviewed a ghastly racist millionaire who had been one of Genet's first patrons and who spoke insultingly of blacks while his black servants waited on us. I interviewed Sartre's male secretary from the years during which Sartre had known Genet and written his huge tome, his literary psychoanalysis, *Saint Genet*. In the end I spent every penny I earned, and then some, on my research and my travels, but my book did win the National Book Critics Circle Award—and the citation singled out my research as what most impressed the judges.

When at last, after the seven years consecrated to Genet, I came back to my own fiction I found that I had been influenced not so much by Genet (whose work I intensely admire but have never attempted to emulate) as by the experience of writing a biography. And not just any biography but a gay biography which, depending on the subject, is marginally different from a biography of a heterosexual. Of course all lives are different, and nationality or profession or period are factors at least as determining as sexual orientation. But I would like to suggest that there are special problems and considerations touching on gay biography. In Genet's case he usually fell for younger heterosexual men with connections to the underworld. Genet several times in his life built houses for these lovers and reserved a room in each house for himself. He invariably befriended their wives and in disputes usually took their side. Because I'm gay myself and just thirty years younger than Genet, I flatter myself that I knew how to interpret these relationships. From my experience of the world I knew that such relationships between older gay "patrons," if you will, and younger heterosexual studs were quite common in the old Mediterranean world and I knew enough not to make too much of them or too little.

Biographers, to be sure, are no better or worse than their fellow citizens and in treating the lives of lesbians and gay men biographers have been guilty of whitewashing or rewriting or even suppressing their subjects' sexual and romantic lives.

Perhaps the prejudices against homosexuals can be said to begin with ignoring many gay writers or relegating them to playing minor roles in the lives of supposedly more important heterosexuals. A figure like Oscar Wilde was always too influential to ignore — too scandalous, too quotable — though at first he was turned into a tragic fop, a witty, epigrammatic Pagliacci, and few biographers were prepared to take him as seriously as everyone took even such an incompetent heterosexual as Nietzsche, for instance, though the parallels are striking (a love of paradox, argumentation through apothegms, hatred of the bourgeoisie, little concern about self-contradiction, an exhortation of readers towards the transvaluation of all values). Only Richard Ellmann's *Oscar Wilde* redressed this balance; moreover, it took another gay man, Neil Bartlett in *Who Was That Man?*, to speculate about the exact nature of Wilde's sexuality. Of course the question is far from being settled and Wilde's grandson, Merlin Holland, whom I've met, is campaigning for Wilde-as-bisexual.

Just as homosexuals themselves were (and often still are) shrugged off as minor retainers at life's banquet, uninitiated in the mysteries of childbirth, adultery and divorce, in the same way an elusive but major gay novelist such as the late Edwardian Ronald Firbank has been largely ignored by biographers, despite the fact that writers as different from one another as Hemingway and Evelyn Waugh all claimed they'd been influenced by him, Hemingway by the practice of representing a crowd scene through unassigned bits of dialogue and Waugh through the exquisite timing of his humor. Brigid Brophy did write a massive biography of Firbank, *Prancing Novelist*, but it is so subjective, capricious and unreliable as to be anything but a standard life. Brophy refused to conduct any original research of her own. She relied on the only other biographer, Miriam Benkowitz, an American librarian, who approached Firbank primarily as a bibliographical problem. Never was a biographer more ill-suited to her subject. Only now is an English gay man, Richard Canning, at last writing Firbank's life, reopening long-closed archives, revisiting all the places Firbank knew, including Rome and North Africa, and studying the effect of Jamaican Creole in Firbank's novel *Sorrow in Sunlight*. Canning has also uncovered the comedy of errors that surrounded the author's burial and reburial in Rome. Such painstaking scholarship is lavished on a writer only when the biographer is convinced of his first-rank value.

In the past sometimes all trace of homosexuality in a statesman or military officer, say, would simply be erased. Cambacarès, for instance, was Napoleon's prime minister and so openly gay that he convinced the emperor to decriminalize homosexuality. Thanks to Cambacarès France had no laws against homosexuals until the pro-Nazi Vichy government came to power during World War II. But when I picked up a French biography of Cambacarès written in the 1950s, there was no mention of his sexuality nor of his influence on France's laws. A misplaced prudishness, in other words, had led the biographer to ignore altogether the legislation for which his subject is most likely to be remembered.

When I was working on my life of Genet the French publisher was worried that I would turn him into a "gay writer." (I had made the mistake in an interview in the French press of calling Rimbaud a homosexual poet.) The French are strenuously opposed to all minority designations of writers, past or present; it's part of the legacy of their universalism dating back to the Enlightenment and the Revolution and it is one of the main cultural differences with the values of the United States, the home of identity politics. Gallimard, the French publisher, was relieved when my Genet manuscript came in and seemed devoid of any special pleading for Genet as a gay hero.

When I wrote my Penguin life of Proust I decided to discuss his homosexuality—how else could I make my book different from the hundreds that had preceded it?—but I was attacked for this approach in the *New York Times Book Review* and in the *New York Review*. The *Times* critic, the English novelist and biographer Peter Ackroyd, took me to task for reducing Proust to his sexuality. Similarly, Roger Shattuck in the *New York Review* struck a blow for Proust's universality against my supposedly narrowing view. And the Egyptian memoirist André Aciman announced that Proust had been a masturbator and not homosexual at all.

I think anyone who has read my book will attest to at least the density and inclusiveness of my brief biography and to my discussion of everything from Proust's crippling asthma to his youthful social-climbing, from his liberating translations of Ruskin into French to his various and prolonged struggles to become a writer, from his dark vision of love and friendship to his strenuous efforts to court prize committees, but I refuse to apologize for my treatment of his sexuality, especially since it presented him with complex literary problems.

Proust himself recognized that homosexuality was a key theme—and a thoroughly original one—in his book and worried that his friend Lucien Daudet had beat him to the punch in his early novel. Only when Proust had examined Daudet's book was he reassured that it was a trivial and inexplicit treatment of the theme and no threat to his own primacy in the field. Proust had promised his publisher, Gallimard, early on that his book might be judged "obscene" since it treated a "pedophile." Indeed many of the female characters turn out to be lesbians and nearly all of the male characters are queer—except "Marcel," the narrator and the stand-in for Proust himself. Since, as Proust told André Gide, all of his sexual experiences had been with men and none with women, he was obliged to transpose his homosexual experiences into heterosexual terms in order to flesh out those scenes, characters and situations. This transposition, I'd claim, was in fact the most creative part of his book, the very area where he had to combine memory of real experiences with objective observations of real women he'd studied in the world and their heterosexual male lovers. In his treatment of Albertine, the great love of Marcel's life and the name that appears most frequently in the book, Proust drew on his affair with Agostinelli, his chauffeur, who met an early death during a flying lesson as a pilot, and with Henri Rochat, a handsome Swiss waiter at the Ritz who eventually moved in with Proust.

When I call these Proustian transpositions of men into women "creative," I'm remembering my own experiences when I was in Ann Arbor as a student between 1958 and 1962. I belonged to the Sigma Nu fraternity but I was also cruising guys in the Union and less reputable places. One of my best friends was arrested for doing what I was constantly doing—and he had to report to a parole officer once a week for the next seven years. Not surprisingly, he became a prison psychologist not long afterwards.

In that period it was impossible to speak openly of one's homosexual adventures. One had to translate them into heterosexual terms, and one had to have a detailed and capacious memory to keep track of all the lies one had invented, often on the spur of the moment. One also needed to be resourceful in finding plausible female activities (sewing, dancing) that would be a counterpart to the real-life male activities of one's partners (sewing, cruising).

I feel that Proust's elaborate transposition of male friends into female characters was an example of the same sort of obsessive and creative mendacity. The transpositions were precisely the most artistic part of Proust's conception of his book, and to ignore them is to miss out on a true literary value peculiarly suited to be analyzed by a biographer.

Just to finish my little disquisition on homosexuality and biography, I'd say that gay lives are not like straight lives. One must know them intimately from the inside in order to place the right emphasis on the facts. For instance, those heterosexual biographers and critics who have attacked Michel Foucault for infecting people even after he knew he was positive for AIDS are ignoring several crucial things. First, Foucault was a sadomasochistic bottom, a slave, unlikely to have infected anyone, since a slave does not transmit his sperm. Second, Foucault certainly didn't know he was positive, since there was no test to determine one's HIV status in Europe until 1984, after Foucault's death. Finally, since he was a friend of mine I can attest that he guessed at his diagnosis only five months before his death. He worried that he might have infected his lover, Daniel Defert, but he knew perfectly well that he'd never infected any of those leather guys in San Francisco. But of course my approach would not please the muckrakers. I'm afraid that all too often biography is the revenge of little people on big people.

Or take another issue, not at all technical or medical but just as telling. Those critics who attacked Brad Gooch's *City Poet*, the biography of the New York poet of the '50s, Frank O'Hara, complained that Gooch had talked too much about his sex life and not enough about the poetry. But in fact O'Hara, the founder of "Personalism," wrote poems to his tricks and had such an active sex life, one might be tempted to say, in order to generate his poems, which are often dedicated to real tricks (who were all also his friends) or imaginary crushes. When Joan Accocela in the *New Yorker* complained that *City Poet* was too "gossipy," she missed the point. O'Hara's grinding social schedule and hundreds of sexual encounters offend people who want his life to be like a straight man's of the same period. If O'Hara had had one or two gay marriages and had made his domestic life more important than his friendships, then he would have seemed like a reassuring translation of straight experience into gay terms. But O'Hara's real life was messy and episodic in the retelling, even picaresque—it doesn't add up to a simple, shapely narrative. It's all day after day of drinks with X, dinner with Y and sex with Z—not what we expect in the usual literary biography. Biographies were originally meant to be exemplary lives, whether they were written as the *Lives of the Saints* or Plutarch's *Lives*, whereas the lives of most gay men, especially those before gay liberation, were furtive, fragmented, submerged—half-erased tales that need special tools if they are to be rendered in glowing colors.

When I turned to *The Farewell Symphony*, the last volume of my autobiographical trilogy, I had just come out of the experience of researching and writing the Genet biography. I was now both a biographer and a novelist, I could tell myself. People often speak of fictional techniques—suspense, shapeliness, narrative flow—influencing the form of biographies, but in my case biographical techniques influenced my new understanding of the novel. Writing Genet's life—which led from his childhood as a peasant foster child in the Morvan into a life of petty crime, prostitution and begging to a flight across Eastern Europe in the 1930s into French prisons under the Nazis and the threat of extermination in the death camps—from such a marginal existence to the consecration of success as a published novelist and produced playwright and the subject of a massive psychoanalytic study by Sartre, the greatest philosopher of the day, and later to contacts with the leading European sculptor, Giacometti, and two other prominent philosophers, Foucault and Derrida, finally to a posthumous master-piece, *Prisoner of Love*, dedicated to the Black Panthers and the Palestinians—writing this amazing story, with its completely unexpected developments, convinced me that no matter how scattered and multifarious a person's activities might be, the fact that they all have happened to one individual moving chronologically through time lends the story a surprising coherence. Having written Genet's life I took on the subject of my own life in the 1970s and '80s in a novel, *The Farewell Symphony*, with a new will-ingness to discuss subjects I had downplayed or excluded altogether in the previous two books—subjects such as friendships, intellectual projects, artistic career and family relationships, sexual peccadilloes and romantic one-night stands—a multitude of subjects I had soft-pedaled in my earlier volumes of autobiographical fiction.

The novel as a genre is essentially a nineteenth century bourgeois concoction. In a Jane Austen novel a small cast of characters, all members of the gentry or nobility, revolve around each other in a village until two or four get married. The mother's bad values, the father's incapacitating eccentricity, the young women's vanity or virtue—everything is properly redressed or punished or rewarded by the last page. As in a Haydn trio the simplest themes are fully exploited and thoroughly developed. For better or worse *Emma* remains our ideal of the novel, the Ur-novel.

There is no way modern gay life could be shoved into this Procrustean bed. Of-ten the most intense and memorable moments in a gay life are without foreshad-owing or consequence. A moment ago I deliberately used the expression "romantic one-night stands" for its shock value, for straight people often imagine that sex at the sauna must be cold and impersonal precisely because it is out of all social context and may never be repeated. Outsiders assume that "anonymous sex" is somehow unfeel-ing or mechanical or merely lust-driven; neither Emma nor Elizabeth would know what to make of it. And yet, as André Gide recalled at the end of his life in his book *Ainsi Soit-Il*, the most meaningful moment of his eventful life had been sex with two beautiful Arab teenagers who'd been assigned to his caravan when he crossed Tunisia at the beginning of the twentieth century. Another French thinker, Michel Foucault, once remarked that if courtship was the most romantic moment for the heterosexual couple, for a gay lover the most romantic moment was after sex and after one had put one's brand-new partner in a taxi. Straight love is all about anticipation, whereas gay love is all aftermath. In straight life love, friendship and sex are ideally all joined in the same person, whereas in gay life these drives can be separated out.

Perhaps assimilation and the safe-sex years have caused gay life in the '90s and in our decade to resemble straight life, but in the period I wanted to cover in *The Farewell Symphony*, the time between the beginning of gay liberation and the onset of AIDS, this period that Brad Gooch has called The Golden Age of Promiscuity, gay life was radically different from anything novelists had ever written about before unless we go back to *The Satyricon* of Petronius. In *The Farewell Symphony* I stretched the boundary of coherence to the breaking point but I had the courage to do so because I'd written a long biography of a man who could not be totalized, whose evolution was always surprising and certainly unpredictable and whose affairs were always messy.

If I had begun my autobiographical series with a cool distance between my adult self as narrator and myself as teenage protagonist, if I had reshaped my life in the first two volumes towards telling a good story and structuring a pleasing narrative, in the last volume, *The Farewell Symphony*, I decided to narrow the distance between narrator and protagonist, even as the story in real time was catching up with the moment in which I was writing the book. It was all a bit like the end of *A Hundred Years of Solitude* in which the last member of the Buendia family, as the allotted century comes to an end, is reading about himself reading before the book and the village catch fire and go up in flames in a great synthesis of conflagration.

Before I began the Genet biography I had imagined I'd turn my autobiographical series into a tetralogy, one volume devoted to the '70s and the heyday of promiscuity and one to the '80s and the tragedy of AIDS. But after the decade that went by following the publication of the second volume I realized that in the late '90s it would be intolerable to read one book about everyone having a great time sexually and even more painful to read another volume about everyone dying. Accordingly I decided to collapse the two books into one and to weave my way back and forth from the '80s into the '70s. The inevitable gloomy trajectory of a strict chronology I would avoid, just as a temporal fluidity would mitigate both the tragic aftermath and the preceding hedonism.

I have not mentioned in these pages many of the issues that have affected my career as a gay author. I have not talked about the gay writing group, The Violet Quill, which I belonged to at the time I took my own leap forward and wrote *A Boy's Own Story*. I could have pointed out how this group was revolutionary because it did not address in its fiction an apology for gay life to a straight reader, as all previous gay writing had done, even Genet's. I could have argued that the gay writing that emerged in the late '70s and throughout the '80s plunged the reader into the midst of gay urban experience. No longer were we writing about lonely and tortured gay men nor about gay couples living in the forest or on a deserted coast. Now for the first time we were showing the gay ghetto and gay friendships as well as gay romances. Nor were we presenting just a few anguished and ever-so-sensitive esthetes; no, we wanted to show the full range of the gay typology, as anthological as that of any society.

I could have written about how this moment in gay writing is now coming to an end and is spawning mindless gay genre writing (murder mysteries and dog stories and teen dating tales) or something more serious, something one could call post-gay writing, in which one or two characters might be gay but in which they are inserted into a more general society. I'm thinking of post-gay writers such as Michael Cunningham or Allan Gurganus or Peter Cameron.

I could have touched on many subjects but I have tried to concentrate on just two or three things, drawing on a career I know well, my own. I've hoped to show how my own writing has evolved away from a traditional conception of the novel towards something broader, more episodic, even picaresque, and how the reach of *The Farewell Symphony* also owes something to a new, more daring conception of gay biography.

Samuel R. Delany

Samuel R. "Chip" Delany (b. 1942) was born to a distinguished African American family. His paternal grandfather was vice-principal of St. Augustine's College in Georgia. Delany's father came to Harlem at seventeen and eventually became owner of Levy and Delany, a successful funeral home in Harlem. His mother was a librarian. In 1993 his two aunts Sadie and A. Elizabeth Delany published *Having Our Say: The Delany Sisters' First Hundred Years,* which became a best seller, a Broadway play, and a television miniseries. Sadie was the first black woman allowed to teach domestic science in the state of New York, and Bessie was the second black woman licensed to practice dentistry there.

Soon after his father's death in 1960 Chip Delany dropped out of college and married the distinguished poet Marilyn Hacker. He was nineteen; she was a year younger, white, and Jewish. In the first year of marriage Delany wrote his first novel, *The Jewels of Aptor* (1962). He was twenty. In the next six years he wrote eight more novels, including *Babel-17* (1966) and *The Einstein Intervention* (1967), which won Nebula Awards as the best science fiction novels of their years.

Delany has gone on to write more than forty books of literary and social criticism, pornography, and memoir as well as science fiction. He has taught at many universities and currently is the director of the Graduate Writing Program at Temple University.

The excerpt below is from his first memoir, *The Motion of Light in Water: Sex and Science Fiction Writing in the East Village* (1998). Although Delany had attended such well-regarded private schools as Horace Mann and the Dalton School, he decided to attend the prestigious public institution, the Bronx High School of Science, perhaps the most demanding school of its kind in the country. This passage records his first days at Bronx Science. What distinguishes Delany's work in general and this passage in particular is that it turns in on itself as a text and includes its own meditation on the very process of composition.

The excerpt is drawn from the University of Minnesota edition (2004), in which Delany has altered the number of the passages from the original edition.

From *The Motion of Light in Water*

6.3.

On the first day of school I took the D train up to 182nd Street, walked the two blocks up the Grand Concourse, and turned left, a block later crossed through the lozenges of sunlight falling through the Jerome Avenue elevated tracks to the concrete, and kept on down the sloping sidewalk beside the telephone company with the other students walking to the Annex, and gathered with them in the basement cafeteria, as we had done three months before at orientation. I spotted the blond boy I'd seen the last time right away—today he was in a white shirt and khaki pants. I probably went up to him and said something immediately. (Ben, a junior by now, was off in the Main Building.) I'd been voted the most popular kid in my grade a year before, and my picture of myself was that I was Someone Who Could Make Friends Easily: so, however scary it was, I'd decided I was going to make them. And as rewarding as friendships with the Bens of this world might be, I'd decided my friends here were *going* to be good-looking, more or less normal people.

The boy's name was Chuck. He'd come to Science from a city Catholic school, Corpus Christi. He'd grown up in Luxembourg. His father was a career man in the US Air Force. (Chuck even spoke some Luxembourgeois.) But he and his younger sister lived with his mother here in the city. His parents were divorced.

We'd been given little cards which guided us to our class, and luck had it that Chuck and I had been assigned to the same freshman homeroom. We took our places together in line and, once again, walked up the crowded stairwell. It was nowhere near as orderly as it had been when half the group had been parents. So there was no running on ahead for Chuck today. We talked a bit more, but for a while, together in the crush, I remember he seemed to lose interest in whatever we were speaking of, and I wondered what I would have to say to catch his attention again while we made our slow way up.

Out on the red-tiled roof, with its high wire fence around the chest-high wall, the student congestion came to a complete halt under the cloud-flecked blue—as it would for three to thirteen minutes every morning for the rest of the year. Finally we crowded into the far stairwell.

6.31.

Downstairs on the fifth floor, I walked into the classroom.

Chuck followed me.

I took a seat in one of the nailed-to-the-floor wooden desks toward the front of the room.

Chuck sat at the desk behind mine.

Our homeroom teacher—standing behind the desk now with his hands in his pockets, greeting us, telling us to take seats, those in the back please hurry up, we have a lot to do this morning—was the freshman algebra instructor, Mr. Tannenbaum. (He turned now to write his name on the board for us.) A thin, homely man, he wore baggy tweeds and had a shy sense of humor. He was a remarkably gentle man, for all his bony forehead and drawn-together shoulders. And he smiled if you made a joke, sometimes in spite of himself. But one of the things Science's average 140 IQ meant was that the teachers respected the students. The school was as strict in hiring instructors as it was in admitting pupils. We all had a sense that the teachers themselves were special, as was, indeed, the whole school—despite its dilapidated housing.

Mr. Tannenbaum began to call out the names of the various kids in the class—"Please answer 'present'"—while I looked around.

Before the end of the first session, I learned that Chuck's full name was Charles Edward Rufus Rastus McSweeney O'Gorman Van Pelt Abramson!

("Is that really your whole name . . . ?"

("Yeah. But Charles Edward Abramson is about all most people can take," and here, on a piece of notebook paper, while I strained around at my desk, he drew a monogram, involving a C, E, and A, and the date—'56—which, over the next year, I would find written on bathroom walls, carved into table tops, or, once, fifteen years later, but still readable, gouged with a compass point into the back of a pew at Corpus Christi Church.)

At Dalton, the classes of twelve and fourteen students had sat in movable chairs at wide blond wood tables, or pushed the tables aside and drawn the chairs into an informal circle for discussion. But here were forty-two students in a single room, desks fixed to the floor and scarred by doodling generations. Even as I was talking with Chuck, it hit me that this was not the entire freshman grade but only one class—that, indeed, there were five others of the same size at the school.

At Dalton, the entire eighth grade had been smaller than this homeroom group.

For the last year, people had been talking to me about the "transition from elementary school to high school." But the transition was really between private school and public school—and nobody had prepared me for that.

Mr. Tannenbaum announced that we were all to get up, leave the seats we had taken, and find seats in alphabetical order, starting with the first seat in the first file and working back, then continuing with the first seat in the second file, and so on.

Well, I thought, slipping out of my desk, that was the end of sitting next to my new friend. We milled around, asking each other our names, laughing, exchanging remarks. Somehow, though, it panned out that (as an "Abramson") Chuck ended up the first student in the first file of desks, and, after we'd gone through the other A's, B's, and C's, I (as a "Delany") ended up in the second seat of the second file. I wasn't in front of him. But I was now one seat diagonally behind him.

The person sitting directly behind Chuck and, therefore, right beside me, was a bright, personable kid from Queens, with glasses, named Danny. He made some comment on some exchange between Chuck and me, and within minutes, had joined the pair of us as friends in a trio that stayed solid through the year.

"Come to order now," Mr. Tannenbaum said, and, once more, the general level of student whispering quieted. "It seems the next thing on our agenda is to elect the class representative to the Student Government Organization."

There was a general groan, and a girl named Debbie raised her hand to protest. "That seems awfully silly right now. None of us really knows anyone else."

Stacking "Delaney Cards" together for his roll book (part of an archaic filing system that only incidentally mirrored my name), Mr. Tannenbaum gave one of his inward, ironic smiles. "I think the idea is that it will help get the process of knowing each other started."

I kind of agreed with Debbie. But diagonally in front of me, Chuck immediately waved his hand. When Mr. Tannenbaum glanced at him, Chuck declared, "I nominate Chip Delany—this guy right here," twisting around and pointing down with his upraised hand at the top of my head.

Danny's hand was up a moment later. "I second the nomination."

"I guess we're getting started then." Mr. Tannenbaum got up to write the nominees on the blackboard. "Any other nominations?"

There were three others—one was a friend of mine from Woodland, named Gene. But he'd been sitting some seats behind me, so we hadn't, in those first minutes, done more than nod and grin at one another.

Another, a golden, good-looking Irish kid like Chuck, was named Mike.

The last was a native Bronx boy called Leo, with an incredible amount of body hair and a winning, easy manner, who, at thirteen, easily looked eighteen or older.

The four of us were called on to say something about ourselves. I don't remember what I said—but Gene used his time to tell a silly joke that fell flat. Moments after our impromptu campaign speeches, Mr. Tannenbaum told us to go out in the hall, where we milled about and glanced at one another, trying not to feel self-conscious; and inside the class discussed the four of us and voted. Somebody came to beckon through the wire-reinforced classroom door window.

We went back in.

I had been elected.

"All the GO representatives are meeting this afternoon," Mr. Tannenbaum told me "in room. . . ." He gave me the number. "It shouldn't take very long. It's just to set things up."

Chuck turned round and whispered, "I'll wait for you, and we can go home together."

Later, I asked Chuck if there'd been any discussion, and, if so, what had been said that got me elected. But he just brushed it off: "Nobody really said anything at all."

At lunch, however, when I got Danny alone (Danny's and Chuck's friendship had been cemented through the happenstance of their ending up in the same German class; and by now, we knew, all three of us had the same English teacher, a rotund gentleman with glasses, Mr. Kotter, who, when a young man had given him a not particularly sharp answer, had planted his hands on his hips that morning and said, "You know, I don't think you'd have sense enough to pour piss out of a boot," at which point we'd all fallen in love with him), Danny explained that when Mr. Tannenbaum had called for comments on the nominees, it came out that all the other nominators had indeed been friends of their nominees at previous schools, and Chuck, logically and coolly, had explained that he had never known me until today, but simply in the few minutes' conversation we'd already had, he'd been struck by my "intelligence, level-headedness, and insight," and these seemed to him better credentials than simply old friends nominating old friends. The argument had carried most of the remaining students—possibly it was a better argument than I was a candidate.

The student representative meeting that afternoon was simple and untaxing. Another math teacher, a woman even taller than Mr. Tannenbaum, gave us a brief rundown of our all but nonexistent duties.

A few minutes before the end of the meeting, Chuck's blond head swerved around outside the window; he waved to me. I kind of nodded back. The teacher saw him gesticulating outside the door, walked over, and opened it. "Are you looking for something?" she asked. "Is there anything I can do for you?"

"I was waiting for a friend," Chuck said.

"Then why don't you just come in," she said, "and sit down quietly." So Chuck came in with his first day's haul of textbooks in his arms and slid into a seat near mine.

About five minutes later, the meeting ended.

As the young reps were standing to leave, the front door of the classroom opened again and, rather breathlessly, a long-haired girl in glasses strode in and announced, half to the teacher and half to everyone else: "This is the student representatives' meeting, isn't it? I'm the GO Alternate. So I belong here."

The teacher looked at her with the smile I was becoming so familiar with. She said: "Actually, I don't think you do."

"Oh, no," the girl said. "I belong here." She repeated, "I'm the Alternate for my class."

"I mean," the teacher said, "the meeting's finished. We're all going home now."

"Well, I *do* belong here," the young woman said again.

Then, realizing what was happening, she said loudly, "Oh. . . ." As she looked around the room, perhaps we saw each other. Perhaps we even smiled. Then she turned and strode out of the room.

Behind me, Chuck said: "Chip, that girl is weird!"

I couldn't help thinking of Ben, though, busy in the Main Building being a genius. Certainly by comparison, she wasn't weird at all.

Chuck and I rode home together on the downtown D train.

6.32.

One other friendship I must speak about formed in that same time. Elements of it coalesced during the same minutes as those I've already written of. It was probably more important, at least to me as a writer, than those with Chuck or Danny. Reviewing it, however, what strikes me is how quickly the written narrative closes it out—puts it outside of language. Reading over what I've already written of that first day, searching for a margin in which to inscribe it, within and around what's already written, I suspect it might well be printed in the column parallel with the above, rather than as a consecutive report—certainly that's the way I experienced it.

Return, then, for a minute, as we came down from the roof. . . .

I walked into the classroom.

Chuck followed me.

As I slid into a seat behind one of the wooden desks toward the front of the room, I glanced aside at the students crowding up the aisle beside me, where I glimpsed a hand—a large hand—on which the broad nails were gnawed back behind a line of adolescent grime. The hand stayed there a second, two, tapped on a denim thigh, and was blocked by another student. I looked up, to see a tall boy—perhaps one of the two or three tallest kids in the class—with dark brown hair, peering over the heads of his classmates. He was wearing a dark brown, long-sleeved shirt. He sighed now, realizing that all the seats near the door were already taken, and began to make his way with the others around the desks to find somewhere to sit.

Chuck sat at the desk behind mine.

Our homeroom teacher, standing behind the desk now with his hands in his pockets, greeted us, telling us to take seats ("Those in the back, please hurry up. We have a lot to do this morning"), turned now to write his name on the board.

Mr. Tannenbaum began to call out the names of the various kids in the class— "Please answer 'present'"—while I looked around.

Once the names had been gone through, behind me Chuck whispered: "I could have really messed up his day and told him my whole name. Charles Edward Rufus Rastus McSweeney O'Gorman Van Pelt Abramson."

I turned around laughing. "Is that really your whole name . . . ?"

Mr. Tannenbaum glanced over, and I looked back.

"Yeah," Chuck went on whispering, obliviously. "But Charles Edward Abramson is about all most people can take." I looked over my shoulder again, where, on a piece of notebook paper, Chuck had begun to draw his monogram.

Mr. Tannenbaum called out more names.

The tall kid was sitting diagonally back in the room from me. I glanced around at the students, correcting their names through the roll call. His name was Joseph Torrent. ("Do people call you Joe?" Mr. Tannenbaum asked.

("Yeah—or Joey. . . ." A kind of squeakiness accented his premature adolescent baritone, as though his voice had not quite finished changing.)

Moments later, Mr. Tannenbaum was announcing that now we were all to get up, leave the seats we had taken, and take seats in alphabetical order, starting with the first seat in the first file and working back, then continuing with the first seat in the second file, and so on. I moved quickly to the back, momentarily losing Chuck (who'd gone forward, knowing his name would put him toward the front), and angling toward the big kid. I nearly bumped into him. With the same determination I'd had when I initially spoke to Chuck, I said, "Joe, this has got to be a lot more confusing than it's worth."

"Yeah," he said. And grinned. "It sure is." Then he frowned again. "What was your name again?"

"I'm Chip." I held out my hand. Not expecting that sort of greeting in the crush of students, he looked a little surprised, and then took it and shook. The skin was dry and warm, and slightly roughish. I liked that. Somebody toward the front said, "Hey, there were some more D's and E's—I know!"

"That's me," I said. And took off, back toward the front of the room, to take my seat, realizing that it was only one seat diagonally behind Chuck's anyway. "This isn't so bad," I told him.

While the kid beside me said, "Was your name Chip? I'm Danny."

"Hi," I said to the kid in the glasses with his spade-shaped face and hair that was nappier than mine, and shook hands. The fingers were thin, the nails ordinary length and clean, and not, to me, interesting at all. "This is Chuck," I said.

Chuck turned around. "Pleased to meet you."

Mr. Tannenbaum said, "Keep it down, now. We're trying to do this with as little noise as possible." He began to stack "Delaney Cards." "It seems the next thing on our agenda is to elect the class representative to the Student Government Organization. . . ."

While I waited outside the room with Gene, Mike, and Leo for the election to be over, I wondered whether Joey had voted for me or not. Someone beckoned us in through the window. As I came in, after Gene and before Mike, I glanced at Joe. He grinned, and I grinned back—then went to take my seat beside Danny and Chuck, as Mr. Tannenbaum announced, "Chip Delany is our GO representative," and I looked at the board where my name was written, the ghosts of the three others just legible on the black slate under the sweeping marks of the eraser. Well, I thought to myself, chances were Joe had.

Between two other classes where neither Chuck nor Danny was involved—I did not want any of my other friends to know about this friend—I talked to Joe some more. There were three lunch periods. Danny's and Chuck's was not the same as mine, that first term. And so I ate my lunch with Joe, asking him about himself, telling him a bit about me—and, every time I could without being obtrusive about it, glancing at his big, heavy-fingered hands, with their permanently grubby knuckles and their gnawed nails.

When Chuck and I came down from the GO meeting, as I walked into the school's dark foyer, out in the sun beyond the stained glass transom I saw Joe and several of his other friends standing around—apparently for some reason they had stayed after school too. They were just turning to leave—but I stepped up to the wall, where a wide bronze plaque hung (commemorating what in the elementary school's nether history, I could not possibly say now) and demanded, "Now who do you think all these people could be?"

Chuck looked back, came up, and in minutes we were joking about this name and that—for at least five minutes . . . time to let Joe get to the corner and out of sight. I even contemplated suggesting I'd forgotten a book upstairs, and asking Chuck to return with me. But certainly Joey was far ahead enough by now to obliterate any possibility of my having to talk with both at the same time—a burden that seemed to lie just beyond the edge of possible endurance.

On days when I didn't ride home on the subway with Danny or Chuck, however, I'd hunt up Joe and ride down with him, occasionally going a few stops past the 135th Street station, where ordinarily I got out, to the Ninety-sixth Street station, where he left the train. Sometimes, I even sat with him on the benches against the station's tiled wall for half an hour, listening to him talk about adolescent problems that ran from his difficulties in getting along with his mother (like Chuck's, Joey's parents were divorced) to misunderstandings he'd had with some friends with whom, from time to time, he played basketball.

Science's 140 IQ average meant, of course, that many students were substantially above it. (I didn't realize at the time that a kind of instinct made me seek out the brighter kids.) But it also meant that there were many below it—students of good or even ordinary intelligence, who had acquired good study habits, who were by temperament hard workers, and who were willing to put real energy into whatever tasks were put them.

Chuck and Danny were students who glittered. Whether they did well or badly, whatever they were involved in was always interesting. Joe, on the other hand, fell squarely into the latter group. (He had done better than I on the entrance exam; no one had had to maneuver *his* name around on a waiting list.) The problem these students had at Bronx Science was that often, if only because of their diligence, they'd been the smartest or among the smartest students in whatever school they'd come from. But now because there was such a concentration of real brilliance around them—and all the eccentricity that went with it—they were reduced to the position of the normal. Often they were not happy with it.

And that was very much Joe.

6.321.

The double narrative, in its parallel columns. . . .

(When, thirty-three years later, I asked Chuck about his recollections of our first day in school together, he told me over long distance from Missoula, Montana, while sunlight through Amherst's leaves dappled my uncurtained storm windows: "The thing I remember about that first day was that Mr. Tannenbaum wore 'space shoes' . . . that this man, who from the way he dressed, should have been wearing the most conservative dark-brown wing tipped Oxfords—he wore space shoes! In the newspaper, every weekend, there used to be that little advertisement, 'Come get your feet poured . . .' or something? And he had them—like your mother. I can remember her wearing them, in the library across from the Museum of Modern Art where she worked. 'Space shoes'—they were really strange to see on someone back then." But because my mother *did* wear them, Mr. Tannenbaum's hadn't made the same impression on me.)

With the two (or more . . .) tales printed as they are, consecutively and not parallel at all, a romantic code hierarchizes them: the second account—full of guilt, silence, desire, and subterfuge—displaces the first—overt, positive, rich, and social—at once discrediting it and at the same time presumably revealing its truth.

Yet reread closely.

Nothing in the first is in any way *explained* by the second, so that this "truth" that the second is presumed to provide is mostly an expectation, a convention, a trope—rather than a real explanatory force.

(The third, Chuck's "space shoes," parenthetical, oblique, idiosyncratic, ironic, simply problematizes the first two, opening the space for a continuation of codes to write, to revise, to develop. . . .)

The more historically sensitive among us will remember an older—and conservative—code from which the Romantic questioning, distrust, and uneasiness with the feelings grew. It holds that, in day-to-day occurrences, the desire- and deceit-laden narrative *always* develops alongside the "socially acceptable" one. Doctors, lawyers, and artists are privileged to discuss it when it impinges on their specialized domains:

the body, ethics, representation. But for the rest of us, the old code says, it *should* be private (rather than subjective: it is the abolition of the private code by active medical, legal, and aesthetic intervention that creates, that necessitates, that constitutes Romantic "subjectivity"). As adults, we have the right—indeed, the duty—to keep it so.

Why speak of what's uncomfortable to speak of?

What damage might it do to women, children, the temperamentally more refined, the socially ignorant, the less well educated, those with a barely controlled tendency toward the perverse?

Since publishing it in most cases explains little or nothing of the public narrative, why not let it remain privy, personal, privileged—outside of language . . . ?

But if it *is* the split—the spaces between the columns (one resplendent and lucid with the writings of legitimacy, the other dark and hollow with the voices of the illegitimate, and even a third aglitter with ironic alterities)—that constitutes the subject, it is only after the Romantic inflation of the private into the subjective that such a split can even be located. That locus, that margin, that split itself first allows, then demands the appropriation of language—now spoken, now written—in both directions, over the gap.

Andrew Holleran

Andrew Holleran's (b. 1943) first novel, *Dancer from the Dance* (1978), evoked the era of New York gay life in the 1970s with a power and haunting romantic lyricism unparalleled by any other work of the time, a power and lyricism that has made the novel a target for those who wish to attack pre-AIDS gay culture and its glamorization of sex and beauty. His two major characters represented the poles of that upper-class white society: Malone is the man whom everyone desires as he, lost, pursues a "career in love"; Sutherland is the campy sophisticate whose sharp tongue is his only weapon to use on life. These two faces of gay life, the knowing camp and the innocent loner, play themselves out in virtually all of Holleran's novels—*Nights in Aruba* (1983), *The Beauty of Men* (1996), and *Grief: A Novel* (2006). The gap of over a dozen years between *Night in Aruba* and *The Beauty of Men* corresponds to the appearance of AIDS, about which Holleran has written with enormous humanity in *Ground Zero* (1988), a collection of essays. For many, Holleran's essays are his major accomplishment. Holleran has also written a haunting collection of stories entitled *In September, the Light Changes* (1999).

Although a shy man, Holleran was part of the Violet Quill group of writers, which included Edmund White, Felice Picano, and Robert Ferro, whom Holleran met while they were students at the prestigious University of Iowa Writers' Workshop. He now teaches writing at American University in Washington, D.C.

The text below is a talk that Holleran gave to an organization of his fellow gay Harvard graduates, and it appeared in the first issue (Winter 1994) of what was then called the *Harvard Gay and Lesbian Review*. It has since been forced by the university to drop the identification with Harvard.

My Harvard

FIRST, THANKS VERY MUCH for having me to speak. My twenty-fifth reunion, dare I date myself, was last year, but I never even considered coming back, even though I was dying to come back and look around, which I've been able to do last evening and today. The reasons I couldn't imagine coming back are what I think I'm going to talk about tonight. The title I gave this talk is "My Harvard," which only seems megalomaniacal, but is not meant to be — it's from a book published in 1982 by a man named Jeffrey Lant, a collection I contributed to of some twenty or more essays written by people who went here. One of them was Erich Segal. Erich Segal — of *Love Story* fame — wrote another novel about Harvard called *The Class*. So did a classmate of mine named Faye Levine, I learned, reading my *25th Reunion Class Report* a few evenings ago. (Faye Levine was a woman who became famous overnight at Harvard after writing an article in *The Crimson* which categorized types of Radcliffe women by comparing them to flavors of ice cream.) Her novel was *Splendor and Misery: A Novel of Harvard*. I don't know if she was alluding to a novel by Balzac, a wonderful novel with a gay character, Vautrin, in it, called *Splendors and Miseries of the Courtesans*, in which a prostitute is sent to a convent to be schooled as the mistress of a jaded Parisian. (Perhaps Faye had a more cynical view of a Harvard education than I did.)

The very first novel I ever wrote was about Harvard, too. I wrote it in a fit of depression after graduation, when I'd lost all my friends and what seemed to me the only place I'd ever been happy. This novel was set not only at Harvard, but in Lowell House, and not only in Lowell House, but on the terrace overlooking the courtyard; it had lots of lilacs, forsythia, roses in it, and the words "balustrade" and "chandelier" occurred a lot; it was, in other words, my sappy attempt at what Evelyn Waugh did so well in *Brideshead Revisited*. What Waugh did in *Brideshead Revisited* was actually make the friends we all have in college, the emotions we feel, the deep nostalgia for that impressionable time of life, objectively matter, seem truly interesting. Because while they are interesting to the people who lived them, they are often very hard to make important to anyone else. Years later, while working as a nocturnal proofreader for a large Park Avenue law firm, one of my co-workers, a graduate of Penn, asked me to read *his* college novel about a classmate who had made a very deep impression on him. It was hard to say anything about his book, since I wanted to be kind, and the simplest thing to have told him was: "Get over it." I recognized my own first novel in his: the nostalgia, melancholy, hero-worship, or at least desire to worship a hero, or be one oneself. But such emotions are mostly sentimental in print and matter all too often to no one but the author. Which is why I was glad Jeffrey Lant, about ten years ago, asked me to contribute an essay to *Our Harvard*—because an essay seems to me about the right size for a college valentine. I got to not only describe my years at Harvard in this piece, but to discover not how happy I'd been during them, but, in fact, how depressed I was here much of the time; and how a lot of that depression was due to a thwarted attempt to come out—an attempt no one at Harvard seemed to want to contemplate, much less assist, or talk about.

There was another chance I had to write about Harvard, I should add, before Jeffrey Lant asked me for an essay—a chance every Harvard graduate who can't manage a *Brideshead Revisited* or *This Side of Paradise* gets, and that is the *Class Report* that comes out every five years after you leave this place. I'm sure most of you are familiar with them. For the first twenty years they are modest paperbacks, easy to carry, to read on a beach. And from the start, they are fascinating. They have been kept since the 18th century and are used by scholars. They read, however, like novels. They're better than most novels, in fact, because they're not contrived, not literary; they're all true. One can see, if you browse long enough, the whole range of human experience in them—the same amazing variety one finds in the people who go to school here, the different ways in which Fate distributes character, and gifts, and good and bad fortune to people. Of course it's impossible to read them and not compare one's own story with other people's—which is okay, because you do it in private, reading, and you can make what you want of it all, draw your own reflective conclusions. Each essay, each five years, amounts to *A Life Thus Far*; a summing up—and, like all summings up, they seem to be divided into the successful and unsuccessful, the happy and unhappy, in their most extreme form, with all the shades and gradations in between. On the other hand, a lot of people do not write in. Ever. I never did, for instance. Enough people do, however, to make the one that just came out for my class, in its twenty-fifth reunion year, over twelve hundred pages long.

The *25th Reunion Class Report* is hardbound, huge, printed on glossy paper, as heavy as a good dictionary or a small one-volume encyclopedia. The overall impression one gets skimming it is that the whole point of going to Harvard is to become a gynecologist. At least, of all the professions represented, doctors seem to write in most often. Doctors, lawyers, and businessmen. Other than that, it's difficult to generalize. Not all who are successful write in. There is nothing next to the name of a woman in my class, for instance, who's had a very successful career as a pianist who specializes in contemporary music, or another who has gone on to be a famous actress, and whom I took sophomore tutorial with: Stockard Channing. The unfamous also write in. The less successful. People write in, thank goodness, who've changed careers in mid-life, who still don't know what they want to do, who are single and living alone and still write lines like, "I still hope to marry one day and live happily ever after." (*Time is running out, dear*, one wants to write back.) There is always an unreconstructed hippy who is *still* in Burma trying to achieve tantric sex, or a man with a scheme that will guarantee world peace forever, or a harassed suburban housewife trying to sustain her commitment to Marxist humanism, or someone building a harpsichord in his basement in Minneapolis. The overall tone, however, is one of unbelievable conventionality. So it's a shock to come upon someone who announces he or she is gay. There are six or seven in my *Class Report*, I believe, without having read all twelve hundred pages to date. The men seem to make more of a point of it than the women. It may be harder, or more necessary, for them to say; I'm not sure. It certainly was for me, which is largely the reason I never wrote in.

One of my classmates who did, however, came out in the very first report my class published—a man I ran into years later in New York at a book signing when my first novel came out. I'd not known him that well at Harvard; I'd seen him, however, because he used to go around campus in a long black opera cloak, which was eccentric even for Harvard. He had an austerely handsome face and majored in medieval history, and this is what he wrote in the latest *Class Report*: "Nothing has turned out as I planned. I planned to be a teacher, probably a college professor. I am an administrator in the bus maintenance side of the New York City Transit Authority. I planned to be a member of a Roman Catholic religious order; I do volunteer work at the Gay Men's Health Crisis of New York. It all started very normally, I wanted to be a medievalist, so I went to Balliol College, Oxford. I was active in the Roman Catholic chaplaincy. I fell in love with a man in my college who denounced me publicly when I hinted at my feelings. I tried suicide, and took a decent honors degree. It was all very commonplace, for Oxford in 1967." And so on. It ends with a description of the grief he feels over the death of friends from AIDS, "a grief," he writes, "that will not go away." This particular classmate, I've thought since the first *Report*, has always been honest. I've always admired his forthrightness, in particular since I could not summon it up myself. And if his entry always seemed to me particularly eloquent, that same courage informs the much briefer opening line of a Radcliffe graduate in this year's *Report*, who writes: "I live in Minnesota with my partner Joan. We lived for many years in the woods."

(*We lived for many years in the woods*—what a novel that might begin.)

At the same time, there are essays in every *Report* that I have always sensed were leaving out an important fact—occasionally, because I happened to know, or know of, the person writing. In my class, for instance, a well-known New York writer has never once divulged the detail that might explain part or much of the sort of life he'd made for himself. Which always seemed to translate into: You can work for *The New Yorker* magazine, and be what the world considers a success, and still not want to have anyone know you're gay, in 1991. The latter surely was one reason I myself never wrote in—what would I say, except the fact that I was gay, and had written novels about gay life? And why did I want to tell them—this mostly straight class—about that?

I was wondering, in fact, as I thought about what I wanted to say here, to this crowd, what it would be like to be at Harvard now, coming to hear this talk. On the one hand, it's impossible to imagine, because this evening would not have occurred when I was here; I couldn't have come to hear me speak; because in 1965 there was no Open Gate, no gay mentor program, no anti-discrimination clause, no newsletter, no Queer Nation going to Brookline High School to distribute condoms and talk about homosexuality, no kiss-ins in house dining halls. Freshman year I was dating a woman I'd gone to high school with who was at Wellesley. Each Saturday night we would return from the French film we'd double-dated at, and stand before her dorm, while the other couples around us puréed each other's lips. Debbie and I talked about Truffaut, then lightly embraced and said good night. Disturbed, I went to Student Health. My question was: Why didn't I want to kiss Debbie? (Debbie's question probably was: What's wrong with my hair and make-up?) At Student Health I had a pre-appointment interview designed to ascertain if there really was a problem; the woman who heard my doubts about my sexuality made a sympathetic clucking noise as she listened—small moans, and sighs; the sound my mother made when watching news of some awful plane crash on TV. I got an appointment the next day with a suntanned shrink whose desk held framed photographs of his sailboat and his family on a lawn in Maine. I told him I thought I was homosexual because I didn't want to kiss Debbie. He listened to me wordlessly and then leaned forward and solved the problem by saying: "Next time, kiss her."

Instead, I stopped dating altogether, and freshman year came to an end in utter isolation. After dinner in the Freshman Union—a meal I waited to eat until three minutes before closing, because it seemed easier to sit by myself in that huge room populated by other loners, staring straight ahead as the stuffed moose heads on the wall looked over us at one another—I would go upstairs to an empty room on the top floor to study, and end up instead staring at a young man modeling a swimsuit for Parr of Arizona, Inc., in the back pages of *Esquire*. I remember going to Widener shortly after my visit to Student Health and looking up Plato in the card catalogue; and I remember being very careful no one was behind me who could see over my shoulder just what I was looking up. I think I also found John Addington Symonds, whose title—*A Problem in Modern Ethics*—seemed an understatement at the time. None of this was decisive; to know that great minds had considered homosexuality not only acceptable but noble did not make much of a dent in a twentieth-century middle-class American Catholic upbringing. Another place I went to read was Lamont. I was taking a course in geology at the time: Nat Sci 5. While sitting in the john one day I noticed the partitions between the stalls were sheets of limestone in which the imprints of trilobites could be seen. I also noticed advertisements for nude wrestling scrawled on the doors in Magic Marker. As everyone knows who has gone to school, one can read certain things at a certain age and just not get it: *Moby Dick*. *King Lear*. Ads for nude wrestling on bathroom walls. Such was the force of my denial, I didn't even associate such things with myself. And when a hand reached under the partition between the toilet stalls one day and stroked my left leg, I stood up, horrified, pulled my pants on, and left. The johns in those days sounded like Niagara Falls when flushed, and the sound, I was sure, let the slimeball who had touched my left calf know just what I thought about *that* sort of activity.

Enter Elizabeth Taylor and Richard Burton. Sophomore year I moved to Lowell House without a roommate. How could I? I still knew no one. The first days there I went to look at places I might live: rooms or suites with people who had no roommates either. One of them was very strange. He chain-smoked while we talked, wore glasses, talked in a low, sepulchral voice and wanted, I learned later, to be a nightclub singer more than anything else in life. Though I ended up in a suite with three sober history majors, I began noticing Richard around Lowell House, with another person—always the same person, a very exotic, aristocratic-looking student who didn't look like the rest of us. He had the sort of expression I'd only seen on the bust of Nefertiti: slanted eyes, wavy blond hair, and a serene but piercing gaze that seemed to regard the world from a mysterious distance I couldn't quite analyze. He often wore a double-breasted blazer, beautiful striped shirts; I decided he must be European, the son of a French count, perhaps. In reality he was the son of a civil servant from the Bronx, and had transferred to Harvard from CCNY. Richard told me about him one day when I found Richard alone at lunch. He said I should get to know Joel, because Joel was in charge of inviting Elizabeth Taylor and Richard Burton to Lowell House for a Ford dinner in the small dining room; part of a series in which undergraduates could invite artists to dinner there. If I got to know him, he might put me on the guest list. The introduction took place. Joel, Richard, and I began eating together, and meeting every night in Joel's room at 11 o'clock. From there we went to Elsie's, ate, came back to Lowell House, and talked till two. They had a remarkable sense of humor—one I liked a lot, but which I knew was not quite right, somehow. When I left Joel's room I thought this was how Macbeth felt after visiting the witches. Harvard, after all, was all about language, the careful and precise use of words. Glib, gabby freshmen like myself soon had ice water thrown on them, so icy my first tutor told me I was "feckless" and I had to rush home to look the word up. Harvard was all about a rational, ironic, critical reserve. Not so with Joel and Dick. I spoke a different language in the room with them. There was a book out at that time about a Princeton student and his relationship with a black prostitute, called *The Hundred Dollar Misunderstanding*, and it had a line of dialogue Joel and Dick used to toss back and forth between themselves that was not very politically correct: "She think hers don't stink, but it do." I couldn't quite fit this in with Henry James, Henry Adams, and Cotton Mather, but after a long day in class learning tropes in Puritan sermons, and the oblivion of Lamont Library, I know I had to go to Joel's at 11 o'clock and hear *some*one say that line.

As it turned out, Elizabeth Taylor never came to Lowell House; she was trapped in her hotel room in downtown Boston—where Burton was appearing in *Hamlet*, shortly after the beginning of their romance. Trapped by fans and paparazzi, if there are paparazzi in Boston, she could not get out to come over to Cambridge. Or so we were told. But by this time, even without Elizabeth Taylor, Joel and Dick and I had become a unit. Or rather I was an appendage; Joel and Dick were the unit, so closely bonded they still seemed to me separate from the rest of the house. They always ate together, for example, at a small table in the corner of the dining hall. Some evenings I would enter that room, see the two of them in one corner, and my roommates at another table, and realize I had to make a terrible choice; a choice Joel watched me make with his penetrating eyes as I walked to the serving line to get my tray—since he knew exactly what I was going through, torn between the conventional and unconventional, respectable and *outré*. Joel seemed to know more about me than I did about myself, in fact. At Joel's I learned a lot of odd things—that perfume is smelled on the wrist, not from the bottle, that Venice is best in September, that I should rinse my face twenty times after cleaning it before bed—but they all seemed mere symptoms of a deeper knowledge he had about what people, including myself, wanted out of life. Really wanted. I of course was too polite to ask, and many nights I simply glanced at Joel and Richard in the corner of the dining room, and sat down instead with my roommates to talk about the closing of the frontier in America.

The frontier may have closed, but finally, in Lowell House, I myself was opening up. I began noticing people besides Joel and Dick; making other friends. One was an assistant professor of English who gave me a part in *An Evening with Oscar Wilde* in the common room, and who led a seminar on Tennessee Williams I took, and whose own book on Emily Dickinson had just come out. Road-signs, it would seem, at this distance. But sexuality is not so easily perceived when young. Once after a lecture on Walt Whitman, we went to lunch in the dining hall, and when we asked if we could sit at his table with him, he looked up, sighed, and said: "If you promise not to ask if Whitman was homosexual." I hadn't been about to, but, like my experience at Student Health, this confirmed my impression that homosexuality was a neurotic bore, a tiresome insecurity of anxious undergraduates and nothing more. Yet I was also aware of this professor's close friendship with another tutor in the house, and the fact that he was thirty-five and unmarried—a fact that must have allowed me to feel closer to him than to other instructors. I was aware, too, of other friendships: another tutor, in particular, and a sophomore, who were both very handsome and went out together in the evening so well dressed they looked like Edwardian fops. And two students, a sleepy-eyed blond and a dark-haired fellow with a faint case of acne, who would walk around our courtyard in spring in black leather pants, actually cracking a big black whip. There was a student playwright whom I saw one morning, just after dawn, walk into the foggy courtyard, while I—having stayed up all night studying for some exam—watched him cross to another entry with his arm wrapped around another man. Cross the courtyard, I sensed (without even making the thought conscious), in a way that was possible only at dawn, in a fog, while everyone else was asleep. There was even a tutor in Slavic studies who looked like the pederast small children are told not to accept candy from—with enormous, liquid eyes, and a pipe at his red lips— a man who contributed drawings to *The New Yorker* and who, rumor had it, flunked his doctoral exams on purpose so he could stay in Lowell House, running both the weight-lifting club and a life drawing class. Both of which seem appealing to me now, but at the time were sub-rosa, off limits, vaguely dangerous. The general atmosphere of the culture, and Lowell House, was macho-competitive. One friend lived with a pack of preppies who would sit in the dining hall Friday nights betting which women coming in as dates were virgins. One of my own roommates was having an affair with a student at Convent of the Sacred Heart, and described his distaste at having to make love in rented hotel rooms with another couple on the adjacent bed. Another room- mate was dating a Wellesley student he did more than kiss; he would hang a red tie on his doorknob to mean they were having sex and were not to be disturbed.

Afterwards, I would see them walk into the dining hall with what looked like a radiant glow on their flushed faces. Like the heroine of a Henry James novel I was reading, I suspected everyone was having sex but me. I suppressed the whole issue by spending even longer hours in libraries, searching for the perfect chair, the perfect desk, the perfect lamp that would enable me to imbibe these books I could hardly remember a word of the minute I finished them. By sophomore year you realize, of course, that reading is, in a sense, all you've been sent here to do. And teaching is all about telling a person to read the right book, the one he or she needs.

My friend the English instructor suggested I read one called *The Last Puritan* by George Santayana fall of my junior year. *The Last Puritan* happens to be about a Har- vard student, a student who transfers to Williams, actually, and his romantic/ideal- istic/platonic friendship with an English sailor his father hires to sail his yacht. It's about a love between two men that can never come to sexual expression; it depressed me deeply; I seemed to recognize in the book an emotion that was my fate, a fate that seemed to close off so much of life that should be hopeful and outgoing in a sort of melancholy resignation. I was also given that year a novel by Henry James called *The Ambassadors*. In a famous scene in *The Ambassadors* a middle-aged man from New England, standing in a garden in Paris, suddenly realizes his life has passed him by, and says to the young man he's with: "Live, live all you can, it's a mistake not to!" The words made perfect sense to me. They do to most of us. The question was: How? In the novel, everyone's upset because a young American has lingered in Paris while having an affair with an older woman. This was hard to translate into the opportunities available to a middle-class college student walking with Joel to Elsie's every night for a piece of mocha cake, hearing him say in his sonorous, nasal voice, "Now, *there's* a face." Faces were all we had, though what the significance of their beauty was, I wasn't sure. We did not always agree on the face, but that we both felt them important, and magical, was one of the bases of our friendship, and the glory of this place. Odd. There was no course at Harvard in Faces, the Beauty Of. There was no seminar that dealt with the powerful hold mere physical beauty had on me—at least, no seminars listed as such. Everything was being transmitted obliquely, politely, it seemed—as seeds that would flower, like so much education, later.

Senior year I took a course on the Life Cycle taught by Erik Erikson that made an impression on a lot of people, I realized, reading my last *Class Report*. The Life Cycle consists, in his conception, of six life crises between birth and death. The idea is to pass each one to get on to the next. It always involved a choice. The one that applied to me at the time I took the course seemed to be the Crisis of Intimacy, or Intimacy versus Isolation. The crisis of intimacy involved a member of the opposite sex. Since I now believed I would never pass that one, I concluded my life was permanently stalled—what people used to, and may still, call arrested development; homosexuality as a sort of eternal and terminal adolescence. Well, thought I, since I can't pass the Crisis of Intimacy, I can never move on to Generativity (parenthood), Acceptance, and Death. Or rather, I'd go straight from Crisis Three to Crisis Six without ever experiencing the other two.

There was another concept of Erikson's that I think of now, because it seems to have perhaps more to do with homosexuality in our culture; and that is Negative Identity. Negative Identity is just that—identifying with the reverse of virtues we are supposed to emulate. That homosexuality was a negative identity was a message I'd received all my life; it was, quite clearly, the complete opposite of the pattern urged on us by family, community, custom, church, school, and law: Marriage and Family.

Marriage and Family: the ultimate Goal. The Crisis of Intimacy, successfully passed. When my favorite professor announced his impending marriage my senior year, I was thunderstruck; appalled; felt deserted, abandoned, as if an adored older brother had just told me the news—so deserted, I blurted out without thinking, "Why?" "To enlarge the circumference of my experience," he said, using a phrase from his book on that famous celibate, Emily Dickinson. To enlarge the circumference of his experience? That sounded like an odd reason to get married—like going to Greece. But then the summer I'd gone to Greece, my travelling companion from Adams House kept saying—each time we found ourselves on some matchless promontory above the Aegean—"I'm going to bring my wife here when I marry." Chilling words: I knew I'd be returning solo. When I was talking with one of my other friends, a math major from Oregon who lived across the entry-way from Joel, one night, I remember telling him the difference between us was that he liked Math, and I liked English. In other words, I thought, you're straight, and I'm gay. "Gay" was not the word then, of course. And Harvard, still sexually segregated, all male, let me finesse the whole issue—the dawning sense of isolation, the failure to pass Life Crisis #3— by ignoring everything. No wonder the novel I wrote in a state of depression after graduation was so awful. No wonder it really seemed my life had ended. If homosexuality was a topic the few adults I asked implied was not worth talking about—Kiss Debbie; don't ask if Whitman was—I might as well ignore it, too. In reality I could not. Even ignoring it I was to waste an awful lot of time afterwards, those years when I sometimes wished I'd never gone to Harvard, had moved right to a city like New York, say, right after high school.

Years later the dear friends I couldn't bear to part with in June of 1965 were all leading separate lives. The math major from Oregon got married, took over the family farm, and had two daughters. The friend who wanted to visit Cape Sounion with his bride did. Joel moved to Paris, met someone, he wrote in a letter, "who sees the world the way I do," and began trying to earn a living. Richard moved to Washington, D.C., to avoid the draft, and taught high school. I took the foreign service exam, thinking I would work for the State Department; but each time I scheduled a personal interview, I cancelled—thinking the FBI or whoever interviewed me would know I wasn't straight. (As Gore Vidal said: "I could've been President except for the fag thing!") Instead I went to a writer's workshop—who cared, in the arts, if you were gay?—and after a stint in the Army, moved to New York and became a clone. The few times Joel and I got together on one of his trips back home, our relationship seemed a bit awkward; it was obvious we couldn't reproduce Harvard on the streets of Greenwich Village. He hated New York, for one thing. I loved it. He wasn't "gay." I was. The period of hilarious innocence was over, and Harvard was behind us, and everything had to be, in a sense, re-negotiated.

One summer evening we were walking through Greenwich Village while he was in New York on business, eating ice cream cones, the way we had in Cambridge, and we passed a newsstand. Writers in the news magazines at that time—1975—were fond of saying the love that dared not speak its name now would not shut up. In the ten years since Joel and I had graduated, not only I had come out of the closet, so had thousands of other people. I even knew the man with whom Joel had gone to Europe the summer after I'd met Joel and Dick—a French teacher who now lived three blocks from me in the East Village, where, though he never visited the bars and discos I did, he lived with one lover after another, always Puerto Rican or black, like some man in a story by Joseph Conrad, one Conrad never wrote. Joel of course had been with the same companion for ten years now; without ever once having gone to a bar, baths, or place like Fire Island—the three staples of my existence at that time, places one went ostensibly to find a companion, again and again and again. Which was the reason I felt a little embarrassed taking him down Christopher Street that evening: Part of me was wondering if he hadn't done it in a better way, and didn't consider this pathetic. In fact, by 1975, Christopher Street had turned fairly trashy, the excesses of the seventies already beginning to transform it into something seedy, and as we walked it all seemed suddenly sordid in a way it might not have had I not been trying to sense, as we walked, his reaction. I was already anticipating his disapproval, perhaps, the failure of the scene to match his own standards in life, whether this was Harvard snobbery or Harvard intelligence, when we passed a newspaper stand covered with porn magazines like *Honcho, Mandate,* and *Drummer.* Joel stopped for a moment to look at them, and then said, as we walked on, in a musing voice: "Why do they make so much of it over here?"

Why do we make so much of it over here, indeed? The question struck me then, and still does: I'd made a lot of it, certainly, in my own life. It had become in a sense everything. So I had to ask my own self what he had, what only a visitor, perhaps, could. The easy answer to his question was to say that in Europe, homosexuality was not the basis for a separate category, community, self-interest group that it was here; that people there lived out their sexual preference while remaining in the context of the larger society and culture. And that you could call this either staying in the closet, or refusing to be ghettoized. What was this mob scene I was involved in, anyway, this stampede of promiscuity, this gay life that seemed all too often toward the end of the seventies as predictable and conformist as any in the suburbs? With its rituals, habits, stereotypes, expectations, and burn-out? Perhaps homosexuality was in fact an essentially private and personal fact, something that had to do with the person in one's bed, and nothing more. I could have told Joel that it was a French man, Renaud Camus, who'd written a book that described gay life as well as any I'd read, a book aptly named *Tricks.* But that was not the answer. So I was back to his simple question as we strolled onto the pier: Why did we make so much of it over here?

Nothing is so diminishing as to realize that one was, after all, part of a trend—an era, an historical moment. American life—the sort journalists sum up in decades, or nicknames—is something Harvard people think, I suspect, they are too smart for, too individual, too different, to be a part of. But I was part of something, I guess, that Joel was not. The Age of Clones, 1971 to 1979 A.D. All movements are merely accumulations of many individuals desiring the same thing, of course. When you are coming out, you do not spend much time thinking about what you are doing—you want simply to live, to have a personal life—an approximation at first of the dreams one was brought up with: domestic happiness, fidelity, affection, trust. You want to solve the Crisis of Intimacy. These concepts translate oddly into homosexual life, I learned. There was no education for the sort of life I ended up leading. We are not brought up to be gay. There was a sense of learning new codes, living in New York as a gay man; of going to school all over again in a society which did not recognize the diploma you'd earned. It recognized other things, mostly unrelated to your education—exactly the problem of all education, Henry Adams had pointed out. I who wondered what James meant in *The Ambassadors* was now wondering how to combine brewers' yeast with my morning milkshake because I needed extra protein for the body-building I was doing at the gym. The thing that had not seemed important at Harvard—the body— was now crucial. My roommate would not travel unless he could continue his workouts wherever he was going, as if he were afraid he would deflate. It often struck me in New York in the seventies that while my friend the math major was writing in letters that Harvard had little to do with farming wheat, I was thinking it had nothing to do with entering the Sandpiper on Fire Island in the right T-shirt and haircut. As the T-shirt said: "So many men, so little time." Life in the seventies was an extraordinary burst of energy and invention. But questions of history and literature were replaced by three: Did you go out last night? Who was there? How was the music? (I did. It was jammed. The music was okay.) In 1977 a Harvard graduate named Toby Marotta came out in his *10th Anniversary Class Report*; he got so many letters, he wrote a book called *Sons of Harvard*—a collection of interviews with gay classmates. One weekend I went down to Washington to visit Richard—Richard who, with classic New England reserve, had never said a word about his private life. Neither Joel nor I had any idea about his sexuality or amorous life. All we knew was that he had been in therapy and was living with 19 cats. One summer evening he and I stood on a terrace of the Capitol, and I asked him what he wanted out of life, and he said: "I want to be successful and have a family." The words stunned me; not only because he seemed far from this goal. When I said goodbye as he dropped me off at Union Station, I did not tell him I felt like the Little Mermaid returning to the sea—the sea of men. I was addicted to cruising. Ten years after graduation from Harvard, where I saw nothing in terms of sex, I now saw everything that way. Re-reading *The Ambassadors* it struck me that the book was really about Chad Newsome's penis—everyone wanted it. And instead of going to Paris to live, live all I could, I headed straight for the Everard Baths the moment the train returned me to New York.

One night the Everard burned down. People died, it was said, because the owners had not hooked sprinklers up. One of the dead was the lover of a man from my neighborhood I used to run into every now and then, infrequently, because he spent six months of the year teaching English in Saudi Arabia and six months back in New York, since, he said, he needed half a year in a strict, puritanical, drugless society to alternate with New York. It was true that, having no limits, thanks to penicillin, there seemed no way the escalation of drugs, muscles, ways to have sex, would stop. The Everard was rebuilt, and now there was also the St. Marks, Man's Country, and the Club. I was reading Henry James now in the waiting room of the Enteric Disease Clinic on 9th Avenue, where I kept running into friends, while waiting for our shit to be analyzed for amoebas. Once I overheard the nurse ask one of the patients the usual question, "Have you been traveling?" and I thought: Yes, in the wrong circles. Yet the moment one was cured, one celebrated by going back into the fray. As a friend said when I asked him what he was going to do with his clean bill of health: "Go to the Mineshaft." In the meantime, a new generation arrived in the City that wanted nothing to do with discos, plaid shirts, or Fire Island theme parties. One day I looked down and saw stencilled on the sidewalk of my block by a group called Fags Against Facial Hair the words CLONES GO HOME. I obeyed. Burnt out by it all, I went home and ended up writing a book about an experience that seemed to have nothing to do with what I'd been educated or prepared for: Gay life. An experience that constituted an odd, mostly invisible, and very foreign country all by itself.

Oddly, all three of us had ended up living apart—Dick in the inner city of Washington, D.C., Joel in Paris, me in gay America, all equally foreign somehow. What was wonderful was our friendship's surviving everything. The awkward reunions spaced over a decade eventually worked themselves out. Joel even introduced me to a man in New York—a friend of his—who became my closest friend in New York. They were pleased about my getting published. We walked around New York together, the three of us, soon after this. Then AIDS hit in 1983 and took the friend Joel had introduced me to, and the next thing I heard were long distance calls from Paris and Washington asking how I was.

Last night I took a walk around campus. I went down to Elsie's—closed and dark and all changed inside, but still there. Then I went, with some wariness, to Lowell House, wondering if I could even go in. I could, and did, and it was quite spooky. The door to Joel's entry was locked, and two women were in the window beside it facing the courtyard; but I could still feel the spell of those evenings in L-14—how happy and romantic I'd been there—and what a dream world we'd lived in, I now realize. At one point I crossed the grass and stood outside the window of my own first room there, looking out onto the courtyard through the fog. I stood there and peered into the window where I'd sat that night, resting my eyes after a night of studying, separated from that moment by twenty-five years of Time, that densest of all mediums through which many things cannot pass. And all I could think, watching the students talking to each other on the walks, saying good-night before the entry-ways, rehearsing music in the common room, was how fresh they seemed, how utterly hopeful.

Homosexual desire isn't easy. It takes, for all its romanticism, an unending ability to face facts over and over again. Sometimes painful facts. What to tell parents, if anything. What to tell friends, people you work for, where to work, how to integrate sex with the other parts of your life and personality. How to settle the issue of generativity. Of intimacy. How to deal with the temptation to shame. How to find what one wanted to begin with—fidelity, intimacy, affection. Henry James wrote a story called *The Beast in the Jungle* in which a man realized his fate was that nothing whatsoever would happen to him all his life. Well, once you act on homosexual, or heterosexual, desire, a lot of things happen. Many writers have painted a not exactly alluring picture of where all this leads. In *A Streetcar Named Desire*, Blanche gets taken away to the insane asylum for kissing the paperboy. In *Death in Venice*, Gustav ends up sobbing on a beach as mascara runs down his cheeks. (For Thomas Mann, a homosexual life was chaos.) In Proust, the greatest of them all, Charlus is devastated when Morel leaves him for a woman. Homosexuality ends up at some point requiring your best thinking and effort: One's education does in fact have to be used, at crucial times. The past twenty-five years have in a sense illustrated Thomas Jefferson's belief that the best way to find out what is true is to let everything compete with everything else in the free marketplace of ideas. We did make much of it over here. It was an attempt to be happy. Now, surrounded by the litter of a certain amount of human wreckage, we can ask ourselves what should be saved, what should be discarded, in the experiment. A point somewhere between gay cheerleading—the recourse of every minority—and despair should probably be found. One has, after all, to go on, whatever the cards dealt. There is a wonderful story by Colette in which a woman who's spent her life going to lunch with friends on the Riviera decides one day that she is too old to continue this existence. So she tells her friends goodbye, takes off her make-up, and stays home. And stays home. And stays home. Till she can't stand it any longer. So she puts on the make-up, and schedules lunch. Exactly. There's a joke I heard Milton Berle tell on TV this winter which describes the same instinct. A Catskills joke, set in one of the hotels where widows used to go to meet new husbands. A handsome man walks into the lobby one day. A woman goes over to him and says, "I don't think I've seen you here before." He says, "That's because I've never been here." "Oh," she says, "a good-looking man like you?" "I was away at school," he says. "Away at school?" she says. "A man your age?" "I was up the river," he says, "in the slammer. The penitentiary. We call it school. I killed my wife. I hacked her into twenty-seven pieces with an ax." "Oh," she says, "so you're single?"

Paul Monette

If Larry Kramer was the Jeremiah of AIDS writing, Paul Monette (1945–
1995) was the Samuel, narrating the agonizing history he was living through.
In *Borrowed Time* (1988), he told the story of Roger Horwitz, his lover, and
Horwitz's battle with AIDS. In *Becoming a Man* (1992), which won the National Book Award, he recounted his own struggle to come out.

Before being stricken with AIDS, Paul Monette was a popular novelist, the author of *Taking Care of Mrs. Carroll* (1978). He was educated at
Phillips Academy and Yale University. After AIDS his work became more
immediate and urgent. With his two memoirs and a book of essays he
also published two novels about AIDS and a collection of poetry. "Puck"
is the opening chapter to *Last Watch of the Night* (1994), the last book he
published before his death.

Puck

STEVIE HAD BEEN in the hospital for about a week and a half, diagnosed with PCP, his first full-blown infection. For some reason he wasn't responding to the standard medication, and his doctors had put him on some new exotic combination regimen—one side effect of which was to turn his piss blue. He certainly didn't act or feel sick, except for a little breathlessness. He was still miles from the brink of death. Not even showing any sign of late-stage shriveling up—let alone the ravages of end-stage, where all that's left of life is sleep shot through with delirium.

Stevie was reading the paper, in a larky mood because he'd just had a dose of Ativan. I was sitting by the window, doodling with a script that I had to finish quickly in order to keep my insurance. "I miss Puck," he announced to no one in particular, no response required.

And I stopped writing and looked out the window at the heat-blistered parking lot, the miasma of low smog bleaching the hills in the distance. "You think Puck's going to survive me?"

"Yup," he replied. Which startled me, a bristle of the old denial that none of us was going to die just yet. Even though we were all living our lives in "dog years" now, seven for every twelvemonth, I still couldn't feel my own death as a palpable thing. To have undertaken the fight as we had for better drugs and treatment, so that we had become a guerrilla tribe of amateur microbiologists, pharmacist/shamans, our own best healers—there were those of us who'd convinced ourselves in 1990 that the dying was soon going to stop.

AIDS, you see, was on the verge of becoming a "chronic manageable illness." That was our totem mantra after we buried the second wave, or was it the third? When I met Steve Kolzak on the Fourth of July in '88, he told me he had seven friends who were going to die in the next six months—and they did. It was my job to persuade him that we could fall in love anyway, embracing between the bombs. And then we would pitch our tent in the chronic, manageable clearing, years and years given back to us by the galloping strides of science. No more afflicted than a diabetic, the daily insulin keeping him one step ahead of his body.

So don't tell me I had less time than a ten-year-old dog—admittedly one who was a specimen of roaring good health, still out chasing coyotes in the canyon every night, his watch-man's bark at home sufficient to curdle the blood. But if I was angry at Stevie for saying so, I kept it to myself as the hospital stay dragged on. A week of treatment for PCP became two, and he found himself reaching more and more for the oxygen. Our determination, or mine at least, to see this bout as a minor inconvenience remained unshaken. Stevie upped his Ativan and mostly retained his playful demeanor, though woe to the nurse or technician who thought a stream of happy talk would get them through the holocaust. Stevie's bark was as lethal as Puck's if you said the wrong thing.

And he didn't get better, either, because it wasn't pneumonia that was killing him. I woke up late on Friday, the fifteenth of September, to learn they'd moved him to intensive care, and I raced to the hospital to find him in a panic, fear glazing his flashing Irish eyes as he clutched the oxygen cup to his mouth. They pulled him through the crisis with steroids, but still wouldn't say what the problem was. Some nasty bug that a sewer of antibiotics hadn't completely arrested yet. But surely all it required was a little patience till one of these drugs kicked in.

His family arrived from back East, the two halves of the divorce. Yet it looked as if the emergency had passed, such is the false promise of massive steroids. I mean, he looked *fine*. He was impish and animated all through the weekend; it was we who had to be vigilant lest he get too tired. And I was so manically certain that he'd pull through, I could hardly take it in at first when one of the docs, shifty-eyed, refined the diagnosis: "He's having a toxic reaction to the chemo."

The chemo? But how could that be? They'd been treating his KS for sixteen months, till all the lesions were under control. Even the ones on his face: you had to know they were there to spot them, a scatter of faded purple under his beard. Besides, KS wasn't a sickness really, it was mostly just a nuisance. This was how deeply invested I was in denial, the 1990 edition. Since KS had never landed us in the hospital, it didn't count. And the chemo was the treatment, so how could it be life-threatening?

Easily, as it turned out. The milligram dosage of bleomycin, a biweekly drip in the doctor's office, is cumulative. After a certain point you run the risk of toxicity, your lungs seizing with fibrous tissue—all the resilience gone till you can't even whistle in the dark anymore. You choke to death the way Stevie did, gasping into the oxygen mask, a little less air with every breath.

Still, there were moments of respite, even on that last day. "I'm not dying, am I?" he asked about noon, genuinely astonished. Finally his doctor came in and broke the news: the damage to the lungs was irreversible, and the most we could hope for was two or three weeks. Stevie nodded and pulled off the mask to speak. "Listen, I'm a greedy bastard," he declared wryly. "I'll take what I can get." As I recall, the idea was to send him home in a wheelchair with an oxygen tank.

I cried when the doctor left, trying to tell him how terrible it was, though he knew it better than I. Yet he smiled and put out a hand to comfort me, reassuring me that he felt no panic. He was on so much medication for pain and anxiety that his own dying had become a movie—a sad one to be sure, but the Ativan/Percodan cocktail was keeping the volume down. I kept saying how much I loved him, as if to store the feeling up for the empty days ahead. Was there anything I could do? Anything left unsaid?

He shook his head, that muzzy wistful smile. Then his eyebrows lifted in surprise: "I'm not going to see Puck again." No regret, just amazement. And then it was time to grab the mask once more, the narrowing tunnel of air, the morphine watch. Twelve hours later he was gone, for death was even greedier than he.

And I was a widower twice now. Nothing for it but to stumble through the week that followed, force-fed by all my anguished friends, pulling together a funeral at the Old North Church at Forest Lawn. A funeral whose orations smeared the blame like dogshit on the rotting churches of this dead Republic, the politicians who run the ovens and dance on our graves. In the limo that took us up the hill to the gravesite, Steve's mother Dolores patted my knee and declared with a ribald trace of an Irish brogue: "Thanks for not burning the flag."

We laughed. A mere oversight, I assured her. She knew that Steve and I had spent a fruitless afternoon the previous Fourth of July—our anniversary, as it happened—going from Thrifty to Target trying to find stars-and-stripes to burn at our party. No such luck: all the flags we found were plastic or polyester, the consistency of cheap shower curtains. A perfect symbol, we realized, of the country we had lost during the decade of the calamity.

We buried the urn of his ashes high on a hill just at the rim of the chaparral, at the foot of a California live oak. The long shadow of our grieving circle fell across the hillside grass where I had buried Roger four years before; the shadow fell on my own grave, as a matter of fact, which is just to the left of Roger's, as if I will one day fling an arm about him and cradle us to sleep. After the putrefaction of the flesh, a pair of skeletons tangled together like metaphysical lovers out of Donne. And my other bone-white arm reaching above my skull, clawing the dirt with piano-key fingers, trying to get to Steve's ashes, just out of reach.

But what has it all got to do with the dog, exactly? My friend Victor stayed with me for the first week of Widowhood II. When at last he went off to juggle the shards of his own dwindling immunity, and I woke to a smudged October morning, my first thought wasn't *Oh poor me*, about which I had already written the book, but rather: *Who's going to take care of Puck?* What nudged me perhaps was the beast himself, who sprawled across the middle of the sagging double bed, permitting me a modest curl of space on the far left side.

You must try to appreciate, I never used to be anything like a rapturist about dogs, Puck or any other. My friend César used to say that Puck was the only dog he knew who'd been raised without any sentimentality at all. I was such a manic creature myself during his formative years that it was all he could do to scramble out of my lurching way, and not take it personally when I'd shoo him away for no reason. This was not the same as having trained him. He rather tumbled up, like one of those squalling babies in Dickens, saved in the nick of time from a scald of boiling water by a harried Mrs. Micawber.

And yet when Roger died, and I thought I had died along with him, the only thing that got me out of bed, groggy at sunset, was that Puck still had to be fed. I could see in his limpid, heartstopping eyes that he knew Roger was not coming back; or maybe he had acquired a permanent wince seeing me sob so inconsolably, hour after hour, gallantly putting his chin on the bed with a questioning look, in case I wanted company. I remember asking my brother in Pennsylvania if the dog could be shipped to him when I died, an event that seemed at the time as close as the walls of this room. But I didn't really like to think of Puck snuffling about in the fields of Bucks County, he whose breeding made him thrive in the desert hills of Southern California.

Half Rhodesian ridgeback, half black lab—or half Zimbabwean ridgeback, I ought to say, since one of my earliest encounters with political correctness occurred in Laurel Canyon Park. In the early eighties it was a place where we could run our dogs off lead, one eye peeled for the panel truck of Animal Control. A sixty-dollar ticket if they caught you—or in this case, if they caught Puck, who left the paying of municipal fines in my capable hands.

He was one of a litter of nine, his mother a purebred ridgeback, tawny and noble, her back bisected by the stiff brush of her ridge, which ran from just behind her shoulders and petered out at her rump. A dog bred to hunt lions, we'd heard, especially prized for being able to go long stretches without any water, loping across the veldt. As a sort of modulation of its terrifying bark, a bay of Baskerville proportions, the ridgeback had developed over time a growl as savage as that of the lions it stalked. Try to get near a ridgeback when he's feeding, you'll see what I mean. You feel like one of those helpless children at the zoo, about to lose an arm through a chain-link fence, waving a box of Crackerjacks in the roaring face of the king.

Ah but you see, there were compensating factors on the father's side. For Nellie, fertile mother of Puck and his eight siblings, had gotten it on with a strapping black lab high up in Benedict Canyon. A lab who was considered most *déclassé*, perhaps a bit of a half-breed himself, so friendly and ebullient that his people were always in peril of being knocked over or slobbered on. Not at all the sort of genes that Nellie's owners were seeking to rarefy even further. We were told all this in a rush by Nellie's starlet mistress, herself the achingly pretty daughter of a wondrously tucked and lifted movie star of the fifties—a pair who looked like sisters if you squinted, beautiful and not much else, the perfect ticket in L.A. to a long and happy journey on the median strip of life.

This was at a Thanksgiving supper in Echo Park—not the year we found the murdered Latino in the driveway as we left, but I think the year after. In any case, Roger and I had been worrying over the issue of a watchdog for some time now, as a security system cheaper by far than the alarm circuits that wired the hills around us, shrieking falsely into the night. The starlet daughter assured us that ridgebacks were brilliant sentries, ferociously protective.

We went back and forth in the next few weeks, warned by both our families that it was just another thing to tie us down. Besides, we traveled too much, and it wasn't fair to an animal to be getting boarded all the time. None of them understood how stirred we'd been the previous spring, when a whimper brought us to the front door one stormy night. A bedraggled one-eyed Pekingese dripped on the tile, matted and scrawny and quaking in the rain. The most improbable creature, the very last dog that either of us would have chosen. But we couldn't send him back out in the whirlwind either, a bare *hors d'oeuvre* for the sleek coyotes that roamed our canyon in pairs.

We put signs on the trees up and down Kings Road, FOUND instead of the usual LOST (for cats, especially, disappeared with alarming frequency in the hills). Nobody called to claim the one-eyed runt, and it started to look as if we were stuck with him. Without consultation, Roger began to call him Pepper and comb him out. I resisted mightily: *This was not by a long shot what anyone would call a watchdog.* I felt faintly ridiculous walking Pepper with his string leash, as if I'd become an aging queen before my time. Thus I withheld my sentiments rigorously, leaving most of the care and feeding to Roger—though now and again I'd permit the orphan to perch on my lap while I typed.

And then about three weeks later we were strolling up Harold Way, Roger and Pepper and I, past the gates to Liberace's spread. We turned to a cry of delight, as a young black woman came running down the driveway. "Thass my mama dog!" she squealed, scooping the one-eyed dustmop into her arms. In truth, Pepper seemed as overjoyed as she, licking her with abandon. The young woman called uphill to the kitchen yard, summoning her mother: "Grits home!" And a moment later an equally joyous woman came trundling toward us, crisp white uniform and billowing apron worthy of Tara.

No, no, of course we wouldn't dream of taking money. This joyous reunion was all the reward we needed. And so we trudged on home, trying not to feel even more ridiculous as we hastily put away the doll-size bowls by the kitchen door that had held Pepper/Grits's food and water. We laughed it off, or tried to anyway, gushing appropriately when the daughter appeared at our door that evening, bearing a peach pie almost too pretty to eat. "This is like Faulkner," Roger declared as we sliced the bounty. Faulkner, I replied, would not have used a Pekingese.

We never saw Pepper again—never even had the chance to ask how he'd lost that eye. But it goes to show how primed we were at the end of the year, when the starlet called nearly every day to say the litter was going fast. We thought we'd go over and have a look, but the only time the lot of us were free was Christmas morning. "Now we don't have to take one," I admonished Roger as we turned up the dirt road. A minute later we were in the kitchen, inundated by the scrambling of nine puppies. "Pick a lively one," I said, though the sheer explosion of canine anarchy didn't seem to have produced a sluggard or a runt. They squirmed out of our hands and yapped and chased. We couldn't have been said to have actually made a choice. The starlet and her human pups were waiting impatiently in the living room to open their gifts. Roger and I exchanged a shrug, and I reached for the one that was trying to crawl behind the refrigerator.

"You don't owe me anything," the starlet trilled. "Just the fifty bucks for his shots." We waved and promised to send a check, clamoring into the car with our erupting bundle. A black lab followed us barking down the drive. The father, we supposed. "He's not going to be *that* big, is he?" murmured Roger in some dismay. By the time we got home we were calling him Puck, in part because some friends of ours had just named a daughter Ariel, and we'd liked the Shakespearean spin of that, the sense that we were bringing home a changeling. The first thing Puck did when he tottered into the house was make for the Christmas tree, where he squatted and peed on a package from Gump's.

I don't remember a whole lot after that, not for the first five years, so assiduously was I trying to avoid the doggy sort of bathos. I do recall how fretful Roger was for the first six months, waiting for Puck to lift his leg instead of squatting. And the moment of triumph when he finally did, on a bush of wild anis. His main lair was beneath my butcher-block desk in the study—where he lies even as I write this, his head propped uncomfortably on the wooden crossbeam that holds the legs in place. We quickly learned that he wouldn't be budged from any of his makeshift doghouses, which came to include the undercave of every table in the house. A lion's growl of warning if you got too close.

I fed him, I walked him. As I say, I was crazed in those years like a starlet myself, frantic to have a script made, fawning as indiscriminately as a puppy over every self-styled producer who left a spoor in my path. I was so unbearably sophisticated, convinced I could reconfigure the Tracy/Hepburn magic, so glib and airy-fairy that my shit didn't stink. For a time I even began to question my life with Roger, and Puck as well, as being perhaps too bourgeois for words.

None of the scripts got made, of course. I was tossed on my ass as a loser and a failure, unable to get my calls returned, no matter how desperately I courted the assistants of assistants. I fell into a wrongheaded love affair with a hustler—literally, the fifty-bucks-a-pop variety—which reminds me, I never paid the debt to the starlet for Puck's shots, which would have been a lot better use of the money. Within a few weeks the hustler had sucked all my marrow and moved on. I careened through a year of near-breakdown, writing plays but mostly whining, and nearly driving Roger away in the process.

Yet we never stopped taking that evening walk, along the rim of the hill that led from Kings Canyon to Queens, Puck rooting ahead of us through the chaparral. I'm not quite sure how he managed to serve two masters, but was clearly far too well-bred to choose sides. We simply represented different orbits, centered of course on him. I was the one who sat at the desk while he slept at my feet all day, and Roger the one who came home at six, sending him into paroxysms of excited barking. The late-night walk was a threesome, no hierarchy of power. I'm not saying it kept Roger and me together, all on its own, but the evening stroll had about it a Zen calm—so many steps to the bower of jacarandas at Queens Road, so many steps home.

I remember the first time the dog howled, when a line of fire trucks shrilled up the canyon to try to cut off a brushfire. Puck threw back his head and gave vent to a call so ancient, so lupine really, that it seemed to have more in common with the ravening of fire and the night stalk of predators than with the drowsy life of a house pet. The howl didn't erupt very often; usually it was kicked off by a siren or a chorus of baying coyotes up-canyon quarreling with the moon. And it was clear Puck didn't like to have us watch him when he did it, especially to laugh or applaud him. He'd been seized by a primal hunger, sacred even, and needed to be alone with it. Usually it lasted no more than a minute, and then he'd be back with us, wagging and begging for biscuits.

We didn't have him fixed, either. More of an oversight than anything else, though I wonder now if it didn't have something to do with the neutering Roger and I had been through during our own years in the closet. It meant of course that Puck could be excruciatingly randy. His favorite sexual activity was to hump our knees as we lay in bed reading at night, barking insistently if we tried to ignore his throbbing need. We more or less took turns, Roger and I, propping our knees beneath the comforter so Puck could have his ride. He never actually came, not a full load, though he dribbled a lot. I can't say if all this made him more of a gay dog or not.

Except for that nightly erotic charge he never actually jumped up on people, though he could be a handful when friends came over, turning himself inside out to greet them. And for some reason—probably having to do with the turkey and ham on the buffet—he loved parties, the bigger the better, wagging about from guest to guest all evening, one eye always on the kitchen and the disposition of scraps.

A dog's life, to be sure, but not really a life destined for heroics—huddling beside a wounded hiker to keep him warm or leading smoke-blinded tenants from a conflagrated house. That was all right: heroics weren't part of the contract. I once read about a woman in England who applied for a seeing-eye dog but specified that she wanted one who'd flunked. She wasn't *very* blind, you see, and besides she wasn't very good at passing tests herself. So she wanted a sort of second-best companion to muck along with her, doing the best they could. My sentiments exactly, I wasn't planning on any heroics in my life either. Puck didn't have to save me and Roger, and we didn't have to save him.

Except he did, save us in the end. I don't see how he could have known about the insidious onset of AIDS, the dread and the fevers, the letting of blood by the bucketful for tests that told us nothing, and finally Roger's exile to UCLA Medical Center, sentence without parole. I suppose Puck must've picked up on my own panic and grief, suddenly so ignored that he probably counted himself lucky to get his supper. I had no expectations of him except that he stay out of the way. It was then that I began to let him out on his own late at night.

Nobody liked that. Several about-to-be-former friends thought it was terribly irresponsible of me, leaving the dog prey to the coked-up traffic that thundered up the hill when the clubs on the Strip closed. Not to mention those coyotes traveling in packs from trash barrel to trash barrel. They didn't understand how rigorously I'd admonish Puck that he not go far and come back straightaway, any more than they understood that they were just displacing the helplessness they felt over Roger's illness. One time Roger's brother had a near-foaming tantrum about the sofa in the living room, grimy and doubtless flea-infested from years of dog naps. "You can't expect people to visit," Sheldon sputtered. "It smells like a kennel in here."

No, it actually smelled like death, when you came right down to it. The whole house did. And frankly, the only one who could live with the stink, the battlefield stench of shallow unmarked graves, was Puck. Those who proposed re-upholstery as a general solution to keeping death away stopped in less and less, good riddance. The ones who thought we were letting the dog run wild were lucky I didn't sic him on them. Only I really understood, because I saw it happen, how Puck would temper his huge ebullience if Roger was feeling a little fragile. Always there to be petted, sometimes a paw on your knee to nudge you into it.

The world narrowed and narrowed, no end to the tunnel and thus no pin of light in the distance. Not to say there weren't precious months, then weeks, then days, that still had the feel of normalcy. I'd cook up a plate of spaghetti, and we'd sit in the dining room talking of nothing at all, just glad to have a lull in the shelling. And we both looked over one night and saw Puck sitting at attention on his haunches, the sable sheen of his coat set off by the flash of white at his heart, head lifted as if on show, utterly still. In all probability he was just waiting for leftovers. But Roger, bemused and quietly beaming with pride, studied the pose and finally said, "Puck, when did you get to be such a noble beast?"

We both laughed, because we knew we'd had nothing to do with it. But from that point on, Noble Beast became the changeling's nickname. If he took the pose beside you, it meant he wanted his chest scratched. Nothing dramatic, you understand, but somehow Puck came to represent the space left over from AIDS. With no notion of the mortal sting that shaped our human doggedness, he managed to keep the real world ambient, the normal one. Filling it edge to edge with what the thirteenth century divine, Duns Scotus, called "this-ness." There gets to be almost nothing more to say about the daily choke of drugs to get down, the nurses streaming in to start the IV drips, the numbing reports to the scatter of family and those few friends who've squeaked through with you. Nothing more to say except what the dog brings in, even if it's mostly fleas.

That last morning, when the home nurse woke me at seven to say it was very bad, Roger virtually comatose, no time to wait for our noon appointment at UCLA, I leapt out of bed and got us out of there in a matter of minutes. I don't remember the dog underfoot. Only holding Roger upright as we staggered down the steps to the car, talking frantically to keep him conscious. Puck would've been perched on the top step watching us go, he'd done that often enough. But I don't really know what he *saw*, any more than I knew what Roger saw—what dim nimbus of light still lingered with one eye gone blind overnight six months before, the other saved by a thrice-daily blast of Acyclovir, but even it milked over with a cataract.

He died that night, and the weeks after are a cataract blur of their own. Somebody must've fed the dog, for I have the impression of him wandering among the houseful of family and friends, trying to find someone who'd lead him to Rog. When we brought home from the hospital the last pitiful overnight bag, the final effects as it were, and Roger's father shook out the maroon coat sweater and put it on for closeness' sake, Puck began to leap up and down, dancing about the old man in a circle, barking deliriously. Because he could still smell life in there.

Have we gotten sentimental yet—gone over the edge? I spent that first annihilating year of grief dragging myself out of bed because somebody had to let the dog out, writing so I wouldn't have to think. I can't count the times when I'd crawl under one of the tables where Puck lay sleeping, to hold him so I could cry. He grumbled at being invaded, but his growl was pretty *pro forma*. And somewhere in there I started to talk to him, asking him if he missed Rog, wondering out loud how we were ever going to get through this—daft as a Booth cartoon. He sat unblinking, the Noble Beast as listener.

I don't know when it started, his peculiar habit of barking whenever visitors would leave. He'd always barked eruptively in greeting, whenever he heard the footfall of a friend coming up the stairs outside. But this new bark was something far more urgent, angry and troubled, a peal of warning, so that I'd have to drag him back by the collar as one bewildered friend or another made his drowned-out goodnights. "He doesn't like people to leave," I'd tell them, but I didn't understand for months what he was warning them of: that if they left they might not come back, might get lost the way Roger did. Don't leave, stay here, I'll keep you safe as I keep this man. Meaning me.

Still, he got over the grief sooner than I, testimony to his blessed unconsciousness of death. He became himself again, inexhaustible, excited anew by the dailiness of life.

I'm afraid I'd aged much more than he, maybe twenty years for the twenty months of Roger's illness. Puck was just six, a warrior still in his prime. I had to do a fair bit of traveling there for a while, the self-appointed seropositive poster child. And Puck would lie waiting under my desk, caretaken by Dan the house-sitter, ears perked at every sound outside in case it was me returning from the wars.

Like Argos, Odysseus' dog. Twenty years old and shunted aside because he was too frail to hunt anymore. Waiting ten years for his master's return from Troy, and the only one in the palace to recognize the king beneath the grizzle and the tattered raiment. The earliest wagging tail in literature, I believe. There was no shyness in that time of gods and heroes when it came to the sentiments of reunion, let alone what loyalty meant. So I would come home from ten days' book-touring, from what seemed a mix of overweening flattery and drive-time call-ins from rabid Baptists who painted me as the incarnation of Satan; I would return scarcely able to say who the real Monette was, indeed if there was one anymore—till Puck ran out to welcome me.

Around that time I began to feel ready to risk the heart again, I who hadn't really had a date in fifteen years. I "lingered hopefully" (to quote the advice that Stevie Smith's lion aunt read out to her niece from the lovelorn column); lingered hopefully, I say, at the edges of various parties, in smoke-filled *boîtes*, even at rallies and protests, looking to connect. Held back by my own sero status as much as anything, unsure if I wanted to find only another positive, or whether a lucky negative might rescue my brain from the constant pound of AIDS.

I was on a stationary bike at the gym, pumping hard and going nowhere (too sweaty to be lingering hopefully), when a young man of thirty or so came up and stood before me, catching my eye with a bright expectant nod. "Excuse me," he said, "but aren't you Edmund White?"

"Not exactly," I retorted. Yet it was such an eccentric pickup line that I let him pick me up with it. At least he was literate. I waxed quite eloquent about Ed's work, was quite modest about my own, and gave no further thought to the not-so-subtle omen that the young man might have no interest whatever in Monette, real or otherwise. After all, if you want to read *Moby Dick*, *Jane Eyre* just won't do.

A few nights later he came over for Chinese takeout. And took an immediate dislike to Puck—nothing personal, he assured me, all dogs really—especially not wanting to sit on the dog-haired sofa in his ice-cream linen trousers. Puck returned the compliment in spades, grumping beneath the coffee table, growling when the young man came too close to me. I apologized for Puck's ragged manners, then deftly turned the subject to AIDS, my own reality check.

His green eyes lit on me. "There's no reason for anyone to die of that," he observed. "All you have to do is take care of yourself. People who die of it, that's just their excuse."

Too stunned or too Episcopalian to savage my first date since puberty, I left the growling to Puck. But I only barely restrained his collar when the young man left, wincing palely at the mastiff shrill of the dog's goodbye.

Stevie had it easier all around. He liked Puck's attitude from the first, recognizing a certain orneriness and perversity that neatly matched his own. If you wanted Puck to come over to you, it did no good to call unless you had a biscuit in hand. In fact I had been bribing him so long—a Meaty Bone to get him outside, another to bring him in—that he acted as if you must be crazy to order him around without reward. It had to be *his* idea to clamber up on the bed or play with a squeak toy. With the latter he wasn't into give-and-take in any case, but snatched it out of your hand and disappeared with it into his lair. Needless to say, "fetch" wasn't in his vocabulary.

I had to learn to back off and feint with Stevie, three months' uncertain courtship. He'd never really made the couple thing work before, and couldn't imagine starting now in the midst of a minefield. It required the barricades for us, going to Washington in October with ACT UP to take over the FDA. A sobbing afternoon spent lurching down the walkways of the quilt, a candle march along the reflecting pool with a hundred thousand others. Then massing at FDA headquarters in Maryland, not even dawn yet (and I don't do mornings), standing groggily with Vito Russo as we briefed the press. A standoff most of the day, squads of cops huddled as if at a doughnut stand, trying not to arrest us.

And then a small gang of six, all from L.A., found a lacuna in the security. Somebody smashed a ground-floor window, and the L.A. guerrillas poured in—Stevie bringing up the rear, impish as Peter Pan himself. When they dragged him out in handcuffs twenty minutes later, the look that passed between us was the purest sign I could've wanted of his being in love with life again. Civil disobedience as aphrodisiac. Within a day we were lovers for real, unarmed and no turning back.

But he wouldn't move in, not to my place. I thought it had to do with the freight of memory, too much Roger wherever you looked. Then I understood how determined he was not to turn the house on Kings Road into a sickroom again—a sickroom that only went one way, to the hospice stage and the last racked weeks. From his own falling numbers, and then the bone-chilling arrival of the first lesion on the roof of his mouth, he knew he'd be out of here sooner than I. (Unless of course I got hit by the bus that seronegatives were forever invoking to prove we were all a hairsbreadth away from the grave—a bus that was always as far behind schedule as we were ahead of it.)

So Stevie began the search for an apartment near me in West Hollywood. Even then we almost broke up a couple of times. He was too far sunk in the quicksand of the endless doctoring, too out of control to be loved. He savaged me one day, calling me blameless even as the arrows found the target of my heart, then fell into a three-day silence. To Victor, who served as go-between in the pained negotiation that followed, he declared: "Why am I breaking up with Paul? I don't know. I like his dog too much."

Oh, that. The fear of getting too attached to the things of life, till you sometimes feel you're better off lying in bed with the shades all down, no visitors welcome. And NO GIFTS, as the invitations all pointedly warn whenever we agree to a final birthday or one more Christmas. No more things to add to the pile that will only have to be dispersed, the yard sale more certain than heaven or hell.

Happily, Puck and I won out. Steve found a place just blocks away, a post-mod apartment behind the Pacific Design Center. And twice a day I'd duck my head under the desk and propose to Puck: "You want to go over to Stevie's?" Then an explosion of barking and dancing, and a long whine of backseat driving as we headed downhill to Huntley Street. As soon as he saw the house, Puck would leap from the moving car to leave his mark on the bushes, then bark me into the downstairs garage as if I were some recalcitrant sheep.

Stevie was usually in bed, his IVs having doubled, with nothing better to do than flip the remote between one numb banality and the next. Television gave him a place to center his anger, I think, railing at the bad hair and the laugh tracks. A business where he had once commanded so much power—and now his big-screen set practically needed windshield wipers, there was so much spit aimed at it.

But his face would brighten like a kid's when Puck tore in and bounded onto the bed, burrowing in and groaning with pleasure as Stevie gave him a scratch. "Puck, you're better than people," he'd praise the beast—a real irony there, for the beast preferred people to dogs any day.

As for sentiment, Stevie carried that off with the effortless charm he once squandered on agents and actors and network VPs. We'd be driving to one of the neighborhood restaurants, pass a street dog rooting for garbage, and Steve would give an appraising look and wonder aloud: "You think he's a friend of Puck's?" No response required from me, as the answer was quickly forthcoming: "I think he is."

In fact, the question went international quite soon thereafter. With so much medicine required on a daily basis, bags of IV drugs to be kept chilled, the only way we could travel was by ship. So we cruised through the final year—Monte Carlo to Venice, Tahiti to Bora Bora, Greece and Turkey—spending the fat disability checks from Columbia.

One day ashore in the Iles des Saintes, a necklace of pirate lagoons below Guadeloupe, we motorbiked to the highest point, winding through denuded fields, for goats were the main livestock here. We sat on a wall of mortared conchs and looked out to sea. It was one of those moments you want to stop time, knowing what torments lie waiting at journey's end. From a shack behind us emerged a gaggle of children, and behind them a tiny black goat still wobbly on its kid legs. No way could it keep up with the children running downhill to the harbor. So the goat crossed the road to where we were, made for Stevie and butted his knee, so gently it might have been a kiss. Then did it again.

"Friend of Puck's, definitely," Stevie observed with a laugh. A laugh fit for paradise, utterly careless, a holiday from dying.

So what do you carry with you once you have started to leave the world behind? Stevie was right that last Monday in the ICU: he was never going to see Puck again. Didn't even have a chance to say goodbye, except inside. For his part Puck made his own bewildered peace, still tearing into Huntley Street as we packed and gave away one man's universe of things, the beast still hoping against hope that Stevie himself would walk in any minute.

I understand that a housedog is yet another ridiculous privilege of having means in a world gone mad with suffering. I've seen the scrawny dogs that follow refugees around in war after pointless war. The dogs have disappeared from the starvation camps of Somalia, long since eaten in the dogless camps of Laos and Bangladesh. There is nothing to pet in the end. Perhaps it is worse than sentimental, the direst form of denial, to still be weeping at dog stories. But I admit it. Puck has gone gray in the face now, stiff in the legs when he stands, and I am drawn to stories about dogs who visit nursing homes and hospitals, unafraid of frailty and the nearness of death. Dogs, in a word, who don't flunk.

And I weep these incorrigible tears. Two years ago I was in a posh photo gallery in New York with a friend, and we asked to see the Wegmans. I maintained a rigorous connoisseur's posture, keeping it all high-toned, for there were those who were very suspicious of the popularity of Man Ray, the supreme model in Wegman's canine fantasias. There was a general wariness that Wegman's audience might be more interested in dogs than art. In my case doubly so, since to me at least Puck could have been Man Ray's twin. Same color, same shape, same humanness.

Now of course Man Ray was gone, and though he'd been replaced in the studio by the sleek and estimable Fay—no mean model herself—prices for a vintage Man had gone through the roof. Anyway, this curatorial assistant, very 57th Street, brought out of a drawer with white gloves three big Polaroids of Man. In one the dog was stretched on his back with his paws up; no gimmicks or costume accessories here, just a dog at rest. You could tell he was old from the shiver of gray on his snout. I found it so unbearably moving that I choked on tears and could not look at another.

After Stevie was buried, I figured Puck and I were set for twilight, seven years for every twelvemonth, a toss-up still as to who'd go first. We didn't plan on letting anyone else in. Not depressed or even defeated yet—just exhausted, hearts brimful already with seized days and a sort of Homeric loyalty, we shared a wordless language and had no expectations. Like the old man and his dog in DeSica's masterpiece *Umberto D*, who cannot save each other but can't leave either. They'd rather starve together.

Then I met Winston. It was a bare two months since Steve had died, and Victor and I had just returned from three weeks' melancholy touring in Europe, weeping in cathedrals so to speak. I recall telling Victor on the flight home that I could probably still connect with someone, but only if that someone could handle the steamship-load of AIDS baggage I carried with me. Somehow Winston could juggle it with his own, or perhaps the risk and intoxication of love made even the dead in our arms lighter. By Christmas we were lovers, and Puck couldn't help but give us his blessing, so showered was he by Winston with rubber bones and pull toys: "This dog has got nothing to play with!"

The dog was not the only one. And because there is never enough time anymore, by mid-January we were deep into the chess match of Winston's move into Kings Road. Just one small problem, really—a four-year-old boxer called Buddy. He'd grown up on a ranch, free to run and in titular charge of a barnful of horses and a tribe of cats. The first meeting of our two unfixed males wasn't promising. Buddy jumped on Puck right off, sending the two of them into a whirlwind ball of snarling and gnashing, leaving Winston and me no choice but to wade in and pull them apart. Buddy was clearly the aggressor here, but then we were on his territory.

The situation didn't improve when Buddy came to stay at Kings Road. Puck was outraged that his slumbering twilight had been invaded. He stuck to his lairs and growled with ferocious menace if Buddy came anywhere near. In fact, if we weren't absolutely vigilant we had a sudden dogfight on our hands. There was nothing for it but to separate them at opposite ends of the house, the doors all closed. It was like a French farce, with the constant flinging and slamming of doors, and enough entrances and exits to rival the court of the Louis.

You get used to compromises when everyone you know is dying. It was clear that Buddy was a pussycat at heart, his gentle spirit every bit as benign as Puck's lab side, except when they were together. And Buddy was meticulously trained as well, as rigorous as a Balanchine dancer, responding with infinite grace to all of his master's commands. Responding to food alone, Puck didn't know quite what to make of the military precision of his housemate.

Puck was fed on the front porch, Buddy in the back yard. It was no more peculiar in its way than families who can't stand one another, sitting silent at the dinner table, invisible lines drawn. If Winston and I hadn't been able to laugh about it, I'm not sure it could have gone on so long. But by April he had bitten the bullet and had Buddy fixed, though we were warned it could take six months for the pugnacity around Puck to abate. Puck's balls followed on the chopping block in June, since the vet assured me Puck would have fewer problems aging, less chance of tumors if he were fixed.

They didn't really seem any different that summer, except that Puck wouldn't hump our knees with the same rollicking passion. He humped all right, but it seemed more of an afterthought, a memory trace, over in a matter of seconds. I didn't have much leisure to notice, frankly, with my own numbers falling precipitously and three ribs broken from taking a dive off a trotting horse. The walls of AIDS were closing in, no matter how tortuous my progress through the drug underground, scoring the latest miracle. It was all I could do not to drown in my own panic, or take it out on Winston. My attitude toward the dogs was more impatient than ever, but Puck had been there before. There were times when dogs just had to be dogs—no neediness, please, and no misbehaving. The merest tick became a problem I couldn't handle.

By the end of summer I'd started to run daily fevers—99.5 at five P.M., like clockwork. My T-cells continued to tumble, under a hundred now. Winston had to fly up to Seattle over Labor Day weekend to visit his former lover, John, who'd taken a very bad turn. It was the first time I'd had the two dogs by myself. All I really wanted to do was sit at the word processor, only three or four pages to go in *Becoming a Man*. And it seemed I spent all day opening and closing doors, a solo performer in a farce.

Finally I'd had it. I called Buddy in from the bedroom, Puck from the fleabag sofa. I sat them down at opposite ends of the study, threatening them direly if they dared make a move toward each other. They both blinked at me as I lectured them: this separate-but-equal shit had got to stop. "Now lie down and be good boys," I commanded with a final flourish.

And they did. Puzzled, I am sure, by the heat of my remark.

There were still rough edges, of course. Now that they managed to be together without attacking, they began to steal toys from each other, swooping in and snatching, the growls just short of a major explosion. The problem was, Puck didn't know how to play—he was as loath to share as a bully in kindergarten or the spoiled brat who takes his baseball home so nobody else can enjoy it. The toys would pile up in his lair, guarded like meat. Buddy—such a prince—was the one who was eager to play in earnest, and yet he'd yield to Puck and forgo the tearing around the house he loved—turning the other cheek, so to speak, rather than bristling. It may have been the loss of balls that let it happen, but clearly Buddy preferred to have a friend than to be on top.

Gradually Puck learned to give a little back, permitting Buddy to do his racing about with a mauled stuffed Dumbo in his mouth, while Puck stood ground and barked. But if Buddy gets credit for teaching Puck the rudiments of play, the pedagogy went the other way when it came to making noise. When Buddy first arrived he didn't make a peep, never having been needed as a watchdog at the ranch. Thus he'd watch with a certain fascination as Puck, alert to every sound outside, especially the arrival of delivery men, ran to the front door bellowing doom. It took a fair amount of time for Buddy to get the hang of it—a softer bark in any case, here too letting Puck be the lead singer—but now they both leap up clamoring, barreling by one another as they scramble to investigate.

In fact it's Puck who's had to yield in the watchdog department. After all, Buddy's hearing is finer, his high-pointed ears like radar. Puck's has dimmed in his twelfth year, so he doesn't quite catch the slam of every car door. More often now Buddy's the one who pricks to the sound of something out there, the first to woof, so that Puck's scramble to join the fray is an act of following.

And Puck has been more than a little grateful to turn the rat chores over to Buddy. We have brown field rats, not so horrible as the gray vermin that haunt the docks and garbage dumps of the world. Sometimes one gets in because the kitchen door is open to the back yard, to give the dogs access. A couple of times Puck and I have surprised a rodent in the kitchen, and I shriek and Puck barks, and somehow the freaked-out rat scoots away.

But Buddy's a ratter. He sniffs them out and waits for them to make their move from under the stove or the washing machine. He'll wait for hours if necessary. And when the rodent makes a dash for the kitchen door, Buddy's on him—unafraid to clamp his jaws around the squirming intruder and give him a bad shake. He doesn't kill them, just scares the bejesus out of them. If I were a rat I would not be coming back soon. And since I can't stand to trap them anymore—that awful springing snap as the trip-arm breaks a leg or neck—I much prefer the Buddy method of pest control.

It would be too simple to call them brothers now, these two dogs, too anthropomorphic by half. Each has retained the marks and idiosyncrasies of his breed quite distinctly. Buddy is what is called a "flashy fawn," because all four paws are white as well as his breastplate and a marvelous zigzag just behind his ears. He can't stand getting wet, doesn't even like to be in the garden after it's been watered, practically walking on tiptoe. While Puck no longer dives into the pool as he used to, swimming laps with Roger, water is still his element. On a very hot day he'll still step down in and dog-paddle in a tight circle to cool off.

Not brothers then, but comrades. Like any other dogs they sleep more than anything else, but sometimes now they do it flank to flank, almost curled about each other. When they sit on their haunches side by side in the kitchen doorway, lingering hopefully for biscuits, they are most definitely a pair. (Puck taught Buddy to beg, by the way, a serious breach in his training.) When they go outside together, Buddy knows he can go no further than the edge of the terrace, not down the steps. Puck on the other hand sprawls himself on the landing at the top of the stairs, one step down from the terrace, his lifelong perch for overseeing the neighborhood. Thus Buddy stands above Puck, though one would be hard put to say who's taking care of whom.

That they look after each other is clear. It's an act of faith among conservative zoologists that there's no homosex in the animal world. Gay is a human orientation, period. But just as I've come to understand, late in my own dog years, that being gay is a matter of identity much larger than carnality, I don't think the mating instinct is all the story. What the two dogs have is an easy sort of intimacy, the opposite of straight men. Thus they sniff each other's buttholes as casually as men shake hands. Not gay then, exactly, even though both have grown up surrounded by a tribe of us: call them different, that comes closest. As if being together has changed them so that they've become more than themselves—a continuum of eccentricities traded off and mimicked, grounded by their willingness to be tamed, loyal before all else. Not unlike Winston and me, and we're as gay as they come.

Meanwhile, twilight deepens. The dogs whoop with delight when Ande the nurse comes to call, once a week these days so I can get my IV dose of Amphotericin. They do not see her as a chill reminder of my sickness, any more than I do. We humans sustain this life as best we can, propelled by the positive brand of denial, the nearest approximation we can make to the bliss of dogs and their mortal ignorance. Thus I can watch Puck age and feel it tear at me, while he can't watch me dwindle or even see the lesions. Somehow it makes him wiser than I am, for all my overstuffed brains, book-riddled and smart to a fault.

We go along as we always have, a household of four instead of two. Every few weeks Puck and I cross Kings Road to visit Mrs. Knecht, our neighbor who lost her husband in '85 to a sudden heart attack. She endures in her eighties, a tribute to her Austrian stalwartness, her family wiped out in the camps. Assaulted by the indignities of age, Mrs. Knecht doesn't have a lot of pleasures anymore, but Puck is one. I'm terrified that he'll knock her down when he barrels into her house, that he'll take her hand off when she feeds him biscuits. But that is what she likes best about him, I think, his indomitable eagerness, his stallion force. Mrs. Knecht is our good deed, Puck's and mine, but also serving to remind all three of us that life goes on among the loyal.

Nights we stay up later than Buddy and Winston, a couple of hours at least. Buddy curls in his basket under the bedroom window, and Winston like Roger sleeps without pills, deeper than I ever get. I can't really say that Puck stays up with me as I potter around in the still of the night. He sleeps too, though always near me, and he would call it keeping me company if he had words. All he knows is, nothing is likely at this hour to bother us or require his vigilance. It will go on like this forever, as far as Puck can see. For his sake I try to see no further, relishing these hours out of time.

It has already been decided: if I go first Winston has promised to care for him, to keep what's left of the family together. If Puck goes first, perhaps a painless shot to end some arthritic misery, I promise nothing. The vets will tell you, there are suicides in the parking lot after the putting down of pets. For some it's the last last straw.

But for tonight I'm glad we have endured together and, as they say in the romance genre, lived to love again. We will not be returning from Troy, either of us, but meanwhile we are one another's link to the best of the past, a matter of trust and bondedness that goes all the way back to prehistory. One of us is descended from wolves; one of us knows he's dying. Together we somehow have the strength to bear it, tonight at least, when the moon is down and no creature howls. What we dream is exactly the same, of course, that nothing will change.

At two A.M. he whimpers at the door to go out, and I let him go. Usually he's back in half an hour, but you never know what will take him further, what trail will beckon him up through the chaparral. He knows me too well. That I'll wait up all night if necessary till he comes panting home. That even if I rail at him like a crabby parent, he'll still get a biscuit before the lights go out. Because all that matters to either of us is that the other one's still here—fellow survivors of so much breakage to the heart, not a clue when the final siren will sound. But guarding the world for dear life anyway, even as it goes. Noble beast.

Jaime Manrique

Jaime Manrique (b. 1949) is a poet, novelist, essayist, and translator who has been hailed by the *Washington Post Book World* as "the most accomplished gay Latino writer of his generation, a picaro prone to shock his readers by pushing the moral standards of his time."

Manrique was born in Barranquilla, Colombia, in 1949 and came to the United States in 1967. He now lives in New York City, where he teaches at Eugene Lang College, the New School for Social Research.

His first volume of poetry received Colombia's Eduardo Cote Lamus National Poetry Award in 1975. In English he has published the volume of poems *My Night with Federico García Lorca* (1995, and a new edition in 1997) and the novels *Colombian Gold* (1983), *Latin Moon in Manhattan* (1992), and *Twilight at the Equator* (1997).

The passage below is from *Eminent Maricones* (1999), a book about Manrique's relationships with three important Spanish-language gay writers—Federico García Lorca, Manuel Puig, and Reinaldo Arenas, the subject of this chapter. Arenas (1943–1990) was one of the finest Cuban writers of his day, but he was imprisoned and tortured by the Cuban government for being a gay critic of the regime. His works are banned in Cuba. The author of such novels as *Singing from the Well* (1967) and *Old Rosa* (1980), Arenas escaped in 1981 to the United States where he died of AIDS complications after writing his acclaimed autobiography *Before Night Falls* (1993).

The Last Days of Reinaldo Arenas:
A Sadness as Deep as the Sea

EARLY IN DECEMBER 1990 the literary agent Thomas Colchie called to say that the exiled Cuban writer Reinaldo Arenas—who lived around the corner from me, in Hell's Kitchen—was in what looked like the final stages of AIDS and that he had expressed a desire to hear from me.

I told Tom that I'd be happy to call on Reinaldo Arenas. I had known for some time that he was sick, but I had respected his decision not to discuss his illness with me. However, that year it became increasingly more difficult for me to run into him at the post office or the supermarket and to pretend that I didn't notice his emaciation and the Kaposi's sarcoma lesions that now gashed his visage. Although Reinaldo applied makeup to the spots on his face, I found it more disturbing to imagine what the lesions looked like than to see them.

I had met Reinaldo Arenas in 1981, when he arrived in New York from Miami after he left Cuba during what became known as the Mariel exodus to Florida. Colchie introduced us. I was thirty then, had returned to New York to settle down after a decade in which I commuted from Colombia to the States. I was then under contract with an American publisher to write a novel. Because I had an American lover, the painter Bill Sullivan, and because I had been educated in this country and felt myself part of New York's art world and writing scene, the differences between Reinaldo and me were huge.

Although he was an internationally known writer, he had lived in Cuba all his life. His parents were peasants, and he grew up as one. He was immensely well read and spoke other languages, but he didn't try to disguise his Goajiro origins. His teeth were crooked and full of cavities, and some were missing. He hadn't yet acquired, as most writers transplanted to New York eventually do, a sense of fashion and slickness. So Reinaldo didn't cut a glittering figure in the image-conscious gay scene. But my mother's family was a peasant family, and I spent time during my formative years living in the countryside, so I felt comfortable with him. Conversely, he must have sensed that I had managed to create an image of myself that was full of artifice and this probably amused him. That we were both openly homosexual Latin American writers was a bond much stronger than all the outward differences.

Something else brought us together: unlike most Latin American authors, I had never been a member of the leftist intelligentsia. When I was an adolescent in Colombia in the 1960s, it was unthinkable for a young intellectual to be unsympathetic to the Cuban Revolution and to the forces that advocated radical changes in countries like Colombia, semifeudal states run with an iron hand by a small group of despotic families. But in 1966 my mother, sister, and I emigrated to Florida. For the first time I came in contact with the Cuban refugees who had fled the island: those who Fidel Castro, and leftists all over the world, labeled *gusanos*—worms. I was torn in my allegiance toward the Cubans I met. On the one hand, many of them provided for us (we settled in Tampa, where few Colombians were living) the vast amount of support that recent immigrants need in order to survive in their new home. Still, I despised their values. They defended American policy in Vietnam, saw John F. Kennedy and the Democrats as communist sympathizers, and, because of their business ingenuity, placed undue emphasis on material success. They were openly racist. A large number of these south Florida Cubans were reactionary, and I, as a sympathizer with the humanistic ideals of socialism, felt alienated by their politics. Yet I was bewitched by their personal warmth, gift for laughter, gaiety, and open and giving nature when they bestowed their friendship upon you. I loved many of them as human beings, although I abhorred them as political symbols.

When Reinaldo Arenas arrived in New York in 1981, I was older, less dogmatic, more understanding of peoples' shortcomings. Also, I had had ample opportunities to become disenchanted with the Stalinist Latin American left. Besides, it was clear that Fidel Castro was no friend of homosexuals—he had persecuted, tortured, and killed many. Cuba no longer appeared to me as an island of hope for a new and more just Latin America. Instead, it seemed an island-jail where nonconformity was punished and where human rights violations were common.

Thus it was with mixed feelings that I entered my friendship with Reinaldo Arenas. Soon after Arenas's arrival my friend, the poet Tim Dlugos, asked me if I could arrange a meeting between the two of them. Tim wanted to interview Reinaldo for *Christopher Street* magazine. Reinaldo agreed to meet him at my apartment. On the appointed day Tim showed up with a tape recorder, and we sat around having drinks and a chat while we waited for Reinaldo. When he was a half hour late, I called to remind him, but there was no answer. Reinaldo had already devised a system for reaching him by phone: you called, waited for the phone to ring three times, and hung up. You called back right away, and then he knew it was someone he wanted to talk to and would pick up. At first I dismissed this and other peculiarities of his social behavior as Latin American eccentricities. I was reminded, for example, of heterosexual poet friends who never answered the phone themselves—the women in their households did. Much later, when I understood Reinaldo better, I realized his behavior was just an extension of the paranoia that exists in the Cuban émigré world. In Castro's Cuba dissidents had to devise elaborate systems of communication to avoid being spied upon; they had transplanted those attitudes to this country, as if here too they felt constantly under surveillance.

Tim Dlugos and I were hurt and disappointed that Reinaldo stood us up. Nonetheless, I made up my mind not to let this incident sour our incipient friendship. Reinaldo gave his first reading in Manhattan in a bookstore in the Village. He read in Spanish, and then his translator read in English. Reinaldo was a dramatic reader: he used his hands expressively and lowered and raised the volume of his voice to underscore key passages. At one startling moment in the reading he boomed a few sentences, letting each word hammer the air like an exclamation point. Before performance art became fashionable, he was doing it.

One memorable evening in 1981 the noted Cuban writer Severo Sarduy called me. (Sarduy died of AIDS several years later.) Because Sarduy lived in Paris, where he was the Latin American editor at Seuil Éditions, I assumed he was the person responsible for bringing Reinaldo's books out in French while Reinaldo was a prisoner in Cuba and his books had to be smuggled out of the country. Sarduy suggested we meet at a Cuban-Chinese restaurant on Eighth Avenue and 50th Street. He had never met Reinaldo. That night my lover and I went with Reinaldo to the restaurant to meet Severo and his French lover. For me it was an exciting moment, two prominent homosexual Cuban writers, who already had an important literary relationship, meeting for the first time. Yet the dinner was anti-climactic: Reinaldo was formal, almost stiff, betraying no emotions. I was disappointed. When the awkward meal was over, we returned to my apartment for drinks and talk. Later that night we went to the now defunct Haymarket, a notorious hustlers' bar on Eighth Avenue and 46th Street. Even there I felt that Reinaldo treated Sarduy strictly as a business acquaintance.

In 1983 my novel *Colombian Gold* was published, and it was met by mostly hostile reviews. Reinaldo's fortunes, on the other hand, rose. He received a Guggenheim Fellowship, and a Cintas Fellowship, which is given to distinguished Cuban artists. His epic poem *El Central* and the novels *Farewell to the Sea* (which Castro's police had destroyed in manuscript a few times) and *Old Rosa* appeared in English. Several other titles came out in Spanish and in many other languages. Reinaldo acquired a set of beautiful new teeth, started working out, and developed an impressive armor of well-defined muscles. With his movie-star smile his handsomeness was irresistible. After a lifetime of persecution and misery, in which he was jailed and witnessed suicides, rapes, cold-blooded murders, and torture, Reinaldo was enjoying success. I was, of course, jealous, but it was hard to resent him because we kept running into each other at the post office and the supermarket and he was unwaveringly friendly and kind. He encouraged me to apply for a Guggenheim and asked me to submit poems to *Mariel*, the Spanish magazine he edited during those years. Yet we stopped hanging out together, and our friendship now had a cautious edge. His all-consuming hatred of

Fidel Castro—and of García Márquez for supporting the Cuban Revolution—combined with the searing intensity of his passions, terrified me. He could be nurturing, but there was, I learned, a truly Dostoyevskian side to his nature. Edmundo Desnoes, author of the celebrated novel *Memories of Underdevelopment* and a supporter of the Cuban Revolution, gave a talk at New York University to an almost exclusively leftist audience. Reinaldo attended and, incensed by Desnoes's favorable report of the revolution, called him a lying s.o.b. A fracas ensued: Reinaldo was thrown in the air and later pinned against a wall where he was hit by some men in the audience. Desnoes was unable to finish his talk. The Latino intellectual community was appalled and from that time on treated Reinaldo as an outcast.

By the mid-eighties so many of my friends had died of AIDS that I wasn't surprised when I realized Reinaldo was ill. His sexual appetite was voracious. Coming home late at night I would see him prowling Times Square or walking out of the sleaziest sex joints.

Reinaldo lived on 44th Street between 8th and 9th Avenues. He had visited my apartment many times yet had never invited me into his home. So when Thomas Colchie phoned in December 1990 and asked me to check on Reinaldo, I thought I'd better get in touch with him right away. Too many friends had died before we had a chance to say things we wanted to say. I called him, and we made plans for me to stop by late that afternoon.

I climbed the steps of Reinaldo's building and rang his buzzer. The building was a walk-up, and Reinaldo's apartment was on the top floor, the sixth. At the top of the steep stairs I knocked on his door. I heard what sounded like a long fumbling with locks and chains, which even in Times Square seemed excessive. The door opened, and I almost gasped. Reinaldo's attractive features were hideously deformed: half his face looked swollen, purple, almost charred, as if it were about to fall off. He was in pajamas and slippers. I can't remember whether we shook hands or not or what we said at that moment. All I remember is that, once I was inside the apartment, he started putting on the chains and locks, as if he were afraid someone was going to break down the door.

We went through the kitchen into a small living room. Besides an old-fashioned sound system and a television set, I remember a primitive painting of the Cuban countryside. A table, two chairs, and a worn-out sofa completed the decor. Reinaldo sat on the sofa and I took a chair. I felt that if I sat too close to him, I would not be able to look him in the eye. Stacks of manuscripts lay on the table—thousands and thousands of sheets, and Reinaldo seemed like a shipwreck disappearing in a sea of paper. When I asked if they were copies of a manuscript he had just finished, he informed me that the three manuscripts on the table were a novel, a book of poems, and his autobiography, *Before Night Falls*.

Reinaldo spoke with enormous difficulty, his voice a frail rasp. "The novel, *El color del verano*, concludes my Pentagony. It's an irreverent book that makes fun of everything," he mused. "*Leprosorio* is a volume of poems. And *Antes que anochezca*," he pointed to the third pile, "is my autobiography. I dictated it into a tape recorder and an amanuensis transcribed it. It's going to make a lot of people mad."

It seemed to me absolutely protean the amount of writing he had managed to do, considering what a debilitating disease AIDS is. I said so.

"Writing those books kept me alive," he whispered. "Especially the autobiography. I didn't want to die until I had put the final touches. It's my revenge." He explained, "I have a sarcoma in my throat. It makes it hard for me to swallow solid foods or to speak. It's very painful."

"Then maybe you shouldn't talk. I'll do the talking," I offered, moving to the sofa.

"But I want to talk," he said curtly. "I need to talk."

I said, "Reinaldo, if there is anything you need, please don't hesitate to let me know. Whatever it is . . . cooking your meals, getting your medicines, going with you to the doctor, anything." I mentioned that the PEN American Center had a fund for writers and editors with AIDS and offered to contact them.

"Thanks so much, *cariño*," he said in the plaintive singsong in which he spoke. It was a sweet, caressing tone: melodious like a lazy samba but also mournful, weary, accepting of the hardships of life. This was a typically peasant trait. "There is a woman who comes to help three days a week. She does all my errands. Besides, Lázaro [Lázaro Carriles, his ex-lover who had remained his closest friend] comes by every day."

Just in case he wasn't aware, I mentioned other sources where he could go for help.

He snapped, "I don't like those men who serve as volunteers. I can't stand all that humility."

From where I sat I could see a bleached wintry sunset over the Hudson.

"But if you contact the PEN Club that would be good," he conceded. "I would like to get away from here before winter comes. My dream is to go to Puerto Rico and get a place at the beach so I can die by the sea."

To encourage him I said, "Perhaps your health will improve. People sometimes . . ."

"Jaime," he cut me off, "I want to die. I don't want my health to improve . . . and then deteriorate again. I've been through too many hospitalizations already. After I was diagnosed with PCP [AIDS pneumonia], I asked Saint Virgilio Piñera," he said, referring to the deceased homosexual Cuban writer, "to give me three years to live so that I could complete my body of work." Reinaldo smiled, and his monstrous face showed some of his former handsomeness. "Saint Virgilio granted me my request. I'm happy. I do wish, though, that I had lived to see Fidel kicked out of Cuba, but I guess it won't happen during my lifetime. Soon, I hope, his tyranny will end. I feel certain of that."

I knew better than to disagree with him when it came to discussing Fidel Castro. Once, in the mid-eighties, I had tried to tell him to put behind him his years of imprisonment and persecution, to forget Cuba, to accept this country as his new home and to live in the present. "You just don't understand, do you?" he had shouted, shaking with anger. "I feel like one of those Jews who were branded with a number by the Nazis; like a concentration camp survivor. There is no way on earth I can forget what I went through. It's my duty to remember. This," he roared, hitting his chest, "will not be over until Castro is dead. Or I am dead."

We talked for a while about the collapse of the communist states. The last thing I wanted was to upset him in any way, yet I had to defend my belief in socialism as the most humanistic form of government. So I spoke to that effect.

"On paper socialism is the ideal form of government," he said, not altogether surprising me. "It's just that it's never worked anywhere. Perhaps someday." Becoming thoughtful, almost as if talking to himself, he added, "Jaime, what a life I've had. Even before the revolution, it was bad enough the agony of being an intellectual queen in Cuba. What a sad and hypocritical world that was," he paused. "Finally, I leave that hell, and come here full of hopes. And this turns out to be another hell; the worship of money is as bad as the worst in Cuba. All these years, I've felt Manhattan was just another island-jail. A bigger jail with more distractions but a jail nonetheless. It just goes to show that there are more than two hells. I left one kind of hell behind and fell into another kind. I never thought I would live to see us plunge again into the dark ages. This plague—AIDS—is but a symptom of the sickness of our age."

As night fell, the neon of the billboards of midtown Manhattan and the lights of the skyscrapers provided the only illumination. We chatted in hushed tones, more intimately than we ever had before. I was aware of how precious the moment was to me, how I wanted to engrave it forever in my memory. When I got up to leave, Reinaldo had difficulty finding his slippers in the darkness, so I knelt on the floor and put them on his calloused, swollen, plum-colored feet. We went again through the kitchen, where he mentioned he would have broiled fish for dinner. Then he unchained the numerous locks, slowly, one by one. We didn't hug or shake hands as we parted—as if neither of those gestures was appropriate.

"Call me any time, if you need anything," I said.

"You're such a dear," he said.

As I was about to take the first step down, I turned around. The door to the apartment was still open. In the rectangular darkness Reinaldo's shadowy shape was like a ghost who couldn't make up its mind whether to materialize or to vanish.

The following day Reinaldo called to ask me if I could get him some grass. He said he had heard it helped to control nausea after meals. I told him that I would try to get some. I called a couple of friends and mentioned Reinaldo's request. Bill Sullivan suggested that I contact the Gay Men's Health Crisis because he thought Reinaldo sounded suicidal. I dismissed this possibility. Because his wish was to die by the sea, I thought he would try to make it to Puerto Rico if he received the grant from PEN. The next day, around noon, Tom Colchie called to say that Reinaldo had taken his life the night before; that he had used pills and had washed them down with shots of Chivas Regal; that he had left letters—one of them for the police, clarifying the circumstances of his death—and another one for the Cuban exiles, urging them to continue their fight against Castro's rule. Reinaldo had died in the early hours of December 7, and his body had been found by the woman who came by to help with his chores. He was forty-seven.

On December 19, at a Catholic church in Manhattan, a handful of Reinaldo's friends attended a mass in his honor. A couple of people eulogized him. His friend, the Barnard professor Perla Rozencvaig, talked about how even though Reinaldo did not attend church, he was very religious. The next orator was Lázaro Carriles, who recited one of Reinaldo's poems, celebrating death in the tradition of Góngora and St. John of the Cross. He finished with a poem also about the triumph of death, by Manuel Gutiérrez Nájera, a nineteenth-century Mexican poet, a poem that, he informed us, Reinaldo loved:

I want to die as the day declines
In the open sea and facing the sky
Where agony will seem like a dream
And the soul a bird taking flight.

Not to listen in the last instants
—Now alone with the sea and the sky—
To other voices or tearful prayers
Than the majestic tumble of the waves.

To die when the sad light withdraws
Its gilded nets from the green sea
And to be like the sun that slowly sinks
Something very luminous going under.

To die, and young: before treacherous
Time withers the graceful crown;
When life still says I am all yours
Although we know it will betray us.

A man in a dark suit and carrying a briefcase sat in front of me; he seemed to be seething with anger and quite determined to hold back his tears. After Lázaro Carriles finished the poem, the priest tried as best as he could to rationalize Reinaldo's suicide, implying that perhaps Reinaldo was not aware of the enormity of this action for a believer. But all of us present knew perfectly well that in the last terrible act of his life Reinaldo Arenas had been fully aware of what he was doing.

Kevin Killian

Kevin Killian (b. 1952) is a poet, novelist, critic, and playwright. He has written a book of poetry, *Argento Series* (2001), two novels, *Shy* (1989) and
Arctic Summer (1997), and two books of stories, *Little Men* (1996) and *I Cry
Like a Baby* (2001). He has also edited a collection of short stories by the
late Sam D'Allesandro, *The Wild Creatures*.

   Although born and raised on the East Coast, Killian is very much associated with San Francisco writing. With Robert Glück and Bruce Boone he
is one of the pioneers of the New Narrative movement, whose members
blur the boundaries between fiction and autobiography, as Killian does in
the chapter below from his memoir *Bedrooms Have Windows* (1989). With
Lewis Ellingham he wrote the definitive biography of Jack Spicer, one of
the central poets of the San Francisco Renaissance. For the San Francisco
Poets Theater Killian has written thirty plays, including *Stone Marmalade*
(1996, with Leslie Scalapino) and *Often* (2001, with Barbara Guest).

   The excerpt below concerns one of the more controversial subjects
in gay life, the relationship between older men and teenage boys. Killian's
relationship with Carey is not a happy one, but he took a secret pride in
having it.

Cherry

SO THERE—I had learned to write, but unless I kept up a rapid pace of living I'd have nothing—or so I felt—to write about.

A year went by, I kept changing college courses and colleges, going to parties, and living in a half-world. Soon I would turn nineteen. I started taking creative writing courses. "One day I'll be *giving* courses," I swore, "in creative living." I met Robbe-Grillet, Marshall McLuhan, Margaret Mead, Nicholas Ray, Marguerite Young, Paul Blackburn, all of whom were living and teaching in New York at the time. And over all of them I felt a half-acknowledged and contemptuous superiority, for who among them but me, I wondered, was having a secret affair with a married man with a son exactly my own age? You can't teach an old fool new tricks, George Grey used to say, and these living masters were, in my considered opinion, hardly of the 70s at all—they belonged to culture, whereas culture belonged to me, by dint of vanity and my increasing self-absorption.

The progress of a life, its growth and development. When we'd met he'd said, "My name's Carey, I want fun with a boy." He smiled sheepishly, as if in on a joke, but it wasn't a big smile. Soon it became clear, soon as he dived in, that he did want fun with a boy, I only wondered if I was that boy. I was fourteen. In his car he took off his coat with the portentousness of Jack the Ripper, and had sex with me, but all the time he kept yapping the most outlandish lines I've ever heard, offscreen or on:

Words of love. Words of adventure. But mostly these *stories* about the ordinary days and nights of his oldest son—Nicky. "I'm me," I thought. "Stop talking about him and pay some attention."

In shadow his face was a moving muscle of fat. I couldn't believe a thing he said; his hands pulled at his cock like they wanted to throw it out the window. Finally from out of it came this enormous spurt of come, dappled in streetlight—green, yellow, lacy, just when he was telling me about Nicky's hobbies. This I found off-putting, but in another corner of my mind I recognized a fellow traveller, another who knew the moves but lacked conviction or intensity. The car door creaked open like a mausoleum, our two bodies slithering to the ground. He swung me around in his huge arms, and threw me onto a patch of weeds. He said, "And so I told him, get a haircut, but sure enough next day rolled round, no haircut, I dragged his ass over to the Singer machine and chopped his damn hair into the needle." He went down on me, gently, and with my cock in his mouth kept talking, barely decipherable words and I think, yes, probably, this was the first time language had ever been used on me quite so intimately. The sensations varied. Fricatives tended to scrape the straight underside vein; sibilants were sucky, babyish, *lisp blowjob*; it were his long vowels and his aspirants that thrilled me. So I got to dislike the word "Nicky" right away, and if his son's name had been "Hugo" who knows? maybe we'd still be together . . .

"Had another little escapade on Tuesday."

"Say the day," I gasped.

"Tuesday," oh it felt so good. "Took Nicky to a Vet's picnic."

Please, no "Nicky," no "picnic," these little bursts of sounds that thudded my balls in rabbit punches. I wrapped my legs over his neck and drove him down into the dirt, but he kept sucking, cupping my ass, talking, and I came and then fell back and let the trees and the wind cool me off and still, after all that, for five long years, Carey kept talking and talking.

Soon I would turn nineteen, so it would be Nick's birthday soon, too, and his father took me shopping to get the young person's point of view. "I don't know the styles," he said, reasonably, in his car, "and you're just Nick's age, same size, build, coloring."

"I don't think I should," I said. "I'd feel funny." We were parked outside a hip store with the unprepossessing name of "Loose Threads," at a deserted shopping mall on Long Island. Carey wouldn't take me anywhere crowded; in too big a crowd there'd be too big a chance of running into someone he knew. One of his wives perhaps. In consequence we spent a lot of time riding aimlessly in his Cadillac, a lot of time in mirrored motels, and a lot of time in different Howard Johnson's, where I learned to go for fried clams in a big way. "I don't want to."

"But you're exactly his size."

"Yeah. Same—same . . . same everything I guess."

Now he was hurt. "What's the problem?" Puzzled too. "Tell Carey. You don't want to do Carey a favor, that it? One little favor and you don't want to help out?"

I pouted for him.

"Well, what's the problem here, I really don't understand." He held open my door and grudgingly I got out, followed him. Four or five drowsy salespeople leaped into life. Here Carey was in his element, beaming broadly, pushing open his fat wallet so they could see all his credit cards. "My son here," he said, "my son here's having a birthday soon. I want to dress him up, the way the kids are dressing nowadays. Carte blanche."

Panic hit me, I don't know why. Yes I do: I was stoned. Each face in the shop seemed to wear a spectral grin of greed and sick pleasure. (You know how these things go.) A young man reached out to touch my shoulder, and I recoiled as if a snake was biting me. "Don't," I said out loud, just like that. Carey waved his hands around like a Texas oilman in a movie, pointing to this and that, craving attention. Now that I think on it, he would have been a perfect shoplifting partner. He liked to distract. When I became involved with him it was for something to do, but as I got to know him I felt all fly and he loomed like a spider. I closed my eyes when he kissed me, when he murmured that he loved my skin and my dick. I always thought that he wanted to make love to his son, Nick, whom I'd never met, and that if I opened my eyes I'd know this for sure, and I kept waiting for the day he'd call out Nick's name instead of mine.

A saleswoman bowed to Carey in a geisha way. "Anything you say, sir."

The young guy's smile was a fixed thing on his skinny face. My eyes begged him: understand me man, this overbearing man I'm with is not my father. At the same time I knew that so very many real son's faces must plead the same thing in connection with their real dads that my look must convey little or nothing to him. This man is not my father. I'm not his son.

"We don't get many clients like you, sir, if I may say so," the young woman said. *Oh boy!* I thought: *she don't know the half of it.* "What with inflation and all."

"What the hell. 'You can't take it with you,' right?" Carey quoted with a sigh.

She nodded sympathetically, as though there was something sad about all this.

"Look at it this way," Carey said. "My oldest son. His birthday. What he wants more than anything else: new clothes. Put them altogether they spell V I S A C A R D, right? Nowadays Dad has to do what Sonnyboy wants or where are you? I'll tell you where: smack in the old generation gap? Am I right, Miss?"

"Absolutely," she replied, still melancholy.

The young man and his gang herded me away to a thin dressing room at the rear of the shop, and threw clothes in at me, clothes so new they smelled of the factory. From floor to ceiling a mirror hung, and velvet nailed over plywood covered the walls. It was just a dressing room, but like a madhouse cell in so many ways. "He's doing all this for Nicky, that goddamn son of his," I said to the mirror. "I'm being used. Or maybe he's going through this whole charade to convince me there really *is* a Nicky, in either case I'm still being used."

From a slit in the velvet the young man poked in his head. "Excuse me," he said. Again he winked at me. "I thought you'd be undressed by now." An unusual thing to say, maybe, but it had its effect. I perked up and said:

"I know you. From somewhere but where?" Because I never went shopping . . .

"You're a friend of George Grey's."

"Oh yeah." This dispirited me all over again.

"I've seen you with him half a dozen times," said the young man, introducing himself. "Acting lovey dovey." He slipped bodily into my room and began to unbutton my shirt for me. I was sad. And this young man—"Roger"—was very much the dextrous pro. "Though I didn't know your name is Nicky, that's cute."

I was about to say it wasn't Nicky. I was about to say, *My name is Kevin. Kevin Killian.* But, embarrassed, I kept mum, thinking of all the dopey things I'd ever done and said and felt in my life. Eyes narrowed, brain sizzling I used, for example, to brag, "I could have that husband in thirty seconds." Just like Joan Crawford in Cukor's film *The Women.* Now some think Crawford's acting is awfully exaggerated. Not me. She's a mistress of understatement compared to my own machinations. A kiss on the hand may be quite continental, but I wanted diamonds, diamonds and cherry, like some Dali valentine. And look where it got me! You tell me, is or is not Crawford a perfect model of representational cool?

"Don't worry, I won't blow your cover," teased Roger. "And no I won't tell your dad the naughty things you do in your spare time; the way you dance or the men you dance with."

"No, don't," I said. Roger stood behind me pulling my shirt off my arms. "Spare him, please."

"He might get upset then."

"He might cut off my hair," I said. Then I laughed. The close dressing room, Roger, the fusty velvet breathed dust and the metallic shiny scent of new pins. "Or my balls," I told him, warming suddenly to the part. "He might cut off my balls with a Singer sewing machine." I flashed: what a part to play! I looked in the mirror and my image wore a funny look on its lips, a look that said, "In for a penny, Carey . . ."

Roger read it a little differently though. "Now try these on, why don't you? Yves St. Laurent. The old man's paying right? Yeah, right. Oh yes, I've seen you in the bars, in the bars with George Grey, right? Now there's your Stud Glorious. He's wasted on the dance floor; he should be lying on his back in bed; my bed; legs pedaling. I tell you what, Nicky: introduce him to me, a real close intro, next time we all meet again. Hear me?"

I was noncommittal.

"He's not yours, is he?" asked Roger in pretended alarm. "What a fool I am!"

"Oh, I'll introduce you," I capitulated, beginning to see the line of complications. I pushed Roger's hands from my waist. "But make me a promise—two promises: don't tell my father anything about me and George; and don't tell George about my dad bringing me in here . . . Promise?"

"Can I call you?"

"Oh, you can call me," I cried, dizzily. My new pants—the pants destined for the son of Carey—rode halfway up my thighs, the tip of my prick chilled in the open metallic air. "You can call me Ray, or you can call me . . ." I wrote down my number. "Call me—any time." I kissed his mouth and his tongue moved beneath mine like Dial-A-Kiss. It seemed logical at the moment. His hands were warm like suds and smooth like velvet, or Black Label. I don't know why I kissed that awful oozing clone, as hard as I did, as much as I cared to. My erection broke me up, broke me in two. Couldn't keep my mind on one man at a time. "You had falafel for lunch," I said. I wrote down my phone number. I gave it to him. I gave it away . . .

About fifteen minutes later Carey and I got ready to leave "Loose Threads," laden with wrapped packages like beasts of burden. "Thank you, Dad," I said for the salespeople's benefit. "You're the ginchiest."

"Sign here, please sir," the young lady murmured, with a breathy, light, floating smile. She should have been a cruise director with that smile. Instead her job consisted of thanking people for spending their money. "Thank you and—have a nice day!"

"Who was that boy," Carey growled in my ear.

"He's the best Dad in the world," I said to the saleslady.

"This better be good," Carey said.

"You're a lucky fella," she told me. "To have a Dad so generous." It brought tears to her eyes, too deepset for tears.

Later I sat among the snappily wrapped gifts that filled the back seat of Carey's car. "Take me home," I said haughtily, regarding him as little more than my chauffeur. "To Shakespeare Mansions." This was the name I called my house, because it was decorated with Victorian lithotypes of scenes from Shakespeare's plays. The car pulled up before it. I didn't want to go in and face my roommates. Shakespeare Mansions, lit from within by candles, now, and glowing in the night like a cathedral or jack-o-lantern. I whispered to Carey wait a second, wait, wait . . . He held up his hand in the dark as a signal, don't open the car door, a light will come on. The Cadillac purred, its motor finely tuned, a great grave smiling cat in the night. Must have been a blackout with all those candles inside. And no electricity anywhere.

"Kiss me," he said.

"Your hands are cold."

"Your ass is red hot," he said. "I want your cherry." (He'd had that, of course, a hundred times or more, and he'd told me I had his. This was Fantasy Life, adult country, where the real and the sore don't matter. Still almost every time we had sex that's what he wanted, I got tired of hearing about it.) "Give it to me!" (The first time it had hardly hurt—it was like giving candy to a baby.) "Give me your ring of fire."

"Thanks for dinner, Carey." Fried clams and hot dogs, wow. "And give my love to your ex-wife and to Nicky and Anita and all the other little people. In your life." In the dark I walked away on rubber soles and found refuge behind a large range of scented bushes. I licked my lips and spat. The huge black car rolled down the hill silently, filled with motive power.

I closed my eyes but the night was so stark I might have left them open. Sometimes when your eyes are shut you see pinwheels of color and light, and stars; that night I saw all these and something more, a band of ribboned colors arcing around my eyelids like a rainbow tipped on its side. Against my back I felt the splintery ridge of a telephone pole; I leaned into it, cracking against it. Somewhere down the pike falling wires had caused this blackout. Above me more wires. If they too fell I'd be electrocuted or would I? Were they dead now too? I was surrounded by a rainbow, inside my skull: Cinerama. Above the dead wires, above them a hundred kinds of constellations, patterns, motives, reasons.

"There's a reason why we're in each other's arms . . . it's because we need each other."

"Some reason," I cried.

"You said you needed a father figure."

"You need a son, Carey? You have two or three of them. Nicky for example."

"Oh fuck that."

"But I am your son in a way, don't get me wrong, don't get mad, I was just wondering."

"Wondering? Wondering what? You can tell me anything, ask me anything, I've shown you everything, I've done everything. All for you, Kevin."

"I don't feel like this is really happening," I said, dazed.

"I've even shown you my house where I used to live with my previous wife!"

I didn't care much for any of his wives, not even the ones I hadn't met.

"I was wondering if you ever did it with Nicky," I said finally. And Carey had turned away, hurt, vicious, his teeth came flying out to bite or chew my cock . . . Maybe then I'd come too close to the truth; who knows! When you're dealing with variables it's hard to say what makes a person's blood boil and what makes the same person say he will love you forever if he can only have your cherry. "Get the fuck away from me with that overbite . . ."

"My boy's no fag."

"I didn't say he was."

Then I remembered to get on my high horse.

"Isn't a crime, you know," I said acidly. "So what if he is. I am. You are. At least you say you are. I don't know what Anita thinks, all she does is rock in the rocking chair and spout Spanish at me."

"I am! I'm a fag in a heterosexual's body!"

"You treat Nicky like shit."

"I treat him swell, he's got everything, he's got a big allowance."

"But he's always got you on his ass."

"Cause I'm his father and I want to see him grow up right, that's all."

I used to slam the car door and run in the night up the flagstone steps, and open my door and tell my roommates, "I'm home, I had a lovely night with the worst shit in the world," angry with him because he'd turned me into some kind of freak. My roommates would blink and say why not drop him, but I considered that what he and I had was little more than a continuous, slow-moving drop, like a glacier melting over all Minnesota and Michigan and making great lakes. But he was ever charming, and bought me plenty of fried clams, grilled frankforts, other treats . . .

Yet despite all his charm if he was conducting a full-blown sex affair with his own son I felt, foolishly, I had the right to know. Once when he and I were at his ex-wife's house and in Nicky's room, making love on Nicky's bed, while the rest of the family was summering in the Poconos, I vomited onto the floor. For no reason. I pictured Carey and Nicky entwined on the bed, creating each other, snaking like a conga line. Only Nicky was smaller than Carey. Not as big. Thin. His child.

"Just don't say you've given me everything, Carey, that you possibly could! I don't want to hear those words any more, cause what you give to Nicky you take away from me, yours truly Kevin!"

I was thinking, these words will be my text, when I grow up, get out of this love, and write my memoirs someday. Carey pulled away from me and stood up, undecided. He got some towels from a linen closet and ran water through them in the bathroom. After a while he came back to the bed and cleaned up the vomit in silence.

I was silent too. I heard nothing but our labored breathing and the moist susurration of the towel swamping the floor. On the wall above the headboard hung a framed photo of Nick winning some trophy or another from a bald portly man dressed in bright warm-up clothes.

"I should more be like Nicky," I finally said. "Turn myself inside out trying to please you. I should grow up and develop a healthy interest in the opposite sex. Go out for organized sport. Learn cunnilingus."

"Maybe you should," Carey said. "Nick's a very good boy. One of these days maybe you'll realize that."

"Maybe one of these days I'll meet him and fuck him," I said. Tit for tat. Of course what happened to me when I finally did meet Nick was something far different. We have a strange way, don't we, of prophesying our futures? Always wrongly, it seems; you'd think after awhile we'd get the hang of it and go by opposites, the way dreams are supposed to? "One of these days he'll be my boy, as well as yours."

POW

Michael Klein

Michael Klein (b. 1954) is a poet and editor whose collection of poems, *1990* (1993), won the Lambda Book Award, as did the anthology he edited, *Poets for Life* (1989).

Klein has not followed the usual route to being a writer. He has been a waiter, a singer-songwriter, a paralegal, and a teacher. His first volume of memoirs, *Track Conditions* (1997), recounts the five years he worked as a groom, culminating in his care of Swale, a horse that won the Kentucky Derby. The passage below is from his second volume of memoirs, *The End of Being Known* (2003), and discusses the taboo subject of incest with his twin brother.

The End of Being Known

THE SEX WITH MY TWIN BROTHER began in the first lap after puberty. We were living near the park in New York City. I can still see the sun set behind the roofs that lead down to the Hudson River, but I can't see the sex as well. I only remember the quality of it and how now it has become a sort of nuance whenever we get on the phone. Sex has given our life of brothers an intonation. We never judge it or marvel at it or allow it to ruin our lives in any discernable way. We just *sound* this way—like brothers who had sex with each other.

When I call my brother, I feel more comfortable leaving a message on his machine. And whenever I do, I'm disarmed sometimes by the outgoing humor of his messages: "I'm off to the sad opening of a girls' school" or "I've been dragged away to the blessing of the ships" or "Are you sure I know you?" or, better, "Are you sure you know me?" The messages could easily have been written by the famous monologists Ruth Draper or Anna Russell because they have this formal hysterical quality to them. They're funny messages, in other words, but not funny to everyone. They're *acquired* funny, like satire.

The messages are particularly not funny to my father, who calls up my brother on the phone occasionally. My brother or me being funny is never funny to my father. My father thinks being funny is something you do when you're not sure about your real purpose in life. Being funny is the summer job. Being funny is extra. But I'm used to my brother's humor. I can see my brother through his humor, no matter what else is happening to him. I can tell what his humor is disclosing or what his humor is obscuring, because my brother is my twin, which makes him differently like me. In that way, nobody sounds like my brother talking into his tape except me. We have the same speaking voice, which wavers somewhere between gravel and gravel and gasoline.

We have become famous for our voices and are known by them more than we're known by our faces or anything psychological, anything under the surface, anything that might throw one off the sound of the voice. We're twins who *sound* alike, not twins who look alike, even if we look alike. Some people have the habit of listening to my voice and not what my voice is saying—loving the music without understanding the lyric. But music can tell you what a lyric means, so some people have this *sense* of me—that it's almost all of me. Me, as my voice. Which can also be intimidating.

Somebody recently said—for the hundredth time of getting told this one thing precisely—that I can be intimidating until you get to know me. But aren't most people? Isn't the human voice always slightly intimidating until it is singing?

I'm sure the gravel and the gasoline come from the early intonation around the language Kevin and I spoke before we learned English. Many twins go through the experience of having the world in their mouths in words only they can understand. It's the way they communicate with each other so they don't have to communicate with anybody else. They strike an early bargain to double private life.

Because twinship begins in narcissism, English can be the thing that breaks the mask—a symbiosis with a dominant but, for the twin, *other* language. A twin joins the world outside his twin world the moment English takes over and the made-up language falls away like a veil between the two dancers. Still, even in English, the twins know that it was that first language that set a tone. They know that the sound they made was filling up the loneliness of being different.

Because I sound like Captain Hook (according to the writer Allan Gurganus), I tried doing voice-overs for a few years but nobody really knew how to cast me. I wasn't a hard seller. I could only sell a voice and not the thing the voice was selling. Whenever I went into an audition, people gasped at my unique sound, but I could never book a job. People didn't know what to do with me. I wasn't marketable. I was too unique. I've always been too unique.

Once I was in a songwriting workshop during the 1970s and ended up being shut out of the big showcase at Reno Sweeney's after the last class because I was too unique. I stood out from my fellow songwriters, which I had thought was the point. Being a twin makes being unique the point. But away from the double, standing out wasn't the point.

Packaging has always been my problem. Nobody knows how to label the box that has me inside it. Because I could never tell exactly what set me apart in the niche sea of voice-over voices, I kept complaining to my agent about not booking work, and she kept telling me it could take five years to really get a career started. It's an audition business—a harried string of appointed times that rules over any actual work. I didn't do a good audition. I wanted people to know I had a famous voice without selling them a famous voice. I don't want to be famous; I want to be loved, unlike a real actor, who switches the love with fame.

The voice-over world is a fantasy world, like every entertainment. All the work is booked by a dozen people who've been in the business since Lauren Bacall, and she was the last of the really unique sounds. Most people, if you listen to them on television selling you the soap or the candy bar, sound pretty much the same. My voice of damage-through-excess isn't popular anymore. I can be ahead of my time, but I'm miserably behind it when it comes to popular culture. I've never made any money from any of my contributions to popular culture. But I'll pay the money it costs to get in, sometimes.

I spent a lot of money on learning voice-overs. I had the best coach, the best agent in New York. Then I couldn't get work. Then somebody said the reason people leave the business is that they run out of money (from all the demo tapes and coaching sessions), which, I suppose, just justifies not making money.

It's a sham in a way, but there were some nice people. I had a nice enough agent. Some of the casting directors were funny—if that's the right word. Sometimes today I'll see a casting director or an agent at a movie. I will be out in the world of no voice-over work, and somebody will say they know *that* voice, they *remember* that voice. I will be in a restaurant or on line for a movie, and someone will say, "Michael, is that you?" as though they can only see me by what they hear—as though they're listening to the voice through a curtain. And only after I've uttered, "Yes, it's me—how are you?" can they put the voice to the face.

It can be tricky on the phone sometimes. When the sex lines were invented I called one, and as soon I started talking, a voice in that sea of chat-room voices cried out, "Klein, is that you?" As soon as I talk, I break my anonymity. People can't *see* me without *hearing* me, which is mostly how I am remembered. And because I am a voice, people don't take the usual photograph of me with their minds. They make a recording.

Like my brother is making a recording. His sound, what he lays down on the outgoing message, is entering the world at large more than it is entering the mind of anyone specific. He doesn't have many people in his life who would call him. There's only me and my father, Roy, most of the time. And sometimes Marie, a half-sister.

My brother isn't a social person anymore. He's trying to stop drinking, so he doesn't go to the bars as much as he used to. He doesn't think very much about knowing people. Sometimes it feels as though my brother thinks that knowing people is a phase that he went through already. I can understand that, in a way. People are a lot to know.

Because he is alone, my brother reads and writes. He freelances. He sees people at the movies. Seeing people is enough of people. He's been hurt by people more than I've been hurt by people. When I look at my brother, he looks back like he's been held up by what hurts him, and so when he's late for something, it's his big-picture pain that makes him late.

There was a story yesterday about a dolphin. The dolphin looked into a mirror for the first time and found himself at exactly the same moment he was alive. As startling as the image was, it also gave the dolphin the feeling that there was more than just one reflection when considering one's self. Self meant he was one among others. I'm a dolphin. Most people are dolphins, I think, especially if they have the capacity to love. My brother can be a dolphin, too, but mostly I think he's fixed in the one gaze he knows will be there—like it was when we only had each other to conquer childhood. We weren't going to make it without each other. There were so many storms my mother and stepfather made outside the room. They were medicated lovers. They weren't going to give us the tools to make any repairs you sometimes have to make in a storm. They didn't have a toolbox that didn't have pills in it.

My parents didn't know how they made it as far as they precisely did make it, so they weren't going to give us that particular experience—the experience of *making it.* They weren't going to give us the American Dream because they didn't go to bed to have it. So, let's say my brother and I had each other because we didn't have our parents. My parents got lost coming home from a dance. Then my brother got lost. Then I got lost. In this way, I'm not my brother's life. I'm at the movies in New York. My brother is at the movies in Boston. We've been at the movies from the beginning, from the beginning of the movie.

There's a coolness at the movies about life. Everyone in the theater shines under the same story in the dark, the smell of popcorn mixed up with the smell of chocolate and perfume. Safe. It meant a lot to us in childhood. Recording moments people were safe. Like what an answering machine does. The person making the message is safe. Safe, in their voice anyway, inside their voice. A voice can live after the person falls away from the voice.

Or a person can only live as long as the voice keeps living. I make up my brother because I got lost. Every fear is a wish. My brother lives in the steel light of a blade. He walks, as if in a dream, toward danger. He improvises with alcohol in a play about an alcoholic who lives in Boston. He keeps a distance. He can't sleep. He thinks there is something going on without him. He is infatuated with the homeless. He smells danger and death when he's drinking. Anything bad can happen to him. By accident. I make my brother up.

My brother is on a street he's lived on for a while, in the neighborhood of the shadows from the lamps in the summer. Everyone knows his name, but no one ever calls him by his name because he's a faggot. They call him faggot because it's the name the world gave him. My brother will die in the world's name for him on a street where someone is killed once a month or so. I make my brother up.

He can't stop living in the bad neighborhoods. I know my brother can afford to live in better places, but he chooses to live close to sudden death. There seem to be more churches there, where they feed the homeless man my brother picks up every few weeks to come live with him—until he can get his shit together he always manages to say when he calls to teach me about the homeless. In the world my brother lives in, the streets give up their homeless. My brother is their king. I make my brother up.

My brother's love suits the men the street gives up to him. He has sex with the homeless man because it's all his heart can afford, what it is already used to, what it has had already—sex with someone who thinks my brother is more powerful. It will not be a homeless man who kills him, finally. It will be a sudden stranger: the addict, the homophobe, the crazed. It will be someone the world has come to name instead of see. My brother doesn't name anything in the world, or he forgets to. And without the naming, my brother doesn't discriminate. He has the ability to get under a person's skin. He makes a wholehearted effort at the beginning of a person in his life to love the person in his life.

The love I have for my brother is different than any other kind of love I have for another person. It's a love with a limit. When it's used up, there won't be any more of it. It's a contract. It's not a love that grows over time, but one that actually diminishes, becomes logical and objective and judgmental in a way I don't like love to be or even thought it could be. I guess it is something other than love. I guess what my brother and I have now is something that happens after love. And something about the love or whatever it is, now that it's had so much life shooting through it, has a force about it that has nothing to do with him, the other one. This . . . whatever it is . . . follows us like a mechanical cloud.

But love won't be staggering up the hill or down the hill or down the street my brother lives on the night he drops the world, the night I make my brother up. My brother would have just closed the bar. Love didn't walk in that night, and he will be almost gone in the vertigo wave of his stagger. And someone will stab him and leave him under the streetlight. The streetlight will be like the end of the movie *West Side Story*, when everything comes down to Bernstein's operatically alone basso ostinato under what's left of the music and the camera suddenly, self-consciously, pulls away from the New York playground. And for the first time in his drunk and sober life, my brother will be amazed that he can hear children on that street because all he has ever heard was the music of craving, and the music of craving doesn't happen to children. The music of craving is not about children. Craving comes from speeding up the heart beyond what it needs to live. Children have all the world they need. They have it, and we want it.

My brother will be amazed that everything has turned out this way. And at the clarity of it. That on that particular day in summer, everything will end with his death pushing into the street and into the sky. And before it ends, he will put his hand over his craving heart, and a line from one of his poems will keep saying itself to him over and over: *the beauty of the broken law, the broken law of beauty*—his imagined life and his unimagined life talking to each other. My brother will die violently and his last breath will have beautiful language in it. Then a crowd will form, the way it always forms around the new dead thing left by a summer tide or storm with nothing left but a story of how the dead thing left came up. A crowd of strangers will make up my brother's life, the way that I have made up my brother's life.

Let's say, for the story's sake, I know I will get that phone call one day, the one telling me my brother is dead. I will be in bed with a book or will have just noticed the

semen on my chest run clear, the way it did on his chest a thousand years ago in a bedroom of recklessness. Let's say, if I go back a thousand years ago to the bedroom that
floats in the time line between two cities, that there's something there and something
after leaving there that my brother would never say, could never face. Something to do
with our father and our mother and death and booze and aloneness and togetherness
and sex the first time. Let's say that maybe I'm not in a love relationship with another
person because it's too specific. Maybe I'm in love with the world.

I don't see my brother very much today. I *hear* from him, as they say. I see him in my
mind, floating above the city shaped like a knife. Or I see him in a dream, arguing. I
see him shaking a tree at me from the bottom of a lake. And when I think of it, if he
does die first—summer, the street, a stranger's blade of light slicing through the air
of a children's playground song—I will not be released. His death will not release me
from his life. It will add to him. But what makes me think it—that *my brother will die
first*? The murder I am so careful to report, in a minutely detailed fantasy, might happen years after I die myself. Or it could never happen. Or it could happen to me. What
is it about my own life that makes me feel compelled to drag the river of my brother
and me for a corpse? Who am I, suddenly, in my mid-forties, alone, and inhabited by
my brother's future ghost?

I have a better life now that I've stopped drinking and managed to, at least, get off
the same road I'm so invested in tracking him down on. But why hasn't this given me
empathy for my brother? Why can't I love him when I have been him—been drunk,
been in the arms of the homeless man, thinking I was home. Why do I imagine violence rather than a plan to save my brother? I can't save him. I don't know how to save
him, even though I've been him. I never saved that part of myself that was him, I just
stopped it. When did I stop loving my brother and why?

My mother never dressed us in the same clothes or sent us to the same schools.
And she hated the curious women in the grocery stores or public parks, peering into
our carriages as though we had just landed from outer space. To those women who
asked "Are they twins?" my mother curtly replied, "No, they're chicken pot pies!"

After being pies together, my brother and I did puberty together in a small apartment in Greenwich Village, while my parents argued about money. I turned up the
radio whenever my parents argued. Or talked.

"I'll never get married," I said.

We were in a kind of marriage. It was a marriage that brought some strange comfort, but it was the wrong thing to be mastering—like having to get used to eyeglasses
at a young age.

The first orgasm I ever had was with my brother. We were twelve, thirteen. We
came to sex like hoodlums. We circumvented authority. My brother and I never got

the talk about sex or anything about what might happen to us. We never got anything futuristic. My parents didn't *pass down* anything experiential or teach us any real lessons because their own experiences, their childhoods, had been filled with utter dread and anxiety.

I think my parents figured my brother and I would pass everything we had to know between each other and it would be enough. They could give us food, clothing, shelter, stuff, but a lot of thinking about the world and what it could do arose out of the twin consciousness that thrived at night when show music and traffic honked through the Greenwich Village of my youth.

My brother and I talked about the world as though we had landed on it. But maybe my parents landed too. Maybe they were still landing, learning to land. Maybe we *don't* choose our parents.

I touched my brother's body for the first time when we were ten years old and we were alone on a stage in the ballroom of the Pine Orchard Country Club in Branford, Connecticut. We were going to be actors/singers when we grew up, we told each other. We were going to write music and plays. Whole universes would spin away from us into an unsuspecting, but soon-to-be adoring, audience. We were going to be famous for what we *thought*.

In the country club my brother and I choreographed a little number (walking with some kind of elaborated arm movements from downstage's powerful left and right diagonals). We were walking in a slanted way toward each other, humming, "All day, all night, a band of angels watching over me, Oh Lord," or was it, "Ain't she sweet, just a-walking down the street, now I ask you very confidentially, ain't she sweet?" After we got to the front of the stage and finished our song, we kissed each other. On the lips.

Eventually, and for about a year, my brother and I were doing it once or twice a week. He would come to my room, or I would go to his, and one of us would just linger there in the doorway until something like permission arose. We kissed. Again. Then my brother sat to the side of me on the bed and ran his hand slowly down my chest and stomach until it reached a beating cock. He kept his hand on my cock a minute, which was when I'd come out of the temporary coma and start reciprocating. I'd grab my brother by his shoulders and push him down to my mouth, which was dry inside but moist at the lips. And we'd kiss again, the second time. And that would be his cue to start climbing up on me, to stay tethered by his tongue inside my mouth but also to move his legs on either side of my body, so that by now he was straddling me. We didn't know what fucking was, or we would have fucked. And so we were oral lovers. And when we sixty-nined (the last move because by then we were always so close to coming and we both wanted to come in the other one's mouth), I always saw us as the snake we had become, swallowing its own tail. It didn't feel like having sex with another person or even having sex with another boy. It felt like an extension of my own sex.

I knew my brother was another body, another cock, another heart. But we were in puberty together, and we always came together. And in that miniature heartbreak I felt just after orgasm when I went back to seeing him as another person—the assigned brother, as everything other than sexual (someone who got up five minutes later than I did and didn't have friends in school, someone lost in books and classical music)—I was struck with something I might now call regret. Or maybe it was an early moment of knowing what it was like to be alone.

Then I knew that my brother and I shouldn't be doing this. When the year of our sex was drawing to its close, he came to my room and I had to tell him that I didn't want to have sex anymore. It wasn't a decision based on anything except how I felt. I didn't think what we were doing was wrong, but I started to want to break away from my brother, in thinking, in feeling, and to become whoever I was supposed to be without him. I wanted to spend time *feeling alone*. The sex became like an animal we had been feeding, and I wanted to let the animal go.

"We should be having sex with other people, not each other. With girls or something."

"Girls?" (As if I'd said gorillas.)

"Yeah. Don't you like girls?"

"I think about them, but I don't know if I like them."

"Well, maybe you need to think about them longer. Maybe we should try it with girls from now on, like other guys."

"I wouldn't know where to start."

"By talking to them, for starters. There are plenty of girls at school who really like you."

"It's you they like."

"That isn't true. I just talk to them more than you do."

"What if we like boys?"

"I don't think so. It's different when it's us. I mean, I don't think of you as a boy, I think of you as my brother."

My brother was beginning the homosexual dream. But I didn't have the homosexual dream until somebody else could give it to me, someone who wasn't in the family. I didn't have the homosexual dream until Henry from school. Henry stayed over one night, and more nights, until we had sex. Then my brother burst into the room. In the weird breeze made from my brother bursting into the room, I felt the secret of sex with my brother whisper to the sex I was having with Henry. Henry was the homosexual dream I was having because I had stopped having my brother. I had woken up from my brother's dream, the dream of my brother. But my brother was still dreaming; *is my brother still dreaming*?

Later my brother and I came up against what sex was like in the world. We went swimming at the YMCA. The swimming counselor, Larry, walked around the locker room one day with an erection and sat down beside Kevin. He started massaging my brother's shoulders. I was fascinated and unnerved by Larry's moves on my brother. As cool as I might have been about the sexual heat of the relationship that was now over, seeing my brother move into the light of another human being made me queasy.

Larry was attractive—tall and lanky, with a shock of black hair. His eyes were gray and they looked frightened, but that didn't make me think he was afraid. I saw the other thing you sometimes find in another person's eyes: the ability to hurt someone. I told my brother I would meet him outside. I waited for almost an hour. When my brother appeared, he was washed out. He was white as the sun. Then my brother said, "He made me have sex with him."

"Made you?" I said, finding it hard to believe it wasn't consensual. Suddenly, in the real world of negotiation, danger, and despair, sex was currency.

"Yeah, I didn't want to do anything."

"Well, what did he make you do?"

"Suck his dick."

It was the first time I ever heard my brother say the sentence, and it shocked me for a minute before I fell under its spell. Sucking anybody's dick was such a specific. I had heard of having someone by the balls, but having someone by the dick was even more possessive, demonstrative.

Larry asked my brother to come along on a sleepover the swimming group was having the next Saturday in the Catskills and to bring me along. The counselor wanted to have sex with me too. But my brother said no. My brother couldn't hold what happened in his mind long enough to think there could be a future in it. He couldn't hold the sex up to the light or share it with anybody.

Then, the way twins do when one of them is talking, I saw what might have happened. I saw the woods in my mind as though they were my experience. I saw myself with Larry. I saw the campfire, pretending to be asleep, waiting until everyone else was asleep before finding Larry in his sleeping bag or Larry finding me in my sleeping bag. I saw myself unzip Larry's sleeping bag from the bottom and crawl between his legs and just be a head moving up and down in the dark. And then I heard Larry groan and cough, to keep the groaning from the other boys.

I looked Larry up in the phone book but never called him. It was important for me to know where Larry lived, to make him real, I suppose. I wanted to see Larry in broad daylight, with clothes on. And for months, after everything had started dissolving into the forgotten and my brother and I settled back into the more familiar confusions that would have calculable outcomes on the future, I liked to imagine Larry walking down the street on his way to swimming class. And I wondered, too (always closing the curtain on the thoughts of him with this), which boys were treading water in his hungry mind now and how long had they been treading there?

I never told my brother about looking up Larry. It was my secret, the way crushes on some boys (*Milo, Milo*) in those days were secrets. And until recently, I rarely spoke about the sex I had with my brother. We're in our forties now and sometimes when I look at him I can't imagine I ever touched my brother's body. It's hard to explain why I had my brother as my lover for that year, however many years. Those glistening, erotic, ecstatic, and dark fragments of time feel like continents breaking off from each other, indistinguishable in the water, floating away from the populations.

In one scenario I make up for the past, I say that the sex with my brother kept us out of the danger zone. The world could unhinge at the dining room table, when my mother was so drugged up that she more than once fell asleep with a lit cigarette in her hand. But with the sex I had with my brother, the cigarette didn't look so dangerous. There was no guilt or shame, just a rash of self-consciousness that broke out sometimes when secret life happened too close to lived life.

And it's easier now to say I don't love my brother anymore, though I still don't understand it. Nothing about love comes with directions, but I know that I should be there for the other person. For example, I should be there to help with my brother's drinking or trying not to drink. I should go stand next to my brother and feel what it feels like just to stand next to him.

But I can't stand next to my brother. My friend A. said once, "You have to go and stand next to your brother and just feel what it's like to stand next to him." Maybe someday, when I am finished being a different person than my brother is. Today I am a different person than somebody who was in love with his brother. I left my brother to go into my life. And he left me to go into his. Or maybe I've just been dreaming. In my dream, I leave my brother alone on a stage in the theater of our time.

David Wojnarowicz

A painter, photographer, filmmaker, performer, musician, and writer, David Wojnarowicz (1954–1992) worked with an intensity that has hardly been matched in America, perhaps because his life seemed so tenuous. Born in Red Bank, New Jersey, he ran away from his abusive home as a teenager and lived for years crisscrossing America and Europe, working as a hustler or farm worker or at any odd job. The pain of his art is often intensified by a pastoral desire for what William Carlos Williams called "the pure products of America."

Because he was untrained in any of the arts, Wojnarowicz was relatively free to use them in conjunction. His paintings, collages, and photographs usually contain language or literary references. But in this practice he was not very different from other people working in the New York downtown scene of the 1970s and 1980s. His work began to appear in such galleries as Civilian Warfare, Club 57, Gracie Mansion, Fashion Moda, and the Limbo Lounge. He achieved prominence when his work was selected for the 1987 biennial at the Whitney Museum.

Wojnarowicz's work had always been political. In his photographic series entitled *Rimbaud in New York* (1977–79) one image is dominated by the graffito "THE SILENCE OF MARCEL DUCHAMP IS OVERRATED." Wojnarowicz did not believe in suffering quietly. With the onset of the AIDS epidemic Wojnarowicz dedicated a large amount of his time and artistic energy in protesting the governmental inaction in combating the disease. In 1989 the National Endowment for the Arts revoked a grant after politicians and religious leaders attacked his work as "pornographic" and "blasphemous." Wojnarowicz challenged the NEA and sued the American Family Association for misrepresenting his work and harming his career. He won both campaigns.

In 1992 Wojnarowicz died of complications from AIDS. "Memories That Smell Like Gasoline" is the title piece in a collection published the year of his death.

Memories That Smell Like Gasoline

IT'S THAT FACE. I knew I'd seen it before. I was standing in the lobby of a movie theater surrounded by crowds of people waiting to enter the auditorium to watch a film about a bunch of teenagers and a dead body and codes of teenage silence. It was the end of the previous show and the doors flung open and hundreds of people were pouring out towards the exits. Suddenly that face. It was one anonymous face in the crowd that tripped the switch in the back of my head. I froze and the face became magnified. It expanded in size until it was five feet tall and disembodied and floating in the darkness of the open doors. I guess he froze too. He was a pale gray color with fastidiously combed hair plastered down around the skull. Thin lips, bloodless and tight. His eyes were colorless and they widened for a moment. We both stood there trying to uncoil each other's private histories and solve the dislocation of familiarity. I had been drugged, tossed out a second story window, strangled, smacked in the head with a slab of marble, almost stabbed four times, punched in the face at least seventeen times, beat about my body too many times to recount, almost completely suffocated, and woken up once tied to a hotel bed with my head over the side all the blood rushed down into it making it feel like it was going to explode, all this before I turned fifteen. I chalked it up to adventure or the risks of being a kid prostitute in new york city. At that point in my life dying didn't mean anything to me other than a big drag. I had mixed feelings about death. When I was trying to get enough money to eat or find a place to sleep for the night, death actually seemed attractive, an alternative. I would go without changing my clothes or bathing for months at a time. I could see my reflection in the legs of my pants if I bent close to them. Periodically if I had a surplus of money from spreading my legs in seven dollar hotels on eighth avenue I would walk into the Port Authority bus terminal and look at all the various names of towns painted on the glass windows of ticket booths. I'd choose one that suggested bodies of water and then buy a ticket, get on the bus and ride it for as long as it took till I spotted a lake or pond in the countryside. I'd then ask the bus driver to let me off, usually having to argue with him because it wasn't a scheduled stop. After the bus continued on its way I would walk across the field and into the water until I was up to my neck. I never bothered to take off my shoes or my clothes. I would float around for hours and then hike back to the road and hitch a ride to a bus-stop or all the way back into the city.

That face. When I noticed his suit and his hands, palms back and manicured nails, I remembered. Maybe it was the quality of light or lack of it in the lobby as the door swung open and people were exiting before the end of the film. Maybe it was the color of his flesh, the look of no oxygen, the look of anticipation or fear, the complexion of anticipation. I remember that night fifteen years earlier. I had spent the later part of the afternoon paddling around this small pond, pushing my face under water looking for signs of life. It was rapidly turning to dusk and I was wet and feeling cold. The town was too small to offer much evening traffic so it was hard to get a ride. I didn't really know where I was. I was gray inside my head and wishing that killing myself was an effortless act.

Those eyes, that face gray and floating disembodied in the dark of the open window. A small beat-up red pick-up truck coasted to a stop along the side of the road. He was waving me into the truck. I remember thinking his skin was fake, like a semi-translucent latex. I asked him how far he was going. Oh, a ways. Thin tight voice layered with a friendliness I couldn't hook into. We drove for a while in silence and I looked out the side window at all the illuminated houses and occasional glimpses of people in driveways, interacting with each other. A stray dog running along the highway in a small panic. He said he worked for a bank in the city. That depressed me for some reason, maybe the formality of it that translated into an image of years and years of writing in ledgers and stale cups of coffee and dealing with people in need. At some point he had his dick out and stared out through the windshield at the beacons of light illuminating the dark roadway. He steered with one hand and jerked with the other. I was leaning against the door and didn't answer when he murmured something about this place he knew where we could go. After a while he made a left turn down a gravel and dirt road winding up through a forest over small hills. I remember moths and bugs diving into the headlights, a small wooden sign with a boy scout symbol on it, and then some scattered cabins. The sound of lake water in the near distance.

He got out of the driver's seat and pulled open the passenger door I was seated behind. Squat down and make it squirt. I didn't move. He had shut the engine and the headlights off. Get out. I felt suddenly much more tired than I ever remember feeling. I swung my legs out from the seat and stood in front of him with my hands in my pockets. A wind was coming up and it was starting to bring with it a light rain. He took me by the arm and led me to the back of the truck and turned a metal latch and swung up the back door of the camper. One of his hands floated up to my face and then encircled the back of my neck and I realized I was being propelled forward towards the black interior of the camper. I crawled obediently inside, it was loaded with blankets and sleeping bags and boxes of indecipherable stuff. It was kind of moist and smelled like earth and grease. He climbed in behind me and pulled the door shut. Everything was reduced to smells and the sound of trees and the squeak of his shoes against the metal parts of the floor. I lay down and curled up on a mass of smelly cloth. I could see his silhouette half-rise before me, blocking out the minimal light and then dropping to my side. The sound of a zipper opening. His hand on my neck again. Pulling. I want to go home, I said. What are you talking about? I realized his head was further back in the truck than I had thought. I couldn't see anything. The rain was coming down hard; sheets of water making the dimness more dark. I don't know, I said, wondering where I would go even if I got out of the truck without him stopping me. You like it in your ass? No. Good, he said and then hit me. Very hard.

I'm blind to the world and he's turning me over and over and over. Where am I? In a muddy field in the back of a stranger's truck and the truck is backed up to a fence and the stranger has put his full weight on my back and I feel like I'm in motion like something flung out of a giant sling shot. A pale length of rope hastily torn out of a wet cardboard box and wrapped around my hands pulled behind my back. I'm on my belly and if I yelled or hollered the only thing to hear me is the dead house miles back on the road dark and empty. Or the handful of rundown shuttered factories on the main road. He's pulling my hair, yanking my head back so his face appears upside down floating before mine and he's smiling. But the smile looks like a frown, it's upside down and he leans in and kisses both my eyes. The windows have fogged up and he opens one slightly and I can hear the occasional shine of an insect. He's slapping my bare butt and driving his tongue into my ear and running it down over the line of my neck and turning me over and over periodically. I'm overwhelmed by the smell of wet metal and the musky thickness of the cloth when my face is ground into a blanket or sleeping bag. What's he doing kneeling on my head, I ain't no doll with replaceable body parts. He's stuffing a rolled up blanket beneath my naked body forcing my ass up into the air. I can't feel my hands any more all the circulation is gone. Funny how everything all my life moved excruciatingly slow until this moment and now I'm just begging for it to stop. He giggles and disappears from the truck. I hear the sound of shoes on the grit and wetness of the road and the truck dips as he climbs back in. He lies on top of me. I'd feel fucking cold but his body is generating intense heat. His shirt's off and his pants are down or gone. He starts slamming his body down on top of mine periodically his arm curving around my face. Lick that bicep. His arm pulls back, fingers shove something in my mouth; It's a wad of mud and sand. He treats me like he owns me. I'm stuck in a drift, lost, no hope, or anything familiar. Maybe now I'll get relief, maybe he'll crush my skull or strangle me. Suddenly I recall something from earlier when he loosened my belt and dragged my pants down to my calves and smacked me as hard as he could and it hurt so bad I tried to make it sexual I tried to imagine it was gentle or that he was somebody sexy or that I was a mile away walking in the opposite direction. Oh hit me I said trying to act like I was into it so maybe he'd get bored. Turning over and over and over what the fuck is he doing that for? He lunges and reaches far into the darkness of the truck and I hear a container of liquid, sounds like a metal container and liquid sounds the image of lighter fluid or gasoline went through my mind. Is this it? I could see the flames; I could see my body being turned over by campers looking like a side of beef left too long in the fire, black and charred with bones poking out of it. I felt the squirt of liquid all over my ass, a memory smell from childhood flooding the truck. Baby oil. I just want to die, I just want to die. I just want to die. If say it often enough will I lose my fear of his hands tightening around my throat? I'm sinking in dark pools of atmosphere and his palm is sliding around the small of my back, into the crack of my ass cheeks. Oh what a gift you're giving me, he mumbles. He grabs my tied arms pressing his full weight on them pinning my elbows at an outrageous angle to the cold metal floor and he shoves his dick into me. Ow. He's biting my cheek. Slap. Slap. Burying his face in my neck and biting again. I'm still sinking and his bites and slaps are so specific I think he hasn't lost control just four fingers in my mouth weight holding me down kissing my eyes breathing hard in my ear pumping like a machine. You like that steady rhythm? Uh.

In the codes that I carry in the sleepy part of my head, personal histories can turn on a dime and either rush away into disintegration or else turn and speed towards me looking to envelop. In the moment he was swept up in the crowd and moving across the lobby towards me I shrunk mentally and in size like a kid with no defenses not even my pocket knife. I wanted walls to suddenly and abruptly burst out of the floor and rise between us. I wanted dozens of walls made of reinforced concrete and steel to keep us separated, to keep his hands from touching me. But I knew he would smash through them like some kind of dream psycho. It was like he was bleeding me right there in the crowded room. All my history and language had suddenly been erased. I knew somewhere that I could finally beat him up but I was stuck looking at him through the eyes of a fifteen-year-old skull. I just kept thinking I wanted to kill his gaze. Something weird happened where I physically shrunk and I took the moment where he and I lost track of each other to duck down the staircase to the restrooms. I went into a stall and sat on the turned down toilet seat for a long time listening to the sounds of dozens of people coming in and out to piss. When I finally went back upstairs he seemed gone. But I could still feel his gaze; it lingered like the stink after a bad fire.

David B. Feinberg

David B. Feinberg (1956–1994) was one of the fiercest voices in the early years of the AIDS pandemic. Unlike Larry Kramer, whose jeremiads about AIDS are more famous, Feinberg used gallows humor to arouse people to action with his "eighties gonzo journalism." He is among the most uncompromising and intense writers of the period, which makes his acidic works more tied to the times in which they were written and harder to bear today.

A graduate of MIT in 1977, Feinberg moved to New York City in 1979 and earned a graduate degree in linguistics at New York University. He published three books, novels *Eighty-Sixed* (1989), *Spontaneous Combustion* (1991), in which, as he admitted, he "filtered [his] own experiences through a fictional persona, B. J. Rosenthal," and *Queer and Loathing* (1994), a collection of essays published shortly before his death. An important member of ACT-UP, he participated in two of its most controversial demonstrations, the ones at Saint Patrick's Cathedral and at the Food and Drug Administration. He died of AIDS-related illnesses in November 1994.

On the Drip

MY REGULAR DOCTOR is in Palm Springs, Wyoming, or at some international conference. I see his charming solicitous partner whose overly concerned demeanor sometimes gives me the creeps. Reading my chart, he recommends that I should consider IVGG: intravenous gamma globulin. Gamma globulin is a protein active against cancer and viral and bacterial infections. It's another part of the immune system, along with T-4 cells. I would make an excellent candidate for this protocol: I have fewer than 100 T-cells and have a history of susceptibility to bacterial infections. His patients on gamma globulin have all managed to stave off CMV infections. I don't particularly feel like getting strep or Hemophilus again, especially after that penicillin nightmare in January 1993.

I tell him I'll think about it.

I think about it.

I am completely terrified.

But if it keeps me off a catheter and daily infusions of ganciclovir or foscarnet, fine.

According to Paul Monette, ganciclovir is now commonly delivered with a pump, not a hanging IV. First toothpaste got the pump, then sneakers got the pump; now it's used for CMV prophylaxis.

I don't mind needle pricks, but an infusion is another matter. I've always had good veins. Back in college, I used to donate large quantities of blood for purposes other than clinical tests. The nurses would always compliment my veins. It's no big deal for me to give two, three, or four test tubes of blood every time I see my doctor. Once my friend Chris, terrified, got me to go with him to the clinic for some complicated protocol. I took the afternoon off from work and waited with him in one of those molded-plastic chairs used in health clinics, fast-food restaurants, and waiting rooms for visiting incarcerated felons in medium-security facilities. Eventually, Chris was called. I joined him as he underwent the procedure. The physician stuck a needle into Chris's arm and took some blood. Big deal.

I decide to wait until I see my regular doctor again.

A month later, my doctor concurs. He also recommends pentamidine infusions, twice monthly. The best prophylaxis against PCP is Bactrim, available in tablets; unfortunately, I'm allergic. I don't feel like going through the desensitization procedure that my doctor suspects won't work on me anyway. I've been inhaling pentamidine for a few years. I tried it at home for a few months, but didn't feel comfortable with it. I would constantly put off doing my inhalation: I would always be a week or ten days late. It didn't feel right. I didn't get that same bitter taste in the back of my throat.

I tell him I'll think about it.

I ask my friend Wayne, the relentless top and control queen who giggles incessantly. Wayne works for the PWA Health Group, which sold me those underground ddC pills that ended up being variably dosed. He says it might be a good thing. The Health Group is selling Kemron (a formulation of oral alpha interferon developed in Kenya); although it is almost assuredly ineffective, it is Wayne's duty in his capacity of guaranteeing quality control that their Kemron be a placebo of proper strength and chemical derivation.

A billion years ago I recall protesting with ACT UP against the pediatric protocol for intravenous immunoglobulin. Infants were getting four-hour drips of IVIG once a month to see if this would help their immune systems against bacterial infections. However, to be scientifically objective, some scientist had decided that in order to avoid the placebo effect, where, given any drug whether useful or not, the patient feels psychologically better, half of the infants received a four-hour sugar drip once a month, putting them at risk of infection from the IV. This was barbaric.

Eventually IVIG was approved for infants and children.

Insurance companies balk at paying for gamma globulin because it's so expensive and it's currently approved only for children. The home-care nurse will be around $400; and the actual substance is around $1,500. There are other infusions for which a nurse can drop off the equipment, set you up, then go to a diner or a matinee performance of the latest Bruce Willis disaster and then return to unhook you. Pentamidine and gamma globulin are the only two infusions that require the presence of a nurse for the duration of the infusion, to monitor for possible allergic reactions.

Gamma globulin is the same thing as immunoglobulin.

Those poor kids suffered so I could try this. I feel guilty. I'm just another overprivileged gay white male with a cushy job and private insurance. Suspicious of the high prices, and slightly taken aback by my doctor's enthusiasm, I wonder if kickbacks are part of the deal. Is this another insurance scam? I don't know anyone else on this protocol. I have a feeling you couldn't get gamma globulin on Medicare. But it's not as if everybody can gain access to d4T, which is still in phase-three trials. Am I just wallowing in Jewish-liberal guilt combined with survival guilt? Should I continue to wallow in it? Better to wallow alive than dead.

Before my first infusion, I have to undergo a nutritional counseling session at Hema-suction's office. I schedule it for 1:00 P.M., during my lunch hour. What could be more appropriate? I had been planning on seeing a nutritionist for the past three years, but I never got around to it. I was a little leery of the ones my friends recommended, especially the vegetarians on kelp diets. Well, one less item to check off from my "to do" list.

I generally try to schedule appointments during lunch or right after work. I seem to have so many appointments with so many doctors that I fear I'll use up all my sick time on regularly scheduled checkups. I also like to keep a little flexibility for those ubiquitous demos I just can't stop myself from going to. And it would be nice to have an occasional vacation. I'm saving those days off from work for a rainy day, and I fear the extended weather forecast is ominous. If I hadn't moved from that hell-hole in Hell's Kitchenette and done the yuppie co-op thing, I wouldn't have to worry about time off at all: I'd probably be on disability. Edmund White himself, the reign-ing queen of gay literature, according to *Time* magazine, where he mysteriously grew to six feet (I'm sure I was mistaken, due to his bad posture), even asked me why I was still working and not just writing before some benefit where we were reading a few months ago. I don't know. Fear of poverty, I guess. Maybe an element of mortal terror of the standard health care in the U.S. for the underprivileged.

I can schedule infusions at home, after work. That means three fewer days a month at the gym. Not that I'm compulsive or anything. The gym thing has sort of gone to hell this past year. Three times a week is a reasonable goal now.

As usual, I bring my anal-retentive self to the Hemasuction office five minutes early. There's no way to go cross-town with public transportation. I have to rush through the jackhammer-filled streets of Manhattan on a balmy afternoon.

It's April 21, Secretaries' Day, which means the entire support staff is out for lunch indefinitely. My nutritional counselor ushers me into her office at twenty minutes past one. I'd be fine if I had eaten something since nine-thirty, because I'm slightly hypo-glycemic. My friend Glenn Person always carried an apple in his backpack. But then, he was a triathlete who burned up to 4,000 calories a day. He died of AIDS back in 1987, half a year after completing the Ironman in Hawaii.

Nancy L. (R.N., M.S.) hands me an easy-to-read booklet about nutrition for people with HIV. It's written in basic English. No Proustian memoirs here. Patiently, she goes over the information in the booklet, a health teacher giving a watered-down lecture with slides for the benefit of the slower members of the class. Surely she's not addressing her concerns toward me? I'll listen out of politeness. She seems to be talk-ing to someone who's already on death's doorstep. I look around and realize it's a class of one.

Am I deluding myself? Am I really sick? Is this stage fifteen of denial? Should I continue the ruse of working and working out? Why waste these last few remaining years, days, hours, in a heinous job, when I could be devoting all my time to writing? Perhaps because I seem to write only about AIDS, and that would make it that much worse, more present.

I lie about my general eating habits. Well, I stretch the truth. I pretend I have been following the American Association of Dietary Fiber and General Roughage's Minimum Adult Daily Requirements religiously. I always eat a well-balanced combination from the seven food groups. I don't eat more than two eggs a week. I have pork only on alternate Tuesdays. I go crazy for big, leafy vegetables. I chew on birch bark to aid digestion thrice daily. But I throw in some snacks just so it will sound plausible. An oatmeal cookie at four. A brownie before bed. And Nancy likes this, even more than my hypothetical well-balanced meals.

Instead of orange juice for breakfast, she suggests one of those nectars loaded with calories. Eat at McDonald's, she continues. Eat your favorite foods. Maybe put on five or ten extra pounds. It's always better to have that margin of safety.

Make foods more caloric. Try Carnation Instant Breakfast. Add milk powder to beverages. Carry around a few granola bars. Use blue cheese or Russian dressing.

To my chagrin, I find that not only is sushi outlawed (I knew that: deadly toxo lurks in raw fish), but so is brie. Soft, runny cheeses are on the list of no-nos. Hysterical, that afternoon I call up my very best friend in the whole world, John Palmer Weir, Jr. "How can I be a card-carrying homo without brie?"

"There's still quiche," he points out. "We'll always have quiche."

"Thank God," I say. "I thought it was Paris," I mutter to myself.

"Check your weight once a week. Watch out for wasting syndrome," warns Nancy. Sure. I'll do my best to keep on the lookout. And I promise never again to get anxious or think of the word *elephant*.

Gamma globulin can take up to four hours; pentamidine can take up to two. I schedule my first two infusions for 5:30 P.M. on successive days one week after my nutritional counseling, which means I have to leave for work at precisely 8:30 A.M. because it takes exactly thirty minutes to walk to work, including a stop to pick up breakfast (poppyseed bagel with butter, orange juice) and the newspapers (*The New York Times*, *New York Newsday*). I'm a little nervous. Binky will be there. He was on his way to Florida for a four-day vacation when he remembered that tomorrow was Davey's first infusion and he decided to come back. I could have asked him, but asking is so difficult for me, because I have heard the word *no* too many times, for the silliest of favors. I asked him if he could take the day off when we moved, and he didn't see why it was that important. "What do you need me for? We have movers." Well, he was in a bad mood because he had to teach a masters' class the day before the April 25 March on Washington and couldn't fly to D.C. because everything was booked and he didn't enjoy crowds in any event. So that Sunday he took off to Florida to visit some friends, who hadn't returned his phone calls because they were still in D.C. I returned from D.C. to see a note on the table. Binky said he would be away for four days. I mentally adjusted my schedule. When the boyfriend's away, the mice will play. I started planning a toga party for Tuesday, and a pool party in the Jacuzzi for Wednesday. Then I remembered I had infusions scheduled on both those nights. He called later that night and told me he was coming back on Monday.

Our latest knock-down drag-out concerned our housewarming. I know we should have discussed it before Binky was faced with the absurd image of my alphabetizing the ninety-five invitations on the floor. I invited everyone that I've fantasized not ex-changing bodily fluids with in the past five years, and a few women, too. Binky wanted to invite only those he would feel comfortable donating ten pints of blood to if they were in a car wreck. We should have had separate parties: one for those who reside in Chelsea, another for ACT UP members, another for pseudonymous drag colum-nists (both were on Fire Island that Sunday, of course), another one for writers, and another one for HIV-positives.

Nurse Perry calls me at work, apologizing. He doesn't want to disturb me on the job, but he's running late today.

Perry comes rolling a steel IV holder down the hallway at ten minutes to six, with boxes and boxes of gifts and exciting new houseware products. Only this time it isn't Hanover House, UPS, or International Male: It's Hemasuction. It's my lucky day! Seventy-five booklets filled with S&H green stamps, and I'm getting my own IV. Should I name it Iman or Twiggy?

"This is yours to keep." I'm so excited. "We try to respect your privacy. The neigh-bors, and all. We'll only be wheeling it in once. Some people use a nail in the ceiling instead of the IV pole." I figure that might cause a crimp in terms of mobility.

"Is it sturdy enough for a sling? I'm sorry, I guess I need two. Binky, would you mind signing up? You'll get your free IV pole, too, and then we can experiment." It's too tall for the bathroom shelves. I have to stick it in the dark, deep recesses of the closet in the bedroom. Can one hang a chandelier from it? I guess it will be useful for Maypole dances and tetherball games.

My visceral reaction is the same a property owner would have after finding out that the city was planning on opening an out-patient methadone clinic next door. NIMBY: Not in My Backyard. I never wanted to have a PC in my apartment; they re-mind me too much of my loathsome nine-to-five job, which involves data-processing equipment. But after my boss was fired I bought one, assuming that I was next in line, or that I would valiantly quit in protest of his firing. That was more than five years ago. Now my apartment is suffused with pills, prescriptions, pharmaceuticals, and prophylactic devices, medical and otherwise. The mirrored bathroom cabinet is nearly bursting with salves, ointments, and drugs. It's a good thing that Binky isn't a hypochondriac. Mercifully, he has escaped the homosexual addiction to expensive skin- and hair-care products that so many are afflicted with. There just isn't any room. If he were HIV-positive, perhaps we could share prescriptions as well as tank tops.

Perry gives me an allergy kit filled with decongestants, anti-inflammatories, hydro-cortisones, and steroids. The supplies come in a box with the Hemasuction insignia. Unfortunately for me, the insignia is on the top and the bottom of the box, so when I flatten it out for recycling, it shows no matter on which side I turn it. Instead of putting it in the compacter room on my floor, I stash it downstairs after midnight with the rest of the recyclables. Thank God for my housewares-supply shelves. I rhapsodize once more on the miles of tiles and endless storage space that Leonard, the former owner of this apartment, has bequeathed me. The infectious-waste container will be stored on the floor of the supply closet, in the back.

"Now, which one of you is David?" asks Perry.

"He is," we say, pointing at each other.

Perry and Binky manage to pry me from the ceiling a good twenty minutes later. I leave claw marks in the paint.

Perry has a British accent. He may or may not be a repressed or closeted homosexual. He's a bit stuffy; he seems to have mild vestiges of that class thing going on: the neighborhood deteriorating, the slightly stiff and superior poise, and all. But I feel no prick when he sticks me.

I look away as he sticks me. I don't like the sight of blood, especially my own. I used to stare as my doctor took my blood, and watch it fill the tubes. "It's quite warm, people don't expect that," he said as he handed me several tubes to drop off with the receptionist. I imagine it's the image of an icy-cold test tube. Blood comes out bright crimson and then bleeds to wine-dark red. I avert my eyes. They remain averted for a long time. Finally, Binky can't resist telling me in a sarcastic voice, "You can look now."

Perry comes to the rescue. "You're next."

I want to be in the ads in *The New England Journal of Medicine* for trouble-free infusion: riding a horse, swimming, at the discotheque, even having my period. I want to be photographed by Annie Leibovitz dragging an IV pole with fluids behind me as I water-ski in the latest Gap wear. I live for publicity. But at the last moment I lose my nerve and tell Binky I'd rather he not take a photo for the album delineating my decline and fall: Davey's First Infusion, smiling ever so bravely, fighting against tears, one arm held high in mock strength: For those of us who are about to infuse, we salute you.

During the infusion there are questions to answer, there is paperwork to sign. Perry is my personal flight attendant, armed with a mélange of items and busywork to keep me amused during the flight. I wait in vain for a first-class upgrade to a pump infusion, or at least for my complimentary soft drink and foil-wrapped peanuts.

I have one pathetic moment: dragging the IV behind me as I go to the bathroom. In that moment I feel like all my friends who've ever been in the hospital. Many never got out. I feel like my grandmother in the Jewish Home for the Aged.

I am left with a bruise on my right arm on the inside of my elbow. I'll just say that my boyfriend and I are exploring our sexuality in new directions that involve electrical cables and bludgeons. I consider marking the sites of future infusions in a connect-the-dots motif so after six months I will have a serviceable tattoo or at least a minor constellation.

Perry warns me that I may be peeing a lot with all this extra fluid. I wake up the next morning with an erection, which, alas, dissipates after I urinate. I used to wake up almost always with an erection (preferably not my own). This hardly ever happens now.

Some people report a huge boost of energy after gamma globulin. With me, it is less a burst of energy than a lack of utter exhaustion. For the past few months I would drag myself home after work and desperately need to lie down for a half hour. I feel more as if I've stabilized to something close to normal—perhaps what I've been missing the past two years without even realizing it. Okay, so I scrubbed the tiles in the bathroom for five hours—is that unusual? Perhaps for me, who finds a scrub brush as alien as a clitoris. I have been exclusively homosexual for the past thirty-six years, and am not about to break a perfect record.

The following night I get my first pentamidine infusion. It is over in an hour. Everything tastes a bit rank and metallic after the pentamidine, for a day or so.

I stuff my gym clothes and towel into the plastic bag with the Hemasuction logo and force myself to take it to the gym. I want to accept this next stage as soon as possible.

"Be prepared" is my motto. Which is why I rushed home after work—I didn't want to miss my infusion—and stacked the six new CDs on my CD player, including the new super-air-brushed Lulu, which looks as if she uses Wite-Out instead of makeup, made sure I had enough reading material and letters to answer, and then I sank into the futon couch, and of course I could not leave without assistance. Wayne came over in the middle of the infusion with the wrong brand of ginger ale and mandarin-orange flavored seltzer water. (Is it possible to be allergic to mandarin-orange flavor?) At least he didn't get peach. So we sat and giggled and looked at photographs in my album, and I apologized for not walking him to the door, since I was encumbered, and he left, and then of course he came back five minutes later because he forgot his sunglasses, which were right on the table, and I had to drag my fucking IV to the door, and it got caught and twisted, and I made faces like the eleven-year-old girl in the movie *Airplane* whose IV keeps getting dislodged when the singing nun strums her guitar and swings it for the entertainment of the plane. I love Wayne. I guess he should have my keys. Binky gets angry whenever I give keys away. I guess that's because that's how we got together. I gave him my keys too early.

My very best friend in the entire world, John Palmer Weir, Jr., to whom my entire writing output is dedicated, came over to sit through the second pentamidine, which was a total of only forty-five minutes of drip. I always used to watch the needles; now I just avert my eyes. But John Weir was making a conscious effort to show me that nothing human offended him; he wanted to show me it was okay. I knew it was okay. I asked him, but *noooooooo*, he had to stare in shock and horror and revulsion as Manny the nurse stuck me, and Manny wasn't that used to doing this sort of thing in the home environment because even though I have excellent veins—indeed, I've entered them in competitions and always gotten at least honorable mention—he was used to hospitals, Perry said, where the patient can be tied down with straps or something or other, and he stabbed me and I bled and John's eyes turned to saucers, and even though I didn't want to look it was as if his eyes were reflecting what was going on, which I didn't want to know; one could see the depth of the sorrow and the pity; it was like watching a twenty-hour movie about the Holocaust in his eyes. Manny tells me that he had a wonderful time skiing in Colorado last winter, and I stifle the impulse to tell him how politically incorrect it is of him to travel to Colorado: Hasn't he heard of the boycott? What about the political ramifications? Because he is the one sticking the needle into me.

Afterward John Weir admitted it wasn't particularly pleasant watching me get sticked. I chided him repeatedly, which both of us enjoyed, as we are unnatural. But afterward we went and saw the new Sharon Stone movie, which was really the new William Baldwin movie, in which he relinquished his shirt repeatedly and he was so entrancing we have no idea at all how badly he acted.

Next month I plan on watching the entire Galsworthy saga on videocassette. Unfortunately, I've run out of William Baldwin movies.

And now I can't stop eating. I never miss my cookie snack in the afternoon, my brownie before bedtime. I'm gaining weight at an appallingly slow rate. Farewell, flat stomach, forever. I fear it would bode ill should it ever reappear, for that would mean I was back on the way down, approaching my Christ-on-the-Cross-in-Auschwitz phase. More likely I will end up with a bloated Biafran belly. Too much gas.

My hunger is uncontrollable. Like Marilyn Chambers, I'm insatiable. I am eating when I'm not even hungry. I have subconsciously internalized the *Diseased Pariah News* maxim "Get fat, don't die!" Like Sylvia Plath, I eat men like air. My sexual hunger has been displaced. And when I become too weak to cook and shop and the boyfriend is anywhere but here, I can always thank heaven for takeout.

But somewhere in the pit of my stomach, I worry. Will my fragile physical equilibrium allow this to happen? I don't think so.

∾

I can think of few sights more terrifying than my itemized statement from Chubb dated 6-15-93, covering three infusions. The bill totaled $3,923.35. Five items listed under medical supplies totaling $3,503.35 are marked with code 53: "Pending receipt of information requested from other sources." The remaining item, "Registered nurse," is marked code 13: "Benefits are limited to the reasonable and customary amount." Chubb feels that $75 is reasonable for a registered nurse, not $300; $75 covered at 80 percent yields $60. Thus Chubb is issuing a draft to Apple Stat for $60 out of a bill for $3,923.35.

After seventeen frantic phone calls to Hemasuction, Chubb LifeAmerica, my doctor, my accountant, my crisis-intervention counselor, my personal trainer, and the Psychic HelpLine, the situation is straightened out. As the Clintons hold a series of private meetings to determine how this country will achieve universal health care, I sit on my futon couch and stare at the plastic bag of precious liquid as it drips into my arm; I sit huddled into a tiny ball, still as a statue, emotionally distraught, wondering who the hell is going to pay for my next infusion.

David Sedaris

Born in Binghampton, New York, and raised in Raleigh, North Carolina, David Sedaris (b. 1956) was selected by *Time* as Humorist of the Year in 2001 and for the Thurber Award. He won national attention with his *SantaLand Diaries*, performed on National Public Radio, in which he recounted his experiences as an elf in Macy's department store during the Christmas season.

With his sister Amy Sedaris he has written several plays, including *Stump the Host* (1993), *Stitches* (1994), *One Woman Shoe* (1995), *The Little Frieda Mysteries* (1997), and *The Book of Liz* (2002), but he is better known for his collections of essays and memoirs, starting with *Barrel Fever* (1994), *Naked* (1997), and *Me Talk Pretty One Day* (2000). He is now a regular contributor to the *New Yorker* and lives in France. The piece below is from *Dress Your Family in Corduroy and Denim* (2004).

Hejira

IT WASN'T ANYTHING I had planned on, but at the age of twenty-two, after dropping out of my second college and traveling across the country a few times, I found myself back in Raleigh, living in my parents' basement. After six months spent waking at noon, getting high, and listening to the same Joni Mitchell record over and over again, I was called by my father into his den and told to get out. He was sitting very formally in a big, comfortable chair behind his desk, and I felt as though he were firing me from the job of being his son.

I'd been expecting this to happen, and it honestly didn't bother me all that much. The way I saw it, being kicked out of the house was just what I needed if I was ever going to get back on my feet. "Fine," I said, "I'll go. But one day you'll be sorry."

I had no idea what I meant by this. It just seemed like the sort of thing a person should say when he was being told to leave.

My sister Lisa had an apartment over by the university and said that I could come stay with her as long as I didn't bring my Joni Mitchell record. My mother offered to drive me over, and after a few bong hits I took her up on it. It was a fifteen-minute trip across town, and on the way we listened to the rebroadcast of a radio call-in show in which people phoned the host to describe the various birds gathered around their backyard feeders. Normally the show came on in the morning, and it seemed strange to listen to it at night. The birds in question had gone to bed hours ago and probably had no idea they were still being talked about. I chewed this over and wondered if anyone back at the house was talking about *me*. To the best of my knowledge, no one had ever tried to imitate my voice or describe the shape of my head, and it was depressing that I went unnoticed while a great many people seemed willing to drop everything for a cardinal.

My mother pulled up in front of my sister's apartment building, and when I opened the car door she started to cry, which worried me, as she normally didn't do things like that. It wasn't one of those "I'm going to miss you" things, but something sadder and more desperate than that. I wouldn't know it until months later, but my father had kicked me out of the house not because I was a bum but because I was gay. Our little talk was supposed to be one of those defining moments that shape a person's adult life, but he'd been so uncomfortable with the most important word that he'd left it out completely, saying only, "I think we both know why I'm doing this." I guess I could have pinned him down, I just hadn't seen the point. "Is it because I'm a failure? A drug addict? A sponge? Come on, Dad, just give me one good reason."

Who wants to say that?

My mother assumed that I knew the truth, and it tore her apart. Here was yet another defining moment, and again I missed it entirely. She cried until it sounded as if she were choking. "I'm sorry," she said. "I'm sorry, I'm sorry, I'm sorry."

I figured that within a few weeks I'd have a job and some crummy little apartment. It didn't seem insurmountable, but my mother's tears made me worry that finding these things might be a little harder than I thought. Did she honestly think I was that much of a loser?

"Really," I said, "I'll be fine."

The car light was on and I wondered what the passing drivers thought as they watched my mother sob. What kind of people did they think we were? Did they think she was one of those crybaby moms who fell apart every time someone chipped a coffee cup? Did they assume I'd said something to hurt her? Did they see us as just another crying mother and her stoned gay son, sitting in a station wagon and listening to a call-in show about birds, or did they imagine, for just one moment, that we might be special?

Essex Hemphill

Essex Hemphill (1957–1995) was born in Chicago and died in Philadelphia, but he is associated mostly with Washington, D.C., where he grew up and was educated. A remarkable and daring performer, he appeared in three films, *Looking for Langston* (1989), *Tongues Untied* (1991), and *Black Is/Black Ain't* (1994). In all three films he helped to make black gay men visible to the black community.

In 1983 he teamed up with Wayson Jones and Larry Duckette to form Cinque, a performance poetry group devoted to black gay life. His break-through came when he appeared in Joseph Beam's important collection *In the Life: A Black Gay Anthology* (1985). As G. B. Mann points out, "Un-like the secrecy which shrouds who Langston loved, questions of who Essex Hemphill loved will never be asked." His writing is dedicated to the black gay cultural movement of the 1980s, a movement that has suffered disproportionately from AIDS. Hemphill died of AIDS-related complications in 1995.

Ceremonies

I STOOD BEFORE HIM grinning, my undershorts and pants were down around my knees. I trembled and panted as he stroked me. After weeks of being coaxed and teased to come by, I had finally succumbed to George's suggestions. I had sneaked up to the store very early that morning, before it opened, after my mother left for work.

The sexual hunger that would eventually illuminate my eyes began then. I was a skinny little fourteen-year-old Black boy, growing up in a ghetto that had not yet suffered the fatal wounds and injuries caused by drugs and Black-on-Black crime.

My neighborhood, my immediate homespace, was an oasis of strivers. A majority of the families living on my block owned their homes. My sexual curiosity would have blossomed in any context, but in Southeast Washington, D.C., where I grew up, I had to carefully allow my petals to unfold. If I had revealed them too soon they would surely have been snatched away, brutalized, and scattered down alleys. I was already alert enough to know what happened to the flamboyant boys at the school who were called "sissies" and "faggots." I could not have endured then the violence and indignities they often suffered.

George was at least thirty years older than I, tall, and slightly muscular beneath his oversized work clothes which consisted of khakis, a cotton short-sleeved shirt, and a white apron. He wore black work boots similar to those of construction workers. Many of the boys in the neighborhood teased him viciously, but I hadn't understood before the morning he and I were together just what motivated them to be cruel and nasty by turn. At that time, I didn't know that George had initiated most of the boys I knew, and some of their older brothers, one by one, into the pleasures of homo sex.

Only months before my visit to him that April morning, I had roamed the parking lot of a nearby country bar—my adolescent desire drove me out there one night, and one night only—discreetly asking the predominately white patrons if they would let me suck their dicks for free. My request was never fulfilled because I believe the men were shocked that I would so boldly solicit them. I was lucky no one summoned the police to come for me. I was lucky I wasn't dragged off to some nearby wooded area and killed.

George was a white man. My initiation into homo sex was guided by the hands of a white man. The significance of this in a racial context was not lost on me, but it wasn't a concern strong enough to check my desire. For weeks George had whispered he wanted to suck my dick. Catching me alone in the store or responding to my request for a particular product, he would quickly serve me, seizing the opportunity to whisper in my ear. *And I was listening.*

Eventually I went to the store on pretense, requesting something I knew they wouldn't have, such as a specific brand of soap or floor wax, just so he would wait on me and whisper. If we had been caught when we finally began fucking, the law would have charged him with molesting and sodomizing me as a minor because of my age, but the law would not have believed that I wanted him to suck my dick. I wanted him to touch me. I wanted to fuck his ass. I, willingly, by the volition of my own desires, engaged in acts of sexual passion, somewhat clumsily, but nonetheless sure of my decision to do so.

When George liberated his equally swollen cock from his pants it sprang out engorged with blood and fire. The head of it was deep pink in color. I was startled to see that the hair surrounding it was as red as the hair on his head.

George again lowered himself to eye level with my cock and drew me into his mouth once more. It was hard to tell which of us was enjoying the cock sucking more. Suddenly, he pulled his mouth off my wet shaft, got up off his knees and hurried to the front of the store. He promptly returned with a short stack of grocery bags, newspapers, and a small jar of Vaseline.

"You're gonna fuck me." It wasn't a statement or a command from him, it was a fact neither of us could turn away from.

After spreading the newspaper and bags on the floor behind the deli counter to create a makeshift paper pallet, George opened the Vaseline, scooped out some with his index finger, and pushed it up into his asshole. He turned his back to me so I could see the pink entrance of his anus being penetrated by the steady in and out motion of his finger. My dick was so hard I thought it would break into a thousand pieces of stone around our feet. The lips of his asshole kissed and sucked his finger as he pushed it in and out, in and out. After thoroughly greasing his asshole, George then scooped out more Vaseline and smeared it all over my dick.

"Ahh! Ahh!" I sighed out in pleasure.

"Yeah, you're ready," he said approvingly, stroking me a few times more. Guided by George, who had now laid down upon the pallet and beckoned me to climb on, my cock, led by his hand, entered his ass in one smooth penetration. I didn't know at that moment that I would mount him all summer, night and day, and pour my adolescence into him. I would lie to get away from home and friends to be with him. I learned then that sneaking, ducking, and hiding were key components of a homo sex life simply because of the risk of exposure and the often devastating consequences.

I continued to visit George early in the morning before the store opened, fucking him at the back of the store behind the deli counter on bags and newspapers. I fucked him at his house at the end of his work day while his mongrel dog sat and watched us. From the spring through the late summer 1971, George was the focus of my sexuality. He was the veracity of my sexual desire.

As it would turn out, I became his sole sex partner that brief summer. I have often speculated that perhaps among all of the homeboys who passed through his hands, I was the one *wanting* to learn more. George knew this, and to the extent that he could exploit my youth for his pleasure I allowed myself to be exploited and fondled and sucked because I wanted this, too. I wanted him. I didn't come back to the store and tease him and curse him as did the other boys who had fucked him. I didn't demand money as some did. After their orgasms they resented him, but what they really resented was the recognition of their own *homo* sexual desire.

I kept silent about our activities. I would dare not say that we were in love. I wasn't sure I loved myself at fourteen but I knew that my dick got hard for George. Never once did I give any thought to the possibility that I might be committing some sin I would be punished for in hell. Sin was the furthest thing from my consciousness. Hell was around me in the ghetto of my adolescence.

My dick did not fall off in his mouth. I did not turn green from kissing him. I didn't burst into flames during our orgasms, nor did he. In fact, during orgasm, I often called out Jesus' name, which seemed appropriate for warding off such evil as I might have imagined we were committing. If anything, I was most concerned about being caught by my buddies or his co-workers. To this day I'm convinced other fellas didn't know that I, too, was being initiated by George. Our group identity and rapport did not allow for this kind of discussion or candor to occur.

I regret that we were never able to talk about our visits to George. I regret, too, that we were not able to sexually explore one another in the same way that we allowed George to explore us. Ours was truly a fragile, stereotypical Black masculinity that would not recognize homo desire as anything but perverse and a deviation from the expected "role" of a man. The ridicule we risked incurring would have condemned us to forever prove our "manhood" or succumb to being the target of a hatred that was, at best, a result of hating *self* for desiring to sexually touch the flesh of another male.

At fourteen, I was astute enough to know my mouth should not reveal any desire that would further endanger me. There was no "older" brother at home to stand watch over my blossoming manhood. There was no father there, either. I was solely responsible for myself—the eldest sibling, the eldest son. Neither of those absences is an explanation for my sexual identity. Only nature knows the reason why.

During that same summer that George introduced me to homoeroticism, my public acceptance as "one of the boys" was severely challenged. The night is so clear to me. It was mid-August, sultry, humid, August, and the anticipation of returning to school was in the air. My buddies, Tommy, Tyrone, Leon, Peanut, and Kevin, we were all across the street from my house talking with some of the older boys—David, George, Doug, Wayne, Kenny, and Leon's brother, Crip.

My mother's bedroom was located at the front of our house and her windows faced out to the street. Her windows were open because there was no air conditioning in the house at that time. The night breeze was as much relief as we could hope for from the oppressive Washington summers.

Across the street from my house, on Douglas's and Kenny's front porch, we were talking about everything from sports to girls. It was the typical conversation of males in various stages of adolescence. We all shined in the streetlights that beat down on our variously muscular frames burnished by the summer sun. Our conversation rose and fell, exerting its brashness and bravado against the night, kicking around in our heads, drawing us into laughter and silence by turns, as we listened to stories of pussy conquests, petty scams and recent ass kickings. The conversation was dominated by the older boys, who by turn tried to impart fragments of street warrior knowledge to us. We were sitting and standing, absorbing all this, relaxing our tough postures, allowing a communal trust to put us at ease and make us glib and attentive.

Crip was standing. I was sitting. It happened that where I sat I could eye his crotch with a slight shift of my eyes. Well, one of the times that I peeked, Crip caught me. I would soon discover that I had cruised very dangerous territory. Lulled by the conversation, I allowed myself to become intoxicated on the blossoming masculinity surrounding me. I might as well have been shooting semen from wet dreams straight into my veins for the high I was on in this gathering of males.

Instantly, Crip jumped forward and got in my face. "I see you looking at my dick!" he hurled at me. I felt as though he had accused me of breaking into his house and violating his mother. Immediately, all conversation ceased and all eyes focused on me and Crip.

"Do you wanna suck my big, Black dick, muthafucka?" he demanded, clutching his crotch and moving up into my face. "Do you, nigga?"

Thank God my instincts told me to stand up. It was this defensive posture that perhaps saved me from *absolute* humiliation, but my "No" was weak.

"Well, why are you looking at my dick? Is you a freak? You must wanna suck it. Are you a faggot? You can suck it, baby," he mockingly cooed, still clutching what was more than a handful of cock.

The fellas were laughing and slapping palms all around by this time. I was becoming visibly angry, but I had uttered nothing more than a meek "No" to his challenge. I then remembered my mother's bedroom windows; they were open; she must have heard him.

The laughter began to die down. The sexual tension in the air was palpable enough to be slapped around. Crip's attitude changed for the worse.

"You shouldn't be looking at a muthafucka's dick unless you plan to suck it," he sneered. It now seemed that all along he had been bellowing at me, so I was even more convinced my mother had heard him.

"Are you funny, nigga?" he asked, deadly serious, which elicited more raucous laughter from the fellas.

"No," I said, attempting to put more conviction in my voice. Crip was but an inch or two taller than me, and a pretty Black male. He carried beauty as agilely as some Black men carry footballs and basketballs and pride. I was surely attracted to him, but to even have hinted at that would have cost me more than the humiliation I endured that night.

So there we stood, me surrounded by gales of laughter punctuated by his booming voice, and all the time, in the back of my mind, I believe my mother was listening, in shock, hearing my humiliation. To her credit, if she overheard this she never confronted me with it.

Crip finally ended his tirade. The conversation resumed its boisterous, brash bravado. Shortly thereafter, I excused myself from the fellas, crossed the street, locked the door behind me, and cried myself to sleep in my bed. It would not be the last time I would cry myself to sleep because a male had inflicted me with emotional pain. It would not be the last time I would lock the door behind me and go to my bed alone, frightened of my sexuality and the desires I could not then speak of or name as clearly as I could articulate the dangers.

My sexual encounters with George ceased several weeks before summer vacation ended. In retrospect, I believe I stopped visiting him at the store and at his home as a direct result of the humiliation I suffered from Crip. I must have thought it would only be a matter of time before we would be discovered. Whatever my reasons, my refusal to engage in any more sex bewildered George. He continued to coax me to climb up on his back, but I could no longer be seduced. He enticed me with money but I refused that, too. When I was sent to the store by my mother, I would go two blocks out of the way to another convenience store just to avoid the longing I recognized in his eyes, a longing that was partially stoked by my mutual desire. I would later discover that such a longing inhabits the eyes of many homosexuals, particularly those who believe themselves to be unable to come out of the closet.

The school year resumed itself uneventfully. The only change, other than those occurring because of puberty, was the increasing burden of carrying a secret. I was learning to live with it safely hidden away, but for how long? It was surely dangerous knowledge. There was no one I could tell about my sexual adventures with George. There was no previous reference of intimacy to compare to sex. I continued nurturing my desire in the long nights of my adolescence, quietly masturbating in my bed as my younger brother slept above on the upper bunk.

Black male adolescent survival in a ghetto context made me realize the *necessity* of having a girlfriend, a female I could be seen walking home after school. It would be my luck to date girls who were "good," girls who were not going to experiment with sex beyond kissing and fondling, and even that was often only tolerated at a minimum if tolerated at all.

I was not the kind of male to force the issue of going all the way sexually. For me, it was enough to have a cover for my *true* desires, and that's what these girls were— covers. But I treated them with respect. They were girl *friends* more often than not.

I had the opportunity to have sex with one of the girls I dated. She agreed to skip school with me one day. We hid out at her house, our mutual motive: sex. After a long morning of petting and kissing the big moment arrived. We stumbled to her bedroom along an unfamiliar path that frightened and excited us. I was nervous because I expected her mother or father or one of her siblings to walk in and catch us.

In our adolescent nakedness we were beautiful, but if caught, we would have been seen as *being ugly*. We were sixteen and fifteen and ripe with curiosity and desire. Her skin was honey gold, smooth, so soft to my touch. Her breasts were full and sweet, the nipples brown and swollen by my tongue. Her hair was plaited in thick braids that coiled atop her head like snakes. We were both virgins. Nothing in our timid sex education classes at school or our evasive discussions at home had prepared us for walking into her bedroom to face our beautiful nakedness.

I believe we both felt we had to go through with the act because we had gone so far. In my mind, George appeared, but that was *different*. He had not instructed me about girls or young women. No one had. I kept hearing the older boys scat about breaking the cherry, but there was no cherry hanging between her legs when I looked. What was there was wet and warm to my fingers.

She laid so still on her bed. I knelt above her, fondling her breasts, kissing her, imagining these must be the things to do to seduce her. Neither of us spoke. As our breathing escalated I grabbed my cock and guided the head toward her vagina. She opened her legs to show me the mouth that was there, wet and waiting. Sunlight poured over us. Sweat bathed our bodies. We were straining ourselves to break rules we were taught not to break. We exerted ourselves against everything we were told not to do.

I pressed my head against the wet mouth. I pushed. She pulled away. I inched forward. Pushed. She pulled away again.

"Am I hurting you?" I asked nervously.

"Yes," she said softly.

"We don't have to do this," I assured her, saying this more for my comfort rather than her own. *I* didn't want to be doing this, after all.

"But I want to," she said. "I want to do this. It will make you—it will make *us* happy."

I rose up off her body. "Maybe this isn't the right time," I said. Looking down at her, I then realized how lovely she was and how little I knew of her. How little she *really* knew of me. I thought of George and a tingle stirred in my loins. I realized I didn't desire penetrating her. I was doing this for my reputation. I thought I needed to walk away with a bloody sheet to prove what—that I could break a hymen? I had no thought about consequences. There was no condom to prevent pregnancy, no pills being taken that I knew of. We were entangled in limbs we couldn't name, dry-throated, sweaty, pursuing different objectives in the afternoon bed we had stolen. My erection slowly fell. I lowered myself onto her again and kissed her lightly on the lips.

"We should probably get dressed," I encouraged her. "Someone might come home soon." That was the last and only time we were naked together. Not long after, we stopped seeing each other romantically.

A year later, she began dating an older boy around school. We saw each other less often, and then one day I saw her in a maternity blouse. I believe she finished school— I'm not sure—but by that time she wasn't my concern. I was seeing another "good girl," walking her home, holding her hand, pretending I was consumed by love—safe, by all appearances, from being identified as a faggot.

Wayne Koestenbaum

A poet and critic, Wayne Koestenbaum (b. 1960) is known for his quick-witted postmodern style and sensibility. The author of the groundbreaking study *The Queen's Throat: Opera, Homosexuality and the Mysteries of Desire* (1993), he has also written a biography, *Andy Warhol* (2001). His most recent volume of poetry is *Best-Selling Jewish Porn Films* (2006). The piece below, "The Aryan Boy," is from *Cleavage* (2000), which places side by side issues of ethnicity, politics, and sexuality in a manner that suggests that they are inseparable and unresolvable.

The Aryan Boy

Story

At some overnight nature retreat, long ago, outside of Berlin, my father woke to discover someone pissing on his head. It was the Aryan boy in the upper bunk. While my father told me this story, I was bathing, under his supervision; a plastic cup floated beside me in the soapy water.

I've often thought of this Aryan boy, circa 1936, pissing on my father's head, and of my position, naked in the tub, while he told me the story—one of the few anecdotes he passed on to me about his childhood in Nazi Germany.

Another story: Hitler paraded through the streets, and my father saluted him because everyone else was saluting. It was the thing to do.

Otherwise I heard little about tyranny.

Who knows if the boy in the story was really Aryan, or if I'm misremembering the story?

Cup

In the bathtub, I pissed in the plastic cup. Pissing in the cup produced a hard-on, but once the penis grew hard, pissflow paradoxically stopped. I liked to use the cup as a ladle, gathering bathwater to rinse shampoo suds out of my hair.

Enjoyable, to place the cup over one's newly emergent penis in the bathtub.

Galicia

On my mother's side, there were some shadowy relatives—I don't know their names—in Galicia. My mother remembers conversations in the early 1940s, late at night, at the Brooklyn kitchen table. Letters from Galicia. Nothing could be done to save these relations. I guess I'm Galician.

The window of my great-grandfather Wolf's jewelry shop in New York was smashed. Did that hate-filled atmosphere shape his son's character? At my grandfather's death, his unfinished project was a book about the Jew in American literature. "When did you stop being an observant Jew?" I asked him, and he said, "What are you talking about? I never stopped."

The Reproduction Story

My older brother had a new book, *The Reproduction Story*, about vagina and penis, secrets of mating, special feelings you develop for members of the opposite sex. I was taking a bath. My mother threw the book into the bathroom, saying "Your brother isn't old enough for this book." She was furious at him for some misdeed, sass, or subversion. He was in the doghouse. "Your brother's not mature enough for this book," she said, meaning, *The bastard's lost his right to learn the reproduction story.* Good. Now the story was my property. Naked in the tub, I read about gonads. I lost track of plot. I pissed into the plastic cup.

More on the Aryan Boy

A miracle, that piss stops once you want to come, that "come" and "piss" functions are dialectical, mutually exclusive.

Did my father consider the boy an Aryan? Was that the term? Or did my father simply call him Gentile? I should ask my father about that incident, but our rapport has diminished. The times of bathing, of pissing into the cup after he left the bathroom, are over. Just as well. But I should figure out whether his aunt's middle name was really Sarah or whether that was just the name the Germans put on her visa to signify her race.

More on the Aryan Boy Pissing

"How are babies conceived?" I asked my older brother, and he told me, "Daddy pisses in Mommy." Therefore from the beginning of time I knew that such relations were degrading.

More on Pissing

Is urine a home remedy? Two scholars—women—were swimming in the ocean. A jellyfish stung one. So the other pissed on her colleague's sting: a proven antidote.

When you piss in the ocean you are not ejecting fluid; rather, you are accepting fluid's absence. You are deciding that you don't want to hold in those muscles, that your liquids sympathize with the saline surround; you want intimacy with coral, crabs, jellyfish, and wrack. That's probably why the little girl in *The Exorcist* pissed on her parents' fancy rug during their dinner party. She wanted to make a big Satanic statement. She wanted to show exactly what she thought of their Georgetown regime. My next step in life is to identify with the possessed girl in *The Exorcist.*

Keith Writes:

"This is how my lover and I met, at a sleaze bar (now closed), getting our fill in the restroom. . . . We both like to give as well as receive golden showers. Meeting others into this 'sport' is becoming impossible. We display our yellow hankies proudly—and sometimes our wet crotches!—only to receive puzzled looks and outright stares. This is in leatherbars! Can you put us in touch with groups, organizations?" (*Honcho*, April 1994.)

Orgasm

I was naked in the tub. My father said, "And I woke to discover I was all wet." Or he said, "I wondered where the liquid was coming from." Or he said, "And I looked up and there was the Aryan bully, pissing on my head." Meanwhile I was ensconced in Mr. Bubble.

There is a time in life when one's own penis—if one has a penis—is a negligible article of faith.

This is what passed through my mind as my very first hand-manipulated orgasm approached: "There's no way I'm going to mess up this clean bathtub with my spermy stuff." So I stopped. For weeks afterward I thought I'd irreparably damaged my potential to come, because I'd interrupted that originary burst.

She Didn't Say a Word

My grandfather said, of his mother, "She never once raised her voice." This was a compliment. She never raised her voice to her husband, Wolf, who translated the Bible into Yiddish at night: during the day he was a jeweler with a broken shopwindow. Wayne stands for Wolf; shared W, meager memorial.

More on the Cup

My fundamentalist friend lay naked on his bathroom throw rug. I said, "I've discovered a neat trick. Look." And I put the bathroom cup over my hard penis. I wanted to teach him secrets of the cup. But he had other plans. He said, "Lie on top of me." My fundamentalist friend wanted me to fuck him. I said, "No way." Then he decided we should stay up past midnight playing World War II strategy games.

Perhaps I misremember the story. I might have wanted to fuck the fundamentalist; he might have said, "No way." Or perhaps no mention of intercourse was made. Perhaps he simply said, "Let me lie on top of you."

In my own fashion I, too, am a fundamentalist. I believe in the fundament and I believe in these fundamentals.

Prosthetic Math

I believed the math teacher's penis was prosthetic because I'd seen it hang loose and inanimate like a stale *bûche de Noël* out of his pants at the urinal.

The squirt named Wasserman who sent a thank-you card to the math teacher: was Wasserman Jewish, too, and did that explain his safari shirt and his friendship with the math teacher with prosthetic penis and recipe for Waldorf salad tucked between algorithmic pages? Even then I thought of Wasserman as Water Man.

Shake It Out

Shake it out afterward, my father wisely said. Smart man. I'm sure he showed me how to shake it out, but there's always more dribble than science can account for. At what exact moment in sexual arousal is the flow of urine stopped? Do you have to wash your hands after pissing? Rumor has it, urine is hygienic. I suppose humiliation has nothing to do with masculinity, my father and I have nothing to do with masculinity, and shaking the penis out after pissing to make sure there are no leftover dribble drops has nothing to do with masculinity.

Tyranny

Kobena Mercer wrote that we have plenty of discussions about desire and pleasure but not enough about "pain and hatred as everyday structures of feeling." I agree. To "pain and hatred," I would add "tyranny." Tyranny is an everyday structure of feeling. We do not have enough discussions of tyranny's mundanity; everyone who analyzes tyranny pretends not to be friends with it, but what if finally we narrated our tyrannic urges?

My Father Saluting Hitler

It was a parade; my father didn't know better. My father, little Jewish boy, saluted Hitler. Someone must have found it cute, someone else must have found it not cute. Up went my father's hand in mimic salute.

One Problem with This Discourse

is that it sounds like a victim's, or like the discourse of someone who considers himself a victim. I must find a way not to sound the victim note. I must find a way to speak as tyrant, not because I want to be a tyrant or become more tyrannical but because there is little about my desire or my death that does not fall under the heading *tyranny*.

Call Masculinity Tyranny and See What Happens

My mother did the disciplinary work—for example, when she threw *The Reproduction Story* like dog food into the bathroom while I lay in the tub.

I always wondered about the difference between breasts in men and breasts in women, and I prayed I would not grow up to become a man with breasts, though now in retrospect I realize that the male chests I feared (men at the beach, men in my family) were just fatty muscles, good pectorals gone to seed. I looked down at my chest to make sure that it did not protrude. I longed for absolute flatness, but also at other moments was eagerly stuffing crumpled paper towels in my shirt to simulate *La Dolce Vita*'s Anita Ekberg.

"Visit the Rabbi while You're in Venice"

my grandfather said, and I wondered why I should waste time in Venice visiting the rabbi. Why squander an afternoon visiting the ghetto, I thought, when there are so many more uplifting tourist sites? My grandfather wanted to prove that Robert Browning was a Jew; I wondered why anyone would bother.

I tell my imaginary son, "Visit the sleaze bars while you're in Venice." I'm sure I feel the same wash of sentiment, anger, pride, self-righteousness, and victimization about queerness that my grandfather felt about Jewishness.

Ice Cube

Ice cube my grandfather sucked as he died: so my mother told me. Hard to take in moisture while you're dying, I suppose, so he sucked an ice cube—or, rather, my grandmother brought the ice cube to his lips. My mother has his features, and I have my mother's: slim mean face, hysteric brown button eyes that will not see the other side of the equation.

Someone must bring ice to the dying man's lips, quenching tyrannic thirst, like the thirst of Prometheus, tied to the rock, liver eaten by vultures. Find the rock we're tied to, find the source of the rivets.

Where Prometheus Pissed

Right on the rock. Tied to rock eternally he pissed right where he was tied. That was part of the Promethean picture. I suppose the rock was in the middle of the ocean, so the piss just washed off the sides of the rock and blended with the wandering sea. You piss where you are bound. When Prometheus was thirsty, my grandmother was not there to give him a taste of ice cube wrapped in handkerchief.

Nun Jew

My mother said "Nun Jew" to refer to non-Jews. "Nun," as in *The Flying Nun*. Does it matter what words you use? It matters what words you use.

Nun Jew Cum

The first time I swallowed cum I didn't care what I was swallowing. The second time I swallowed cum I gargled afterward with Listerine. The first two times were Nun Jew Cum. I don't remember the third time I swallowed cum. That's how it is with origins.

Agoraphobia

I once knew a therapist who treated agoraphobics in their own houses. She'd visit them, help them overcome their fear of agoras. My father voted for Nixon because of the Israel question. My father usually based his votes on the Israel question. Long ago as part of a Sunday-school project I gave money to plant a tree in Israel. I didn't know what Israel was. I thought Israel was a country that needed shade. The space of this discourse—these words, here—is agoraphobic. I am visiting my own discourse in its house to see if I can help it overcome its fear of the agora. If you never leave your house, can you do damage? You can do damage inside your house, but can you do damage outside your house if you never leave it?

I Imagine

that the Aryan boy was once my father's friend but then the boy turned Aryan in ideology and pissed on my father's head, but the pain of the incident lies in the Aryan boy's betrayal, his flight from peaceful boyhood into Aryan identification, his movement from friend-of-my-father into Aryan thug. It is not possible today to say something absolute about history or hatred, but it is possible to say I was naked in the tub and that a story infiltrated my constitution; it is possible to speak about the bathwater and my water-logged skin; it is possible to say I remember my father laughing as he told me this story. Have I misconstrued it? Maybe the boy who pissed on his head was actually a Jew. In 1936 (or a few years earlier) could my father have shared a bunk bed with an Aryan? In any case, I remember my father chuckling as he told me the story.

Transferred to a Jewish School

My father liked to eat mashed carrots, sweetened, in a bowl.

Before long, he transferred to a Jewish school.

Idyllic black-and-white photo of my father at five years old in Berlin, naked, in the yard of his house, unselfconsciously urinating on the flowers or the ferns with a small and not yet interesting penis: if I were merely imagining this picture, I would tell you, but I am not merely imagining it.

Why Didn't Someone Just Shoot Hitler

In *Triumph of the Will*, Hitler moves along a row of soldiers, shaking their hands. Leni Riefenstahl filmed it so that he stares directly into the viewer's eyes, as if to shake the viewer's hand. I stare right into his eyes when he reaches his hand out to clasp mine. That is how Riefenstahl planned it. I have no other place to look.

I find many propagandistic manipulations seductive, including Wagner, but I draw the line at *Triumph of the Will*: I do not find its panoramas seductive. I expected I would find the near-naked Nazis boys attractive, showering in preparation for the rally. I'm relieved to find them scrawny. I'm relieved to know that I might not have found the Aryan boy attractive as he leaned over and let pour onto my head his golden arc.

Gil Cuadros

Gil Cuadros (1962–1996) published only one book, *City of God* (1994), and it was written under the specter of AIDS. Writing the book, he wrote, "literally saved my life or at least extended my life." Given two years to live in 1987, he did challenge the odds. But the selection below is not about AIDS; it is about a childhood memory of growing up in a Hispanic family. It is a recollection of the childhood play that occurs just before sexual awareness.

Chivalry

WHEN I TURNED NINE, my relatives thought there must be something genetically wrong with me, some inherent defect in their first-born sons. My cousin Rolando, crib death. My cousin David, "half-retarded." Me, they couldn't put their finger on it. They were annoyed whenever I spoke, and they thought I whispered intentionally, kept things hidden. And then one day I cut my wrists.

Every Easter my Grandma Lupe would pray novenas for David and me. I would receive a letter from her with a charcoal drawing of Jesus at Gethsemane, and a note saying a novena had been prayed for me. When I was younger, she'd send along five dollars, folded in tissue. My mother fussed and said, "Your grandma isn't rich, you should be very grateful to her." When I turned nine, a week before Easter, I cut my wrists. Then she sent twenty dollars and a bronze medallion of St. Christopher. My mother called her and made arrangements for me to visit during the summer for the month.

It was my second near-death experience. The first had been a near-drowning the year before. Grandma had then sent ten dollars with a novena. It was an incident I couldn't explain. Near where my family was having a reunion, I suddenly found myself underwater. My feet were tied in fishing line and algae at the lake's bottom. The story of cutting myself was similar; my wrists were bleeding, my arms were outstretched, and I had no idea how it started. I tried to explain to my folks, "I was taking out the trash and . . ." Both looked in horror as I came through the kitchen door, my father leaving for work on the night shift. My mother could only say "Aye!" as she grabbed kitchen towels to hold my blood in. My father sat back in a chair and said, "You won't be satisfied until you're dead."

My grandma lived with my Uncle Steve and Tia Gloria off the highway near Delano. They shared a small farm with four other families. My uncle looked like my father only thinner, the back of his neck wrinkled and dark. He worked for Del Monte fixing machines, conveyor belts, and irrigation systems. Sometimes my cousin David worked there, during canning season, throwing bad fruit off the line, taking home a crate of bruised peaches or tomatoes and a few extra dollars. Grandma would pack bean burritos for his lunch. It was simple work for him, the family said. Driving me up, Uncle Steve said few words, used hand gestures to say, "Can you move the side mirror to the left?" Their driveway had a gravel embankment that didn't allow for a surprise visit, small rocks banged off tires and into the truck's sidewalls. David jumped up and down, his tall thin body spinning around when he saw us drive up. His father sucked in his breath, a tinge of disgust that his fourteen-year-old would act like this. My uncle tried to shoo David away from the truck, yelling out the window, "What did I tell you, David, just what did I tell you?" The front yard was fenced in with tall white-washed planks, on top, weather vanes of all kinds spun from the traffic's wind. On the other side of the highway, tracks ran through a field of wheat grass and barbed-wire fences. As I got out of the cab, David kissed me on the cheek, spun me in his embrace. I let out a nervous laugh. He was the only one I would let do this.

David rambled on about how he caught a ton of pollywogs in the stream nearby. "We can go tomorrow." And that we could sleep in the farmhouse all summer and there was the lake. You can grab sun fish with your bare hands. We can go swimming and he can teach me. My tia came out of the back kitchen door, her hands drying a wet casserole dish. "Don't you think you should see your grandmother first before you go running off?" David grabbed me by the arm and said "I'll show him."

Grandma had the calmest room in the house. It was dark, with fans blowing from every corner, a sweet aroma of rose water mixed with mentholated ointment. The rest of the house sweltered. A small TV flickered a Mexican soap opera while my grandmother sat on the edge of her bed. She smiled from the craziness; a fat man in a multi-colored polka dot shirt talked loudly, his voice changing octaves every sentence. Her *panza* giggled as she laughed, repeating the words the man said. "*Mijo*, come here," she said. I let her rock me in her arms, my hands pressed to the side, the cold wrinkles of her face against my eye. There wasn't much I could say. She spoke only Spanish and I was taught only English. She took my hands up, looked at the insides of my wrists and then led me to another part of her room. On a table stood a plaster statue of Mary, pictures of the Virgin Guadalupe and Saul pasted to "Eternalux" candles. There were pictures of David and me in small brass frames, a porcelain manger with baby Jesus between us. Behind our pictures was an old postcard photograph of my grandfather, long dead, his wife curled in his arms. Not so much a demand, but almost a plea, she said, "You will come back and pray? David and you?"

"Sure, Grandma, whenever." David shook his head and told Grandma we were going to the lake. She smiled and nodded, placed her hand on David's cheek. She took a green Tupperware bowl from the nightstand, pulled a chunk of dough and started kneading tortillas, getting lost again in her soap opera, her hands becoming powdery.

It was too hot to play outside most afternoons; the temperature reached a hundred and ten. That's when Grandma would pull us in her room and we'd pray for an hour or more, until we did a whole rosary. A single candle would flicker, curtains closed, black beads turned over in our hands. The silence seemed to create more space, the small room swelled to a cathedral, inducing awe and delirium in me. During prayers, I thought I could feel Jesus in my heart, the blood speeding through my arms, the belief that my actions would lead to heaven. The fan's air oscillated past my back, sending shivers through my body. Then the fan's blades turned on David. His sweat filled my nostrils. The heat and the odor made me warm and somehow I wanted to move closer to David, to inhale deeply next to him, to place my head against his shoulder, to rub my nose in his armpit. When we were done, Grandma lay down on the crochet-covered bed, her hands over her stomach as if she were out of air. My tia flicked her cleaning rag at David and me to get us outside. She'd looked in on Grandma to see if she was all right and if she left the candle burning. "You'll thank her later in your life for this," my aunt told us, as I followed David out the back door, letting it slam like he did. As my uncle said, I was David's little shadow.

David had secrets, secrets he never told anyone but me: the newspapers he set on fire in the bathtub, then stepped in; the space below his knees where he'd dig with his dinner fork until the pain felt too good. The first night in the farmhouse where David and I would sleep, he pulled up the carpet and underneath were old magazines filled with black and white photos of men and women nude on the beach. I pretended to be studious of the women's figures, pointing out their breasts. What intrigued me were the men, the abundance of hair around their dicks and asses, how many different shapes they came in, the strange musty odor of the pages themselves. I wanted to hold their crotches to my nose, let my tongue taste the magazines. Then David asked, "Do you have a boner?"

I had no idea what he was saying, like it was a word my grandmother had taught him, that it was part of some ritual. I did feel different, extremely flush, the same buoyancy inside as if I were held underwater, a similar dizziness to losing blood. Then David grabbed my dick. It made me jump, and I noticed how it swelled and felt good having him hold it, having him bend it and explain that this was a boner. I wasn't sure if I should, but he let me lightly touch his dick too, let me outline the shape, then squeeze.

As we passed the farmhouse, our usual destination after prayers with grandma, David asked if I wanted to see something special. He said I couldn't tell anybody about this either. He walked quickly, deliberately, to the old barn on my uncle's lot. The door was locked but we could pull the bottom corner out and slip through the crack. It was dark inside. The smell of gasoline and hay made me nauseous. I thought he was going to show me some more dirty pictures and I started to get hard. We walked over to a workbench where there were flower pots and hand tools. There was just enough light streaming from the ceiling, punctured with holes. From the highest shelf he pulled down some red clay pots. He said, "Shh, you can't tell anyone or they'll make me bury them." I still held a smile, my dick pressed against my zipper. He brought the first pot low enough for me to look in. "Go ahead, take one out." I wasn't sure what was inside, they were small and white. When I paused, David said "They won't hurt you." As I placed my hand inside, I touched something dry and porous. I wanted to pull my hand out, but David pushed on my back. My fingers found holes to slip into, so I pulled it out quickly. Even then I wasn't sure what it was. I turned it over in a crevice of light. The shape was unintelligible, but as I looked closer teeth smiled back at me and I dropped it, the fine dirt floor absorbing the impact. David giggled, "They're mouse heads. I find them in the fields all the time. And over here are some birds." I wrinkled my nose, not sure if he shouldn't bury them. I almost didn't want to see the pot with the bird heads. Holding the pot to the light, I could make out small bluish lumps; a horrible smell came up. I could see small feathers still attached, a bit of rotted eyes, whereas the mouse skulls were sun bleached. David said over and over, "Aren't they cool? Aren't they cool?" He put his arm across my back, "But this is the best." He pulled down the last pot, "Go ahead and grab one." I did, slowly felt my way around the edge of the pot, till I felt something like very dry-textured skin. I moaned, my stomach felt sick. It was shaped like a cone or a shell. As I pulled it to the light again I couldn't make it out. It sounded as if there were tiny beads inside the shell. I shook it a little harder and asked what is it. "It's a rattler tail. Cool, huh?"

I was a little incredulous, "Oh right, come on, what is it?" I was sure it was going to be something disgusting.

"No really, it is, I'll show you." On the other side of the barn, snake skins were pinned to the old boards of the barn; he had several up, each at least a yard long.

"Yuck, did you find them dead, too?" I asked.

"No, I kill them. I go walking down the old dirt road, past the tracks. I always find them near an edge of grass. I just use rocks. I try to hit them below their heads first. I like it when their bodies squirm." I ran my finger down one of the skins, the texture feeling much drier than I imagined. David smiled, a smile I usually liked to see, a smile that meant he had pride in me, that he taught me something. He said, "The guys at the cannery buy the skins off me, they put them on their hats, but I'm going to give you one before you have to leave."

David started to put the pots back up on the shelf, almost as sacred as my grandmother's table of religious statues and family photographs. As David put the last pot up, the old shelf started to tilt, small nails came out of the wood brackets and all the pots came crashing down. Skulls fell everywhere, rattles seemed crushed under planks of wood and other pots. My tia heard the noise and came running out through the kitchen. "You boys, are you in there?" David and I looked at each other, afraid to answer. "So help me God, you better answer."

David said, "Yes, Mom."

"What are you kids up to, and what made that noise?" She tried to peek through

the crack in the door, but couldn't see clearly. David and I tried to kick the skulls under the workbench, my white tennis shoes turning brown. "Get out here," my aunt
yelled.

David said under his breath, "Oh Jesus, oh Jesus." I left the barn first, scraping my
arm against the cracked wood, lodging a small splinter.

"God blessed, am I going to have to go get the key from the house? I want to know
what happened, I want to know now!" David slipped out, holding two broken shards
of my tia's pots. "Oh God, what happened?" David started to try to explain, his words
jumbled and mixed up. "I guess you want your cousin to see you cry," my tia said to
David. David whimpered, shaking his head. "Give me your belt, and don't give me any
of your lip, boy." David stared at the ground, slowly slipping off his belt. He handed
the leather weaved belt to her; she grabbed it quickly. "Bend over," she screamed. "You
should be embarrassed that your cousin is going to see you cry." I was afraid, too, and
stood stiffly by him. David pulled down his pants, exposing just his cheeks. When he
finally stood absolutely still, she swung the belt hard. Each hit made David cry more
distinctly, until his entire body crumpled onto the ground, his hands brought to his
mouth, his knees pressed to his stomach. "Now pick this mess up," my aunt scowled.
My grandma came outside, wanting to know what was going on. My tia gave her a
look like they'd discussed something before, then walked back in the house. I tried to
follow David into the barn, holding the corner of the door open. Grandma reached
for my arm, wanting me to come into her room, saying it was best for David to clean
up the mess himself.

"Grandma is doing another novena for you," I said. David and I were stripped to our
white briefs and ready for bed, the night had not yet cooled down. David had been
quiet for the whole day. Tearful from being belted, he didn't look me in the eye, tears
along the edges of his eyelids, even after he'd cleaned up the mess and walked into
grandma's room to join me. I pulled up the carpet in the farmhouse, our normal routine. I would read what I could to David, who was looking over my shoulder, trying to
understand. David looked mad tonight. Above his head the moon was shaped like a
nail clipping. I slept badly near the stash of porno magazines and the open window.

"I don't think you should look at those magazines," he said.

"Why not?" I asked.

"Because I'm going to tell."

"They're your magazines." David looked down on his hands, studying their shape,
their strength. He then got up on his knees, then his haunches. I looked up at him, not
sure what he was going to do. He then pounced on me, striking my face with a good
slap, placing all his weight on top of me like a "dog pile" at school, where everyone
jumps on top of one another and the bottom guy is crushed. I started to cry, afraid he
was going to beat me up. I told him I was going to snitch on him, tell my uncle what

he showed me. David just lay on top of me, not moving, his weight nearly crushing me. I knew I wouldn't really tell, somehow I wanted him to go farther, do something more to me, and I wondered if David knew what I wanted. I began to get hard, my body getting used to his body's weight, he then rolled off. He turned the light off and crawled into his sleeping bag. The windows sparkled with stars. I knew he had closed his eyes.

I was a light sleeper, would wake from any sound. From cracked eyes I could see David getting out of bed; it must have been near past midnight now. Standing at a window, I could make out David's hands behind his back. He turned to look at me. I got up quietly, so as not to make the floors creak. David's body was outlined by moonlight and the fine tracing of body hair. When I stood by him, he moved over slightly to let me look outside too. At home the street lights would allow only a few stars to show. Here you could see the stretch of the Milky Way. It made me feel small, made me want to hold onto David these last few days. There was a smile on David's lips as he put his arm around my waist, as he pulled me close.

With hand signals, David got me to put my socks and hiking boots on. I whispered, "Why?" and felt unsure. He held his palm over my mouth. We both sneaked outside, careful not to make too much noise with the door. It felt good to be outside, almost naked, the night's cool temperature finally present, the strange smell of cows, dry grass, the feeling of insects grazing on my skin, chest, legs, the back of my neck. I crossed my arms over my chest, not sure someone couldn't see. David motioned me to the fields, the other side of my uncle's fence. The neighbors grew strawberries and David climbed over. I stepped on the sturdy 2x4 rung, but David insisted on helping me over. "Watch for nails," he said, his hand holding mine. When I was over he said, "Walk ahead." I led, walking in a furrow, afraid of snakes, and that my aunt and uncle would look out their window and see us. In the middle of the field David said, "Lie down."

"Where?" As I turned around, David had stepped over to the other furrow and had lain down in it. On his chest were strawberries that he was plucking from plants nearby. "Lie down!" I did it this time, uneasy at first. The back of my calves, and my shoulders felt the unfamiliar touch of soil. I, too, started picking strawberries, slowly placing them on my chest, wondering what this was all about. I took a bite of one, it didn't taste ripe. I held it up to the moon, but could barely see even with the sky nearly white in pinpoints. David said, "Now crush them on your body." I looked over and he was covered already. He had smashed them on his face, over his crotch, and was smearing the waste over his mouth, across his forehead.

It felt stupid at first, the seedy skin breaking, the aroma of strawberries blanketing me. "Inside your underwear, too," came David's voice. I watched as he put some down his shorts, his face turned to the sky. I put one strawberry inside, pressing it down with my hand, the skin breaking near my dick. He stepped over from his furrow and offered me a hand up. His white underwear looked as if he were bleeding. Small skins fell off his stomach and his arms, leaving discolored patches on his flesh, dark and unnatural. His face was nearly shadowed; my uncle's farm was behind him. He held onto my hand and reached for my other, pulled me in an embrace. David had a pleasant odor. With my nose buried between his arm and chest, he started to rub his body against mine and I helped, sliding the juice between us, his laughter reassuring me. He stepped back and looked me over, saw the extent of our handiwork. "Now we're brothers," he said.

Hand in hand, we went further up the furrows till we came to the highway. We stood there red-stained, our hair uncombed, our underwear blood red and dirt brown. Cars would drive by and honk. No one would stop. A driver in a big rig dropped his hairy jaw as if that were all he could do. David and I looked both ways down the highway, running across the road then into the weeds. My cousin spoke softly, softer than he had ever spoken to me before: "Be careful, there might be snakes this time." The weeds grew high until we hit rocks again, a small rise in the open field, then tracks. "The train should be coming soon."

It started to get cold. I felt an urge to leave, to go back inside and wipe the strawberry marks off me. My grandma had warned me never to go near the tracks with David. David said, "Please wait, I can see the front light of the train not far away."

As the train came close David said, "Close your eyes." When I did, he made me move closer to the tracks, my body stiff and almost unwilling. He told me not to move an inch either way. I could hear the metal wheels on the metal tracks, I opened my eyes. David covered my eyes, said, "Trust me, please." When I stood absolutely still like he wanted, his hands came off me, lifted off the back of my arms. Somehow I felt comforted, as if invisible threads linked us. From across the tracks he yelled, "When it's over look over here." I could barely hear the end of the sentence. With that, all I could hear was the noise of the train, the honking of a horn, the rush of wind the train made across my body, across the field, kicking up dirt, pushing out exhaust. I thought I would fall forward, I could feel the near miss of the train, maybe inches away, an occasional light piercing my closed eyelids. The screech, whoosh, the banging of track seemed to take forever before I could open my eyes again, until the last car went by with a final perishing gust. I looked across the tracks. I didn't see David. I turned all the way around, the train now far down the track leading to Delano. I was alone and I looked back at the farm, wondering what I should do, if I should go to Grandma's room and tell her. At that moment David popped up behind the tall weeds, laughing and saying, "I told you to trust me, I told you." I stood perfectly still, unable to speak or breathe. I knew I wouldn't until he said so, my body glistening in sweat under the moonlight.

Without David telling me to be silent, I held my words as we walked in the small wooden building to the far end of my uncle's lot. Along the wall I could see a sink and hose, a large tin bucket leaning on a cabinet, a bare bulb hung above. As I stepped in the wash basin, I remembered how a boy my own age I hadn't known had pulled me out of the lake as I was choking up water, his hands pressing rhythmically against my stomach, his eyes full of intent on saving my life. My grandma stood behind this boy, her hands folded, saying Hail Marys, tears running down her face to the ground. Now David pressed his hand against my chest. His touch seemed to burn somewhere deep inside me, the warmth quickly extinguished by the cool water. Strawberry skins filled the drain. I watched David's hands work, how they rubbed over the front of my body, how sturdy his wrists appeared, their strength. And still I knew where weakness ran. I looked at my own wrists, then David's. I noticed the patterns of veins stretched up his arms, they flexed as he washed me, lifting the elastic band of my briefs, spraying gently inside. He was just as thorough drying me off, with old cloth towels, stiff and musty, smelling of car wax and window cleaner. A cool breeze, like a fan, passed over us. I wanted to rush David, as if I was called for a mission, to say, "Now it is my turn, let me do you."

Justin Chin

Justin Chin (b. 1969) was born in Malaysia. His father was a doctor; his mother was a nurse. Chin was supposed to be a doctor. He was sent to live with his grandmother in Singapore to further his education, but he did not do well in school. When he was eighteen, he came to the United States as a student and soon found his way into writing. In 1990 he came to San Francisco to study journalism. Instead, he became a performance artist, essayist, and poet.

The passage below is taken from his performance piece "And Judas Boogied until His Slippers Wept," included in *Attack of the Man-Eating Lotus Blossoms* (2005), which he performed between 1993 and 1996. According to Chin, "The show was decidedly Gen X," with lots of seventies and eighties pop culture references. It centers on the intersection of ethnicity and sexuality with rare frankness and humor.

And Judas Boogied until His Slippers Wept

Who the Fuck Am I?

I am Chinese. (I am part of the Chinese diaspora.)/I am gay. (At any point in my life, I always seem to be in love with a man that I'm not sure is in love with me.)/I am a writer. (Once, after a reading, a man came up to me and said, "I didn't understand a word you said, but your reading was very powerful.")/I have an accent./I shave my head./I have tattoos./I am damaged./I am a Joni Mitchell fan./I hate my body./I love my feet./I am a cat owner./I have allergies./I am from what is known as the Third World./I feel invisible./I feel powerless./I feel unattractive./I am bitter./I feel normal./I belong to what they call GENERATION X./I feel alienated./I feel like ASIAN AMERICA'S bastard retard child./I am in pain./I have more closets than I care to imagine./I have bad clothes sense./I like fucking./I like being fucked./I like sucking dick./I like swallowing cum./I like red meat./I am nearsighted./I am un-circumcised./I am vaccinated./I don't know my HIV status anymore./I hate a lot of people./I hate fruit desserts./I like rough sex./I have insomnia./Sometimes, I think I might fall in love with Linda Ronstadt./I want to know for sure./I want to be loved./I hate anyone who loves me./I am drowning./I am the day of openness./I am a plague of locusts./I am crucified./I am bones and paper./I am nothing but dust./I am a work in progress./I am abandoned./I am fucked up./I am totally fucked up./I am a freak./I am between worlds./I am drawing a line in my skull./I am sick./I am re-covering./I am in recovery./I am a fucking shit./I am fucking shit out of someone's asshole./I am grim./I am brain-dead./I am a chink./I am a fag./I am ticklish./I am violent when provoked./I am soft-spoken./I am nervous./I am a butterfly./I am a whore./I am a virgin./I am nothing./I am mad./I am a dog./I am repentant./I am baptised./I am saved./I am going to go straight to hell./I am going to visit heaven just to say hello./I am in need of something good./I am the premature ejaculate of a cheap trick./I am short./I should know better./I am a rat./I smell bad./I am not who I want to be./I am regret./I am remorse./I am happy./I am delirious./I am cruel./I am fate./I am poison./I need poison./I need oxygen./I need to be abused./I want to scream./I want to cry./I am floating./I am a boring fuck./I am a vegetable./I am a child./I was curious yellow./I am a burden./I am repulsive./I am the splendid parsnips./I am the form of a mouth./I am a dinner of lilies./I am subterranean./I lie like mad./I am in agony./I am spiteful./I am baited with ambition./I am baited with lust./I am naked./I am a black sleeve./I am a cut sleeve./I am the secret life./I am the lines of pleasure./I am mud and honey./I am choking on honey./I am drooling./I am noise./I am not a pipe./I am the last one to be picked./I am broken./I am shame./I am a blade./I am sad./I am empowered./I am not angry anymore./I am numb./I am everything I shouldn't be./I am everything I want to be.

Fagtown

I need a man. I'm running out of time. I know the men in my family, and by the time we hit thirty, we fall apart. Okay, perhaps if we really took care of ourselves, followed all the steps in Lea Salonga's *Health & Beauty for Asian Skin*, perhaps, just perhaps we can make it till thirty-five, but then, it all falls apart: we develop the huge hard round belly, and we all start to smell like my Uncle Jeck Juan—raw pork marinated with beer. It's really quite tragic.

But I live in San Francisco. My friends think that I should have no problems meeting my dream man because they think it's one big huge-ass fag block party. Sort of like it was one huge long concrete *Love Boat* episode. And I live so close to the Castro, too, they tsk at me.

When I first came to San Francisco, I knew I had to find this place called Castro Street. It was February, it was raining, it was cold, I only had a corduroy jacket, I didn't have a map, I just walked and walked and walked. Down Van Ness. Up Market. And amazingly, I ended up on Castro Street. It was as if there was this homing instinct, the same thing that guides salmon to spawn, halibut to the Arctic circle, carrier pigeons with vital information taped to their toes to their destinations. It's really amazing, because I could have just turned off anywhere along the way and I could have ended up in Pacific Heights or Cow Hollow or Coit Tower or the crookedest Street in the World or (*shudder*) Pier 39. I mean, my first visit to San Francisco would have taken such a different turn. But thanks to my little queer radio signal, that little blip in all our heads that goes FAG/FAG/FAG, that guides us to wherever it is we have to go. (The nonthreatening PC version of that line would read GAY-LESBIAN-BISEXUAL-TRANSGENDERED/GAY-LESBIAN-BISEXUAL-TRANSGENDERED/GAY-LESBIAN-BISEXUAL-TRANSGENDERED; the beat is a little bit off, I know.) But it's true this little blip guided me in my trip to New Orleans. I managed to wander right through the French Quarter right into a fag-bar where a stripper wearing Batman briefs kissed me and I drank way too many $2 Hurricanes and puked all the way back to the Marriott.

But the Castro. The mystical, exciting, exotic, intangible Castro.
Home of butch men with nelly dogs, nelly men with butch bodies.
Home of those annoying little homosexual mustaches.

Yes, the Castro. The alien, intangible, stinking Castro. Literally. I mean with all these fag-dog owners letting their little pooches shit all over the memory of poor little Harvey Milk. And when it rains — whoo — those dried up clumps of dogshit just soak up the water like Body Shop Organic Sponges and they just puff up with their aromatic treasure. And the whole fucking neighborhood smells like the playroom at Gravy Train headquarters.

But to know know know the Castro is to love love love the Castro.

I want to share: I approached my first visit to the Castro like White Folks on their first visit to Chinatown. "Ooooo, how exotic, how bizarre, how thrilling. I wonder if this is a good place to eat. I see a lot of homosexuals are eating here, so it must be an authentic homosexual diner, serving authentic homosexual food."

But as I have known the Castro, let me be your guide to knowing the Castro so you may love the Castro. Using the area's bars as markers and group cluster, the Castro can be socio-geographically divided into

1. drunken desperation
2. pathetic desperation
3. desperation in denial
4. upper-middle-class desperation
5. desperation.

V. *Do You Love Me? (Real letter. I no kid you.)*
An Open Letter to Justin Chin:

My reaction to your awful whining writing, Justin? Well, I reacted on several different levels. I was immediately struck by the anger, the hatred, the rage, the venom that poured forth from your pen and I thought to myself, "This guy has really been hurt. He's in a lot of pain." And thinking this, my eyes got moist, as indeed they are as I write this. I've never been into S&M. I don't enjoy pain, either my own or someone else's. And when I imagine the pain that you had to go through in order to be filled up with so much rage, my heart goes out to you.

Justin, you seem to rage at everyone: you're angry at us whites who are prejudiced against Asians; you're angry at those of us who are attracted to Asians and even Asian culture, ridiculing even our mismatched collections of Asian art, our attempts to use chopsticks and to learn other cultural customs. You are even angry at other Asians who are attracted to whites. I wonder, do you ever wear blue jeans or use a fork?

Justin, none of us likes to be nothing more than a sex object. More than once an Asian has been disappointed in me because I *didn't* have hair on my chest. And, on the flip side of that, I have experienced many times the silly gushing of an Asian over my blue eyes. But, Justin, in all of these cases, we went beyond that initial reaction and developed relationships (not just sexual ones, either) that were based on more than my blue eyes or their silky smooth hairless skin.

We are all humans, Justin, and how can we explain what it is that makes our crotches tingle? Can you honestly say to us that your own physical attractions to others have been totally without objectification? Have you never experienced fetish-like qualities in your own sexual urges?

Your anger is destroying you, Justin. It is poison that is eating you alive. And that's such a waste. Yes, Justin, there is injustice in this world. There is racism, discord, prejudice, discrimination, evil, pollution, hunger, poverty, and all kinds of wretchedness. And we should all work to change this.

And we can do this, motivated by love and compassion. Like Mother Teressa (sic).

Or with anger and rage. Like you.

And one more thing, Justin. My name is "D——." What does my name mean, you ask?

It means "Beloved."

D—— S——, Psychologist
Dallas, Texas

An Invocation for Mr. S—— and People Like Him in the Hopes That Their Moist Eyes Would Blind Them So They Stumble Off the Pavement Into the Path of a Beer Truck.

Dear Mr. S——.

Thank you for giving me your bleeding heart. I promptly took it to the organ bank. They were quite pleased. I got 76¢ for it. It wasn't enough for bus fare. I walked home. When I got home, there was a message on the answering machine. It was the organ bank. They couldn't use the heart after all—it had bled itself blue. I could keep the 76¢ though, they said. So I'm sending you back your heart postage paid. Enclosed are a couple of tissues for you to wipe your eyes too. We wouldn't want your tears to blind you lest you fall off the pavement and get crushed by a truck loaded with Miller Drafts.

Because I was so excited when I received your heart, I rushed straight to the organ bank instead of writing a thank-you note immediately. Where are my manners! So I am writing now to thank you for your heart and tears and to respond to your kind kind note.

I'm feeling much better now. I have been able to feel so much more centered and calm ever since you explained to me that the roots of my oppression, the pain and the anger that I was feeling, were something that I consciously chose to enjoy, like anchovies on an extra-cheese, deep-crust pizza, boxer shorts, armpit sniffing, and sadomasochism.

Also, I'm glad you so understand the racism and the marginalization that I've experienced and am able to advise me on how to deal with all these oppressions. Honestly, without you, I'm nothing! I did notice all that sexual imagery in your note — all those spurting pens, etc. Why, Mr. S———, if I didn't know better, I'd think you were being quite naughty indeed!

Oh yes. How I wish I was more like Mother Teresa. Then I too could be worshipped and adored as a wrinkled colonialist. She's the last of a pure breed, you know. I'm sure there's nothing I like to do better than rescue poor sick folks and make sure they know their class and place in this world, all so they can get their true reward in the glorious golden realms of heaven. (But Bless Me Father for I Have Sinned.)

Don't tell anyone this, but since you asked, I've always wanted to be an ice-pick-wielding fag given to stabbing the poor hapless sap I just fucked. Oh dear, I wish I could just be satisfied with frottage, heavy kissing, and foot-licking.

Oh dear me, I have to run now. Got to fire up the Norelco Wet/Dry Shaver™ so I can keep my silky smooth hairless skin up to par. Once again, thanks so much for your kind love and compassion.

Hugs and kisses,
Justin Chin
San Francisco, California

P.S. I'll just simply die of hunger without my lacquered chopsticks! And I'm rarely seen without my slit-up-to-my-hips cheong-sam!

VI. Epilogue

When I was little my whole family said I looked like a seal. Growing up, the image of beauty and attractiveness was always the other: the Japanese, the Korean, and especially, the Eurasian. And in my family, my brother was the good-looking one. When there was a family gathering, there would always be some remark that my brother was so damn good-looking (and his good grades and footballing skills probably helped in their estimation). Then the gaze would turn to me and they would ask me what I was going to do with my life.

The funny thing about all this is that the last time I went home, my family said that I was beginning to look Japanese. As if that wasn't bad enough, store owners also thought I was Japanese, and greetings of *Konichiwa* followed me as an enticement to enter their store. And when I did and when they found out that I was merely local, they refused to sell me an under-the-counter cheap knock-off imitation Titoni watch.

Perhaps I'm being terribly shallow, whining on and on about beauty and attractiveness. Why do we care so much about beauty and image? Why do children's stories and fairy tales tell us that good people are beautiful and bad people ugly?

But more than that, researchers have found that attractive people tend to get further in life. They found that attractive people do better in school, work, and relationships.

In one experiment, researchers attached to an eight-year-old child's dismal school and test records an attractive photo of a child and to the same copy of the report, an unattractive photo of a child. Nearly twice as many of the teachers who reviewed the file recommended that the unattractive child be sent to a special-education class.

In another experiment, a mediocre college-level sophomore essay (about some inane topic like WHY I LIKE SUMMER) was sent to teams of graders. To the very same essay, the researchers attached photos of the supposed writer, again attractive and unattractive people. The essay with the attractive photo attached consistently received higher marks.

No shit.

Researchers have found that people who think themselves unattractive are more prone to mental illness later in life.

In a study of 17,000 professional men, researchers found that those over six feet received a higher salary and were promoted faster.

When I was seventeen, I tried to commit suicide twice. The first time, I swallowed a handful of antihistamines. It didn't produce the desired effect and I only woke with incredibly dry nostrils. The second time, I swallowed a handful of blood pressure pills. Again, it didn't produce the desired effect, which was to let my blood flow slow down until it became a trickle and then the entire circulation calmed down like the Dead Sea. But that didn't happen and I only woke the next afternoon with a strange buzz, a massive headache, a terrible nausea, and a fucking depressed bitchy attitude about it all. Of course like most suicide attempts, failed or successful, I thought a lot about the means of the act. I thought a lot about more drastic means like:

Jumping off a building. Hanging. Slashing wrists. So dramatic. So Hong Kong melodrama.

But I felt that these were either too painful or way too messy. It's hell trying to commit suicide while not being able to put aside that Virgo compulsiveness. So I decided that blood was the best way to do it. But unfortunately, or fortunately, I cheated blood.

You may cheat blood but you can't cheat its flow.

I have a recurrent dream about this. In this dream, I'm sitting in the kitchen. I'm looking for the veins in my left arm. I'm holding a knife and slowly using the tip to nip into my skin, the little bit of flesh, and eventually flicking the membrane of the vein open, all with a delicacy reserved for dissection and cake-making. I'm sitting on the kitchen floor with the top of my vein in my left arm, the skinnier arm, open as if the vein were a water hose and I merely peeled the top off to look into the tube. I watch my blood flowing down my arm and, under that vein, the blood flow up the arm. In reality, blood in your arteries flows as fast as a midnight bus on an open road, but in my dream, the flow merely trickles, a garden hose in the middle of a drought. Then someone, different people each time, enters the kitchen and I will wake—thrown back into the slow-motion roller-coaster ride that is my life.

When you die, you may become either one of three things: angels; ghosts; demons.

Consider the options:
    Angels get to gently whisk around and inspire people to do good things and beautiful things. Ghosts get to strike a pose and look winsome—strictly for the poseurs. Demons get to dart about and possess the living.

When I die, I want to come back as a demon and possess all those attitudinal shits in all those clubs and bars that have wronged me and make them have horrible breakouts, bad hair, potbellies, the pox (maybe syphilis if I really feel like working it), and best of all, a proclivity for bad fashion decisions.

When I die, I want to come back as a demon and possess various people in my life who judged me wrong. I want to drag them out to some cheap motel with the scuzziest trick, get them on their knees and to beg to lick cum/spit/shit off the floor. I want to make them want to take it in their ass while citing prophetic scriptures. I want to leave their body the very precise moment they feel that regret of hot jism squirt up their rectum.

Think of all the ramifications of being able to possess bodies. Anyone from politicians or lawmakers to your neighbors and friends. Think of all the sheer fun. Think of all the people you could fuck over and nothing would be able to save you.

But for the living,
somewhere, something is always waiting to save you

Somewhere, Jesus will crawl down from his cross, discard his loin cloth at yr feet and kiss you until it's all better

Somewhere, Buddha's bones will flavor yr tea

Somewhere, yr therapist wants to finger-fuck you

Somewhere, Louise Hay and Marianne Williamson will get out of their limousines, sneak into yr bed and whisper sweet affirmations into yr skull until you go blind

Somewhere, the Virgin Mary is making you lick her pits

Somewhere, the Prophet is watching her

& somewhere, the suicide man is never sad

& somewhere. & somewhere.

My mother tells me that I was born a Christian.
My father tells me that I was born with potential.
My grandmother tells me that I was born with little fuss.
The queer community tells me that I was born gay.
The United Nations tells me that I was born in the Third World. (Got the vaccina-
    tion scars to prove it.)
Politicians tell me that I was born at the most opportune time in the nation's history.
Scientists tell me that I was born with a bit of my brain bigger than 85 percent of the
    population.
The church tells me that I was born a sinner.
Psychologists tell me that I was born to learn.
Science tells me that I was born.
All this is supposed to make me feel mighty real.

I was going out with this man
& he said to me,

HE SAID "why do you have to do that to your body"

& I SAID "do what"
& HE SAID "you know"

& I SAID "no, what"
& HE SAID "why do you have to sleep with all those other men"

& I SAID "well, not much I can do about that now is there"
& HE SAID "you're exactly my type but why do you have to
do that to your body"

"I wish you were really shy and bookish, you'd spend all day in the library and you'd
have big balls with big loads of cum to shoot in my mouth" HE SAID
"well, except for the big balls and big load of cum, I can pretend, but that wouldn't
be the same, would it" I SAID
"no, no, that's okay, just pretend" HE SAID

People always want to know.
When was the first time I had sex with a man.
When was the first time I had sex with a man and liked it.
When was the first time I took some cock in my mouth.
When was the first time I was in love.
When was the first time I knew I liked dick.
When was the first time I saw my father naked.
When was the first time I saw my mother naked.
When was the first time I noticed hair growing on my dick.
When was the first time I got my balls licked in a toilet.
When was the first time I swallowed.
When was the first time I had a good load of cum dripping out of my ass.

Nobody ever wants to know when was the last time I had a good load of cum
      dripping out of my ass.

The first time I ever had sex was at the age of thirteen just before shop in the first-floor
toilet of Swiss Cottage Secondary School. This man sat behind me on the bus to school
and put his foot in the crack of the seat. It was an old bus and the seats were two cushions: seat and backrest, both in a metal frame; there was a split between the two and
he pressed the tip of his shoe against me.

    I glanced behind and caught his reflection in the window as the bus shuttled
along a row of trees that would darken the window enough to allow me to catch
a glimpse of him: ugly, skimpy mustache, looked like the kind of man you'd see at
shopping malls hanging out with nothing to do, the sort I'd walk across the street
to avoid because he looked like the "short, tight-fitting polo shirt, polyester slacks,

slim gold jewelry" type that would stab you with a bearing scraper if you looked at him wrong.

He followed me when I transferred buses and sat beside me. He apologized for touching my rear. I ignored him. After a fidgety silence, he suddenly but nervously placed his hand on my crotch and frantically asked, pleaded, panicked for me to cover that touch with my school bag, and the Adidas canvas shielded some pervert's embarrassed thrill from the rest of the passengers.

Now when people ask, I remember it as different: he was the most gorgeous hunk, he worked in a bank, he smelled good, and we came together after he sucked me. I did not gag on his dick. I did not nearly vomit up my breakfast from the smell of his dick. I did not try to run out only to be grabbed from behind, slapped across the face. He did not force his dick into my mouth while leaning over to whisper in my ear how I would get expelled if I was caught. I was not late for class because I shitted on myself after he tried to stick his dick into my ass without telling me. I did not spend a half hour crying in a toilet stall, cleaning myself up while praying to the Almighty Lord God Jesus Christ for forgiveness. All that did not happen: we just sucked a little, he kissed me on the mouth but I did not like it, and we watched each other come.

Only I can fuck with my memories:
And all those pity fucks. (Did not happen!)
All those boring fucks. (Are suddenly great!)
All that rough sex when I didn't want it. (Was so tender you could cry!)
That incident in the restroom of the mall that made me bleed up the ass for three days. (Was the hottest sex ever! And he called!)

Only I can fuck with my memories and I can't stop there:
H. who was beaten to near death for looking too damn good in a dress. (Snapped his way out of there with so much shade, you could have put on a shadow play!)
And J. who killed himself. (Was hit by a bus like you see on Hong Kong melodramas!)
And L. who died after so much pain. (Died in his sleep!)
And D. who died alone in the hospital with no one to claim his body for weeks. (Died with all his friends around him. Someone made a joke and everybody laughed and when the laughing and repetition of the punchline died down, D. had passed away with a smile; his mother cried for months!)

This is the way I know how to live and nobody has the power to fuck with my memories but me, so this body, baby, this body better play along.

Selected Gay Autobiographies and Life Writings

Als, Hilton. *The Women* (1996).

Arenas, Reinaldo. *Before Night Falls* (1993).

Bell, Arthur. *Dancing the Gay Lib Blues* (1971).

Benderson, Bruce. *The Romanian: Story of an Obsession* (2006).

Bowles, Paul. *Days: A Tangier Diary* (2006).

———. *Dear Paul, Dear Ned: The Correspondence of Paul Bowles and Ned Rorem* (1997).

———. *In Touch: The Letters of Paul Bowles* (1993).

———. *Without Stopping* (1972).

Boykin, Keith. *One More River to Cross: Black and Gay in America* (1996).

Brodkey, Harold. *This Wild Darkness: The Story of My Death* (1996).

Brown, Howard. *Familiar Faces, Hidden Lives: The Story of Homosexual Men in America Today* (1976).

Brown, Ricardo. *The Evening Crowd at Krimmers': A Gay Life in the 1940s* (2003).

Chase, Clifford, ed. *Queer 13: Lesbian and Gay Writers Recall Seventh Grade* (1998).

Clarke, Lige, and Jack Nichols. *I Have More Fun with You than Anybody* (1972).

Cooper, Bernard. *The Bill from My Father: A Memoir* (2007).

———. *Truth Serum* (1996).

Crane, Hart. *O My Land, My Friends: The Selected Letters of Hart Crane* (1997).

Darling, Candy. *Candy Darling* (1992).

———. *My Face for the World to See: The Diaries, Letters, and Drawings of Candy Darling, Andy Warhol Superstar* (2001).

Delany, Samuel R. *Longer Views: Extended Essays* (1996).

———. *Times Square Red, Times Square Blue* (1999).

Doty, Mark. *Dog Years: A Memoir* (2007).

———. *Firebird: A Memoir* (1999).

———. *Heaven's Coast: A Memoir* (1996).

Eighner, Lars. *Travels with Lizbeth: Three Years on the Road and on the Streets* (1993).

Fellows, Will, ed. *Farm Boys: Lives of Gay Men from the Rural Midwest* (1996).

Fisher, Gary. *Gary in Your Pocket: Stories and Notebooks of Gary Fisher* (1996).

Ford, Charles Henri. *Water from a Bucket: A Diary 1948–1957* (2001).

Fries, Kenny. *Body, Remember* (1994).

———. *The History of My Shoes and the Evolution of Darwin's Theory* (2007).

———, ed. *Staring Back: The Disability Experience from the Inside Out* (1997).

Gibson, Wesley. *You Are Here: A Memoir of Arrival* (2004).

Ginsberg, Allen. *The Book of Martyrdom and Artifice: First Journals and Poems 1937–1952* (2006).

———. *Family Business: Selected Letters between a Father and Son* (2001).

———. *Indian Journals* (1996).

———. *Journals: Early Fifties, Early Sixties* (1994).

Glück, Robert. *Jack the Modernist* (1995).

Harris, E. Lynn. *What Becomes of the Brokenhearted: A Memoir* (2003).

Hartley, Marsden. *Somehow a Past: The Autobiography of Marsden Hartley* (1998).

Heath, Gordon. *Deep Are the Roots: Memoirs of a Black Expatriate* (1992).

Holleran, Andrew. *Chronicle of a Plague, Revisited: AIDS and Its Aftermath* (2008).

Hughes, Langston. *The Big Sea: An Autobiography* (1940).

———. *I Wonder as I Wander: An Autobiographical Journey* (1956).

Isherwood, Christopher. *Christopher and His Kind, 1929–1939* (1997).

———. *Diaries: Volume 1, 1939–1960* (1996).

———. *Lost Years: A Memoir, 1945–1951* (2000).

———. *My Guru and His Disciple* (1980).

James, Henry. *Notes of a Son and Brother* (1914).

———. *A Small Boy and Others* (1913).

Johnson, Anthony Godby. *A Rock and a Hard Place* (1993).

Johnson, Fenton. *Geography of the Heart* (1996).

Jones, Bill T. *Last Night on Earth* (1995).

Kleinberg, Seymour. *Alienated Affections: Being Gay in America* (1980).

Kramer, Larry. *Reports from the Holocaust: The Making of an AIDS Activist* (1989).

Leavitt, David, and Mark Mitchell. *In Maremma: Life and a House in Southern Tuscany* (2001).

LeSueur, Joe. *Digressions on Some Poems by Frank O'Hara: A Memoir* (2004).

Lisicky, Paul. *Famous Builder* (2002).

Mass, Lawrence D. *Confessions of a Jewish Wagnerite: Being Gay and Jewish in America* (1999).

Melson, James. *The Golden Boy* (1992).

Merla, Patrick, ed. *Boys Like Us* (1996).

Michaels, Eric. *Unbecoming* (1997).

Miller Tim. *1001 Beds: Performances, Essays, and Travels* (2006).

———. *Body Blows: Six Performances* (2002).

———. *Shirts & Skin* (1997).

Monette, Paul. *Becoming a Man: Half a Life Story* (1992).

———. *Borrowed Time: An AIDS Memoir* (1988).

O'Hara, Scott. *Autopornography: A Memoir of Life in the Lust Lane* (1997).

Peters, Robert. *Crunching Gravel: A Wisconsin Boyhood in the Thirties* (1993).

———. *For You, Lili Marlene: A Memoir of World War II* (1995).

Picano, Felice. *Ambidextrous: The Secret Lives of Children* (1985).

———. *Art and Sex in Greenwich Village: A Memoir of Gay Literary Life after Stonewall* (2007).

———. *A House on the Ocean, a House on the Bay* (1997).

———. *Men Who Loved Me* (1989).

Preston, John, ed. *Hometowns: Gay Men Write about Where They Belong* (1991).

———, ed. *Member of the Family: Gay Men Write about Their Families* (1992).

———. *Winter's Light: Reflections of a Yankee Queer* (1995).

Preston, John, and Michael Lowenthal, eds. *Friends and Lovers: Gay Men Write about the Families They Create* (1995).

Preston, John, and Joan Nestle, eds. *Sister & Brother: Lesbians & Gay Men Write about Their Lives Together* (1994).

Price, Reynolds. *A Whole New Life: An Illness and a Healing* (2000).

Rechy, John. *About My Life and the Kept Woman: A Memoir* (2008).

Rorem, Ned. *Knowing When to Stop* (1994).

Rumaker, Michael. *Black Mountain Days* (2003).

———. *Robert Duncan in San Francisco* (1996).

Schneebaum, Tobias. *Keep the River on Your Right* (1969).

———. *Where the Spirits Dwell: An Odyssey in the Jungle of New Guinea* (1988).

———. *Wild Man* (1979).

Schuyler, James. *The Diary of James Schuyler* (1997).

———. *Just the Thing: Selected Letters of James Schuyler* (2000).

———. *The Letters of James Schuyler to Frank O'Hara* (2006).

Sedaris, David. *Dress Your Family in Corduroy and Denim* (2004).

———. *Me Talk Pretty One Day* (2000).

———. *Naked* (1997).

Smith, Bob. *Openly Bob* (1997).

———. *Selfish and Perverse* (2007).

———. *Way to Go, Smith!* (1999).

Solomon, Andrew. *The Noonday Demon: An Atlas of Depression* (2001).

Stambolian, George. *Male Fantasies/Gay Realities: Interviews with Ten Men* (1984).

Sterry, David Henry. *Chicken: Self-Portrait of a Young Man for Rent* (2002).

Taylor, Paul. *Private Domain* (1987).

Tobias, Andrew. *The Best Little Boy in the World* (1973).

Vidal, Gore. *Palimpsest: A Memoir* (1995).

———. *Point to Point Navigation: A Memoir, 1964 to 2006* (2006).

Warhol, Andy. *The Andy Warhol Diaries* (1989).

———. *The Philosophy of Andy Warhol: From A to B and Back Again* (1975).

———. *POPism: The Warhol Sixties* (1980).

Whitaker, Rick. *Assuming the Position: A Memoir of Hustling* (1999).

White, Edmund. *My Lives: A Memoir* (2006).

White, Edmund, and Hubert Sorin. *Our Paris: Sketches from Memory* (2002).

Whitmore, George. *Someone Was Here* (1988).

Williams, Tennessee. *Notebooks* (2007).

———. *Tennessee Williams Memoirs* (1975).

Woodlawn, Holly. *The Holly Woodlawn Story: A Low Life in High Heels* (1991).

Living Out

Gay and Lesbian Autobiographies

Joan Larkin and David Bergman
SERIES EDITORS

Raphael Kadushin
SERIES ACQUISITIONS EDITOR